Exodus

THE GENESIS OF GOD'S PEOPLE

Zvi Grumet

שמות

Exodus

The Genesis of God's People

Maggid Books

Exodus
The Genesis of God's People

First Edition, 2025

Maggid Books
An imprint of Koren Publishers Jerusalem Ltd.

POB 8531, New Milford, CT 06776-8531, USA
& POB 4044, Jerusalem 9104001, Israel
www.korenpub.com

The publication of this book was made possible
through the generous support of *The Jewish Book Trust*.

ISBN 978-1-59264-703-3, *hardcover*

A CIP catalogue record for this title is
available from the British Library

Printed and bound in the United States

Dedicated in loving memory of our parents

Ephraim and Harriet Grumet

אפרים בן יעקב דוד הכהן ז״ל
הענטשא בת שמחה ז״ל

Who raised us with a love of עם ישראל*,*
תורת ישראל *and* ארץ ישראל

Shelly and Barry Dorf
Lynn and Joel Mael

Contents

Acknowledgments

The evolution of the ideas in this book began more than thirty years ago, when I was privileged to study with my friend and *ḥavruta* Michael Berger. He helped me formulate some initial thoughts on the second half of Exodus, particularly with regard to the *Mishkan*. Over the course of the last twenty years, I've had some extraordinary students at Yeshivat Eretz HaTzvi with whom I learned the opening chapters of Exodus in private study. While I fear that I may be omitting some names, and I apologize for that, I deeply appreciate the give-and-take which forced me to sharpen and repeatedly reformulate my thinking. Ikey Setton, Alex Schindler, and Ray Braha are noteworthy for their textual acuity, depth of thought, and brutal honesty. Sonny Setton and Naftali Shavelson brought their thirst for learning and shared with me their notes from our learning, both written and recorded. Steven Galitzer forced me to think about textual issues I had overlooked, and Sam Stonefield added a breadth of perspective – both from Tanakh and general thought, which forced me to look beyond the texts as well. Additional thanks goes to Sam for reading through the initial draft and offering constructive feedback to help improve it.

While writing this book I was involved in a joint project of The Lookstein Center and The Rabbi Sacks Legacy. That project not only engaged me with the inspiring writings of Rabbi Jonathan Sacks, but also challenged me to delve deeper into a wide range of commentaries on Exodus and explore its major themes. My work on preparing the content for that project and my interactions with the inspiring teachers I was mentoring both broadened my knowledge and forced me to translate heady ideas into those that might speak to an audience of laypeople.

Throughout this book I quote from the Talmud, midrashic sources, and traditional (usually medieval) commentaries. There are two contemporary writers whom I cite frequently, Elhanan Samet and Leon Kass. Samet's extraordinary essays are built on fidelity to the text, the ability to see structures and patterns in the text of the Torah, and the gift of understanding that those structures are designed to accentuate and convey meaning. Leon Kass's philosophical-political insights provoked me to think and rethink, provided a meta-view of the text, and opened me to new worlds of wisdom which illuminated the Torah for me in entirely new ways. Both provided inspiration and challenges, and represent for me the finest levels of what I might call meaningful scholarship – maintaining simultaneously rigorous reading and compelling contemporary relevance.

I am indebted to Matthew Miller, publisher at Koren Publishers Jerusalem, and Rabbi Reuven Ziegler, editor of the Maggid Studies in Tanakh series, whose confidence encouraged me to take on this project. The patience and professionalism of the editorial team of Nechama Unterman, Debbie Ismailoff, Ita Olesker, and David Silverstein improved the initial draft considerably.

I appreciate the support and understanding of my wife Naomi and my three children, Ruti, Yair, and Haviva. Much of the work on this book was done during trying times, both on a personal and a national level. My mother's passing nearly coincided with the massacre of Simḥat Torah and the ensuing war – both of which have clouded our lives, albeit in different ways. All the normal stresses of life along with the needs that accompany being a teen, or raising three of them, have been amplified in ways which we could never have imagined. Despite all that, my family learned to be patient when I needed to say, "Can it wait just a few minutes; I need to finish writing this thought." My love and appreciation for them knows no bounds.

No words can express my thanks to my parents, Harriet and Ephraim Grumet *z"l*. While they initially would have preferred that I become a lawyer, computer programmer, or diamond cutter, they quickly embraced my passion for Jewish education. Having themselves raised four children and ensured that they all received a proper Jewish education, regardless of the sacrifice involved and under sometimes difficult circumstances, they took pride in my choice of career and celebrated my milestones along the way. My father was gifted in his ability to see things differently than did others, and he was a masterful storyteller; my mother always took the attitude that it's never too late to start something new. Together they inspired me to seek truth and not be satisfied with standard, sometimes superficial answers. I am grateful for what they gave me – their memory is embedded in every page of this book, and nothing could have made them prouder than to have their names inscribed in it. I am deeply grateful to my sisters and brothers-in-law, Shelly and Barry Dorf, and Lynn and Joel Mael, for dedicating this book in their memory.

Finally, my thanks to God – for giving us the Torah, whose beauty and brilliance is endless, and for helping me to overcome obstacles only He knows about to have been able to learn, to teach, to discover new insights, and to share them with others.

Jerusalem, Israel
Tishrei 5785

Introduction

In the Torah scroll, five blank lines separate between one book and the next. On the one hand, each book stands alone, with its own style and tone, with its unique focus. On the other hand, all five books are joined in a single scroll – the sanctity of the Torah scroll depends on all five books appearing side by side in the proper sequence. The core ideas and themes which receive unique presentations in each of the five books are inseparably linked. To properly understand Exodus, we must place it in the context, first and foremost, of Genesis.

The bulk of Genesis describes its key heroes – Abraham, Isaac, Jacob, and Joseph – and, more importantly, their paths, which mark them as archetypal figures.[1] In the Bible, great characters are not born great; they achieve their status through a growth process in which they overcome challenges and obstacles.[2] Abraham must negotiate between the competing loyalties to family and God. Isaac struggles to carve his own path even as he lives in Abraham's shadow. Jacob learns to protect his dignity, to stop running from his problems, and to conduct himself

1. Technically, only the first three are identified as patriarchs. God speaks with them and formally includes them in the covenant.
2. See my work *Moses and the Path to Leadership* (Urim, 2014), 16–17.

with integrity. Joseph needs to learn humility, understand God's role in his life, and embrace the covenantal destiny of his people in their promised land.

As much as the lives of the individuals and their families are compelling on a human level, their stories are but part of a grand divine design. God created a world so that He could have meaningful interactions with humans, created in His image. That seemingly simple aspiration is repeatedly frustrated by human missteps resulting from the very fact that they are human.[3] Cain is banished from God's presence[4] and nine generations later God decides to start all over with one righteous man and his family, this time introducing some basic guidelines[5] for humanity in the hope that they will help people achieve their potential. That attempt, however, failed in a different direction. Instead of people abusing their ability to choose freely, as they did before the Great Confusion (commonly called the Flood), the crushing of human freedom in Babel required yet another divine intervention. With humanity divided by geography and language, God recognizes that His plan needs to be adjusted to accommodate the human side of humanity. Thus, Abraham is instructed to uproot himself and move to Canaan, where he will teach God's message of *tzedek* (righteousness) and *mishpat* (justice) to his family and the people he encounters, introducing humanity to Godliness.[6]

But a single individual is inadequate to become God's standard-bearer. What is required is a family, a clan, a nation which will hold fast together to bring God's message forward. Jacob, with the help of Joseph and Judah, builds a family which eventually bonds and stays together. That family will form the nucleus of the nation that will become God's partner,[7] and it – like Abraham – will need to be centered at the

3. See Gen. 6:3.
4. Gen. 4:14.
5. Gen. 9:1–7.
6. See Gen. 18:17–19. Genesis Rabba 54:6 describes Abraham's tent as the place where he welcomes guests, feeds them, and teaches them to bless God (rather than himself) for their food.
7. For a somewhat different articulation of this idea see *Haamek Davar*, introduction to Exodus.

crossroads of the world where it will be able to interact with and impact upon all three branches of Noah's descendants.

One of the fascinating features of Genesis is that God's presence dominates the opening of Genesis but slowly fades into the background as we progress through the book. The Creation, the Great Confusion, and the Dispersion from Babel all feature God as the prime mover. After He identifies Abram-Abraham as His partner, God shares the stage with that new partner. And while God is involved, speaking to Abraham, commanding him, entering into a covenant with him, there is a shift to focusing on human behavior rather than divine action. That shift continues into Isaac's life, where God speaks to him only twice and is involved behind the scenes in making Isaac successful, and it likewise persists through Jacob's tumultuous journeys. By the time we get to Joseph, He is completely silent – we, the readers, are aware of His presence only because the text tells us, but Joseph seems oblivious until he discovers God's workings behind the scenes.[8]

This brings us back to the five blank lines separating Exodus from Genesis. That space represents a fast-forward of an extended period of time – perhaps one or two or three hundred years – about which we know very little. Was Jacob's family still isolated in Goshen or did they spread out? Did they maintain a distinct identity as shepherds, or did they assimilate into Egyptian culture and society?[9] How long were they

---

8. This pattern will repeat itself in the latter books of the Bible. The initial battle in the conquest of the Promised Land has God miraculously bringing down the walls of Jericho, but from then on God recedes further and further into the background. The books of Samuel and Kings have intermittent overt interventions by God, evidenced especially by the lack of success of the prophets in bringing any awareness of God's involvement into the public and royal consciousness.
9. Varying sources take different positions regarding this. On the one hand we have Moses's family apparently living near enough to the royal palace that they can secrete him in a basket in the reeds. We also find a description of Israelite women asking for silver, gold, and clothing from their Egyptian neighbors and housemates (3:22). Later, the Israelites are instructed to eat the *pesaḥ* in their homes and mark the door frames with the blood of the sheep (12:7), again indicating that they had their own homes. Exodus Rabba 14:3 and 16:3 also describe the Israelites living among the Egyptians. A conflicting position is evidenced in 8:18, describing Israel as living in Goshen and hence being spared the wild beasts. When it comes to their spiritual

in Egypt before the slavery began? And together with the unknowns about the people, there is God's absence. Has God abandoned Jacob's family? Has God abandoned His covenant with the patriarchs with its focus on the special land? Has God given up on the people founded by Abraham, Isaac, and Jacob as being His ambassadors to humanity?

These are the questions which drive the opening of Exodus. In fact, they drive all of Exodus. The fulfillment of the Abrahamic covenant looms large, but there is another layer lurking just beneath the surface of – and sometimes peeking through – the entire saga of the liberation from Egyptian slavery. That hidden agenda, in which God seeks His national covenantal partners, slowly emerges and finally bursts forth as the central thrust of the story when Israel arrives at Mount Sinai and enters into a new covenant with God. Nurturing and negotiating that covenantal relationship closes the book with the construction of the Tabernacle along with the incident of the Golden Calf and its aftershocks.

Lest we think that it is just the modern reader imposing questions about the link between Genesis and Exodus, the opening chapters just about make those connections explicit. The opening five verses of Exodus are an abridged version of – including some of the same language as – the passage in Genesis 46:8–27. They both open with *Ve'eileh shemot benei Yisrael haba'im Mitzraima,* continue with a listing of those who descended to Egypt with Jacob (minus Joseph, who was already there), and close with the total count of seventy family members who ended up in Egypt. Following that (v. 7), the text describes the dramatic growth of the family as *paru vayishretzu vayirbu vayaatzmu bimeod meod, vatimalei haaretz otam,* language which echoes God's blessing to humanity in Creation (Gen. 1:28) and His subsequent blessings to Noah and his sons (Gen. 9:1 and 9:7). The parallels continue into chapter 2 of Exodus (2:2), where Moses is described as *ki tov,* a phrase which reminds the reader of that same phrase which dominates the first chapter of Genesis.[10]

---

stature, the Torah does not reveal much, but rabbinic literature does refer to this. On the one hand, the Zohar (*Yitro*) describes Israel as being on the forty-ninth level of impurity in Egypt (had they reached the fiftieth level, they would have been unredeemable), yet Exodus Rabba (1:28) praises Israel for not taking on Egyptian names, language, or dress, maintaining a distinct cultural identity.

10. Similarly, the first key turning point in Genesis is the Great Confusion, after which

There are many more such references, especially in the beginning of Exodus.[11] These parallels lend themselves to a variety of interpretations. One possibility is that Exodus is the genesis of Israel,[12] the story of how a family became a clan, the clan a nation, and the nation a holy people in covenant with God. A variation on that shifts the focus from the people to God – Exodus is where God's plan for creation and the desire to have a relationship with humanity is finally getting close to fulfillment. The difference between these two formulations is subtle, but significant. Is it the story of the formation of the Israelite nation or does it represent a path toward the ultimate completion of creation?[13] The first is particularistic, the second universal, and that is one of the tensions framing Exodus.

After all, if God really does care about all people, not just about His chosen ones, how are we to understand the seeming capriciousness of the plagues brought upon the Egyptians even after they urge Pharaoh to release Israel? The detail of those afflictions occupies more than a tenth of Exodus, including a description of God's actions in Egypt as

---

God introduces the seven Noahide laws which are to guide humanity in its relationship with God. The centerpiece of Exodus is the Revelation at Sinai, where God introduces an updated version of those laws – the Ten Commandments – which serve as the foundation of Israel's relationship with God.

11. There are also instances of contrasts. For example, the ten generations following Noah saw the rapid expansion of humanity and the emergence of a populated world which seems to be the product of men begetting men – not a single woman is mentioned until Abram and his brother are described as marrying. That is contrasted with the opening chapter of Exodus, which describes the rapid expansion of the descendants of Israel and the land of Egypt being populated by the descendants of Israel as a result of the courageous midwives and the "vigorous" Hebrew women who manage to bear their children even before the midwives arrive. Similarly, the bulk of Genesis focuses on the three patriarchal figures, while the opening of Exodus emphasizes the mothering qualities of the midwives and of Moses's nurturing mother, sister, and adoptive mother.
12. See the introduction to Exodus by Rabbi David Zvi Hoffmann.
13. Or perhaps it is both. God's plan for humanity cannot come to fruition without the Israelite nation as His partner, and the emergence of the Israelite nation is important inasmuch as they will be God's partner. This is much like the *Aleinu* prayer, in which the first paragraph celebrates the uniqueness of Israel while the second affirms that Israel's uniqueness is not an end unto itself but a means to God's ultimate hope for humanity.

making the Egyptians a "laughingstock" (10:2). Does that reflect a universalist-oriented God? That question is not a modern one; it is inherent in a careful reading of the text, and we find echoes of discomfort with the suffering of the Egyptians in a midrash which cites God rebuking the angels for wanting to join in Israel's song at the Reed Sea.[14]

Exodus introduces us to the birth of the nation of Israel, their slavery and liberation, their struggle to adapt to the dramatic transformation from a disorganized, oppressed people to an independent nation. It highlights their and God's struggle to establish, build, and maintain a meaningful relationship, one which will hopefully eventually bring them into sanctified partnership with God but seems hopelessly mired in the petty details and travails of daily life.

THE *MISHKAN*

Nearly a third of Exodus is dedicated to the design and construction of the Tabernacle, the portable sanctuary Israel carried with them through their travels and which served them for nearly half a millennium, well into their entry into their promised land. Despite its significance as the *ohel moed,* literally, the tent in which God meets His terrestrial partners, the lengthy technical details of the plan are mind-numbing to most readers when they are first presented in chapters 25–31 and frustrating when they are repeated in chapters 35–40, as the Torah describes the actual construction. A quick survey of many of the traditional commentaries reveals that there is a lengthy stretch in that repetition for which the commentaries have absolutely nothing to add.

When we understand the Tabernacle in the context of God establishing a dwelling place, in Hebrew a *Mishkan,* among His partner nation, the details of that *Mishkan* reveal a significant amount of symbolic meaning about how God envisions the relationship with Israel. Even more, when we understand the nature of that *Mishkan* and its context in Exodus, it sheds a new light on the incident of the Golden Calf and

14. Sanhedrin 39b. This is a fascinating midrash. As angels are divine messengers incapable of independent thought, the desire of the angels is an expression of God's will. God wants to rejoice in the downfall of the Egyptians but cannot, as their demise reflects a failure in God's plan for their divine image to inform and direct their actions.

its aftermath (chapters 32–34), which seems to interrupt between the plan for constructing the *Mishkan* and its implementation. In fact, the interruption is not only in the textual narrative, but also in the nascent partnership between God and Israel. The entire vision for the *Mishkan* and what it represents is threatened by Israel's sin; there is the real possibility of a rupture between God and His people.

It is in that light that the actual construction of the *Mishkan* takes on new meaning and significance. Every detail, even if described earlier, needs to be described again, and every nuanced difference between the plan and its implementation takes on profound significance. When we include the full narrative of the Golden Calf and its aftermath as an integral part of the *Mishkan*, it turns out that this occupies nearly half of the book of Exodus and deserves substantive study.

A TALE OF TWO COVENANTS

Much of the first half of Exodus is almost expected. After all, God established a covenant with Abraham, which was passed on through Isaac and Jacob. In that covenant, known as the Covenant Between the Pieces (Gen. 15:9–21), God informs Abraham that his descendants will be strangers in a foreign land where they will be subjected to oppressive slavery for an extended period of time, after which they will be freed with great wealth and returned to their ancestral land. That covenant is referenced explicitly at the end of Exodus 2 and again in God's speech to Moses at the beginning of Exodus 6. Fulfillment of that covenant would involve the liberation of Israel and their direct transit into their promised land.

That, however, is not the trajectory of Exodus. The trip from Egypt to Canaan is delayed, most significantly by a detour to Mount Sinai, where God offers Israel a new covenant. Unclear to the reader is the relationship between those two covenants. Is the latter built on the former or does it stand independent of it? What would have happened had Israel rejected that second covenant? Does their violation of that second covenant with the Golden Calf annul the patriarchal one?

An initial analysis suggests that the two covenants are dramatically different. The first is about what God will do for Israel – it is one-sided. All Abraham's descendants need to do are endure their fate and await God's deliverance. By contrast, the second covenant is two-sided.

It requires Israel's initial acceptance and demands adherence to a set of rules and code of behavior. In contrast to the Abrahamic covenant of fate, this is a covenant of chosen destiny.[15]

MOSES

No discussion of Exodus is complete without a serious exploration of its hero, Moses.[16] Moses is unquestionably the most central human figure in Exodus, and he will remain the Torah's most important character through the end of Deuteronomy. We hear about him from before his birth until his death. He is the prototype of the unwilling prophet who eventually embraces his mission with extraordinary passion. We are witness to his passionate defenses of and commitment to both God and his people. As I noted earlier, the most significant heroes in the biblical tradition are those who grow into greatness, grappling with challenges along the way and growing from both their successes and failures. Moses is no exception. Born auspiciously, saved audaciously, raised in Pharaoh's house, he shows promise as a popular savior only to disappear soon afterward into a quiet pastoral life as a Midianite shepherd (imagine – an Egyptian prince serving as a shepherd, a profession despised by the Egyptians[17]). When approached by God, he seems genuinely uninterested in getting involved, and when forced into the task only to see it fail, brazenly confronts God. Exodus portrays Moses alternating between challenging God and representing Him, between faithful oracle of God's message and creative interpreter of that message, and between frustrated leader of a difficult people and their staunchest advocate.

As much as Moses is described in Numbers (12:7) as "loyal" to God, in Deuteronomy (34:10) as prophetically unique, and in Joshua (1:1) as God's servant, there is little indication in Moses's early life of loyalty, prophecy, or servitude. Moses is independent. A careful reading of the Torah text reveals a Moses who defies God, evades God,

15. This framing was first articulated by Rabbi Joseph B. Soloveitchik in an address he delivered in 1956 and was later published as an essay titled "Kol Dodi Dofek" in *BeSod HaYaḥid VeHaYaḥad,* ed. Pinhas Peli (Orot, 1976).
16. For a more extensive examination of Moses, see my work *Moses and the Path to Leadership.*
17. See Gen. 43:33 and 46:34.

challenges God, changes God's instructions, and forces God's hand. It will also reveal multiple aspects of who Moses is and, more importantly, who he becomes. Ironically, the same Moses whose antinomian streak balks against human law is the one who brings God's law to the people and rails against its violation.

Why does God choose him, and does He stick with Moses despite Moses's rebellious streak or because of it? How does a man with seemingly no connection to the Hebrews in Egypt and no apparent spirituality become the most important figure in forging a national identity for Israel and bringing them into a covenantal bond with the Divine, enabling God's hope for humanity to get that much closer to fruition?

MOSES'S INITIATIVE

One of the ideas which will emerge is that Moses is not simply a passive loudspeaker for God's message but is an active participant in delivering that message, to the extent that he repeatedly challenges God, modifies the message delivered to Israel, and takes his own initiative. While there are ample examples where that will be readily apparent, there are other places where it is open to interpretation. For example, God's version of the commandment regarding consecration of the firstborns is brief, covering but a single verse (13:2); Moses's version of that spans six verses (13:11–16) and adds many elements which are not even hinted to in God's command. Did God say all those details to Moses but the Torah chose not to record them, or did Moses add them on his own? Nahmanides addresses this question in multiple places throughout the Torah and is open to both possibilities, although many traditionalists would be wary of suggesting that anything is Moses's original idea. The approach I take is based on the way the Torah presents it. When Moses's words are different from those of God, appear to be a significant expansion of God's words, or appear to be a condensed version of God's words, my assumption is that it is probably presented that way for a reason, and is not simply for variety of expression.[18] That being said, even if we assume

18. Ibn Ezra's approach is generally the opposite, as he understands that the variations are insignificant as long as they present the same general idea. See his commentary on 20:1.

those to be Moses's additions, that does not detract from their significance, as their inclusion in the Torah implies God's approval.[19]

GOD AS LEARNER

The idea of God testing man is first introduced in Genesis, when God tests Abraham. The very notion of testing generated intense discussion among the midrashim and traditional commentaries struggling to explain why an omniscient God needs to test people.[20] That challenge is magnified in Exodus, which thrice explicitly describes God as testing Israel[21] and where many of the explanations offered in Genesis are less relevant.

I've argued elsewhere[22] that to create man, an independent being endowed with *tzelem E-lohim* – the divine quality of independence and creativity – omniscient God may have intentionally self-limited His knowledge of what people will do. In fact, it may even have been a necessary precondition for creating the type of being God sought to create, for how could humans be truly God-like, free to choose their paths, if their choices are known in advance? This self-limiting is what makes it possible for the Torah to describe God as disappointed when humanity doesn't meet His hopes and expectations (Gen. 6:2, 5–7), necessitating a restart of creation in the Great Confusion and another significant intervention as He disperses the people from Babel (Gen. 11:1–9). God had hoped that things would have turned out differently but truly did not know – because He chose not to – how people would act until after they did.[23]

19. See Abrabanel's introduction to Deuteronomy.
20. For example, Rabbi Saadia Gaon suggests that the test is to provide the righteous with an opportunity to receive extra reward, Rashi understands the test as providing an opportunity to improve the one being tested, Rashbam sees the test as a form of punishment, and Nahmanides understands the test as a means of bringing out the potential in the one being tested.
21. 15:25, 16:4, and 20:16.
22. Zvi Grumet, *Genesis: From Creation to Covenant* (Maggid Books, 2017), 17–27.
23. This presentation of an omniscient God whose knowledge of people is suspended is mirrored by a talmudic aggada (Nidda 30b) which describes unborn children as having mastered all of Torah and being made to forget it just prior to birth.

The possibility for an omniscient God to not know what people will do provides an elegant solution to the conundrum of God repeatedly testing people, as this is how He learns about people.[24]

In Genesis, God's "blind spot" regarding humanity is expressed as frustration,[25] regret,[26] or a need to intervene in the affairs of humanity.[27] In Exodus the focus shifts from humanity to Israel, and God's disappointment – which generates His learning about them – is expressed as anger or even as a rhetorical question. Thus, God is angered when Moses repeatedly looks for excuses to avoid engaging in his mission (4:14), is frustrated that Israel fails to trust Him (16:28), and threatens to destroy Israel (32:10) or remove His presence from them (33:3) in response to the Golden Calf. Later, His anger will flare at them for their unjustified discontent (Num. 11:1), their ingratitude regarding the manna (Num. 11:10), and their distrust regarding the quail (Num. 11:33). He will be frustrated by their rejection of the Promised Land (Num. 14:11–12) and their rejection of Moses and Aaron as their leaders (Num. 17:6–10). His disappointment in the ability of Moses and Aaron to meet the challenge of the new generation (Num. 20:7–13) will impel Him to bar them from continuing to lead the people.

Beyond God's reaction to disappointment with His chosen partners, God learns about them and adjusts. In Genesis, God adjusts the rules for humanity following the Great Confusion (Gen. 9:1–7), forces diversity into a world lacking independent thought (Gen. 11:1–9), and ultimately changes course, electing to work with Abraham and his descendants as His ambassadors rather than continue to try to deal directly with all of humanity.[28] In Exodus, we will see that God

---

24. For a different angle on God adapting to human intercession, see Jonathan Sacks's work *I Believe* (Maggid Books, 2022), 117–21.

25. The word *etzev*, meaning pain or frustration, is used to describe God's reaction to the difficulty in creating humans who rise up to His expectations (Gen. 6:6). This is parallel to the frustration and pain decreed upon both men (Gen. 3:17–18) and women (Gen. 3:16) in their efforts to be productive.

26. Gen. 6:6.

27. This is particularly evident in the stories of the Great Confusion, the Dispersion from Babel, and the destruction of Sodom.

28. For a thematic exploration of the idea of God adjusting for the reality of humanity, see my article "The Ideal and the Real" (*Tradition* 34:3).

introduces Aaron as a partner to Moses in response to Moses's reticence to speak with Israel and Pharaoh, adjusts the covenant with Israel in response to their inability to quickly shift from a slave people to a covenantal one, shifts Moses's role in that covenant, and even adopts some of Moses's innovations.

Much like a parent who needs to adapt to children with different needs to ensure their growth and success, the God of the Torah is one who learns about people in general and His people in particular, and He adapts to them and their reality in His commitment to help them grow and succeed on their multilayered journeys. We should therefore not be surprised that God tests His people to learn about them, much as they repeatedly test Him.[29] As God and Israel seek to build a relationship, they each learn about the other.

This continues into Exodus as well. It is expressed repeatedly in God's dealings with Moses's[30] as well as in His interactions with Israel. Each brings its own source of frustration, like when Moses repeatedly refuses his mission and when Israel's trust in God falters again and again, and God shows signs of changing His plan to adapt to the human nature of those with whom He is dealing. As we will see, God not only adapts His expectations, but may even modify the covenant with Israel as a result.

WHAT COMES NEXT?

Exodus is the second of the five books of the Torah. Although it stands on its own, and we've seen it in the context of Genesis, its predecessor, it will be valuable to briefly explore how it connects to the books which follow, especially Leviticus and Numbers. Both of those books are sequels to Exodus, each following a different core theme of the book. Leviticus

29. Exodus thrice describes God as testing Israel (15:25, 16:4, and 20:16) and twice describes Israel as testing God (17:2 and 17:7). In an extraordinary parallel, Deuteronomy – reflecting on the historical relationship between God and Israel – thrice references God testing Israel (Deut. 8:2, 16, and 13:4) and has two references to Israel testing God (both in Deut. 6:16). Strikingly, Numbers 14:22 speaks of ten tests in the wilderness, and it is not surprising that the Mishna (Avot 5:3) refers to ten times that God tested Abraham.
30. For one example of this, see Netziv's commentary on 4:14.

primarily explores the notion of Israel as a sanctified nation, following the theme first introduced in the preamble to the Revelation at Sinai (Ex. 19) and developed further in the lengthy discussion of the Tabernacle. As we will see, the aftershocks of the Golden Calf dominate not only the end of Exodus but also significant parts of Leviticus. By contrast, Numbers is focused on the development of the nation, its structure, and how it transforms over the course of forty years in the wilderness. It continues much of the thrust of the first half of Exodus, focused on the people, and highlighting their transformation from a band of liberated slaves with the psychological baggage of generations of servitude to a confident and unified nation poised to enter and fight for their ancestral lands.

Exodus thus serves not only as a sequel to Genesis, developing its core theme, but as the unifying book of the Torah, creating the bonds holding the first four books together as a unit.[31] The links between Exodus on the one hand and Leviticus and Numbers on the other will be explored in the epilogues.

THE LEGAL SECTIONS

Beginning with the instructions for preparing the *pesaḥ*,[32] Exodus introduces a new genre of literature into the Torah. Whereas up until now the Torah is essentially a narrative, that narrative will now be interwoven with legal sections. Some are brief and explicitly linked to the narrative, such as the mitzvot directly related to leaving Egypt in Exodus 12 and 13, and some are lengthier and not explicitly linked to any narrative, especially the extended list of laws in chapters 21–23. My approach to those is to understand them in the context of the narrative, so that they enrich the story and add new perspectives. Thus, aligned with the approach taken by Rashbam to 13:9, "the sign on the hand and the reminder between the eyes" are metaphors for keeping God's salvation in our hearts and minds, as if they were inscribed there. That does not mean that the

31. Deuteronomy stands out as unique. It serves as a reflection on the previous three books, with an eye toward preparing Israel for their future as a people settled into a land without the leader who forged them. See Micah Goodman, *The Last Words of Moses* (Maggid Books, 2023).

32. Exodus 12. In its initial usage, the word *pesaḥ* refers to the special meal prepared by the Israelites for the night of their redemption.

Torah does not require men to wear tefillin, but it understands that the source of that mitzva is not necessarily in the text of the Torah, but is in the Oral Tradition (or Oral Torah), which was passed from generation to generation. What the written text provides is an understanding of underlying principles and values which drive these mitzvot, but it is not intended as a source from which the legal, halakhic requirements of these mitzvot can be learned.

This is a significant departure from the approaches popularized in the nineteenth century by Malbim, Rabbi S. R. Hirsch, Rabbi Yaakov Zvi Mecklenburg, and others, who sought to demonstrate the inseparability of the Written Law from the Oral Tradition. In my understanding, separating the Oral Torah from the Written Torah allows for each to shine independently as they complement one another – since the text of the Torah provides a conceptual framework for understanding the meaning of the mitzvot while the Oral Torah elucidates the technical requirements of their performance. To return to our example from Rashbam, the written text of the Torah provides the religious significance of the mitzva of tefillin which the Oral Law teaches.

ASSUMPTIONS

There is a dance between theology and textual reading. Every reader brings his or her own theological biases to the reading. Were we to leave it at that, there would be few revelations about biblical text other than the creative ways of demonstrating that the text supports our predetermined ideas. To truly uncover the theology of the text requires shedding theological preconceptions. That is both difficult, if not impossible, and rather frightening to those for whom their theological assumptions are of primary importance. And yet it is important to be able to do so, to some extent, if we are to begin to uncover the Bible's theology (as distinct from theologies developed over many subsequent centuries). As a result, some of what I write here may be jarring to some readers in its boldness, while other readers will be disappointed that I did not go far enough. I hope that my fidelity to the voice of the text is not colored by preconceptions.

It is this preparedness to explore the Torah's initial intent which impels me to try to read the text as if I am encountering it for the first time, without preconditions. For me, this includes taking the text at face value. For example, there is no reason to assume that the Israelites were substantively different from other enslaved groups, with some kind of distinctive cultural heritage but not necessarily deeply knowledgeable about the intricacies of their ancestors' lives. In other words, while we readers have access to intimate familiarity with Genesis, they did not, so and they may have less knowledge about their past – and their God – than contemporary readers, whose knowledge of the Bible comes from childhood stories. The extension of this is that the Israelites leaving Egypt had a very steep learning curve. This is certainly true in matters of faith (having been entrenched in Egyptian culture for multiple generations), so that their newly found faith would have shaky foundations – despite God's repeated miraculous demonstrations. It is also true regarding their sense of identity and self-worth – having grown up generation after generation as second- or third-class people with slavery as their perceived past and destiny.

This approach also means taking the same position regarding Moses, whose stature in Jewish tradition is unparalleled. That stature is the product of a lifetime of work, but he was not born that way. Despite assorted midrashic comments, the text provides no reason to assume that Moses's early life is marked by any particular knowledge of God or the history of the Israelites, or even an identification with the latter, other than what he might have learned as an infant in his mother's home or from his adoptive mother. There is also no reason to assume that he had any idea of the God of Israel prior to his encounter at the burning bush. The result of this approach is that he, too, has a steep learning curve in matters of identity, history, Israelite theology – a curve perhaps significantly steeper than that of the rest of the Israelites.

All this allows for a fresh reading of many of the scenes in Exodus, scenes which otherwise generate questions from readers who may be puzzled after assuming that the ancient Israelites – and certainly Moses – knew at least as much as the contemporary educated Jew. Thus, when Israel first receives the manna, neither they nor Moses were aware of the concept of Shabbat or of restrictions associated with it.

Despite my professed desire to read the text as if it were my first time, I do have some basic assumptions which guide me in this work.

First, the biblical text is a unified work, and any attempt to disassemble it into its disparate components does violence to the text (unless accompanied by an equal attempt to reassemble it into a meaningful and coherent whole). Much of the classic academic study of the Bible is devoted to the deconstruction of the text. Typically, that process involves two phases – noticing the anomalies within the text and drawing conclusions about the multiple origins of the texts based on those observations. While the observations made in academic Bible study of the anomalies are often astute and filled with insight, I find that the solutions provided are usually unconvincing, since they, too, often reflect a predetermined bias of the scholar. Further, I find that this approach robs the text of even the possibility of meaning. As such, I assume that the Bible must be read as a single, focused work with a distinct message and focus.

My second assumption is that the meaningfulness of the Bible emerges organically from a close reading of it and should not be superimposed on it from external sources. The enterprise of Midrash (rabbinic homiletic readings) is meaningful as its own discipline but should not be confused with the meaning which is inherent within the biblical text. With regard to Midrash, it should be noted that many midrashim were born out of deep readings of the Bible for which the Rabbis used homiletic rather than exegetical language to express those ideas. As such, it should not be surprising that many of the insights coming from contemporary literary readings of the Bible can be found in midrashim. I will sometimes point those out.

Third, I assume that the reader has at least a minimum familiarity with the biblical story. The more knowledge the reader has, the better he or she will be able to appreciate the nuances which support and develop the arguments I present, and those with access to the original Hebrew text will benefit even more. That being said, I aim to have the content accessible to those who do not already possess comprehensive knowledge of the text, but they should be prepared to open the Bible and read along.

Fourth, there is often temptation to draw conclusions from a single passage without context. While that may be appropriate for homiletic purposes, I believe that it is misleading, like drawing conclusions from an individual photo when a video is available. I believe that a broad and comprehensive reading of the text reveals patterns and themes which contain the lasting truths which make reading the Torah as compelling today as ever.

As mentioned earlier, this applies to the great biblical heroes as well. They are heroes because they became giants grappling with challenges. Those struggles sometimes reveal steps forward, but we should not be surprised to find slipping backward or mistakes. It is precisely their humanity which makes them meaningful characters from whom we can learn. The Torah never asserts that its central heroes are models of perfection,[33] and the assumption made by some that they are flawless characters forces those readers into complex apologetics as they try to rationalize ethically questionable behavior.

Fifth, despite the notion popularized by Rashi[34] that the Torah is not written chronologically, this book assumes (like Nahmanides[35]) that – unless there is a compelling reason to suggest otherwise – the Torah is very much chronological and sequential. This takes on particular significance in Exodus when discussing the sequence of events in the second half of the book, about which the classic medieval exegetes Rashi and Nahmanides take dramatically different positions.

Finally, I believe that the Bible is written with exquisite care so that close attention must be paid to its nuances. These include choice of words and wordplays, theme words, pacing, patterns, developing themes, and literary structures embedded within the text – even nuances in spelling can sometimes reveal significant insights. It is only through an exploration of those that deep meaning emerges from reading the text.

TERMINOLOGY AND CONVENTIONS

The Hebrew term "Torah" literally means teaching, or a guiding manual. In its most narrow sense it refers only to the Five Books, or the Pentateuch, and in its broadest sense encompasses all of Jewish teaching from the Revelation at Sinai to the latest commentaries, law codes, and religious instruction. In this volume I use "Torah" to refer specifically to

33. This approach is adopted by Rashbam, Nahmanides, Radak, and many others.
34. See Rashi's comments on Gen. 35:29; Ex. 18:9, 19:11, 21:1, 21:12, 31:18; and Lev. 8:2.
35. See Nahmanides's comments on Gen. 11:32, 35:28; Ex. 24:1; Lev. 16:1; and Num. 16:1.

the Five Books, and the term "Bible" to refer to the rest of the Hebrew biblical canon (what Christians would call the Old Testament). Biblical references to Exodus are identified by chapter and verse, often without mentioning Exodus. References to other books in the Bible are identified by book as well.

The terms "Jew" and "Jewish," used colloquially today to refer to the entirety of the people, originated as a reference to those who were associated with the biblical Judean monarchy of First Temple times, as opposed to those identified with the monarchy of Israel. To use those terms in the context of the Exodus is anachronistic, as the Judean monarchy was first established hundreds of years later. The Torah refers to the people God liberated from Egypt as "Hebrews" (*Ivrim*) or "Israelites" (Benei Yisrael, literally, "the children of Israel"). I try to be careful to use the nomenclature employed by the Torah.

Exodus is filled with multiple names for God, some of which are specifically highlighted in its early chapters. Academic and mystical writing insists on distinguishing between them, and indeed most translations make those distinctions. Unless there is particular significance to the name, I do not make those distinctions, as they are mostly unimportant to what I am exploring. When the Torah emphasizes God's four-letter name, I use A-donai. While God is neither masculine nor feminine, convention refers to God using masculine terminology (with the exception of the *Shekhina*, the Divine Presence, which is distinctly feminine). This book will stick with that convention, including using masculine pronouns to refer to God.

When referring to humankind, I try to remain gender neutral, using terms such as humanity, and when I use the terms man or mankind it refers equally to both genders.

The main characters in Exodus are well known in the English-speaking world, as are the conventional renditions of those names. Moses, Aaron, Joshua, and Pharaoh are ubiquitous in the English language and Western culture. For purposes of convention, I use those names which are familiar to the native English speaker, even though to the student of the Bible in its original they sound awkward. Other biblical names which are less prominent I will present in transliteration of their Hebrew pronunciation.

Rendering the biblical text in translation is difficult and robs it of the power of nuance and wordplay embedded in the Hebrew text. Translations in this book are my own and are adapted to demonstrate some of the power in the original Hebrew, although I regularly consulted Robert Alter's sensitive translation in his *The Five Books of Moses: Translation and Commentary* (Norton, 2004) and Everett Fox's *The Five Books of Moses: A New Translation with Introductions, Commentary, and Notes* (Schocken, 1995).

TORAH AS INSTRUCTION

Ever since the Torah was written it has been studied as a source of guidance. With the Enlightenment, in many circles the study shifted from seeking moral or religious direction to academic study. That academic examination challenged some of the most fundamental assumptions and sensitivities of the religiously oriented, and for much of the past two hundred years there has been an antagonistic relationship between those who study the Bible from an academic perspective and those who see it as a sanctified, core religious document. In recent decades, however, a new approach has begun to emerge – one which is aware of and enlightened by the contributions of two centuries of academic literature while remaining committed to preserving the Torah as its Hebrew name means, a book of instruction.

In these pages I attempt to participate in this emerging trend. I have been fortunate to be exposed to an extraordinary and growing body of literature written by people with deep reverence for the text and astonishing insights, including those derived from history, philosophy, philology, archaeology, and most importantly, an exquisitely refined literary sensitivity. The marriage of traditional reverence for the text with an array of new tools for exploring it has the potential to reveal extraordinary insights into the text coupled with deep religious inspiration which otherwise would have remained hidden. I write these pages in an attempt to share with others my own religious experience emanating from this multilayered exploration of the Torah.

Exodus 1:1–22

Genesis Revisited

While Genesis opens with the breathtaking Creation, Exodus falls rather flat by contrast – a list of names, Israel's children who descended to Egypt, information abbreviated from Genesis 46. There is nothing new in the beginning of the second book.[1]

Then again, perhaps we should not be so surprised. After all, Genesis is comprised of an introduction followed by eleven chronicles of *toledot*, almost every one of which begins with a review of some key piece of information told earlier.[2] If Exodus is the natural continuation of Genesis, then perhaps the repetition is to be expected. But Exodus is a different book, with a different focus, and absent the *toledot* structure so prominent in Genesis, which begs us to rethink the opening.

One of the characteristics of this passage is its brevity, the effect of which is twofold. First, it highlights the explosive expansion of this family – from twelve to seventy to an uncountable multitude, all in the

1. This question was addressed by many of the traditional commentaries. See Rashi, Ibn Ezra, and Nahmanides for a variety of approaches.
2. For more on this, see Grumet, *Genesis: From Creation to Covenant*, xvii–xviii. A similar approach here is taken by Bekhor Shor.

span of seven verses.[3] Second, the fifth verse pauses the rapidity ever so briefly to identify the number seventy. Each of these deserves a fuller explanation.

GENESIS FULFILLED

We will eventually learn that the people numbered in excess of six hundred thousand males. To get from seventy to six hundred thousand in the span of a few hundred years seems unreal, and this is precisely what the Torah is trying to convey. The growth of this people cannot be explained naturally; there must have been another factor involved. In fact, the continuation of the chapter highlights two factors – the oppression of the people (1:12) and divine intervention (1:20), and those two factors may very well have been connected. Pharaoh's plan to oppress the people is, in part, also an attempt to prevent their growth – *pen yirbeh,* lest they multiply (1:10). Describing the result of his plan, the Torah states that "as they were oppressed they multiplied" – *ken yirbeh* (1:12). Using the same word to describe his intention and how that was foiled suggests that there is some other force ensuring that Pharaoh would fail, as if to say, "Let's see whose plan will actually work."[4]

Beyond that, however, the Torah devotes an entire verse (1:7) to describe their extraordinary fecundity. *Uvenei Yisrael paru vayishretzu vayirbu vayaatzmu bimeod meod vatimalei haaretz otam.* At first glance, readers will recognize language from God's blessing to the first people (Genesis 1:28), *peru urevu umilu et haaretz,*[5] suggesting that the children of Israel are finally reproducing as God initially intended all humans to do. Yet our verse adds two verbs (*vayishretzu* and *vayaatzmu*) as well as a double adjective, *bimeod meod* (very, very much), to describe their growth – all of which are absent in that initial Genesis blessing. Those additional words, however, do appear elsewhere in Genesis. The first appears in God's instruction to Noah and his sons following the Great Confusion – *peru urevu shirtzu vaaretz* (Gen. 9:7). The second verb

3. See Rashbam.
4. Exodus Rabba 1:12.
5. The continuation of the Genesis verse speaks of conquering the land, which is precisely what Pharaoh fears.

is used to describe God's blessing to Abraham – Abraham will be a great and *atzum* nation. As for the double adjective, it is also first used to describe Abraham's fruitfulness (Gen. 17:2, 7, and 20)[6] and is used nowhere else in the Torah.[7]

One way to summarize this opening passage is that God's blessing to and hope for humanity – including from the first people through Noah and finally Abraham – which were not fulfilled in Genesis, are finally being realized in the opening of Exodus with the descendants of Israel.

This takes on additional depth when we consider the closing phrase of this opening passage, *vatimalei haaretz otam* – the land was filled with them. This phrase echoes the opening of the story of Noah, in which God felt compelled to undo His creation, which is introduced by the phrase *vatimalei haaretz ḥamas* – the land was filled with injustice (Gen. 6:11).[8] As opposed to Genesis, where God's designs went awry in every generation, in Exodus they are finally being actualized. The growth of Israel's descendants is the fulfillment of God's blessing to all of humanity, to Noah, and to Abraham – the three major pivot points in Genesis.

The filling of the land brings to light another interesting parallel with Genesis, as well as an important contrast. The story of populating the earth is recounted in Genesis through a series of genealogical tables, most prominently in chapters 5 and 10. There is something curious about those tables, as they list twenty generations of men begetting men. There is a not a single woman identified by name; the closest we get to hearing about a woman is that the named men sired both sons and daughters. By contrast, the opening of Exodus – which also tells a story of population growth – highlights the role of women. Two women, in particular, are featured in the first chapter of Exodus – the midwives[9] who are integral to the survival of the Israelite nation – and they are

6. This third reference is actually to Ishmael, whom God blesses to become a very large nation, as he is Abraham's son.
7. It does appear twice in Ezekiel 9:9 and 16:13.
8. Most translations render *ḥamas* as violence. Its usage in Genesis 16:5 convinces me that it means injustice.
9. The Hebrew term used in the Torah is ambiguous, either meaning the midwives who themselves were Hebrews (Rashi, Rashbam) or the midwives to the Hebrews (Bekhor Shor, Abrabanel, Rabbi Shmuel David Luzzatto).

identified by name. That highlighting continues in the second chapter, in which three anonymous women are featured as conspiring to secretly save a single Israelite boy.

Finally, when we consider the number seventy, which is highlighted by the brevity of the opening passage, we are reminded of the seventy nations descended from Noah.[10] Those seventy nations represent all of humanity, that same humanity which disappoints God a few generations later, eventually necessitating that God shift plans. The children of Israel, presented in Exodus as God's new focus, represent God's new hope for all of humanity; their success in fulfilling the promise of Genesis holds the key to the fulfillment of God's initial plan for all of creation. As God says to Abram, "Through you will come blessing to all the families on the earth" (Gen. 12:3).[11]

FROM CHILDREN OF ISRAEL TO THE ISRAELITE NATION

It is difficult to know precisely what kind of identity Israel's descendants maintained in Egypt. Joseph set them up to live separately in Goshen yet made sure that they all had Egyptian clothes so that they could blend in.[12] We later find Egyptians and Israelites living side by side, even integrated into the same homes.[13] And while Joseph insisted that his bones be reinterred in Canaan, there is no record in the Torah of any of his brothers making a similar request.

Regardless of whatever integration there may have been, there were likely barriers as well. Egypt was a conservative and traditional culture. Kings came from long-lasting dynasties protecting ancient traditions and ways and were accorded a level of divinity which was passed from father to son. Moreover, Egyptians were Hamites, while the Israelites were Semites, which would have automatically set them apart as

---

10. Gen. 10:1–32. The idea of there being seventy nations in the world is reflected in multiple talmudic and midrashic comments.
11. This idea is repeated in Gen. 18:18 when God shares His thinking in choosing Abraham.
12. Gen. 45:22. While he set them up to live in Goshen, he gave them permanent land holdings in the land of Rameses (Gen. 47:11). This appears to be different from the Raamses the Israelites built in Ex. 1:11.
13. See 3:22.

being different. We will later learn that it is likely that they had an oral tradition of a divine promise that they would be taken from Egypt[14] and that Moses assumed that there was a code involving a name of God that they associated with that tradition.[15] Further, the beginning of Exodus 2 and the brief genealogical table in 6:14–25 suggest that there were tribal identities,[16] and we later hear that there was some kind of native leadership in the form of the elders.[17]

Whether they identified as Semites, as members of related clans, or as members of a family with a common ancestor, there is no sense that they identify as a nation. In the latter part of Genesis, Jacob's progeny is called either *benei Yaakov* (the children of Jacob)[18] or benei Yisrael (the children of Israel),[19] with Jacob and Israel being interchangeable. They are a family. Indeed, the opening verse of Exodus – echoing Genesis 46:5 – also speaks of benei Yisrael, the children of the man named Israel, and that same term is used again in 1:7 as the Torah describes the spectacular proliferation of the family.

In the transition from the review of Genesis to the story of Exodus that same term is used, but it takes on an entirely different connotation. Just two verses after it was used to describe a growing family Pharaoh describes Benei Yisrael (which I now capitalize as a proper name) as the Israelite nation. "Behold, the nation, Benei Yisrael, is more prolific[20] and mightier than us" (1:9). Pharaoh is the first to identify them as a separate national entity.

Ironically, it may have been his pronouncement which helped the descendants of Israel forge the beginning of a national identity, as

14. This is why they believed Moses when he first approached them in 4:31. Note that when Moses and God speak in chapter 3, Moses is not concerned that they will not believe in redemption, but rather that they will be skeptical of him being the redeemer.
15. 3:13.
16. *Pirkei DeRabbi Eliezer* 42 expresses this idea midrashically, suggesting that the sea split into twelve distinct paths, one for each tribe.
17. 3:16–18.
18. Gen. 35:33, 49:1.
19. Gen. 46:5, 8.
20. This translation is based on the comments of Rabbi Abraham, son of Maimonides, and Ralbag.

they are marked by the Egyptians as non-Egyptian, and as a subjugated minority they found new ways to bolster themselves. "The more they [the Egyptians] oppressed him [Israel], the more he [Israel] multiplied and spread" (1:12). This switch is portrayed subtly yet powerfully in the opening narrative of the enslavement and oppression in which every reference to the Egyptians in verses 9–12 consistently describes the Egyptians using plural pronouns and verbs while every reference to Israel describes it in the singular.[21] Notice the highlighted words in this passage:

> Behold, the *nation*, Benei Yisrael, *is* more prolific and mightier than *us*. Come now, let *us* outsmart *it*, lest *it* become even more numerous and then, if there should be a war, *it* will be added to *our* enemies and *it* will go up and away from the land. So, *they* set upon *it* officers of the labor tax to afflict *it* with *their* burdens, and *it* built storage cities for Pharaoh, Pitom and Raamses. But as *they* oppressed *it*, *it* continued to increase and *it* spread out, and *they* loathed *Israel*. (Ex. 1:9–12)

In fact, two words stand out as they contrast the children of Israel with the Israelite nation. Describing the phenomenal growth of the people (1:7), the Torah uses five verbs in succession, including *vayirbu* (they became numerous) and *vayaatzmu* (they grew mighty). These two verbs, along with the others in the succession, are in the plural. They – the many individuals who reproduced greatly and mightily – are transformed. Pharaoh uses those same verbs to describe the Israelite nation, but this time they are in the singular. The nation is *rav* and *atzum*. It is a large and mighty nation.

This switch begins one of the most important projects in the history of Israel – building a national identity. The endeavor begins in the very first chapter of Exodus and continues throughout the book. In fact, forging that national identity emerges as one of the most significant effects of the forty years in the wilderness and is one of Moses's great

21. This is overlooked in most translations of the Torah. Notable exceptions are Everett Fox's *The Five Books of Moses* (Schocken, 1983) and *The Steinsaltz Humash* (Koren Publishers, 2018).

achievements – even managing to prevent the secession of two of the tribes just months before the entry into the land.[22]

The riddle of the opening verses highlights the transformation of the people. Indeed, the opening sounds like Genesis 46, which speaks of Jacob's family. But as we race through the generations in less than ten verses, we understand that the opening is designed to serve as a contrast to what they were when they descended and what they became, in no small part due to Pharaoh's efforts. In that sense, the opening verses begin to frame the story of the genesis of the nation of Israel.

PHARAOH AND BABEL

It is not just the introductory passage which links Exodus and Genesis, but the story of the enslavement of Israel echoes one of the key events of Genesis, the story of Babel.[23] Chapter 11 of Genesis depicts all of humanity living in a single place, the floodplain of the Tigris and Euphrates Rivers, speaking in a single voice and single language. A technological development, the ability to create bricks by firing mud, enables construction in ways previously unimaginable. That sparks a movement to build a city with a tower that will "reach the heavens" to prevent them from spreading out over the land, and the tower to maintain watch over – and control – the inhabitants. God, seeking to thwart the plan to dominate, introduces multiple languages so that the residents lose their ability to cooperate effectively. Not only is the construction plan thwarted, but the inability to communicate impels people to disperse from that centralized place.[24]

Both the thematic framing of the story and the language used are echoed in our present narrative of the subjugation of Israel. There is an attempt by the powerful to control others.[25] A major construction project

22. See Grumet, *Moses and the Path to Leadership*, 163–65. Maintaining that national identity is one of the most important challenges of the rest of the biblical narrative, eventually faltering with the splitting of the Kingdom of Israel (I Kings 12) – a rift which has never healed (Ezekiel 37 is a prophecy about a future reconciliation).
23. For a fuller explication of this parallel, see J. Klitsner, *Subversive Sequels in the Bible* (JPS, 2009), 31–62.
24. For a fuller explication of this, see Grumet, *Genesis: From Creation to Covenant*, 101–8.
25. Genesis Rabba 23:7 identifies the leader in Babel as none other than Nimrod, the

to build a city – *ir* – is introduced with the call of *hava* – let us – which is designed to thwart – *pen* – some anticipated danger involving people leaving the land – *aretz* – and which is eventually foiled when intervention brings about precisely the very thing which was feared. Bricks – *leveinim* – and mortar – *ḥomer* – are described in both as essential elements of the design to subjugate. The initiative in Babel was designed to prevent the fulfillment of God's desire for humanity to fill the earth, which is precisely what Israel does in Egypt, and divine intervention is the only way to prevent the human plan from succeeding. Here is what the linguistic parallels look like:

Exodus 1	**Genesis 11**
***hava** nitḥakma lo* (v. 10)	***hava** nivne lanu ir* (v. 4)
***pen** yirbeh* (v. 10)	***pen** nafutz* (v. 4)
*ve'ala min **haaretz*** (v. 10)	*al penei kol **haaretz*** (v. 4)
vayiven (v. 11)	***nivne*** (v. 4)
***arei** miskenot* (v. 11)	***ir*** (v. 4)
beḥomer uvileveinim (v. 14)	*vatehi lahem **halevena** le'aven vehaḥemar haya lahem **laḥomer*** (v. 3)
ken yirbeh (v. 11)	*vayafetz* (v. 8)

A deep reading of the Babel story reveals that the attempt to control humanity threatens to undermine God's role. After all, if the tower provides for control over those who are lower, then a tower which "reaches the heavens" is designed to control everything under those heavens, replacing God as sovereign over humanity. The mirroring of the stories suggests that Pharaoh's designs to dominate Israel are equally an attempt to subvert God's role on earth, in essence painting Pharaoh as God's rival.[26] Indeed, a passage from the Passover Haggada emphasizes this

first man to lord himself over masses of others (Gen. 10:7–10).

26. God's absence in Exodus 1, which is dominated by Pharaoh, is striking. Leon Kass, *Founding God's Nation: Reading Exodus* (Yale University Press, 2021), 35, notes that

very point: "Had God not taken us out of Egypt, we and our children and our children's children would still be slaves to Pharaoh in Egypt."

This parallel provides the setting for one of the central themes of the first half of Exodus. If Pharaoh's plan is to dominate humanity, that is, to challenge God, then it is not sufficient for God to free Israel. Rather, it will become necessary for God to demonstrate to Pharaoh, and to all those who look up to him, that he is not the god, that there is a Being before whom Pharaoh will necessarily submit. This is an idea which we will see repeatedly throughout the first half of Exodus.

The passage involving the midwives is interesting (1:15–21) as, on the surface, it sems to be unnecessary. What would we be missing had the Torah omitted this entire section, going straight from the intensified slavery (1:14) to the decree to throw all male babies (presumably only the Israelite ones) into the river? This omission would not affect anything in the subsequent narrative, and their subversion does not ultimately derail Pharaoh.

The seeming superfluousness of the section challenges us to explore its significance. True, the narrative of the oppression and the parallel to Babel draw our attention to the danger of unchecked power concentrated in the hands of the few, in this case, Pharaoh. The second half of that narrative, however, the story of the midwives, ignites a new hope. True, Pharaoh seems unstoppable, except that a group of women surreptitiously subvert him. And while they are not the saviors of the people, they are the saviors of the innocent newborns, exposing Pharaoh's weakness.[27] In the face of tyranny they demonstrate a different kind of freedom – one which is not dependent on external factors but which results from their deciding to act like free people and refusing to

---

the end of Genesis highlights Egypt's desire to control death, while the beginning of Exodus describes Pharaoh's effort to control birth. As the Talmud (Taanit 2a) reminds us, however, those realms are solely in God's hands.

27. In the Bible, one of the greatest disgraces to an authority, especially a man wielding power over others, is being undone by a woman. Thus, the great disgrace to the Canaanite general Sisera (Judges 4:21) is being killed by Yael using household tools, and Avimelekh is mortified by the thought that he could have been defeated by a woman using a kitchen implement (Judges 9:53–54).

have their conscience controlled. Pharaoh's might and power are challenged by the basic decency of ordinary people.[28]

It is precisely in this that the Torah defines the difference between the Babel story and the present one about Pharaoh. In Babel, God must intervene, and without that intervention the plot to derail God's hope for humanity will succeed. By contrast, in Egypt, God is surprisingly absent from the story, but that does not mean that all hope is lost. Quite the opposite. There are decent people, women committed to bringing life into the world, who will not be swayed to betray their sacred commitment.[29] In fact, they play an active role in ensuring that the babies survive. Note that both the Torah's description of their actions (the end of 1:17) and Pharaoh's challenging them (the end of 1:18) use the identical phrase, "*Vateḥayena et hayeladim*," "They gave life to the baby boys."[30] These midwives, Shifrah and Puah, follow their ethical cores and use their cunning to undermine Pharaoh's intentions. "The midwives feared God and did not do as the king of Egypt ordered them" (1:17).[31]

---

28. Natan Sharansky reported that his Soviet oppressors mocked the "housewives and students" rallying to free him, and how it was indeed those very housewives and students who defeated the might of the KGB.
29. See Kass, *Founding God's Nation*, 32. J. Klitsner notes the irony that while Pharaoh feared the male babies it was the females who undid his plan. The Torah text itself is ambiguous about the identity of these midwives. Are they the Hebrew midwives or the midwives to the Hebrews? While many of the classical commentaries debate this, it seems irrelevant to the story, which may explain why the Torah intentionally used ambiguous language. The actions of these two women serve as an indictment of the rest of the Egyptians who did not find ways to resist Pharaoh's murderous decrees, perhaps serving as the backdrop for why the plagues affected the Egyptian people and not just Pharaoh and his advisors.
30. See Ibn Ezra (1:17).
31. Rabbi David Zvi Hoffmann notes that the term "God-fearing" refers to living by a set of ethical values. See also Nehama Leibowitz, *Iyunim BeSefer Shemot* (WZO, 1975), 32–33, where she argues that this is only when referring to God-fearing non-Israelites. The Torah states that as a reward for their behavior God "made for them houses." The expression to "make a house" as opposed to "build a house" is rare, and means to build someone up, whether with wealth or progeny. See Ibn Ezra and Bekhor Shor on 1:21. Michael Hattin (https://etzion.org.il/en/tanakh/torah/sefer-shemot/parashat-shemot/shemot-pharaoh-god-king) notes that the name Pharaoh means "Great House." In that context, this expression suggests that these brave women earned their own great houses to rival that of Pharaoh.

SLOW DESCENT INTO SLAVERY

It is hard to know whether Pharaoh genuinely feared the Israelites or contrived this fear to serve his political needs and ideology. Did he really not know who Joseph was or, as some suggest, did he choose to bury Joseph's legacy because it accorded Joseph too much credit for the Egyptian success story?[32]

After all, the traditionalist Egyptian monarchy was responsible for guarding the purity of Egyptian heritage, a purity which made it unbearable for Egyptians to eat together with Semites,[33] much less have them play a significant role in Egyptian society or grow into a significant force. Hence the first step taken by Pharaoh was to identify the Hebrew nation as "other" – a foreign implant that is not native to the land. In doing so he plants the seeds of fear in his people. Not only are there foreigners in the land, but they are multiplying faster than the Egyptians and will soon present a significant threat.[34]

It is here that Pharaoh faces a problem. He does not like, and may even be genuinely fearful of, the foreigners. On the one hand, he may be tempted to expel them, as he sees – or presents – them as a potential threat. On the other hand, they are way too valuable to expel. In fact, he is afraid that they will leave the land on their own.[35]

> Behold, the nation, Benei Yisrael, is more prolific and mightier than us. Come now, let us outsmart it, lest it become even more

32. At the end of Genesis, Joseph is directly responsible for bringing his family and settling them in Egypt as well as serving as the architect of the plan to turn Egypt into a mighty empire. He is also responsible for showing favoritism to his own family while the Egyptians starved for food (Genesis 47), perhaps planting the seeds of animosity between the Egyptians and the Hebrews. Further, he created institutionalized slavery in Egypt, which laid the foundation for the eventual enslavement of Israel.
33. Gen. 43:32.
34. A similar argument can be found in Haman's presentation of the Judeans as a fifth column in the Persian Empire. See Est. 3:5.
35. Rashi (v. 10) attempts to solve this conundrum by reading "it will leave the land" as a euphemism for "we will be forced to leave the land." This, however, strays from the meaning of the text.

> numerous and then, if there should be a war, it will be added to our enemies and it will go up and away from the land. (1:10)

Having marked Israel as other and identifying his conundrum, Pharaoh comes up with a plan. They will stay, but they will be disempowered and marshaled to build the Egyptian infrastructure. The text tells us *what* he did: "So they set upon it officers of the labor tax to afflict it with their burdens, and it built storage cities for Pharaoh, Pitom and Raamses" (1:11). What the text doesn't say is *how* he did it. How did he manage to get decent Egyptians to agree to such a plan? How did he get Israel to participate so readily?

When we think about it, it is not too difficult to use our imagination to fill in those gaps. Identifying Israel as foreign invites the question of loyalty. Are they truly Egyptian, or do they have a subversive agenda? Imagine that Pharaoh announces a national plan to meet some great Egyptian need – perhaps storage cities to preserve Egypt's precious resources.[36] To prove themselves as genuine Egyptians, the Israelites offered their services, and once they did it was difficult to pull back. Were they no longer concerned with Egypt and its needs? Having been shamed into continuing to work it became enshrined in law, with officers in charge of the labor tax to ensure compliance – institutionalized, justified, and legalized servitude. This is the meaning of the Torah's expression *lemaan anoto besivlotam* – in order to intensify the servitude of Israel by making Israel carry the burdens of the Egyptians.[37] In fact, the word *anoto* comes from the Hebrew *inui*, often translated as oppression but which, at its core, means to intensify the servitude in a way which marks the worker's status as a servant.[38]

36. Notice how this plays on the story of Joseph, who collected the grain during the years of plenty and warehoused them in cities in preparation for some future event. See Gen. 41:48.

37. Note that Israel (in the singular) is being held responsible for the burdens of the Egyptians (in the plural).

38. This is what Sarah does to Hagar (Gen. 16:6) in response to Hagar's rejection of Sarah's authority as the mistress of the house. She establishes her own authority over Hagar, which Hagar, having tasted the hope of freedom, cannot bear. See also Code of Hammurabi, no. 146.

Pharaoh may have successfully established control over Israel, but Israel's fecundity despite the servitude impels him to take the next step, intensifying the burden so that it would literally crush them. That is the word which concludes both 1:13 and its expansion, 1:14. In fact, the root E-V-D, meaning slave or labor, appears four times in in a single verse – *Vayemareru et ḥayeihem* ***baavoda*** *kasha beḥomer uvilveinim uvev khol* ***avoda*** *basadeh, et kol* ***avodatam*** *asher* ***avedu*** *bahem befarekh* (1:14).

Within just eight verses, the slippery slope designed by Pharaoh took Israel from being "them" (as opposed to "us") to volunteerism, forced labor, servitude, crushing slavery, and ultimately infanticide. Facing a problem that instead of going away just keeps growing, Pharaoh first instructs the Hebrew midwives to kill the male babies secretly, as if they had died in childbirth, and when that does not succeed, ultimately charges all Egyptians to participate in drowning the male Hebrew children.[39]

Ironically, it is Pharaoh's desire to control Israel that leads to its emerging national identity and uncontrolled growth. It is his decree against the babies which brings the redeemer of Israel to be raised in Pharaoh's own home.[40]

There is a universal message here as well. What Pharaoh does not understand, the readers see clearly. If the only way to rule people is through control and power, then you don't really have control and power. He successfully makes the lives of the Israelites miserable, but he cannot control the divine spirit – the *tzelem E-lohim* – which is an integral part of who people are as God created them. Pharaoh may be powerful and wily, even able to outsmart his adversaries, but God has already planted the seeds of humanity in people, and it is within those people – as we will see in the next chapter – that the seeds of rebellion will take root and begin to unravel his plans.

FINDING THE SAVIOR

Where does this leave us? Israel is transformed from a family into a nation as it provides the spark of hope for the fulfillment of God's Genesis hopes.

---

39. The foundations for this reading can be found in the comment of Nahmanides on 1:10.
40. Kass, *Founding God's Nation*, 34.

God prepares to reenter history after an extended absence, but faces the challenge of Pharaoh, who assumes God's role and, if not stopped, will prevent God's plan from coming to fruition. If God is going to be reintroduced to humanity, that must involve not only the liberation of His people and the fulfillment of His promise, but the humbling of Pharaoh and Egypt so that they – and the rest of the world – acknowledge God.

That humbling, however, has a twist. In the first chapter of Exodus, God does not intervene directly to prevent the reversal of Israel's growth; it was the midwives, His human agents, who did that. In that sense they act in Abrahamic fashion, as God's involvement with the world is going to necessarily entail human agency. Similarly, as much as God will be involved in humbling Pharaoh and liberating Israel, He will insist on using people to accomplish that.

The catch is that people are human. They have their own wills and desires and opinions. The midwives inspire hope, but they are not the answer. Recruiting and grooming the right messenger will prove to be a more significant challenge than anyone realizes.

Exodus 2:1–22

The Missing Hero

From where do heroes come? Are they born into greatness, or do they need to develop that unique character which sets them apart from others?

The grand sweep of the introductory chapter focusing on the emergence of the nation despite – or perhaps as a result of – Pharaoh's decree, and the unsuccessful attempt of two courageous women to subvert the evil decree, fades into the background. The noise of Pharaoh's furious efforts, the growth of the people, and the clatter of construction disappear as the Torah shifts our focus to one anonymous couple, their unnamed child, a sister-in-waiting, and an anonymous but gutsy princess. The story is quiet; we hear silence and subdued conversation with the rustle of the reeds in the background.

The dramatic change in setting gives the feeling of watching a movie filmed in shades of gray with only a single scene, or perhaps even a single character, shown in full color; we don't know if this was the only story of its kind or if there were thousands of other brave and desperate attempts by Hebrew mothers to save their sons, perhaps with very different endings.

An initial reading reveals a beautiful chiastic structure:[1]

(A) The boy is in his mother's home, but is hidden
(B) The mother places the child in the water as the sister watches
(C) Pharaoh's daughter finds the child
(C') Pharaoh's daughter is filled with compassion for the child
(B') The sister schemes to return the child to its mother
(A') The boy is returned to his mother's home

This is an elegant scene. The child who was cared for clandestinely can now be nurtured openly; the mother who thought she had lost her son has him miraculously returned. The progression takes us from the loving mother to the caring sister and ultimately to the dangerous stranger. After all, she was the daughter of the Pharaoh, the one responsible for the decree. We move from the one we imagine would be most caring to the one we anticipate would be the least.

The progression is accentuated even more by the timing of the scene. The introduction of the story takes months, maybe a year, followed by a slowing – a three-month period of hiding the infant at home. Preparing the basket[2] slows the pace of the storytelling, which slows even more as the Torah describes the meticulous placing of the basket into the water as the sister anxiously watches from a safe distance. The pace slows even more as the tension rises when Pharaoh's daughter discovers the basket:

> She opened it and she saw him. The child. (v. 6)

This moment freezes the scene completely. It is only in the second half that the tension is relieved as the reader is pleasantly shocked to discover

1. See Elhanan Samet, *Iyunim BeFarashat HaShavua,* Series 2, Volume 1 (Maaliyot, 2004), 230–46. See also David Ti, "Moshe – HaYeled VeHaIsh," *Megadim* 22 (1994): 30–42.
2. Various midrashim note the parallels between this scene and the story of Noah. Both involve a *teiva* (ark or basket) coated with tar for waterproofing and whose inhabitant who is saved from the water ends up saving an entire world, or at least the world which God is trying to save.

that Pharaoh's daughter's first reaction is compassion toward the crying Israelite child. At that point the pace picks up with the intervention of the sister and the return of the child to its mother to be nursed for a few years.

The chiastic structure and the pacing of the text draws extraordinary attention to Pharaoh's daughter as the key to the child's survival. We expect the mother to be loving, we expect the sister to be caring, but we don't expect anything positive from an Egyptian, much less the daughter of Pharaoh. In that slow-motion moment, motivated by maternal instinct and human decency, she rises as the heroine of the story.

As a beautiful sequel to the end of Exodus 1, which featured two brave midwives seeking to undermine Pharaoh's decree on a large scale, this is a story of three anonymous women conspiring to save a single child. It is a tale in which placing the baby in the very river which is supposed to drown him ends up saving his life.[3]

This reading of the story, however, leads to a false conclusion. The scene doesn't end there; the boy doesn't live happily ever after with his birth family. After he is weaned, he is returned to Pharaoh's daughter, probably before he has the chance to form any conscious memories of his family. We never know what they named him at home, what his birth name was. For the rest of his life he carries the name given by his adoptive mother. Moses, she calls him. A beautiful Egyptian name meaning "My son,"[4] with a Hebrew play on the name identifying him as the child drawn from the water, but not the name given by his birth parents.

This is a beautiful scene within a tragedy. A boy is miraculously saved, but the only way for him to be saved is for his mother to give him

3. Contrary to popular belief, placing him in the river initially is not an act of abandonment. He was not floated down the river but hidden in the reeds. The location would provide visual shelter as well as prevent him from floating downstream. His sister standing guard would look for opportunities to go to him, provide him with food and care, and return him to his hiding place. Ibn Ezra (long commentary) on 2:3 invokes the image of Hagar tossing Ishmael under the bush (Gen. 21:16), apparently to demonstrate how different this woman's action is to Hagar's.
4. See M. D. Cassuto, *Peirush al Sefer Shemot* (Magnes, 1944). The Hebrew twist on the name was perhaps an attempt by his mother to preserve a sense of identity with the Hebrews.

up. The boy has a loving and caring foster mother but is severed from his biological family.[5]

The tragedy is even bigger than we imagine. This private scene, a sequel to the previous chapter describing the intensifying hardships faced by the people, gives the reader a sense of hope. Amid the darkness there is a ray of light; the child is born. Described by his mother as *ki tov*, that he is good, a phrase echoing the perfection of the Creation in Genesis 1, surrounded by caring women, standing out as the only person in the story to be named, we anticipate that this child will bring salvation to his people. Surviving against the odds, saved miraculously from the river, even returned to his mother, we await his arrival on the scene, only to be disappointed when he leaves his mother and is raised by Pharaoh's daughter. The hero is lost.[6]

MOSES'S IDENTITY

Fast-forward. Moses is raised as an Egyptian by the daughter of the Egyptian monarch. While his birth family likely knows about him, it is unlikely that he knows who they are. After all, his sister cleverly hid her own identity and that of her mother from Pharaoh's daughter. He seems to have been sheltered in his childhood, only venturing to see conditions outside the palace when he grows up. Does he know that he is an Israelite? Did his adoptive mother, who acted rebelliously against her own father, share with him the story of how he was saved and that he was born into a Hebrew family? It certainly is possible, yet we have no way of knowing that Moses sees himself as anything but an Egyptian.

---

5. The scene provides a narrative backdrop to the later command to return a lost object to its owner. The sister arranges for the "lost" child to be restored to its rightful family. The complication is that the identification of the rightful mother is unclear – is it the mother who birthed him or the one who gave him a second chance at life? For more on Pharaoh's daughter as "birthing" the child, see Samet, *Iyunim BeFarashat HaShavua*, Series 2, 230–46.
6. Both ancient and contemporary culture is filled with stories of miraculous salvation of specially endowed children. For a discussion of one parallel to this story in Ancient Near Eastern literature, see Joshua Berman's *Created Equal* (Oxford University Press, 2008), 135–66. In contemporary culture this theme has found expression in popular series such as *Star Wars*.

For the royal family he is clearly not one of them, yet he is raised among them. As a lowly Semite associated with a proud, royal Hamite family, it is unlikely that he has any sort of royal status. Otherwise, the taskmaster he eventually kills would have been obligated to heed his command rather than lose his life and Moses would not have had to hesitate – looking to see if there were any witnesses, and the quarreling Israelites would not have spoken to him with such impudence: "Who placed you over us as the man, the officer, the judge?" (2:14). Further, as a prince he would not have to fear for his life from Pharaoh. He may have been reprimanded, but probably not killed. In fact, his killing of that taskmaster may have given Pharaoh the excuse he had been long seeking to rid himself of this foreign implant in the palace. Finally, when he arrives in Midian he is identified by Yitro's daughters as an Egyptian man, not an Egyptian royal (2:19).

And yet, being raised in the palace affords him a perspective unlike other Egyptians and certainly different from the Hebrews. He has lived as a free man with protection, privilege, and dignity. He understands the inner workings of the palace and the intrigues of the royal family.[7] He is less likely to be intimidated by people with money, prestige, and power.[8]

It is this Moses who goes "out to his brethren where he sees their burdens (*sivlotam*)," and witnesses "an Egyptian man beating a Hebrew man, one of his brethren," which raises a significant question: Since when does Moses identify as a Hebrew? It is easy to imagine midrashic comments seeking the backstory to explain this, and yet it is glaringly absent in the text.

Perhaps the word *sivlotam* (their burdens) holds the key. That word was first introduced in Exodus 1: "So *they* ([the Egyptians] set upon *it* [Israel] officers of the labor tax to afflict *it* [Israel] with *their*

7. Ibn Ezra (long commentary 2:3) writes: "God's thoughts are deep; who can understand His secret? Perhaps God arranged that Moses should grow up in the royal house so that his spirit would be noble and princely, not ordinary or lowly like one raised in a house of slaves."
8. Moses's position in the royal palace is portrayed suggestively by Exodus Rabba 1 as beloved by Pharaoh but despised by the royal advisors. The midrash includes a tale of Moses being unimpressed by gold and the royal wealth.

[the Egyptians'] burdens" (v. 11). Earlier we noticed that, consistently, Israel is referred to in the singular while the Egyptians are identified as many. When we reread that verse with the bracketed identifiers, what emerges is that it is not Israel who has the burden but the Egyptians. The verse describes how the Egyptians tried to make Israel bear their – the Egyptians' – burdens.

This is not a mere semantic issue but reflects the extent to which the Egyptians wanted Israel to own responsibility for Egypt's labor. Later, when Moses and Aaron first come to Pharaoh, Pharaoh dismisses them by telling them, "*Lekhu lesivloteikhem*," "Go to your burdens" (5:4). He wanted the burdens to be Israel's. God, however, sees this differently, instructing Moses to tell the Israelites that He will "take them out from under the Egyptian *sivlot*, burdens" (7:6). Despite Pharaoh's best efforts, the *sivlot* remain those of Egypt.

This observation bears great significance for understanding Moses's initial identity. He goes out to his brethren and sees their *sivlot*. Since the *sivlot* belong to the Egyptians, the brethren he goes out to see are his Egyptian brethren. It is then that he sees what he cannot accept – the Egyptians take no responsibility for their own burdens; they instead inflict them upon another people, even mercilessly beating those others in the process. It is at that moment that he identifies with the oppressed – either because of some innate quality of compassion, a deep sense of justice, or perhaps because of his own second-class status in Pharaoh's palace. The brethren that he goes out to see in the opening of the verse are Egyptian, but those with whom he identifies at the end of the verse are the Hebrews. The experience of witnessing oppression is transformative on a core level – he can no longer dream of being an Egyptian.[9]

But, as we well know, real transformation does not happen in an instant. On the second day he again goes out and sees two quarreling Hebrews (note that they are not identified as his brethren). When he intervenes to stop a beating, he is impudently rebuked by the aggressor. In their eyes Moses is neither a fellow Hebrew nor a master, but

---

9. As Leon Kass writes, Moses kills not only the Egyptian, but the Egyptian within himself. *Founding God's Nation*, 614n26.

an ordinary Egyptian. His identification with the oppressed, even his willingness to take action against the oppressor, did not win him an insider's status to the people who truly suffer that subjugation. Neither an Egyptian nor a Hebrew, he is a man without identity.

Belonging to no group and fearful for his life, Moses flees to Midian. He is identified there by Yitro's daughters as an Egyptian and soon afterward marries one of them and remains in Yitro's house, tending his sheep. The irony is extraordinary. The Egyptian man, raised in the house of Pharaoh, takes on an occupation that is the most anti-Egyptian imaginable. Recall that when Joseph's family descends to Egypt, he instructs his brothers to tell Pharaoh that they are shepherds, guaranteeing that they remain geographically separated from the Egyptian, "for the Egyptians find all shepherds abominable" (Gen. 46:34). Becoming a shepherd completes Moses's rebellion against Egypt but also highlights his alienation. He has rejected his Egyptian identity, never fully embraced a Hebrew one,[10] and marries into a Midianite family where he will spend many decades as a nomad.

WHO WAS MOSES?

Moses's identity can perhaps be summarized as a "nowhere man sitting in his nowhere land." Just look at the explanation he provides for the name he bestows upon his son, Gershom: For I was a stranger (*ger*) in a foreign land (*sham*, meaning, "there").[11] This sense of alienation may have been what he and Yitro, the man who became his father-in-law, shared. After all, one might expect that the daughters of the priest of Midian would be accorded some privilege, that his status would provide them a measure of protection. That is not, however, the case, as they are regularly pushed aside from the watering hole by the other shepherds. Neither Yitro nor Moses truly belongs and they are thus drawn to each other.

10. It could be argued that becoming a shepherd prepares him unconsciously to identify with the Hebrews, especially their ancestors, who were all shepherds.
11. While most commentators understand that he is referring to Moses's status in Midian, Rabbi David Zvi Hoffmann suggests that he is referring to his being an "other" even in Egypt. The past tense used in Moses's explanation – I was a stranger – coupled with the use of the word "there" as opposed to "here," support this reading.

Lack of belonging, however, is not necessarily synonymous with a lack of character (or depth). We could indeed argue that Exodus 2 is actually devoted to laying the foundations of Moses's character and thus reveals some of what defines Moses.

At this point, we do not as yet know who his parents are; they, like everyone else he encounters in Egypt, remain anonymous. We do, however, know something about them – they are both Levites. A Levite man went and took a Levite woman (2:1). That makes Moses a pure-bred Levite, the significance of which is clear to anyone familiar with Levi in Genesis. He was a zealot who, together with his older brother Shimon, massacred the town of Shechem as punishment for the rape and kidnapping of their sister, Dinah (Gen. 34). We should not be surprised, then, that the first story we hear about Moses highlights his zealous nature as he kills the Egyptian who is beating the Hebrew man. And while it is unclear if Moses intended to kill the Egyptian or merely to strike him,[12] the rage which impelled him to intervene violently should not surprise us given his pedigree. It is that same outrage which pushes him to intervene on the following day, when he encounters the two quarreling Hebrews and later to save the daughters of the Midianite priest from the male shepherds who were bullying them.

While there is a pattern in his behavior, there appears to be a lessening of the intensity of his reaction. While he kills the Egyptian offender, he verbally rebukes the assaulting Hebrew and we do not even know how he "saves" the Midianite women. It could be argued that Moses is so shaken by the fact that he killed a man that he restrains himself, and even runs from the source of provocation so that he should not have to deal with it again. That makes Moses, with deep convictions and values, the zealot who does not want to be one.[13]

Beyond the zealotry, there seem to be two additional, intertwined elements of his character which emerge from this opening series of

12. The word used to describe Moses's act, *vayakh* (2:12), comes from the same root as the word used to describe that which the Egyptian was doing to the Hebrew in the previous verse, as well as what one Hebrew was doing to the other on the subsequent day (2:13).
13. For a more in-depth exploration of this, see Grumet, *Moses and the Path to Leadership*, 27–45. Leon Kass points out that neither killing the Egyptian nor rebuking

events: his compassion for those being abused by others who are more powerful, and his sense of justice. While it seems that his zealotry may have been part of his Levite heritage, his compassion seems to be have been nurtured by the loving women who hovered over him in his early years – the loving mother who hid him for three months and prepared to continue to do so in the Nile reeds, the caring sister who stood guard from a distance and creatively leapt into action to return him to his mother, and the compassion displayed by Pharaoh's daughter from the moment she saw him through his maturity. The fearlessness of all those women in doing the right thing, despite the risks and dangers, may have contributed to his sense of justice.

Again, with Genesis lurking in the background, these values do not stand in isolation. God and Abraham found each other because of their shared value of justice and righteousness, *tzedaka* and *mishpat* (Gen. 19:19).[14] The sense of compassion and responsibility that are evident in Abraham's relationship with Lot (especially Gen. 14), the value of hosting in his hospitality to travelers, and the qualities of kindness which Abraham's servant sought in a spouse for Isaac (Gen. 24) reflect on Abraham's values as well. Not only does Moses's commitment to justice echo Abraham, the scene at the well supersedes Abraham's hospitality and Rebecca's kindness at the well, as Moses is the uninvited guest performing the kindness for the ones who do not know yet that they will be his hosts.[15]

A zealot, filled with compassion for the weak and committed to justice, and reflecting the core values of the patriarchs. Could there be a more suitable savior for the people?

---

the Hebrew actually change anything. In this sense, Moses's actions are similar to those of Shifrah and Puah – morally courageous, lifesaving on the micro-scale, but naively ineffective in the broader picture.

14. See Grumet, *Genesis: From Creation to Covenant*, 201.

15. Jacob at the well (Gen. 29:1–10) similarly inverts the scene in which his mother offers Abraham's servant water, as he is the guest offering assistance to the host. In Jacob's case, he is inspired by having arrived at his uncle's house and by the arrival of his cousin Rachel. In Moses's case, he has no prior knowledge of who these women are.

MOSES THE MAN

One of the interesting features of the description of Moses's birth and early life is the disappearing man, the *ish*. The narrative opens by telling us about a man, and we think that the story will be about him. To our surprise, the man is never to be heard from again.[16] Instead, Moses is surrounded by strong, compassionate, devoted women, who dominate the first half of the chapter.

The second half of the chapter is marked by no fewer than eight appearances of the word *ish*, referring to the Egyptian taskmaster, the Hebrew slave being beaten, the two quarreling Hebrews, Yitro, the non-existent witness to Moses's smiting the Egyptian[17] – and three times to Moses himself. Moses emerges as the *ish* where there is no other,[18] and is identified as the *ish* as he rebukes the Hebrews, saves Yitro's daughters, and is invited by Yitro to dine.

Highlighting Moses as the man in Exodus 2 builds on the patriarchal qualities he displays and strengthens our sense that God has identified the savior. Which only accentuates our disappointment to discover that he has disappeared. That same frustration experienced when the boy is returned to his mother in the false happy ending and subsequently ends up in the house of his adoptive mother is magnified even more when we meet him and learn about his character. He is bold and audacious, raised by a rebellious mother in Pharaoh's own house, compassionate and just, and a blend of the qualities we respect so much in our ancestral heroes.

---

16. The type scene of the disappearing man appears a number of other times in the Bible. Manoah, Samson's father, is introduced that way but the rest of the story mocks him as irrelevant (Judges 13). Elkanah, Samuel's father, is similarly introduced, even though his wife, Hannah, will take centerstage (I Sam. 1). Elimelech, Naomi's husband, is also presented that way in the opening lines of Ruth (1:1–2); he dies in the following verse.
17. Moses's realization that there was no *ish* to witness his act was the precursor to his striking out. There were obviously Hebrews around, as revealed in the subsequent scene, but Moses was unafraid of them as witnesses, as there would be little reason for them to report one Egyptian (Moses) smiting another.
18. The juxtaposition of the lack of there being an *ish* with Moses's rising to the occasion is likely the foundation for the Mishna (Avot 2:5): Where there are no stand-up people (*anashim*), strive to be one (*ish*).

But he runs – from Pharaoh and perhaps even from his own self. Unable to bear witness to suffering and injustice, he settles into the quiet pastoral life as a Midianite shepherd.[19] He is the anti-Egyptian who keeps company with sheep – gentle creatures incapable of cruelty. He is the rock, the island, who allows no one to touch him.

But he, in turn, touches no one.

The story begins with his birth and closes with the birth of his own son, a son he names. Moses transforms his story into an ordinary life cycle – birth, marriage, and another generation. There is nothing unusual or special about him.

The hero has gone missing.

GOD'S RETURN

The disappearance of the savior frustrates not only us, the readers, but God Himself. The entire story of Moses's birth and rescue were a departure from the opening narrative describing the intensifying suffering of Israel under Pharaoh's increasingly harsh decrees, a departure which was designed to introduce hope into a bleak, seemingly hopeless situation. Perhaps the accidental concert of the mother, the sister, and the princess was not happenstance; perhaps there was a guiding hand which brought Pharaoh's daughter to exactly that place at that time to help facilitate Moses's emergence on the scene. But the great hope that God shepherded has fled the scene to live as a Midianite shepherd.

It is at that point that the narrative returns to Israel's story, not that of Moses. Pharaoh dies, but instead of bringing relief to Israel it seems like Israel's position in Egypt has been sealed, fixed, permanently institutionalized as slaves.[20] They groan from under the load.[21]

---

19. There is a parallel between this story and the story of Cain. In both, the central character begins in a land of agriculture. There is a killing, perhaps unintended, followed by a flight into exile where the central character marries and has children. The story of Cain continues with a shift in Cain's way of life, with his becoming a city dweller rather than a farmer, while the story of Moses concludes with his becoming a shepherd, the quintessential Hebrew lifestyle.
20. See the comments of Bekhor Shor; Rabbi Abraham, son of Maimonides; and Rabbi Samson R. Hirsch on 2:22.
21. It should be noted that the text does not say that they cried out to God. Their cry

Little do they know that there was a potential savior who decided not to be involved. But God knows, and in the absence of a human actor, He decides that the time has come to act. He hears their cries, sees their pain, and remembers the covenant with their ancestors.[22] Bound by His oath to the patriarchs, God's intervention is inevitable.

Unlike His involvement in Genesis, where He single-handedly undid the Creation with the water of the Great Confusion or overturned Sodom with fire and brimstone, God is committed to freeing His people and fulfilling His covenant through partnership with a human agent. On one level, this is a continuation of the shift which began with the patriarchal covenant, in which God prefers to interact with His partners who, in turn, interact with humanity. On another level this will serve a purpose to which the Torah has only hinted until now. The people who will be freed from Egypt need to be forged into a nation – a nation which, despite its special relationship with God, will be like many others, with internal structures and institutions. That nation will need leadership, human leadership. God's partner will be that leader.

Recruiting that partner will prove more challenging than anticipated.

---

was one of hopeless anguish, not a prayer or a call for assistance.

22. Rabbi Abraham, son of Maimonides (3:6), notes that the four verbs in the text – seeing, hearing, remembering, and knowing – are precisely those God mentions in His opening monologue to Moses in Exodus 3.

Exodus 3:1–4:16

Recruiting Moses

Moses, the Midianite shepherd, seeks nothing more than good grazing for his sheep. That's what the wilderness is for. The particular area he was in at that moment may have been drier than others,[1] but it was fine for the low bushes which grew there and on which his father-in-law's sheep could feed – and it minimized the likelihood of his running into other shepherds there.

The initial encounter between Moses and God is unlike the ones between God and the Genesis heroes – Noah, Abraham, Isaac, and Jacob. God approaches each of them without introduction, providing a command, a promise, or a message of comfort. They were apparently primed for those messages, as they did not flinch when God spoke with each of them. But Moses is different. He is a man who fled his past and seems content with his newfound life. God needs to draw him in, to draw his attention, to spark his curiosity. That's what the bush is for. Will Moses notice it, the way he noticed suffering in Egypt? Will he look at the bush long enough to realize the curious nature of this fire – that it burns but does not consume?

1. The name Horeb (Ḥorev) means "dry." See, for example, 14:21.

Moses sees, and, behold, the bush is on fire but does not burn up.[2]

THE INITIAL ENCOUNTER

Here we have our first bridge between young Moses in Egypt and mature Moses in Midian. In Egypt, Moses sees the suffering of the people (2:11), which is matched by God seeing their suffering (2:25). Here, too, Moses notices the bush (3:2), which is mirrored by God observing that Moses notices (3:4). In fact, it is Moses's seeing which opens the door to God's initial communication with him.

> God: Moses! Moses![3]
> Moses: *Hineni* (Here I am)![4]
> God: Do not come close to here.
> Remove your shoes.
> For the place on which you stand is sacred land.[5]

God's initial communication to Moses presents a puzzle. First, God identifies the place as holy, but nowhere else do we find that the place is

---

2. This same language, *vayar* ("he saw") and *vehinei* ("and behold") is used to describe the initial encounter between Pharaoh's daughter and the baby in the basket (2:6). While Moses initially thinks that it is the bush which is unusual, it turns out that the bush is quite ordinary – it is actually the fire which is unusual. In fact, it is not a fire at all, but a visual manifestation of God's presence. The Hebrew word identifying the bush is *seneh*. This word appears in the Bible only in the context of this mountain, perhaps providing an etiology of the mountain's name, Sinai.
3. This double call is used with Abraham (Gen. 22:11) and Jacob (Gen. 46:2), apparently to signal a need to make a dramatic change. Abraham needs to withdraw the knife about to slaughter Isaac, and Jacob needs to shift from acting as Israel to assuming the position of Jacob. Similarly, God summons Samuel with the double language (I Sam. 3:10) to signal the beginning of Samuel's prophecy and the end of the extended era of the Tabernacle in Shiloh. It is also used, in an interesting twist, when God calls to Moses to teach him to transform God's wrath into mercy (Ex. 34:6).
4. This is the same response that Abraham and Jacob have to their double call. It usually indicates readiness to act and an understanding of the significance of the moment. See Gen. 22:1, 7, and 11, which demonstrate the tension of conflicting commitments and their resolution. See also Gen. 27:18, 37:13, and 46:2. Ironically, the text attributes *Hineni* to Moses but, as we will see, he is anything but ready to heed God's call.
5. This division of the verse is supported by the cantillation marks.

sanctified; even if that place is the same as Mount Sinai, its sanctity was temporary, lasting only as long as the Revelation itself. Second, the link between the three clauses is unclear. If Moses is standing in a holy place, then why should he not draw closer to the fire? Third, in what way are the three clauses linked? Fourth, while Moses is instructed to remove his shoes, there is no indication that he actually does.[6]

The resolution of the puzzle reveals God's message to Moses. The reason for Moses to not approach the bush is not because the bush – or the fire – is sacred. They are not holy at all; their existence was simply to catch Moses's attention and bring him to the encounter with God. When "God saw that he detoured to see" (3:4), that triggers God's appearance to him; the instruction to remove his shoes is to ensure that he goes nowhere, not toward the non-sacred bush and not away from the divine encounter. God's opening message is that Moses needs to disabuse himself of the notion that the bush or the fire are special; in fact, what makes the place holy is that Moses is there. "The place on which *you* stand is sacred land." Moses is special; that is the dramatic message for him to hear before God entrusts him with a mission that will change the direction of humanity, and this is his inauguration into the role as the savior God has been seeking.

So important is this potentially history-making message that the text marks it with a special word, *kadosh*, "sacred." This is the first appearance of the word *kadosh* since the Creation story; God was saving it for this moment. In Genesis, it is only God who sets things aside for elevated purposes, sanctification. With the appearance of Moses, who

---

6. In a parallel scene (Josh. 5:9), also apparently an inaugural encounter, the text explicitly notes that Joshua does remove his shoes. The other significant difference between these two encounters is that Joshua is not explicitly instructed to remain in his place. As Moses's "lad" he learned that one does not cavalierly walk away from the divine encounter; once he understands that he is speaking with a divine figure, he accepts his own sanctified status and removes his shoes as instructed. Regarding the shoes, a mishna in Berakhot (9:8) records a prohibition of entering the Temple compound with shoes, apparently as a way of signaling that one does not leave the Divine Presence hastily.

will ultimately lead Israel to their liberation, the process of sanctification is handed over from God to God's appointed people.[7]

While Moses refrains from approaching the bush, there is no indication that he removes his shoes. Moses does not think that he is special in any way, and it certainly does not make sense to him that he can generate sanctity. In his mind he is a man without an identity, a permanent refugee, a shepherd who finally found his peace in Midian. It is for that reason that, after a pregnant pause,[8] God continues to speak. And it is in that continuation that God makes explicit what Moses doesn't accept at first.

God's second speech is short. In Hebrew, it consists of a total of nine words: "I am the God of your forefathers, the God of Abraham, the God of Isaac, and the God of Jacob" (3:6). This short speech, to which Moses reacts by hiding his face, touches on two essential ideas – each of which is new to Moses.

First, God introduces Himself to Moses. Moses had heard the voice but was apparently unaware of who was speaking with him.

Second, God introduces Moses to himself. The child with no birth family, the man who was welcomed by neither the Hebrews nor the Egyptians, the individual who belonged in no place, is suddenly informed that he has ancestors: Abraham, Isaac, Jacob. Moses, whose core identity was heretofore defined by who he was not rather than by who he was, for the first time in his life learns that he has a past, a history, an ancestry.

Did Moses know who Abraham, Isaac, and Jacob were? Perhaps he heard it as a nursing infant, from which time it remained buried in his subconsciousness. Perhaps his adoptive mother told him what she knew about the Hebrews and their past. And perhaps he was hearing these names for the first time. Regardless, the man with no identity suddenly discovers that he has one.

---

7. Rabbi Joseph B. Soloveitchik often noted that in the eyes of the halakha, it is human creativity which generates lasting sanctity.
8. In the Torah, when we find a character speaking and the character continues to speak only after the Torah inserts another *vayomer* ("he spoke"), that indicates a pause between the two speeches.

No wonder he hides his face. Not only is he afraid of looking at the deity,[9] he is afraid of learning about himself, upending a lifetime of constructing and deconstructing his selfhood.

A TEXTUAL PUZZLE

It is at this point that God informs Moses of the purpose of their encounter. God has a nation which is suffering greatly under Egyptian oppression. He has decided to save it and bring it to a land flowing with milk and honey, that is, a land appropriate for shepherds[10] – the ancestral land from which it descended. So far so good. But what does that have to do with Moses?

God (A-donai) continues. Since the cries of the Israelites are reaching Him and He sees how the Egyptians squeeze them, He intends to send Moses to Pharaoh and to take the Israelites out of Egypt.

Here's the logical leap that God makes which Moses may have a hard time absorbing. If this is God's nation, and they are suffering, and He wants to save them, then why doesn't He save them? He is, after all, God. What could Moses do that God can't? Even more, why should Moses get involved in a fight which isn't his? He does not identify with Israel, and as far as he can remember, they certainly did not identify with him.

It could be that this is precisely what Moses means when he challenges: "Who am I that I should go to Pharaoh and that I should take

9. The Torah describes Moses as hiding his face, for he feared "looking at the deity." Ironically, it is this same person who in short time will commune with God on Mount Sinai and will communicate with God "face-to-face" (Deut. 34:10). This irony is noted in the Talmud (Berakhot 7a), suggesting that the glow on Moses's face was a reward for his hiding his face in this encounter.

   Regarding describing God as "the deity," there are three terms used in this passage. One is the unique name of the God of Israel, A-donai, which will be addressed implicitly in the Torah text. A second is E-lohim, which means "the Almighty" (as in, "All Powerful"). The third is *ha'elohim*, which is used here as a generic term describing a powerful being. In this passage, identifying the different names helps the reader understand to whom Moses thinks he is speaking and what God is actually trying to teach Moses.

10. The milk is from the livestock; the honey is from the wildflowers upon which the sheep graze.

the Israelites out of Egypt?" I am a non-Egyptian fugitive from Egypt, at best persona non grata in Egypt, at worst an unknown shepherd living in Midian. Moses's reluctance is understandable, but God persists.

It is at this point that we need to take a careful look at the text, as it presents a number of oddities, the resolution of which will reveal a number of surprises. Here is God's initial response to Moses's reluctance:

> For I will be (*ehyeh*) with you,
> and this is the sign for you that I have sent you,
> when you take the nation out of Egypt,
> you will worship the deity on this mountain.

While we understand the first line, essentially God's reassurance that Moses will not be doing this alone, what follows sounds bizarre. How could an event which will only occur *after* the Exodus be a sign which will help Moses *now*?

The continuation of the conversation is also unusual. Moses is concerned that the Israelites will ask for the name of the God who is sending him, and he does not know that name. God apparently has three distinct responses:

1. E-lohim said to Moses: I will be what I will be (*Ehyeh asher ehyeh*).
2. He said: This is what you should say to the Israelites. "I will be (*ehyeh*) sent me to you."
3. E-lohim further said to Moses: This is what you should say to the Israelites. "God (A-donai),[11] the God of your ancestors – the God of Abraham, the God of Isaac, and the God of Jacob – sent me to you. This is My eternal name, the way I am mentioned for all generations."

11. The name A-donai, as it is written in the Bible, is built on the same Hebrew root as *Ehyeh*. The play on this name carries through the entire opening dialogue of the scene at the bush.

A single question generates three responses, and the responses to the question about God's name yields at least two, if not three names (E-lohim, A-donai, and perhaps Ehyeh), a cryptic "I will be what I will be," and a historical reference to the God of their ancestors. There seems to be too much repetition, variation, and lack of flow from one sentence to the next.

UNRAVELING THE PUZZLE

The first step toward solving the puzzle of this dialogue is to recognize its structure. This is not a dialogue; rather, it is God's attempt to recruit Moses which Moses repeatedly interrupts. God responds to those interruptions, after which He continues with His message to Moses. When we separate the "interruption dialogues" we get a better picture, both of the message God intended to deliver and of the nature of God's responses to Moses.[12] What follows is a suggested reconstruction of that dialogue, beginning with God's initial request of Moses.

God's intended message	Dialogue resulting from Moses's interruptions
(10) So now, I am going to send you to Pharaoh, and take My nation – Israel – out of Egypt	
	(11) Moses said to the deity: Who am I that I should go to Pharaoh and that I should take the Israelites out of Egypt? (12) He said: For I will be (*ehyeh*) with you, and this is the sign for you – that I have sent you
when you take the nation out of Egypt you will worship the deity on this mountain.	

12. See Grumet, *Genesis: From Creation to Covenant*, 170–74, where a similar analysis reveals new insights into the Covenant Between the Pieces.

	(13) Moses said to the deity: Behold! I am going to come to the Israelites and say to them, "The God of your forefathers has sent me to you." They will say to me, "What is His name?" What should I say to them? (14) E-lohim said to Moses: I will be what I will be (*Ehyeh asher ehyeh*). He said: This is what you should say to the Israelites. "I will be (*ehyeh*) sent me to you. God (A-donai), the God of your forefathers – the God of Abraham, the God of Isaac, and the God of Jacob – sent me to you." This is My eternal name, the way I have been invoked for generations
(15) E-lohim further said to Moses: This is what you should say to the Israelites. "God (A-donai), the God of your forefathers – the God of Abraham, the God of Isaac, and the God of Jacob – sent me to you. This is My eternal name, the way I am mentioned for all generations." (16) Go and gather the Israelite elders and tell them, "A-donai, the God of your forefathers, appeared to me – the God of Abraham, Isaac, and Jacob – saying, I recall[13] you and what was done to you in Egypt"	

13. The Hebrew root P-K-D, often translated as "to remember," frequently has the added

When we read the left column, we see the message God would have delivered to Moses had Moses not interrupted. It begins with an overview of the mission – Moses will go to Pharaoh and to Israel, and he will take Israel out of Egypt and bring them to the mountain to worship the deity. It then continues with a more detailed version of what will happen. Moses will go to the Israelite elders, who will believe him, after which they will all go to Pharaoh to request a three-day furlough for worship. Pharaoh will reject the request, leading to God smiting Egypt and ultimately to Pharaoh sending Israel out. This reading also helps us to understand that God's earlier mention of worshipping at the mountain was not intended as a sign for Moses. Rather, it was the continuation of God's description of the initial plan (which Moses interrupted).

The right column captures the dialogue generated by Moses's questions. To his first question, in which he asks by what right is he going to Pharaoh, the answer is simple. It is not you, Moses, who is going to Pharaoh; it is I, God. The only sign Moses needs is the knowledge that it is God who is sending him.[14] Embedded within God's response of, "For I will be with you," is the word *ehyeh* ("I will be"). That word suggests to the reader that God is anticipating Moses's second question, as His response to that question will place *ehyeh* at the very core.

As we saw earlier, that second dialogue is complex. At first glance we thought that there were three responses to a single question; now it appears that there are two. But why is there a need for two responses? And what is the purpose of what appears to be the third response, given that it adds little to the previous two?

---

implication of being remembered for a particular destiny (e.g., Gen. 21:1 and 50:24). As such, it takes on the meaning of being appointed, as in Gen. 39:4, 40:4, and Num. 27:16. The language God uses, *pakod pakadti,* mirrors the language used by Joseph as he instructs his brothers about their future destiny in their ancestral homeland (Gen. 50:24–25). This likely served as a key phrase for the Israelites awaiting redemption, so that when Moses uses this internal language of the people as he informs them of God's return to the scene it probably triggers a greater sense of familiarity and hope for them than does the name of God Moses uses. See Rashi, 3:13.

14. See Exodus Rabba 3:4. A similar approach is presented by Rabbi Judah HaLevi in *Kuzari,* IV:4.

WHAT'S IN A NAME?

Egypt, and likely Midian too, like all other ancient Mesopotamian cultures, were absolutely polytheistic societies. There were gods of the sun, the moon, and the river. There were gods of death, gods of life, and gods of fertility. Every geographical region had its god, including the wilderness.

These gods were temperamental. The gods would feud and fight, sometimes violently (with obvious repercussions for humans). They would mate and bear offspring. They had needs and desires, and it was the job of humans to provide for them. Literally. They needed to be fed and tended to. When they were satisfied, life would go well for the people. When their needs were not met, they became enraged and would unleash their anger upon the people.

There was no Supreme Being in charge of all or who was all-powerful, and there was no concept of a God who would care about people. Part of the great revolution of the Abrahamic faith, which had not as yet spread beyond Abraham's clan, was that God cared about people. Even more outrageous was that God wanted to have a meaningful relationship with people, expressed as promises and even as covenant.

Moses was raised in Egypt and until this time lived his adult life in Midian. His conceptions of God were most likely those of the cultures of all the societies of that part of the world, save that of the Abrahamic family.[15] In this context, Moses's question about God can be understood on two planes. On the simplest level, he was asking which God was sending him to the Israelites. After all, Egypt had some powerful gods. If this was the god of the wilderness, what power would he wield in Egypt, where he would likely be overwhelmed by the obviously superior ones there.

On another level, Moses's curiosity may have been piqued by God's introduction. This is a god who claims to maintain a historical bond with people, even to care about them. This is a god who maintains his commitment to the descendants of people with whom he once

---

15. This is an approach which most traditional commentaries could not entertain. It was incomprehensible to them that Moses would have less knowledge of God and of theosophy than themselves.

interacted. "I am the God of your forefathers, the God of Abraham, the God of Isaac, and the God of Jacob." Odd, indeed. This is a god who cares about people and their suffering, not for his own benefit but for their sake. "I am descending[16] to save it from Egypt...the cries of the Israelites have come before Me." Moses wants to understand more. In fact, while his question is phrased as "What shall I tell the Israelites?" it is not a stretch of the imagination to suggest that Moses is asking for himself too. Who are you? Just what kind of god are you?

To this question God offers two responses – one to the question Moses implies and another to the question he actually asks.

To Moses He says, "*Ehyeh asher Ehyeh.* I will be what I will be." This is the first of a number of cryptic replies God will offer to Moses's questions.[17] On the most basic level it means that He is undefinable. He is neither a god of this nor a god of that; He is the God of all existence whose expression is unpredictable and will change with His choosing. Expanding on God's earlier statement that *Ehyeh* will be with Moses, He says that the concept of a name, which limits the gods with which Moses is familiar, is completely irrelevant. This response is Moses's second lesson in the God of Israel. The first taught him that the Israelite God cares about people, establishing relationships with them. This second lesson further teaches Moses that this God is unlike any others he may have heard of.

It is only after this that God addresses the question Moses actually asks. Now that Moses has some sense of who God is, or perhaps, what God is not, he is instructed to tell Israel that the God of existence, *Ehyeh,* sent him to them.

---

16. The language of God descending first appears in Gen. 11:7, as God decides to confuse the language of Babel, and again in 18:21 as God is deciding whether to destroy Sodom. The language indicates God's decision to intervene in the course of human history; hence, He "descends" from the heavenly spheres to get involved in what happens on earth.
17. Two other examples are in 33:14 and 33:19. There are other incidents in the Bible in which an apparently angelic figure is asked to identify himself, only to elicit a refusal to respond. See Gen. 32:29 and Judges 13:18.

GOD CONTINUES AFTER BEING INTERRUPTED

Now that God has responded to Moses's interruption, this time with a double response, He continues His original message to Moses, with specific instructions about what to say to Israel and to Pharaoh, what the results of each of those missions will be, and how the divine plan will ultimately unfold. Yet, as we look at this continuation, it sounds too familiar. In fact, it sounds like a repetition of the previous verse. As we continue reading, we notice that the continuation also sounds like a repetition. As you can see below, verses 14–16 are linked like a chain, and by examining that chain we will reveal an extraordinary twist.

(14) [E-lohim] said, *a* – This is what you should say to the Israelites, *b* – "*Ehyeh* sent me to you"	(15) E-lohim further said to Moses, *a* – This is what you should say to the Israelites, *b* – "A-donai, the God of your forefathers – the God of Abraham, the God of Isaac, and the God of Jacob – sent me to you." *c* – This is My eternal name, the way I am mentioned for all generations	(16) *a* – Go and gather the Israelite elders and tell them, *b* – "A-donai, the God of your forefathers appeared to me – the God of Abraham, Isaac and Jacob – saying, *d* – I recall you and what was done to you in Egypt"

When we line the verses parallel to each other we cannot but notice the linkage between them. All three clauses of verse 15 clearly echo those of verse 14, with the third line of verse 15 being an expansion of its parallel in verse 14 – even though they are distinct speeches. As we move on to verse 16, the opening line is a clarification of the second clause of both verse 14 and verse 15. That is, the way that Moses will address "the Israelites" is via speaking to the elders. The continuation of verse 16, along with the rest of God's plan (vv. 17–22), brings us away from the discussion of the name and into God's message to Israel of their impending redemption. What is behind all this apparent repetition?

Before we address the repetition, let us remember that verse 15 is not part of God's response to Moses's question. Rather, it is intended as the continuation of God's original charge to Moses. If that is the case, then why does verse 15 close with a brief flashback to the discussion of God's name, where it seems that God is actually providing a name, especially since He hesitated to do so earlier?

What seems to be happening here is that as God returns to His originally planned speech to Moses (v. 15), He alters, ever so slightly, His message. Had Moses not interrupted God with his question about the name, God would never have discussed it. Why would the Israelites need to know God's name – wouldn't they simply be thrilled to hear that the God of their ancestors was coming to rescue them? Moses's interruption alerts God to the idea that perhaps it could be relevant to them. After all, if Moses needed to know, wouldn't it be reasonable to expect that the Israelites might want to know as well?

It is for that reason that when God returns to His initially intended message, He refers back to His responses to Moses and amplifies them before continuing. God learns from Moses what the people need, incorporates that into the instructions, and invokes the name by which He was known for generations.[18]

The final part of God's mission to Moses also seems to have shifted as a result of Moses's interruption. As God spells out the plan (3:16–22), He says that Moses will go to the people, who will listen to him, but that when he goes to Pharaoh with a request for a three-day furlough to worship God, the request will be denied. Pharaoh's denial of the request will trigger God's direct involvement in sending afflictions, after which Pharaoh will free the people completely.[19] In this plan, it is

18. The name A-donai is apparently a play on the cryptic *Ehyeh asher Ehyeh*. It incorporates past, present, and future, and is sometimes rendered as The Eternal. Introducing the name here with the explanation that this is how He was also known presents somewhat of a conundrum, as 6:2–3 suggests that this was not the name by which the forefathers knew Him. Rabbi David Zvi Hoffmann (3:13) suggests that while the patriarchs knew this name, they did not pass it on to their children.

19. This is the first time God introduces the request of the three-day furlough, which

God who frees the people from Egypt. This contrasts with God's opening words to Moses, in which he suggests that it is Moses who will free the people from Egypt. "So now, go! I will send you to Pharaoh. Take My nation, Israel, out of Egypt" (3:10). This subtle change is apparently a response to Moses's resistance, in which he proclaims, "Who am I that I should go to Israel and that I should take the Israelites out of Egypt?" (3:11). You, says God, will not take them out. I will, but I want you to go to Pharaoh to set up the conditions for My intervention.[20]

There is a great irony in this interpretation. Moses has yet to accept the mission, and as we will see, he will continue to resist. He thinks that he is unworthy, that he is the wrong person. Yet his questioning of – even challenging – God prods God to adjust His message to the people. Inadvertently, Moses displays just how appropriate he is to be the intermediary between God and the people. When Moses eventually delivers the message to the people, he will have turned out to be the bridge between God and the people.[21]

MOSES'S DOUBTS AND GOD'S RESPONSE

While the text reveals to us, the readers, what makes Moses the right choice for this mission, Moses himself is filled with doubts. For sure, God promised that He will be doing all the hard work of releasing the people from Egypt, but Moses doesn't think that he will have credibility with the people. He is not an Israelite insider – why should anyone believe that God approached him to save them? Many traditional commentators[22]

---

will be repeated many times throughout the story. In this presentation it is a ruse. Pharaoh's resistance to this minimal request – in essence a challenge to God – demonstrates the need for God to teach Pharaoh who He is, ultimately resulting in Pharaoh chasing the Israelites out of Egypt and releasing them completely from slavery. For a survey of literature on this and a dramatically different conclusion, see Elhanan Samet, *Iyunim BeFarashat HaShavua,* Series 1, Volume 1 (Maaliyot, 2002), 178–84.

20. This intervention of God reflects a new stage in God's interaction with the world. In contrast to Genesis, where God acts solo to change the course of history, here He insists on working together with a human agent.
21. What this also means is that verse 15 serves as a bridge between God's tangential conversation with Moses and the continuation of His charge to Moses.
22. See Exodus Rabba 3:15; Rashi, 4:2; Ibn Ezra, 4:1.

are troubled by Moses's lack of faith in the people – after all, didn't God just assure him that the people would listen to him?

To be sure, God had assured Moses that the people would listen to him. *Veshamu lekolekha* (3:18). Moses is not as concerned as to whether they will listen to what he has to say, but whether they will accept and obey what he tells them – *velo yishme'u bekoli*. The difference between *lishmoa **le**kol* and *lishmoa **be**kol* is that while the former means to listen, the latter goes further, including accepting the authority of the speaker. If they don't believe that God actually spoke with Moses, then he has no standing among them. They may like what he has to say but will have no reason to follow him.[23]

Once again, God is patient with Moses's questions. He provides Moses with three signs, ostensibly to win the trust of the Israelites. Initially this sounds like a good idea, but it does raise a few problems. First, we remember that Egypt is filled with magicians; Pharaoh will later reject Moses's "proof" of God's power by replicating the wondrous displays Moses presents. Why would we think that the Israelites would be any more convinced that Moses was God's messenger as a result of a performance of magic? Second, God did not seem concerned that the people would not trust him as God's messenger. From His perspective, the signs were completely unnecessary for the people.

These questions lead to two possible paths for exploration. One is that the signs were not intended to wow the people out of disbelief, but that there was something about them – about *these* particular signs – which was intended to convey a message to the people. The other is that the signs were actually not for the people at all.

THE SIGNS

To explore the first option, we need to dig a little deeper into the signs themselves. First, it should be noted that God only identifies the first

---

23. Taking this one step further, is it possible that Moses is expressing not only his doubt in himself, but his doubt in this entire encounter? Remember that this is his first encounter with God and with the unique God of Israel. Surely the speaker identified Himself, but does Moses himself believe it? And while he will not express that doubt as his own thought, perhaps he can express it by putting it into the mouth of the people.

two as signs (God refers to them as the "first sign" and the "last sign" in 4:8). The third is a performance which Moses is to enact in front of the people, but never identified as a sign.

What is interesting about those two signs? They both invoke images of death and salvation from it. The story of the snake in the Garden identifies it as the agent of mortality and, in the ancient world, being afflicted with *tzaraat* signified the end of a productive life.[24] The intended message would have been clear. You thought that you were dead, that you have no future. God, who controls both life and death, can turn that around. We should add that in Egyptian culture, death and the afterlife played an outsized role. The gods who controlled death, and the priests who influenced them, were inordinately powerful. Therefore, restoring a worldly life to one considered dead was an anti-Egyptian message.

Further, while we have little knowledge about the oral traditions of the Israelites in Egypt, the theme of being saved from near-death (or total slavery) form the core of some of the most ancient traditions. Barren Sarah is miraculously renewed with youthfulness as she bears and nurses Isaac; Isaac has a brush with death and is saved by a last-minute divine intervention; Jacob is enslaved by his uncle Laban and nearly swallowed up into the culture of Haran, saved only by God's command to leave;[25] Joseph, the godfather of the Egyptian exile, was also taken for dead, only to be discovered to be very much alive.[26] The purpose of the signs God gives Moses is not to impress the people, but to demonstrate that Moses understands their internal story. He is not an outsider, but someone with a deep understanding of their past, their distinct culture, and their hoped-for future.

Perhaps this explains why the third performance, water-blood, is not considered a sign at all. It demonstrates the transformation of

24. In the Bible, this is demonstrated in the incident of Miriam's *tzaraat*, in which Aaron pleads with Moses not to leave her for dead (Num. 12:11). It is also a key element of the fate of King Uzziah, who when afflicted with *tzaraat* ceased to be able to function as king, despite his extraordinary achievements and generally good standing with God (II Chr. 26). In rabbinic literature, this is expressed explicitly in Nedarim 64b.

25. See Grumet, *Genesis: From Creation to Covenant*, 336–51.

26. Gen. 37:33 and 45:28.

the Egyptian source of life into one of death. It does not invoke Israel's past, but Egypt's future.

To examine the second alternative, it is worthwhile doing a careful reading of the text:

> God said to him: "What is that in your hand?"
>
> He [Moses] said: "A staff."[27]
>
> He [God] said: "Cast it to the ground."
>
> So he cast it to the ground and it turned into a snake. Moses fled from it.
>
> God said to Moses: "Extend your hand and grab its tail."[28]
>
> Moses extended his hand and held the tail – it became a staff in his palm.
>
> [God said,] "In order that they should believe that the God of their forefathers – the God of Abraham, Isaac, and Jacob – appeared to you."
>
> God further said to him: "Bring your hand into your breast."
>
> He brought his hand into his breast and it became afflicted with *tzaraat*, like snow.
>
> He said: "Return your hand to your breast."
>
> He returned his hand to his breast, and when he withdrew it, his flesh was restored.
>
> [God said,] "Should they not believe you or not listen to the first sign, they will believe as a result of the last sign. And should they not believe even these two signs and still not listen to you,

---

27. In the Hebrew, this part of the conversation is marked by an exquisite wordplay. God asks Moses *Ma zeh,* ("What is that?"), to which Moses responds with the assonant, *mateh* ("a staff"). The rhetorical question invites Moses's single-word response, which is followed up by that *mateh* being transformed into a non-*mateh*, as if to say, what you thought was a *mateh* is anything but that. This scene, opening with the rhetorical question, provides Moses with a concrete challenge to recalibrate his understanding of the world, similar to the one experienced by Abraham at the Covenant Between the Pieces (Gen. 15:5).
28. The tail is the most dangerous way to pick up a snake as it can easily contort its body to bite what it sees as its attacker. The demand to pick up the snake by its tail required an extraordinary leap of faith, especially considering how fearfully Moses reacted when the staff became a snake.

> you should take some water from the river and spill it on the dry land – the water which you take from the river will become blood on the dry land."

This is an odd passage. God does not tell Moses in advance that He is providing him with signs. In fact, He does not even tell Moses to do these acts in front of the Israelites. Rather, He instructs Moses to perform an act, which turns his staff into a snake, and then undoes it. Only after Moses is sufficiently frightened does God identify this as a sign. We don't even know if Moses is supposed to perform this in front of them or tell them about his experience. The only thing that Moses is told to do in front of the people, and only should they still not believe him, is to spill water from the river onto the ground where it will turn into blood – and that act is not even identified as a sign.[29]

This opens the possibility that the first two signs were not intended for the people at all. God never told him to do them in front of the people and, as we recall, from God's perspective the people need no convincing. If they were not meant for the people, then the logical alternative is that they are for Moses himself; he is the one who needs to be convinced that it is God who is speaking with him and sending him on this mission. Moses couched his concern in terms of the people's disbelief, but it is his own, unspoken doubt which is expressed in the manner of, "I have a friend who has a problem." God respects his hesitancy and discretion, teaching him how to help "his friend," but the absence of a direct instruction to perform this in front of the people suggests that perhaps it is Moses himself who is God's intended audience for these signs.

A key word, "hand," contributes to this reading. In the first sign, the staff-serpent, Moses's hand is mentioned three times – "What is that in your hand?" (4:2), "Extend your hand" (4:4), and "Moses extended his hand" (4:4) – making it the most prominent feature in that sign.[30]

---

29. This, of course, Moses cannot try in the wilderness where he has no access to the river.
30. Interesting, there was an option for a fourth mention, but the Torah (4:4) opts for the word meaning palm (*kaf*) rather than the word for hand (*yad*).

In the second sign, the *tzaraat,* Moses's hand is mentioned another three times, as the condition of Moses's hand is the sign. The third performance, water-blood, is never identified as a sign and is absent any mention of Moses's hand.

Thus, the purpose of the scene is not to show Moses how to convince Israel that God is coming to redeem them but rather to convince Moses himself that he is truly being sent by God with the hope that he will accept the mission. If only it were so simple.

MOSES STILL DEMURS

Despite God reassuring Moses that He will be the one taking Israel out of Egypt, responding to Moses's query about the name, and even providing Moses with signs to demonstrate to himself and others, Moses is still not ready to take on the task. Not that there hasn't been progress. For the first time Moses addresses A-donai, not just the generic deity, and for the first time Moses describes himself as God's servant – perhaps the signs were actually helpful to him. Nonetheless, Moses prefers to decline, averring that he is of "heavy mouth and heavy tongue."

Not to be deterred, God promises to be with Moses's mouth as well. "Who gives man a mouth or makes him mute or deaf or seeing or blind? Is it not I, God?" (4:11). In case it was unclear to Moses, the God asking Moses to undertake His mission is not simply the God of Moses's ancestors but the God of Creation itself. God can ensure that Moses will be able to speak if that is what is necessary.

At the same time that God responds to Moses's objection, there are indications that God's patience is beginning to wear thin. Rhetorical questions are often a rebuke. Both Pharaoh and Avimelekh rebuke Abraham for suggesting that his wife was his sister, Abraham rebukes Avimelekh for stealing his wells, Laban rebukes Jacob for stealing his idols, Jacob rebukes Laban for pursuing him without cause – and all these use rhetorical questions. This is even more true in the Torah when the rhetorical question is asked by a divine figure. God asks the man in the Garden, "Where are you?" and He asks Cain, "Where is Abel, your brother?" An angel asks Hagar, "From where are you coming and to where are you going?"

God's response to Moses is substantive but phrased as a rhetorical question. This happened earlier, but more subtly, when God asks Moses,

"What is in your hand?" The rebuke is not readily apparent, as Moses actually responds to the question. Here, however, it is unquestionable. God is not simply informing Moses that He has the capacity to turn a mute person into a speaking one; He is letting Moses know that He is displeased with Moses's demurral.

God's displeasure becomes even clearer when we look carefully at the substance, not only the tone, of His response. There are five characteristics listed – speech, muteness, deafness, sight, and blindness. Four of these characteristics form pairs of opposites. Speech contrasts with muteness, sight contrasts with blindness. The central one is deafness, which has no match. God can make the blind see and the mute talk, but he cannot make someone hear if they are determined to be deaf. Moses thought that the people would be deaf to him, but God is growing impatient with the one who is being deaf to God's entreaties.

We, the readers, have the luxury of studying the text. Moses did not have that. If God is hinting, it does not seem like Moses understands. For the fifth time he declines going on God's behalf, but this time is different. He has no substantive argument – not that the people won't listen, not that he has no position to stand before Pharaoh, not that the people won't trust him, not that he doesn't know what to say or what name of God to use, and not even that he has a speech impediment. Send someone else, anyone else, anyone else that You choose.

It is this unjustified refusal which provokes God's anger. God was patient with all of Moses's excuses, but a non-substantive refusal goes too far. God stops asking. He now commands. Go. Take your staff to do the signs. Aaron, your brother, your fellow Levite – also a zealot – he knows how to speak and will be happy to join you.[31] I will instruct you, you will in turn instruct him, and I will be with both of you.

31. If, indeed, Moses's flight from Egypt resulted from his fear of what caring about Israel could make him do, God reassures him that his brother is also a zealot but knows how to temper that with words.

Moses called himself God's servant; once he does, God commands His servant.[32] Moses no longer has a choice. He will go because he has been commanded and because he has God with him.

And, for the first time in his conscious life, he learns that he has a brother.

32. Zevaḥim 102a notes that if not for his hesitation at this point, after identifying himself as God's servant, Moses would have been appointed high priest.

Exodus 4:18–6:1

Buying In

Having learned about his brother, Aaron, and having been commanded by God, we would naturally expect that the next verse would begin with something like: "So Moses went to Egypt, as God had instructed him." In fact, the next verse does begin as expected, "So Moses went," but surprises us with the continuation: "and he returned to Yeter, his father-in-law."[1]

The conversation between Moses and Yeter is no less surprising.

> Moses: I will go, please, and return to my brothers in Egypt to see if they are still alive.
> Yitro: Go in peace.

Rather than telling Yitro about his life-altering encounter with God and his mission to save Israel, Moses presents what sounds like a roots trip, a reunion with long-lost family. Aside from being disingenuous,

1. Yeter and Yitro are likely the same person. According to a rabbinic tradition, he is known by seven names, including Reuel (Ex. 18) and Ḥovav (Num. 10:29). Ibn Ezra (3:1) suggests that Yeter-Yitro is Moses's brother-in-law.

it is surprising that he seems to be asking for permission. Was he not commanded by God? What would he have done had Yitro not granted him leave?

When we survey other stories in the Bible involving fathers-in-law, we discover that there is a distinct pattern – fathers-in-law do not let their sons-in-law leave. Jacob, upon completing his fourteen-year stint working for Laban, asks permission to leave, and is convinced by Laban to stay.[2] When Jacob eventually does leave, sneaking away while Laban is out of town, Laban chases after him to try to force him to return. In the scene which sets up the closing narrative in Judges, the father-in-law of the Levite he is hosting repeatedly tries to prevent his son-in-law from leaving.[3] Later, Saul's fraught relationship with David is marked by his alternately trying to kill David while keeping him close.[4]

What this suggests is that when Moses asks his father-in-law's permission, he is expecting to be refused. Both he, and we, are surprised to hear that Yitro freely grants him permission.[5] Yet even after Yitro's permission, it seems like Moses is not moving, to the extent that God needs to speak with him again to encourage him to go. "God said to Moses, in Midian: Go,[6] return to Egypt, for all the people seeking to

---

2. Gen. 30:25–34. There are multiple parallels between Moses and Jacob. Both flee to foreign countries when they sensed that their lives were in danger; both met their future wives by performing an act of kindness at a well; both end up tending sheep for their fathers-in-law for a longer-than-expected period; both are told by God to leave, and both ask permission to do so from someone they expected would deny that permission; both end up in a mysterious encounter which threatens their life; both are reunited with long-lost brothers who are happy to see them. Later, the Exodus of Israel from Egypt will also parallel Jacob's trip from Haran back home. Both end up leaving their enslavement with greater wealth than they anticipated, and both are chased by their former oppressor who wants to return them back to servitude. Deuteronomy (26:5) draws subtly on these parallels, weaving together the stories of Jacob's sojourn in Haran with the experience of the Israelites leaving Egypt.
3. Judges 19:4–9. The language of *Vayaḥazek bo*, "He held onto him firmly" (19:4), convincingly conveys the father-in-law's intent.
4. I Sam. 18–20.
5. By contrast, when Moses approaches Pharaoh, expecting him to refuse, Pharaoh reacts as we would expect.
6. God's instruction to Moses to go, *Lekh*, appears four times (3:10, 3:16, 4:12, 4:19),

kill you have died" (4:19).[7] And when Moses does go, his actions look more like planning a family reunion than of preparing to save a nation from slavery, as he takes his wife and children, packing them onto a donkey for the long trip.[8] Apparently, God was less successful than we originally thought in His attempt to recruit Moses.[9]

GOD CHANGES THE MISSION

As we reconstruct the sequence of events, a different possibility emerges. While God instructs Moses to go, the messenger is not yet ready to embrace that mission. There is, however, one thing that God says that piques Moses's curiosity. He has a brother. Aaron is his name. The man with no identity or affiliation discovers that there is someplace that he might belong.[10]

As Moses returns to Yitro after the burning bush, he has no intention of going to Egypt, but he cannot get out of his head the news that he has a family. The nagging sense that he can finally discover who he is, like the adopted child (which he is!) who discovers that he is adopted

---

yet Moses hesitates each time. This contrasts with God's instruction of *Lekh lekha*, to which Abraham responds immediately both times (Gen. 12:1 and 22:2).

7. This echoes Pharaoh in 1:8 who forgot Joseph. Just as a new generation of Pharaohs enables the descent into slavery, a new Pharaoh allows for the reentry of the savior into the story.
8. Ibn Ezra (4:20) is perplexed by Moses taking his wife and children. Rashbam (4:24) understands that God's "desire to kill Moses" is a response to Moses's delay in fulfilling God's mission, a delay indicated by him taking his family with him.
9. For alternative approaches to this question, see Nahmanides (4:19) and Rabbi David Zvi Hoffmann (4:18).
10. This parallels Joseph's decision to reunite with his family. Although he was estranged from them for many years, even naming his first son as a tribute to his ability to forget his past, he recovers his past when he rejoins them. There are multiple parallels and contrasts between Joseph and Moses. Both live significant parts of their lives separated from their birth families, both are uprooted geographically from their homes, both have Egyptian names. Perhaps the most significant difference is that Joseph is the architect of Israel's settling into Egypt while Moses engineers their departure. Joseph builds Pharaoh and his kingdom while Moses is responsible for dismantling that kingdom. Further, the word chosen by the text to describe Moses being hidden by his mother comes from the root TZ-F-N (2:3); the only other place the Torah uses that root is in Joseph's Egyptian name, *Tzofnat Paane'aḥ*. For more on Joseph, see Grumet, *Genesis: From Creation to Covenant*, 407–16.

and seeks out his birth family, impels him to go to Egypt – not to fulfill God's mission but to seek out his kin. When Moses tells Yitro that he wants to see if his brothers are still alive, he is not being disingenuous – that is exactly what he is seeking. God's instructions neither motivate him nor do they compel him to obey, but the news of the brother tempts him. For Moses, this indeed holds the hope for a family reunion; hence he rightfully takes his family with him.

God apparently recognizes this, accepts it, and decides to work with what He has.[11] Listen carefully to what He says to Moses in Midian: "Go, return to Egypt, for all the people seeking to kill you have died." There is no anger expressed at Moses's procrastination, and if this was another push for Moses to fulfill the previously discussed mission, mentioning the safety of the trip would be irrelevant. The very fact that God offers him that reassurance points to the reality to which God must adapt – He did not succeed in getting Moses to follow His command, but He has found a different way to bring Moses to Egypt: the brother, the possibility of discovering an authentic identity.

In this context, God's second message to Moses in Midian takes on an entirely new meaning. "As you travel to Egypt, see all the wonders[12] that I have placed in your hand – do them in front of Pharaoh." This is no longer Moses's prime purpose, but as he is already going to seek his family, God requests that he stop at Pharaoh's palace to deliver a message.

This switch in plan is similar to one we find with Jonah. In chapter 1 of Jonah, God commands Jonah to go to Nineveh and prophesy to the people. Jonah refuses, running away to the sea. When it becomes clear that he cannot escape God's will, God repeats the command in

---

11. *Haamek Davar* (4:24) suggests that God's anger at Moses is the result of the need to change the plan.
12. This is markedly different from what was described earlier at the burning bush (4:2–9). There, God has Moses perform signs, ostensibly to help Israel believe that he is God's messenger, while here God describes wonders Moses is to perform in front of Pharaoh. Interestingly, in both descriptions it is Moses's hands which play a central role. Ibn Ezra (4:21) suggests that the wonders of which God speaks here do not refer to those signs at all but to the future wonders that Moses will display before Pharaoh and the Egyptians.

chapter 3, with a subtle difference between the initial command and its repetition.

Jonah 1	Jonah 3
1. The word of God came to Jonah ben Amitai, saying:	1. The word of God came to Jonah a second time, saying:
2. Rise up, go to Nineveh the large city, and call upon it, for their evil has come before Me	2. Rise up, go to Nineveh the large city, and announce to it the announcement that I will tell you

The similarity between the two verses highlights the differences. When God first comes to Jonah, He instructs him to "call upon" Nineveh, for God has taken note of their evil. Calling upon the city is what prophets do – they use their oratory skills and creativity to shape and deliver a message that will hopefully bring about a change in behavior. That is what God expected of Jonah initially. The second call to Jonah comes after Jonah ultimately accepts that he has no choice but to do God's bidding, even though he still does not want to. Recognizing that, while God insists that Jonah go to Nineveh, He changes the mission – all Jonah needs to do is to recite the words God gives him, to "call upon it the call" that God will tell him. God no longer expects Jonah to invest his energies; instead, he will simply be a mouthpiece repeating God's words. In fact, this is precisely what Jonah does. He takes one day to run through a city that would normally take three days (Jonah 3:3–4) and repeats the five words God dictates: *Od arba'im yom veNineveh nehepakhet*, "Another forty days and Nineveh is destroyed." No explanations, no call for repentance. God wanted Jonah to go but understood that it was unreasonable for Jonah to pour his heart into a mission with which he strongly disagreed – so God changed the mission to accommodate His chosen messenger.

Similarly, God initially wanted Moses to be His partner, inspiring the Israelites with the message of redemption and humbling the arrogant Pharaoh until he released Israel from bondage. Moses openly refused that mission five times and passively ignored it after God's insistence. Recognizing that Moses would not cooperate, God capitalizes on Moses's interest in searching out his family, asking Moses to do one thing while there – to make a stop at Pharaoh's palace to deliver a message while Moses was going for a family reunion.

ON THE WAY

What does Moses's wife, Tzippora, know about his encounter at the burning bush? Does she think that they are going to reunite with Moses's birth family, or does she understand that her husband is following a divine command? We have no direct knowledge, but there is a mysterious encounter which sheds some light on this.

On the way to Egypt, at a rest stop, God wants to kill Moses.[13] Tzippora takes a sharp flint stone and circumcises their son.[14] Moses is saved when she touches the severed foreskin to Moses's leg, proclaiming him to be the bloody bridegroom. Afterward she says that the bridegroom was bloodied by the circumcision.

What does any of this mean?

Here is one suggestion. As much as God adapts to the reality of what Moses is prepared to do, He is not satisfied with Moses simply being a message courier to Pharaoh as a side trip to his family reunion in Egypt. Hence God expresses His displeasure by "wanting to kill" Moses.[15] To be sure, God could have killed Moses instantly – but that was not His intention. He wanted to convey just how serious this is; it is a matter of life and death. Ironically, God had reassured Moses that it was safe to go to Egypt because the people who sought to kill him were dead. That message now takes on a new twist – it is not safe to avoid going to Egypt. Moses shouldn't be worried about the people who want to take his life but about the God who is prepared to do so should Moses continue to defy Him.

---

13. Some authors suggest that God wanted to kill the uncircumcised son. Ibn Ezra (4:20) rejects this. The rest stop, *malon*, is referred to only one other time in the Torah – it is the place that Joseph's brothers spent the night on their way back to Canaan and where one of them discovered that his silver remained in his satchel.
14. This is apparently Eliezer, whose name is hinted to in God's reassurance to Moses that the people who want to kill him are dead.
15. God's displeasure was earlier (4:14) expressed as anger. See Rashbam (4:14).

Tzippora understands that Moses is generating obstacles for God's fulfillment of His covenant, so she invokes that covenant by circumcising their son. Tzippora apparently heard Moses's earlier prevarication and decides – like the other women in Exodus who understood what the men surrounding them missed – that God's plans are greater than those of man, that destiny demands being able to see beyond the immediate.

The vision of destiny is at the core of covenant. God's Covenant Between the Pieces with Abraham demanded that Abraham look to the very distant future before seeing any benefit to the covenant. Circumcision is an essential act of covenant because it obligates the next generation, and even the generation afterward, as it sanctifies the procreative process. It was thus inconceivable to Tzippora that Moses was bringing a child who had not as yet entered the covenant to the event marking the fulfillment of that covenant.[16] Her act of dedication to the covenant redirects Moses, and that redirection allows God to permit Moses to continue.

We can barely imagine what is running through Tzippora's mind. She met Moses many years earlier as a kind Egyptian who was helpful to her and her sisters and who eventually married her and settled in with their family. He was the unassuming man who tended her father's flocks, freeing her and her sisters from their daily micro-oppression at the hands of the other shepherds. When Moses returns from the burning bush he must have shared with her his encounter, or at least what he thought was his encounter – what the voice told him, what he did with his hand and the staff, and Moses's reluctance to get involved, perhaps even his doubt afterward if the encounter ever happened.[17] Moses's doubts and curios-

---

16. Ironically, Moses's children were not present at the moment of the fulfilment of the covenant (see 18:2), as Tzippora had apparently returned to Midian. This scene evokes a modified version of the binding of Isaac, as both involve God apparently wanting to kill the bearer of the future of the covenant. The differences between them are profound. While Abraham was supposed to have included Sarah as his covenantal partner, he did not; she dies soon after the story of the *Akeda*. By contrast, Tzippora was never intended to be Moses's partner; in fact, she too was not present at the Exodus, despite that fact that ironically, it was she who understood the covenantal nature of Moses's trip and rescued that mission by circumcising their child. Bringing the child into the covenant should, in theory, have drawn Moses into it as well. As we will see, that is not necessarily the case.
17. This is similar to Jacob's dream. When he wakes in the morning, he is unsure of

ity became hers, only she heard it secondhand and may have doubted even more. When the mysterious force tries to kill her husband, she realizes that the man with whom she has lived for decades is not who she thought he was at all. Her bridegroom is a man of divine covenant, a man of the covenant of blood.

MOSES ARRIVES IN EGYPT

The encounter at the rest stop apparently has an effect on Moses. His reunion with his long-lost brother lacks any of the pathos of Jacob's reunion with Esau or Joseph's with his brothers.[18] It is all business. Moses's roots trip has been completely coopted; he shares his mission with Aaron[19] and the pair proceed to fulfill it. Yet despite the fact that Moses accepts his charge, there is good reason to suggest that he does

---

whether it was actually a revelation or a dream, the product of his wishful thinking. See Grumet, *Genesis: From Creation to Covenant,* 317–324.

18. While Aaron kisses Moses (4:27), there is no indication that Moses reciprocates. The word used to describe their meeting, *vayifgeshehu,* is exactly the same as that which is used just three verses earlier to describe God's encounter with Moses and desire to kill him. The contrast between these two encounters on the way to Egypt could not be greater.

19. Aaron is first introduced by God as Moses's spokesperson, ostensibly after Moses avers that he cannot go to Pharaoh because he is not a man of words (4:14–16). From a political perspective, Aaron will serve a significant role. In contrast to Moses, who is unknown by the Israelites (he fled from there many decades earlier and was never known as an Israelite), he is an Israelite of some standing (see 6:23, where he marries into an elite Judahite family). Aaron will provide entry and legitimacy to Moses as Moses speaks with Israel. Aaron's status – even vis-à-vis the Egyptians – is attested to by the fact that he is free to leave Egypt to meet Moses in the wilderness. Aaron is someone with whom God speaks, and without much fanfare. God's instruction to Aaron to meet Moses in the wilderness is perhaps the shortest prophecy in the Bible, consisting of only four words, and is contrasted with Moses's dialogue with God, which is the longest in the Torah. The contrast between Aaron and Moses is accentuated when Aaron responds immediately to God's command while Moses hesitates even after a lengthy discussion.

    Leon Kass suggests that the brotherhood of Moses and Aaron marks a dramatic departure from the antagonistic brotherly relations which marked Genesis. He argues, however, that there are underlying unspoken tensions, which surface occasionally through the stories of the Golden Calf, the deaths of Aaron's sons, and the incident in which Miriam and Aaron speak against Moses.

not embrace it. In fact, it seems like he labors to ensure that everything happens exactly as God told him, so that afterward he can say that he did what he was asked to do and then return to his quiet life in Midian.

As he was instructed initially, he goes straight to the Israelites, more precisely, the Israelite elders. Aaron tells them about God's salvation and performs the signs God gave Moses, even though God told Moses to display them only should the people doubt him and his prophecy, and there is no sign of that doubt. Leaving nothing to chance, Moses has Aaron perform the signs immediately. Moses's plan, slightly altered from God's plan to ensure absolute success, works. "The people believed; when they heard that God appointed them and saw their suffering, they bowed and prostrated themselves" (4:31).

When they arrive at Pharaoh's palace Moses wants to ensure that this part of the plan goes exactly as God said, that is, that Pharaoh rejects their request. To accomplish that Moses delivers God's message – but makes some subtle modifications to guarantee Pharaoh's rejection.

God's instruction (3:18)	**What Moses says initially (5:1)**
You should say to him: A-donai, God of the Hebrews, happened upon us, so let us now travel on a three-day trip in the wilderness so that we may slaughter to A-donai, our God	They said to Pharaoh: Thus said A-donai, God of Israel, "Send My people out so that they may celebrate to Me in the wilderness"

It is not difficult to see the difference between God's instructions and what Moses says. First, Moses changes the name of the nation from the Hebrews to Israel. Second, Moses spoke about celebration while God spoke of a slaughter (presumably a sacrifice). Third, God mentioned a three-day trip which Moses omits. And fourth, Moses mentions that God spoke to them.

Changing the name to Israel was surprising to Pharaoh. From his perspective, his predecessor had coined that name in order to identify the growing clan as outsiders to the rest of the Egyptians. Given that the name was an Egyptian invention, how could some deity claim to be the god of that artificial entity? Second, while feeding the gods was a norm in the Ancient Near East, Moses speaks of something entirely different, a celebration. What is it that slave people celebrate? Third, Moses omits the three days, suggesting that Pharaoh understands that he is not asking for a furlough but to be sent free,[20] and perhaps the celebration of which he spoke was a celebration of their freedom. Fourth, as we saw earlier, in the ancient world gods were to be tended, fed, and taken care of. That was the sum total of their interaction with people, except for showing their displeasure when their needs were not seen to. The notion that a god would speak to people was foreign, especially for a Pharaoh who deigned himself a god.

With these changes, Moses ensures that Pharaoh will find every element of the request absurd, likely fabricated by Moses. "Who is A-donai that I should listen to Him to send out Israel? I know not A-donai and I will also not send out Israel." Moses has succeeded. Israel listens and accepts, Pharaoh rejects. This was the plan.

Now that Moses has succeeded in earning Pharaoh's emphatic "No!" he understands that he must deliver God's message, not his own. Listen to what he says now and compare that, too, to God's initial instruction.

God's instruction (3:18)	What Moses says secondarily (5:3)
You should say to him: A-donai, God of the Hebrews, happened (*nikra,* ending with a *heh*) upon us, so let us now travel on a three-day journey in the wilderness so that we may slaughter to A-donai, our God	They said: The God of the Hebrews called (*nikra,* ending with an *alef*) upon us; let us travel on a three-day journey lest He strike us with pestilence or sword

20. The root SH-L-Ḥ, meaning to send out, is one of the theme words of the Exodus story, appearing sixty times.

Notice that this second oration matches God's instructions more closely. Moses omits God's name and restores His identity as the God of the Hebrews; he speaks of a three-day journey rather than hinting at being set free, and he refers to a god who may strike out at the people, a concept familiar to Egyptians. The content and tone match, and there are only two minor discrepancies between God's instruction and Moses's words. First, God spoke of a slaughter while Moses refers to the fear of divine retribution. Given what Pharaoh has already heard and the Egyptian mindset, Moses's words may be slightly different from God's, but they convey precisely the same message. The other difference is much subtler. While God told Moses to say that He happened upon them, *nikra* (with a *heh* as the final letter), Moses uses the homophone *nikra,* He called upon us (with an *alef* as the final letter).[21] Moses's *nikra* matches what he said earlier, that God spoke to them. He speaks his heart but allows the listener to believe that he is simply repeating God's words.

It turns out that before Moses delivers God's message, the second one he says to Pharaoh, he delivers his own – one which he is sure Pharaoh will reject. Now that Pharaoh is in a mode of rejection, Moses delivers God's words, knowing that Pharaoh will hear them as identical to the initial message.

With that, Moses has completed his mission. God told him to speak to Israel, who would listen. He spoke with Israel and ensured that they would listen by giving the signs even before they had a chance to doubt. God told him to speak to Pharaoh, who would reject his words. Moses speaks with Pharaoh and ensures that Pharaoh will reject his words. With that, in Moses's eyes, he has done as he was instructed and is now free to leave. The rest is in God's hands, as God had previously assured him.

But he does not leave.

A CHANGE OF HEART

What caused Moses to stay? Was it his newfound relationship with his brother? Or perhaps his rediscovery of his identity as a Hebrew? These are certainly possible, although the text gives no indication of either.

21. Rabbi Shmuel David Luzzatto (5:3) and Ibn Ezra (3:18) note the difference but suggest that they have the same meaning.

What the text actually does say is that he hears Pharaoh's reaction to his second request. Pharaoh did not simply reject him, but he decided to intensify their labor as a result of Moses's second speech, the one he needed to say to clear his conscience with God.

> The Egyptian king said to them: "Why, Moses and Aaron, do you disturb the people from their work? Go to your burdens." Pharaoh said: "There are many people in the land, and you want to cause them to desist from their burdens?" (5:4–5)[22]

Even more, on that day Pharaoh issued new decrees to make the Israelites work harder, accusing them of being soft, weak in their work habits. They will now need to gather the straw to make bricks rather than having it provided for them.[23] While Moses did not want to get involved, it turns out that his attempt to ensure Pharaoh's denial of the request generated some unexpected and distressing consequences. Within a day or two[24] the Israelites are being beaten for not fulfilling their quotas of bricks.[25] Rather than God taking charge, as Moses understood would happen, God seems absent, and Israel's suffering – which God

---

22. Apparently, Pharaoh's attempt to transfer the burdens from the Egyptians to the Israelites is bearing fruit. The extra *vayomer* (Pharaoh "said") in the beginning of 5:5 suggests that after Pharaoh told Moses and Aaron to go to their burdens they did not leave, necessitating another directive from Pharaoh.
23. The word for gathering the straw is *mekoshesh*. This word appears one other time in the Torah, referring to the man gathering wood on Shabbat after the incident of the scouts (Num. 15:32). It is possible that that individual was trying to remind the Israelites, who called for the appointment of a new leader and return to Egypt, what that would look like: gathering wood/straw with no days of rest, unlike God's mandate when they entered the covenant at Sinai.
24. The text describes the taskmasters complaining that the Israelites did not fill their quotas of bricks as they had done *temol shilshom*, "yesterday and the day before" (6:14). This phrase echoes Moses's earlier comment to God that he has never been a man of words (4:10). I use the term "taskmaster" as a poor translation for the Hebrew *nogess*, which is not a title but a description of what they do – oppress, drive, and wield power.
25. The language used by Pharaoh includes the words *lo tosifu* ("you should no longer continue") and *lo tigre'u* ("you should not lessen"). This pair of phrases is echoed in Deuteronomy (4:2 and 13:1) as Moses commands to neither to add to nor diminish

said motivated Him to begin this process – is only getting worse. Moses needs to see what happens.

When the Israelite team leaders, perplexed about the new rules and frustrated with the impossibility of them being able to meet the expectations of them and their brethren, approach Pharaoh for an explanation, he tells them what he earlier said to the Egyptian officers in charge. "He said: You are soft, weak. That is why you say, 'Let us travel to worship A-donai'" (5:17).

Moses is aware of Pharaoh's decree as well as of the meeting between the Israelite team leaders and Pharaoh. He was waiting for them outside Pharaoh's palace, eagerly hoping to hear the result.[26] What he hears moves him deeply.

> May God look down upon you and issue judgment, for you have made us smell bad in the eyes[27] of Pharaoh and his servants; you have given them a sword to kill us. (5:21)

Their accusation that Moses brought injustice upon them evokes some of the most powerful moments from Genesis. Barren Sarai, suffering humiliation at the hands of her Egyptian servant, demands that God judge between herself and Abram (Gen. 16:5). Similarly, Jacob, outraged at having been accused of theft by Laban, declares God as the judge of which of them has stolen from the other (Gen. 31:36–42).[28] The language

from God's commands, and in Numbers (36:3–4) in the context of the request by Zelophehad's daughters to receive his portion in the land and the follow-up request by the leaders of Menashe.

26. The text describes Moses and Aaron as *nitzavim*, usually translated as "standing," waiting to greet the Israelite leaders. The word *nitzav* is often used in the Bible to describe someone standing ready, in a guarding or anticipatory position, prepared to act. See, for example, Gen. 18:2, 24:13, 28:13; Ex. 7:9, 17:9; and many others. When objects are set in place by someone to serve a significant function they are described as *nitzav*. See, for example, Gen. 21:28, 28:12, 33:20, 35:20. This may be the reason that although the patriarchs set up *matzevot* (Gen. 28:18, 31:45, 35:15, and 35:20), God later rejects them (Ex. 34:13; Lev. 26:1; Deut. 7:5, 12:3, and 16:22), as they suggest attributing significance to an object which is a gateway to idolatry.
27. Ibn Ezra notes the mixed metaphor of smell and eyes.
28. God's judgment often includes a reference to God seeing. See Gen. 6:5, 6:12, 18:21,

of "making us smell bad" and its linkage to the fear of being slaughtered by the sword feature prominently in Jacob's rebuke of Shimon and Levi after their massacre of Shechem (Gen. 34:30). While Moses may not be familiar with Genesis, the impact of those words upon him is immense. The man whose early adult life was dramatically defined by his response to injustice, both in his killing the Egyptian and in his saving Yitro's daughters (one of whom became his wife), is now accused of perpetrating the very kind of injustice against which he once raged.

Moses is now enraged. He did not want to go to Egypt in the first place. He only agreed to go because God made him do so, and because God assured him that his going would bring God into the picture and bring salvation for these people. Now he is brought face-to-face with the reality that his actions, forced upon him by God, brought intensified suffering and even more injustice. That is too much for him.

He doesn't return to Midian. For the first time in his life, he initiates a dialogue with God, or, more accurately, summons God to a monologue. He launches into a series of rhetorical questions, rebuke, against God: "Why have You done evil to these people? Why did You send me?" (5:22). Moses does not suffice with his accusatory questions but provides his own response: "From the time I came to Pharaoh to speak in Your name he acted even worse to this people – and You did not save Your people!" (5:23). Moses accuses God of injustice, much as Abraham did when he heard God's intent to destroy Sodom: "Will the judge of all the world not do justice?" (Gen. 18:25).

One would think that God would be offended, even angered, by Moses's impudence – but His response seems to be the opposite. We can imagine God smiling as he reassures Moses, "Now you will see what I will do to Pharaoh, for he will send them out – even chase them out – as a result of My strong hand" (6:1).[29] This is not simply a reassurance to Moses; it is God's delight at Moses's rage. Moses challenges

---

31:42. Perhaps this is the source of talmudic aphorism that the judge must rely only on what he sees (Sanhedrin 6b).

29. According to the standardized chapter breaks, attributed to Stephen Langton (the fourteenth-century archbishop of Canterbury), this verse opens the next chapter. In doing so, God's primary response to Moses opens with the discussion of God's name and the reiteration of the mission in the beginning of Exodus 6. According

and confronts God more than Abraham does, making him more Abrahamic than Abraham himself. Moses cares. He cares enough to burst out at God. He is moved by injustice, regardless of whether it is Pharaoh or God who perpetrates it. He is committed to these people and their future, and he knows where he belongs – he has discovered his identity. Moses has proven himself worthy of being the agent for fulfilling the covenant God initiated with Abraham, the first to recognize God as the Master of Justice. What God could not accomplish in His lengthy dialogue at the burning bush He accomplished by cajoling and enticing Moses to travel to Egypt.

With Moses on board as a committed liberator, the table has now been set for the unfolding redemption.

---

to the Masoretic division, however, this single verse stands as a significant closure to God's attempt to recruit Moses and is distinct from the communication which comes afterward.

Exodus 6:2–7:13

Again, and Again

With God's secure assurance that He will hold Pharaoh accountable and ensure that Israel exit, and with Moses committed to the people, we expect that the next verse will mention God's instruction that Moses return to Pharaoh. Surprisingly, that does not happen. At least not yet. Instead, we are faced with a series of puzzling, seemingly repetitive passages.

The first, 6:2–13, seems to repeat the encounter between God and Moses at the burning bush, including the following elements:

- E-lohim introduces Himself as A-donai
- References to the patriarchs
- God witnesses the suffering of Israel
- God decides to save Israel from Egypt and to bring them to a different land
- Moses is reticent to accept the mission due to a speech defect
- God introduces Aaron as a spokesman

Every one of these was already described in the lengthy narrative of the burning bush.

The second passage, 6:14–27,[1] opens with a genealogical tree. Starting with a brief mention of the descendants of the eldest two tribes, Reuben and Simeon, it provides a detailed map of the family of Levi leading to Moses and Aaron – the brother-team of the book's heroes – including the wives of Amram (Moses's father), Aaron, and Elazar (one of Aaron's sons).

The third passage, 6:28–7:7, opens with God introducing Himself to Moses yet again, an instruction to Moses to go to Pharaoh, Moses's refusal to go because he has a speech defect, and the introduction of Aaron as his spokesman. That is followed by an outline of the divine plan, including Aaron addressing Pharaoh, Pharaoh rejecting the request because God will harden Pharaoh's heart, God sending multiple signs and wonders, God bringing Egypt to recognize Him, which will ultimately lead to God taking Israel out of Egypt.

How are we to make sense of this unexpected, redundant, and seemingly unnecessary interruption?

THE FIRST PASSAGE

Rabbi Elhanan Samet's[2] analysis of the first passage demonstrates not only its beauty, but also the uniqueness of its message. I will share an abridged version of it here. He highlights that the passage is written chiastically, an ABBA structure, as follows:

I am A-donai

A (3) I appeared to Abraham, Isaac, and Jacob in the name El-Shaddai, but by the name A-donai I was not known to them. (4) I also established My covenant with them, giving them the land of Canaan, in which they dwelled temporarily.

1. Ibn Ezra (6:28) notes that although the Masoretic break joins 6:28 with the previous passage, its content suggests that it belongs as the opening of the next one.
2. *Iyunim BeFarashat HaShavua*, Series 1, Volume 1, 167–77.

B (5) I also heard the cry of the Israelites as Egypt enslaves them, and I recall My covenant. (6) Therefore say to the Israelites:

I am A-donai.

B' I will take you out from under the Egyptian burdens, I will save you from the enslavement, I will redeem you with an outstretched arm and great judgments, (7) I will take you to Me as a nation and I will be your God; you will know that I, A-donai, am your God, the one taking you from under the Egyptian burdens.

A' (8) I will bring you to the land that I promised to give to Abraham, Isaac, and Jacob; I will give it to you as a legacy;

I am A-donai.

The A and A' sections mention the patriarchs; in the A section they are the ones to whom God made the promise of the land; in the A' section it is God's commitment to fulfill that promise and bring them into the land. That land will be transformed from the one in which the patriarchs dwelled temporarily (A) to the one which will become part of the Israelite legacy (A'). The B and B' sections mention Israel's status vis-à-vis Egypt; in the B section they are suffering at the hands of Egypt, and in the B' passage God promises to take them out of that place of suffering.

The first half of this message (A and B) refers to the past, both the distant past (the patriarchs – A) and the near past (the suffering of Israel in Egypt – B) as background which God shares with Moses. That framing explains why God is about to do what He plans, in both the near future (taking them out of Egypt – B') and the distant future (bringing them into their promised land – A').

In the first half God speaks *about* the Israelites; in the second half He hands Moses a message to be delivered *to* the Israelites.

Finally, framing this entire speech is God's self-identification as A-donai. It opens the speech, closes the speech, and is at its very center.

What does all this mean? The core of this new charge highlights two key issues. One is the centrality of the covenant[3] as the motivator for God's reentry into history. God established a covenant, and He has every intention of fulfilling it. Hence, here the land is not described as a generic "good" land or a land flowing with milk and honey, the way it had been described earlier (3:8), but as the land of the covenant. The second key issue, intimately intertwined with the first, is God's desire for Israel to know who He is and to build a relationship with Him. For that reason, the phrase "I am A-donai" frames the entire oracle and stands at its center. It is also what is highlighted in the B' section, culminating with, "I will take you to Me as a nation and I will be your God; you will know that I, A-donai, am your God."

It turns out, then, that despite the similarities to God's initial interaction with Moses, this is not a repetition of it but a further development with a new focus. Covenant. Relationship. Both are completely new to Moses – neither was mentioned even once at the burning bush but both are central here. What triggered covenant to suddenly emerge? Israel's intensified suffering. This was precisely what God had told Abraham. When his descendants become strangers, are enslaved, and are oppressed, that is when their redemption will come (Gen. 15:13).

UNANSWERED QUESTIONS

Rabbi Samet's analysis demonstrates the elegance of the passage and is both insightful and meaningful. At the same time, however, it leaves many questions unanswered. First, the covenant actually was mentioned earlier, not in the dialogue between Moses and God but in the preamble to it.

> During those many days the king of Egypt died; when the Israelites groaned[4] from their work their cries from their work rose up to God. God heard their anguished groaning,[5] and God

3. Specifically, the Covenant Between the Pieces (Gen. 15:9–21).
4. This verb appears only here in the Torah.
5. The Hebrew word for this is *ne'aka*, which we will discuss shortly.

> remembered His covenant with Abraham, with Isaac, and with Jacob. (2:23–24).

If the covenant is introduced earlier, why then does God not mention it even once in His initial encounter with Moses? Second, while we understand that God wants to introduce Himself to Israel, why does He need to reintroduce Himself again to Moses? In fact, the passage opens with an unusual formulation: "E-lohim spoke with Moses and said, 'I am A-donai'" (6:2).[6] That is not part of the message to Israel, but to Moses himself. Given the extensive earlier dialogue about God's name (3:13–16), it seems highly unusual that God would need to repeat it, especially since Moses himself used the name A-donai in his first dialogue with Pharaoh (5:1–3). Third, why would God engineer the conditions that would cause Israel to lose hope after they had just recently prostrated themselves before Moses in thanks of the message of redemption he brought (4:31)?

Beyond this opening passage we have two additional ones. The genealogy of Moses and Aaron seems out of place; it should have come immediately after the scene at the burning bush, where Moses seems to have been willing to go to Egypt and where Aaron is first introduced. And the opening of that genealogy seems disconnected from what came before. Here's how it reads:

> These are the heads of their households. The children of Reuben, Israel's firstborn, are Enoch, Pallu, Hezron, and Karmi. These are the families of Reuben. And the children of Simeon. (6:14–15)

Assuming we can explain why the Torah wanted to put the genealogy of Moses and Aaron here, why would it open with those of Reuben and Simeon?[7] Even more, to what is the Torah referring when it opens with

6. This verse and the following one drew the attention of many of the traditional commentators, both because of its content and because of its unusual use of the word *nodati*.

7. This question was addressed by many of the commentators, yet those explanations do not really answer the core question of what this passage is connected to and why – if the focus is truly on Levi – the Torah felt a need to mention the others at

"These are the heads of their households"? Reuben and Simeon have not been mentioned at all in this story.

There are other puzzling elements which Rabbi Samet does not address. After the genealogy there is an additional passage in which God introduces Himself yet again and in which Moses demurs because of a speech impediment (6:29–30). That entire passage seems like a verbatim repetition of 6:10–12. And when Moses finally does go to Pharaoh (7:10–13), it is Aaron, not Moses, who uses the staff which turns into a crocodile, not a serpent (as at the burning bush). Rabbi Samet's analysis is deep and thoughtful but leaves too many unanswered questions.

A MULTIDIMENSIONAL APPROACH

Based on the evidence in the text, it seems like there are three different times that God introduces Himself to Moses as A-donai, three times that Moses declines to do God's bidding – each of which involves a speech impediment – and three times that Aaron is introduced as Moses's assistant. And while there is some overlap between them, each paints a distinctly different image of Moses as well as offering a different motivation for God's involvement.

When we consider the characters involved, this should not surprise us. God is not unidimensional; He has many modes of functioning in His interactions with humanity.[8] The Sages spoke of this – sometimes

---

all. Rashi suggests that it could not start with Levi, as it had to go through his elder siblings first. Rashbam offers that these were the three sons whose blessings from Jacob were highly critical, so the Torah needed to restore their positions. Rabbi David Zvi Hoffmann suggests that it comes to point out that Levi's uniqueness was earned, not inherent, as he was only the third child and not the firstborn. These explanations seem unsatisfying in that they do not address the question of why this genealogy is brought here.

8. For a more extensive overview of this approach to reading the Torah and its applicability to the traditional reader, see Mordechai Breuer, *Pirkei Mo'adot* (Horev, 1989), and Mordechai Breuer, *Pirkei Bereshit* (Tevunot, 1999). In English, see his article "The Study of Bible and the Primacy of the Fear of Heaven: Compatibility or Contradiction?" in *Modern Scholarship and the Study of Torah: Contributions and Limitations*, Shalom Carmy, ed. (Jason Aronson, 1996), 159–80. For a critique of the approach, see Shnayer Z. Leiman, "Response to Rabbi Breuer" in that same volume, 181–88.

He functions with the characteristic of strict justice, other times with the characteristic of kindness or compassion. In an infinitely complex universe, every move God makes has multiple ramifications. Imagine, for example, a simple rainstorm. While farmers and hydrologists delight, travelers and tennis players are frustrated. God's decision to bring rain is simultaneously compassionate and troublesome.[9] Similarly with regard to the famine at the end of Genesis. It brought immense wealth and power to the Egyptian Empire and brought Joseph into a position of considerable power and influence, yet caused great suffering to average citizens throughout Egypt and Canaan and brought Jacob and his family out of their ancestral promised land, even as it reunited Joseph with his brothers and his father, setting the stage for great suffering followed by ultimate redemption.

As for Moses, we have already seen that he is a complex figure. Beyond the initial portrayal of him as a conflicted zealot and a reluctant savior, we later find that he is as close to God as one can imagine – he survives walking into a fiery mountain (19:18–20), lives for forty days without eating or drinking (34:28), has an otherworldly glow emanating from his face (34:29–30), and shows no sign of aging or infirmity until his death (Deut. 34:7).

Given the complexity of our two central characters in this book, it should not surprise us that the Torah describes them from multiple perspectives. Indeed, as we explore further, we can begin to distinguish specific features of each of the three introductions, including how they each portray Moses and describe God's purpose in intervening in Egypt.

WHO IS MOSES?

We've already examined the first portrayal of Moses: born in secrecy to anonymous parents, hidden by his mother for three months, saved by Pharaoh's daughter, nursed by his birth mother, and adopted by Pharaoh's daughter. Neither an Egyptian nor a Hebrew, he is moved by unjust suffering and lashes out in rage, only to soon afterward move to

9. The Mishna in Taanit (1:3) describes the tension between the need for life-giving rain and the desire to ensure that pilgrims who came to Jerusalem for the festival get home unimpeded by washed-out roads.

Midian, where he settles in as a shepherd for countless years. He is the man with no identity who finds peace with sheep in the wilderness, only to be jarringly forced into acting on behalf of a people whose memory he tried to erase, ultimately identifying with their suffering a second time and committing himself to them. This Moses needed to be introduced to himself, to his family, to his people (to whom he is an outsider), to his ancestors, and to God. He doubts, certainly himself and perhaps God, and has a staff with which to perform signs for the people. He is far from passive with God, arguing repeatedly why he should not have to do God's bidding, and even resisting after God commands him. And when he finally follows God's instructions, he tries to ensure that he can get out as quickly as possible, only to discover that he cares too much to leave the people. His brother Aaron is to be his spokesman, speaking to the people (but not to Pharaoh), because he believes that he is "heavy of mouth and heavy of tongue" (4:16). His initial job is to speak with Pharaoh and Israel, but God will be the one taking Israel out of Egypt (3:19–20). His commitment, which he displayed in our first snapshot of him and at the close of the first section, is to the people. This Moses is depicted in Exodus 2–5.

The second portrayal of Moses is much vaguer. We know nothing of his early life – perhaps it is the same as in the first version. Somehow, this Moses has an identity and knows who his ancestors and God are, but does not yet know about A-donai or about God's covenant with his ancestors. When God tells him to go to the people of Israel, he goes without question (6:9) but fails (in contrast to the first presentation, in which Moses succeeds when he goes to the people), and it is that failure which impels him to resist God's instruction to go to Pharaoh. His brother Aaron will join him, but it is not clear what role he will play other than being Moses's partner (6:13). This Moses, presented in 6:2–13, is charged with introducing Israel to A-donai and His covenant with their ancestors, and it is his job – together with Aaron (even though Aaron's role is unclear) – to free the people from Egypt (6:13). His commitment is not to the people, as it was in the first instance, but to the covenant of which he only recently learned.

This second image of Moses doesn't come out of thin air; it is actually linked textually to an earlier passage. We earlier looked briefly at the end of Exodus 2 (vv. 23–25), describing Israel's anguished cries after the death of the Egyptian king and God's decision to act upon the patriarchal covenant. We were also surprised that the covenant was not mentioned, even once, in the extended conversation between God and Moses at the burning bush. It appears that the covenant is not part of God's motivation in recruiting that first Moses, but it is central to sending the second Moses to Israel. It turns out that that earlier short passage does not introduce the scene at the burning bush, but it does serve as the opening to the one in the beginning of Exodus 6. Both have covenant as the central feature sparking God's intervention. There is another textual link binding those two passages – they are the only two places in the Torah where the word *naaka*, anguished cries, is used (2:24 and 6:5), and in the same context. In both places God hears the *naaka* of the Israelites, remembers the covenant, and decides to act upon it.

The third image of Moses is altogether different.[10] His tribe is presented with great fanfare. Much like the descendants of Seth (Gen. 5:1–32), who are the ancestors of the humanity who survived the Great Confusion, they are presented with their lifespans. Like the patriarchs, many of their wives are named and they, too, are from the elite. Amram marries Levi's daughter; Aaron marries the sister of Nahshon, the leader of Judah.[11] Moses is not an outsider to Israel, nor are he and his family anonymous (as in the first portrayal) – quite the contrary, he comes from one of the most distinguished clans. Moses and Aaron are presented together, as equals, in the mission to speak with Pharaoh and take Israel out of Egypt (Ex. 6:26–27), but God will soon clarify that Aaron's role is to speak with Pharaoh, not Israel (7:1).[12]

10. Aaron's role is also different. In the first presentation he is a spokesperson to the people; in the third he is a spokesman to Pharaoh. In the first Moses is described as being an authority (E-lohim) to Aaron (4:16); in the third Moses is described as being an authority (E-lohim) to Pharaoh (7:1) while Aaron will be the spokesman/prophet.

11. Elazar, Aaron's son, marries a daughter of Putiel. While we have no direct knowledge of who Putiel is, the name rings of Egyptian aristocracy, like Potiphar and Potiphera (Joseph's father-in-law).

12. Rashi (Ex. 6:26, s.v. *hu Aharon uMoshe asher amar*).

We earlier questioned the context of this genealogy – to whom, or to what, is the text referring when it opens with "These are the heads of their households." It appears, surprisingly, that this passage is not linked to what precedes it directly but it is a direct continuation of the opening passage of the book. Look at how it flows naturally:

> These are the children of Israel who came to Egypt; together with Jacob, they came with their families. Reuben, Simeon, Levi, and Judah. Issachar, Zebulun, and Benjamin. Dan and Naphtali; Gad and Asher. A total of seventy people who emerged from Jacob's loins, and Joseph who was in Egypt. Joseph, his brothers, and that entire generation died. The children of Israel were fruitful and they swarmed, they multiplied and became exceedingly mighty, so that the land was filled with them. (1:1–7)
>
> These are the heads of their households. The children of Reuben, Israel's firstborn, are Enoch, Pallu, Hezron, and Karmi. These are the families of Reuben. And the children of Simeon. (6:14–15)

If this analysis is correct, then this third presentation of Moses, the aristocrat, skips entirely the story of Moses's early life. In fact, it even skips the intense enslavement and oppression of Israel, which – as we are about to see – carries extraordinary significance.

Each of the three "Moses introductions" is distinguished by both theme and language.

WHAT IS GOD'S GOAL?

As we noted earlier, this approach suggests not only a three-dimensional portrayal of Moses (and, by extension, of Aaron's role), it also opens a new window into understanding the multiple purposes God sees in His involvement.

The initial conversation with Moses focuses explicitly on two targets, Israel and Pharaoh. Regarding Israel, God's primary motivation seems to be relieving the people from their suffering. Just look at how many descriptions of that suffering He mentions in His opening words to Moses.

> I see the *suffering* of My people who are in Egypt, and I hear its *cries* as a result of those who *oppress* it, for I know its *pain*. (Ex. 3:7)

> So now, the *cries* of the Israelites have come to Me, and I see the *pressure* with which the Egyptians are *pressing* them. (3:9)

Secondarily, He will bring them to a land of shepherds, a land flowing with milk and honey, restoring them to their ancestral culture.[13] There is no mention of covenant, only to the restoration of their ancient way of life. What God refers to is Joseph; it was he who brought them into Egypt and who, before his death, recognized that Egypt could not be their destiny. The double language of *pakod pakadti* (3:16) Moses is instructed to use is intended to awaken the memories of Joseph's last instructions to his brothers, *Pakod yifkod E-lohim etkhem*, completing the cycle of descent into Egypt and their rising up from it. Finally, when they do leave, they will leave with their dignity, not as slaves running away but as free people, loaded with parting gifts, as the Torah later mandates for all freed Hebrew slaves (Deut. 15:14).

Regarding Pharaoh, God explicitly acknowledges that Pharaoh will not accede to even a three-day furlough. What, then, is the purpose of asking for it? Apparently, God is interested that Pharaoh conclude on his own that the people need to be freed, permanently. Had that been the initial request, then all Pharaoh would have eventually done is bow to God's pressure. "I will send My hand and smite Egypt with all of My wonders that I will do in its midst" (Ex. 3:20). What God wants is more than Pharaoh's surrender; He wants Pharaoh's acknowledgment that he is not the master of the people.

The humbling of Pharaoh is directly related to the opening of Exodus. We already examined parallels between the building project in Egypt and its counterpart in Babel; both are designed to have an individual dominate humanity and thus push God out of the affairs of man. But just like in Babel, where God intervenes to block those attempts,

13. Abraham, Isaac, and Jacob were all shepherds. The milk refers to that which the sheep produce; the honey is the produce of bees who eat from the copious wildflowers which serve as grazing for the sheep.

God will step in to thwart Pharaoh's plans. This is the subtext of God's second focus.

This opening conversation with Moses sets up what Leon Kass calls the contest between God and Pharaoh.[14] God's goal is not simply to save Israel from their suffering, but to demonstrate to Pharaoh who the real God is. That is also why God speaks of His strong hand. Joshua Berman[15] argues that the language of God's strong hand, which is unique to the Exodus story, is chosen specifically because Pharaoh's boast was of his strong hand.[16] God tells Moses that it is His strong hand, not Pharaoh's, which will dominate the story.

The second version of the conversation between God and Moses is dramatically different from the first. In this second one there is a singular focus – God's covenant with the people (mentioned twice in the opening verses and the proximate reason for His involvement) and His desire to establish a relationship with them (which dominates the second half of the speech in Exodus 6). Israel is in Egypt not because of Joseph but because of the covenant, and they will leave Egypt because of that covenant. The land is no longer described as "the good land" or "the land of milk and honey" but instead is referred to as *their* land, the land of their eternal heritage, the land of the covenant. Moses's goal is not to introduce Pharaoh to God but to introduce Israel to God. "Therefore, say to the Israelites, I am A-donai" (Ex. 6:6). The purpose of God's involvement is not that Pharaoh should know who He is, but that Israel should know. "I will take you to Me as a nation and I will be your God, you will know that I, A-doni, am your God, the one taking you from under the Egyptian burdens" (6:7).

This is what makes the unfolding of the events following this second version of the mission so startling – the one thing God sought in this entire process was the relationship with Israel, and they reject it.

---

14. Kass, *Founding God's Nation*, 130.
15. Joshua Berman, *Ani Maamin* (Maggid Books, 2020), 55–56. In our context the phrase is used in an unusual way, and the traditional medieval commentators debate whether it means despite God's strong hand (Nahmanides, Ibn Caspi), until God shows His strong hand (Rashi, Ralbag), or as a result of Pharaoh's belief in his strong hand (Rashbam, Ibn Ezra, Bekhor Shor).
16. In the British Museum is a carved stone statue of Pharaoh's outstretched arm with a fist.

"They did not listen to Moses from their shortness of spirit and the hard labor" (6:9). The noble message of covenant with God was too much for a slave people, who know nothing more than following instructions, to absorb in any meaningful way.

Only after that major disappointment does God mention Pharaoh with the sparsest message. "Let him send the people out of his land" (6:10). No demand, no threat of consequence, no prediction of Pharaoh's refusal, and no presentation of any contest. In this communication Pharaoh is nearly irrelevant. And this second speech doesn't end well for God – Israel rejects His message and Moses refuses to go to Pharaoh. "Behold, the Israelites did not listen to me, how will Pharaoh listen to me, and I am of uncircumcised lips" (6:12).

The third version is also distinct. Here, Moses and Aaron are presented as a team from the outset, scions of a prominent Levite family.[17] Moses has no issues of credibility with the people and no need for an introduction from God other than "I am A-donai" (6:29). This version is the inverse of the second; there is no mention of covenant, no discussion of a relationship with the people, and no message to the people – the sole focus is Pharaoh. It is here that we see the full explication of God's plan vis-à-vis Pharaoh; for the first time God speaks explicitly of hardening Pharaoh's heart.[18] This is accompanied by the multiplicity of signs and wonders God will demonstrate, which will still not convince Pharaoh.[19] God will take Israel out of Egypt despite Pharaoh's obstinance (not that Pharaoh will send them out, as in the first encounter), and that is how

17. This would also suggest that both Aaron and Miriam also had elevated status vis-à-vis the people. Aaron's position as Moses's assistant (Ex. 17:10), stand-in for Moses at Sinai (24:14), and eventually his elevation as high priest all make sense, as does Miriam's public role at the Splitting of the Sea (16:20–21).

18. This was mentioned briefly in God's message to Moses at the rest stop but was not part of the initial mission.

19. This is distinctly different from what we saw earlier. At the burning bush God gave Moses two signs (*otot*, singular *ot*), which he was to perform in front of Israel if they did not believe that he was sent by God. Those signs were performed in Moses's first encounter with the people (4:30). Here, God prepares Moses with a single wondrous deed (*mofet*) which Aaron is to perform in front of Pharaoh (7:9–11). Further, at the burning bush one of the signs was to take water from the Nile and pour it on the ground, where *that* water would turn into blood. This is not the same as the

Pharaoh will know who God is. The Exodus is not the goal but the means to achieving a broader goal – recognition by the Egyptians and their monarch that there is a true God, unlike any known heretofore, which is why in this version the Torah describes the "contest" between Aaron's staff-crocodile and those of the Egyptian sorcerers. Both Aaron and the sorcerers are avatars for those they represent; this begins the showdown between God and the Egyptian pantheon, including Pharaoh himself.[20]

BUILDING THE COMPOSITE

Separating the overall narrative into its three components affords the reader a rich, multidimensional picture. Moses is far more complex than we realized initially. Although born into a noble Israelite family, that nobility is hidden because of his secretive birth and infancy, yet it will be revived with a twist as he is "reborn" as a noble Egyptian. That identity will be challenged when he flees Egypt and again when he is summoned back to Egypt. Moses is both an Israelite insider and an outsider, he is simultaneously of humble and noble origins, and those tensions will likely accompany him for many years to come.

God's role is complex as well. On the one hand He is moved by the suffering of Israel, and that alone is enough of a reason to free them and relieve them of their pain. Yet even though that is enough to justify His involvement, there is a much bigger picture involved. Pharaoh has deigned himself as the supreme ruler, forcing God into the background. But God's decision to humble Pharaoh goes far beyond a petty contest.

God created humanity so that they could have a relationship with Him. The first attempt faltered, as humans deconstructed their very existence as they became consumed with injustice, which, if left to continue, would have led to the complete failure of creation. God's

first of the plagues, in which the water in the Nile turns to blood (7:17–21). The sign of the blood, as opposed to the plague of the blood, may have served as a signal to Israel – but not to Pharaoh – that God would humble the Egyptian pantheon.

20. Genesis 1:21 describes God as the creator of the great crocodiles, apparently as a polemic against many of the Mesopotamian cultures which saw the crocodiles as gods. Kass (*Founding God's Nation*, 134) notes that the Egyptian god Sobek, the god of crocodiles, was credited with creating the Nile, and that the hieroglyph for "sovereign" included two crocodiles.

commitment to the success of humanity could not allow for that, and so, saving the kernel of goodness that was left, He recreated the world in the Great Confusion. In Babel He faced a different crisis, no less serious than the first. The domination of the masses by the few threatened to crush human creativity and snuff out the divine image, the *tzelem E-lohim*, with which every human was endowed. The response to that was to strengthen the human spirit and creativity by multiplying the languages and, by extension, the very thought processes which allow people to be people. That was successful, but people still found it challenging to establish a meaningful relationship with God – it was much easier for them to relate to concrete objects and heavenly symbols. So God tweaked the plan yet again, opting to reach humanity through the mediation of a single individual and his family.

In Egypt, the ghost of Babel came back to haunt creation as Pharaoh nearly eliminated the spirit of the very people God chose to be His ambassadors to humanity. Had he succeeded there would have been no value left to creation itself, and that is a prospect God could not entertain. That is why the covenant is so significant – not only does it represent God's solemn commitment to a particular people, it is at the core of God's commitment to all of humanity. It is that commitment which demands that Israel be freed, that Pharaoh be humbled, that Egypt learn who God is, that Israel learns who God is, and that God manifest Himself to the entirety of humanity as He did at Creation itself – because it is all at risk.[21]

What should also be obvious is that it is not just restarting God's relationship with humanity which is at stake. Every attempt to supplant God is marked by a human desire to dominate and is accompanied by a perversion of fundamental morality and human dignity. The need to demonstrate Pharaoh's impotence is intrinsically bound with the effort

21. Interestingly, the Covenant Between the Pieces mentions nothing of God reasserting Himself into the affairs of humanity. This additional element was necessitated by the specific nature of Pharaoh's asserting himself as an alternative to God. A similar approach was suggested by Nahmanides (Gen. 16:11) to explain why the Egyptians were punished for something which was preordained in the Covenant Between the Pieces. He offers that the Egyptians went above and beyond the enslavement and oppression God had fated for Abraham's descendants.

to restore the dignity of all humanity. Divinity is not about power or control but about morality.[22]

Separating the components of this grand vision is a necessary step in identifying them. Putting them back together into a coherent whole reframes the entire story. With our three-dimensional image of Moses and our deep understanding of God's goals, the scene for the showdown has been prepared.

WHY MOSES?

All this leads to the question of why we care so much about Moses, or more accurately, why does God care so much about Moses. Couldn't God have done all this without him?

Apparently not. Earlier God chose to work through Abraham, and even earlier He elected to have Noah build the ark. God could surely have saved Noah without an ark – it would have been no less of a miracle. The point, however, was not just to save Noah, but to have Noah as a partner in saving himself, along with his family and the nucleus of the new world. The same is true for Abraham. God could have forced His way onto humanity, but that would have made the entire project meaningless, much like programming a computer (or an angel) to endlessly recite one's praise. Empowering Abraham as the partner, the messenger to humanity, was an essential step in the plan to have people seek out a meaningful relationship with God.

The same is true now that God is reasserting His place in the world. He certainly could do so solo, but that would be self-defeating in the bigger picture. It is the partnership with humanity, built through the partnership with Israel, built with the direct intervention of Moses, which makes the project meaningful.

One additional point on this. Moses is a man who had to find his identity. Israel will struggle with the same. We see it countless times throughout Exodus and for much of Numbers. They need to forge themselves into a nation; they need to create for themselves a corporate identity with a destiny. Who better to lead them than the man who struggled to find his own identity?

---

22. I thank Sam Stonefield for this formulation.

Exodus 7:14–11:10

The Plagues

Perhaps no part of the story of Exodus is as beloved to children as the plagues. They delight in hearing how God punishes Pharaoh and the Egyptian people for their cruelty to Israel and the repeated refusal to deny their petition. They love hearing about all the creative ways God finds to make the evil oppressors suffer. There are songs in Hebrew about Pharaoh in his pajamas running door to door looking for Moses in the middle of the night, there are songs in English about frogs, there are Passover Seder kits for reenacting the plagues, and there are customs at the Seder involving dipping fingers into wine for each of the plagues as well as for the acronym which summarizes them.[1]

Perhaps no part of the story of Exodus – in fact, of the entire Torah – is as strange, perplexing, and troubling as the plagues. The cycle of bizarre afflictions interspersed with Pharaoh's stubbornness and

1. *De.TZa.KH, A.Da.SH, Be.A.Ḥa.V.* The earliest mention of his acronym appears to be in Exodus Rabba (5:6) but it does not include the attribution to R. Yehuda. Heinrich Guggenheimer, in *The Scholar's Haggadah* (Jason Aronson, 1995), 303, suggests that R. Yehuda is identified as the author because he was known for generating acronyms as mnemonic devices (see Menaḥot 96a).

God's encouraging of that stubbornness sounds like a cat playing with the mouse it caught, taunting and torturing it repeatedly before finally finishing it off. The powerful God sounds simultaneously whimsical and cruel, and the plagues seemingly random – as if God is having fun finding new ways to make Pharaoh squirm as the children squeal in delight. Is this the God of the Bible?

Aside from the theological-ethical problem there is an additional challenge deeply embedded in the story of the plagues – the issue of Pharaoh's free will. Can Pharaoh be punished for decisions which God impels him to make? This goes beyond Pharaoh – while we understand that there are consequences to decisions we make, we struggle to comprehend how God can punish people for decisions they do not make. In the language of Abraham as he challenges God over the decision to destroy Sodom: "Will the judge of the entire land not do justice?" (Gen. 18:25).

PHARAOH'S HEART

We are certainly not the first to address these questions. A midrash records R. Yoḥanan as complaining that God's making Pharaoh's heart heavy (10:1) opens the door to complaints that God is preventing him from repenting, leading to heretical conclusions that divine justice is fundamentally unjust.[2] Multiple medieval thinkers struggled with this question, offering a diverse palette of explanations. Maimonides asserts that it is possible for individuals, like Pharaoh, to cross a threshold of evil beyond which repentance is impossible.[3] One variation on this theme is to suggest that the cumulative effect of Pharaoh's evil deeds, including his obduracy in the first five plagues, warranted all the plagues which came afterward, meaning that the last five plagues are not punishments for his continued refusal but for all that he had done earlier. Rabbi Ovadia Sforno,[4] a fifteenth-to-sixteenth-century Italian commentator, suggests that all God did was to provide Pharaoh with the willpower to

2. Exodus Rabba 13:4.
3. *Hilkhot Teshuva* 6:1–3.
4. See his comment to 7:3. This is a more developed version of an idea expressed by Rabbi Joseph Albo (fifteenth-century Spain) in his *Sefer HaIkkarim* 4:25.

do what he really wanted to do in his heart – hold on to Israel – and to resist caving to external pressures exerted by the plagues, his advisors, and eventually the Egyptian populace.

Twenty-first-century thinkers added their own insights. Rabbi Jonathan Sacks offers an interpretation based on a psychological insight. When we consider addictive behavior like substance abuse or abuse of power – they begin with free will but end up with a behavior that is compelled by repeated poor decision making. The alcoholic loses the ability to desist, and the power-hungry dictator, like Pharaoh, who has buried himself in a hole by refusing to cede to others, is unable to see the bigger picture.[5] Leon Kass suggests that the entire story of the plagues is intended as a "contest" between God and Pharaoh, but for that contest to be meaningful, it is necessary that both contestants be "at the top of their game." Strengthening Pharaoh's heart elevates him – both in the eyes of the Egyptians and in the eyes of the biblical reader, so that God's triumph is not over a minor potentate but over the most formidable opponent mankind could muster.[6]

An examination of the texts themselves reveals considerable nuances which suggest that the philosophical, theological, and psychological approaches – as appealing as they might be – may not be aligned with what the Torah text actually says. Those details include distinctions such as:

1. Sometimes Pharaoh's change of heart is attributed to himself, while at other times it is identified as being the result of God's intervention.
2. Three different roots are used to describe the change of heart: Ḥ-Z-K (strengthen), K-V-D (heavy), K-SH-H (hard).
3. Sometimes the Torah speaks about what God says He will do, while at other times it describes what God did.

---

5. Rabbi Jonathan Sacks, *Essays on Ethics* (Maggid Books, 2016), 85–89. In his work *Judaism's Life-Changing Ideas* (Maggid Books, 2020), 71–75, Rabbi Sacks suggests that this is grounded neurologically as well. See also his book *Covenant and Conversation: Exodus* (Maggid Books, 2010), 47–51.
6. Kass, *Founding God's Nation*, 83–85, 130–32.

4. Some describe the process regarding Pharaoh's heart as active, while others describe it as passive.

The approaches offered by the commentaries, both medieval and contemporary, largely do not pay attention to those distinctions. As we examine the evidence in the Torah we may discover that the nuances point not to a single approach but to a complex set of understandings.

The following chart lays out the different expressions:

Pharaoh changes his heart	God changes Pharaoh's heart	When
	4:21 God said to Moses: When you return to Egypt see all the wonders that I placed in your hands; do them before Pharaoh. I will *strengthen* his heart and he will not send the people out	At the rest stop as Moses initially returns to Egypt
	7:3 I will *harden* Pharaoh's heart; I will multiply My signs and My wonders in the land of Egypt	As God introduces the idea of the plagues to Moses
7:13 Pharaoh's heart *became strong* (passive) and he did not listen to them		After Aaron's staff swallows the staffs of the Egyptian sorcerers
7:22 Pharaoh's heart *became strong* (passive) and did not listen to them		After the plague of blood

8:11 Pharaoh saw that there was an easing, his heart *heavied*[7] (passive) and he did not listen to them.		After the plague of frogs
8:15 Pharaoh's heart *became strong* (passive) and he did not listen to them.		After the sorcerers identify the plague of lice as an act of God
8:28 Pharaoh *heavied*[8] his heart (active) this time too.		After the plague of the animal swarm
9:7 Pharaoh's heart *heavied*[9] (passive), and he did not send out the people.		After the plague of cattle death
	9:12 God *strengthened* Pharaoh's heart and he did not listen to them, as God told Moses.	After the plague of boils
9:34–35 He continued to sin, he *heavied* (active) his heart, both him and his servants. Pharaoh's heart *strengthened* (passive) and he did not send out the Israelites, as God told Moses.		After the plague of hail

7. This is the first time that Pharaoh reneged on a previous commitment to let the people go.
8. This is the second time that Pharaoh reneged on a previous commitment to let the people go.
9. This is the third time that Pharaoh reneged on a previous commitment to let the people go.

	10:20 God *strengthened* Pharaoh's heart.	After the plague of locusts
	10:27 God *strengthened* Pharaoh's heart; he did not want to send them.	After the plague of darkness
14:5 Pharaoh's heart, as well as those of his servants, *turned around.*	14:8 God *strengthened* the heart of Pharaoh.	After Israel left Egypt

The first thing we notice is that although immediately prior to launching the plagues God says that He would harden Pharaoh's heart (7:3), there is no record in the text of that ever happening.[10] Similarly, every time the Torah mentions heaviness in Pharaoh's heart, it is Pharaoh who is doing the heavying, not God.[11] Second, God's opening and closing statements to Moses regarding Pharaoh's heart (4:21 and 11:10) refer only to strengthening Pharaoh's heart (not to the heaviness of his heart),[12] and, in practice, that strengthening is mentioned as occurring only four times in the story.[13] Those four apparent mirror the earlier four times that Pharaoh's heart strengthened without God's input, so that God's actions on Pharaoh's heart seem to act as a reinforcement of Pharaoh's will (which sounds like Sforno's idea). Third, seven out of the twelve times the Torah describes a change in Pharaoh's heart (including the first four), it describes it using passive language, as if it were the result

10. Moses later (Ex. 13:14) describes Pharaoh as making it hard to release Israel, and Deut. 2:30 tells of God hardening the spirit of Sihon, king of the Emorites, as he refuses to let Israel pass peacefully. Ironically the term is used seven times in the Torah to describe Israel as a hard-necked nation.
11. In 10:1 God tells Moses that He heavied Pharaoh's heart, yet the earlier narrative (9:34) ascribes that to Pharaoh himself.
12. While the Torah never explicates the difference between strengthening and heavying God's heart, 9:34–35 makes it clear that these are two distinct processes.
13. I do not include 11:10 as that is not part of the narrative describing a specific response exhibited by Pharaoh; rather, it is part of the narrator's summary of the events which includes the previous three times that God strengthened Pharaoh's heart.

of a natural process requiring no effort on either God's or Pharaoh's part (much like Rabbi Sacks's explanation).

It should also be noted that the phrase "heaviness of the heart" has a particular meaning for those living within the ancient Egyptian milieu. Egyptians believed that the path to everlasting life was determined by a ceremony called the Judgment of Osiris, in which an individual's heart was placed on one side of a balance scale and a feather on the other. Good deeds and maintenance of the natural order of the universe made the heart light, and if the heart was lighter than the feather then the individual could proceed to the afterlife. If the individual, however, did not pursue justice and harmony, then the heart would be judged as heavier, condemning its owner to the underworld.

In that context, the language of Pharaoh's heart growing heavy means that Pharaoh was acting against the principle of order and justice, the kind of behavior which would bar him from the afterlife. To describe Pharaoh as making his heart heavy (9:34) meant that he was actively choosing to act in ways for which he would be judged negatively even by the standards of Egyptian theology. It is also particularly notable that God never says that he will make Pharaoh's heart heavy, as that would violate the fundamental principle of a person being judged based on his or her own deeds.

When we put the observations together, it turns out that although God was prepared to strengthen Pharaoh's heart, in reality that was almost unnecessary. For the first five plagues as well as in the introductory scene with the crocodiles, Pharaoh's heart strengthened and heavied on its own, seemingly with no need for effort from Pharaoh and certainly not from necessitating divine manipulation. It is only in the second half of the plagues that God intervenes, strengthening Pharaoh's heart in four of the five instances, one of which is to help Pharaoh resist the pressure from his advisors rather than to resist the pressure of the plague itself (9:12) and another fifth was seemingly unnecessary, as Pharaoh already had a change of heart (14:5–8).

In summary, God's strengthening of Pharaoh's heart seems to mirror or reinforce what Pharaoh was already doing on his own, and despite His threats to harden Pharaoh's heart, God never does, nor does He make it heavy. Which brings us back to a fundamental question: Why does God even introduce the idea to strengthen or harden Pharaoh's heart?

THE PURPOSE OF THE PLAGUES

Before we attempt to answer the core question of why God would want to intervene in Pharaoh's decision making, let us look at the plagues themselves. They seem to be whimsical, random afflictions intended to make the Egyptians suffer. Yet the sheer volume of biblical real estate devoted to them suggests that the Torah does want us to understand them better, as they are an integral part of the broader story.

We are not the first to struggle with these questions. One midrashic opinion suggests that God is acting toward the Egyptians as would any king toward a province which rebelled against him, applying gradually increasing pressure to get it to accept his authority.[14] Another suggests viewing the plagues as "measure-for-measure" responses to the Egyptian oppression of the Israelites.[15] Modern scholars add perspectives based on their understanding of ancient Egypt. Nahum Sarna[16] cites an ancient Hellenistic-Jewish work which portrays the plagues as a mockery of Egyptian paganism, developing the idea by identifying how individual plagues challenge specific figures in the Egyptian pantheon. The attack on the Nile directly challenged the Nile god, Hapi, and indirectly the god Osiris; the plague of frogs made a mockery of the Egyptian goddess Heqt, a fertility goddess, as retribution for the Egyptian decree to drown Israeli babies; the plague of darkness humiliated the Egyptian sun god, Re. Rabbi Jonathan Sacks[17] extends this idea to the plague of lice, pointing to the conclusion of the sorcerers who could not reproduce it that it was "the finger of [a true] God" (8:15).

As we try to approach the plagues through a fresh lens, we begin with an analysis of the way the Torah presents them. As in the acronym found in the Haggada, the plagues are easily organized into three sets of three plagues each, followed by a tenth which is unique.

14. *Midrash Tanḥuma Bo* 4.
15. Ibid. 5.
16. Nahum Sarna, *Exploring Exodus* (Schocken, 1986), 78–79.
17. https://www.rabbisacks.org/covenant-conversation/vaera/lice-and-men/.

First set	Second set	Third set
Blood	Animal swarm	Hail
Frogs	Cattle death	Locusts
Lice	Boils	Darkness
Death of firstborn[18]		

In the first of each set God sends Moses to station himself[19] (N-TZ-V) before Pharaoh early in the morning,[20] where Moses is to warn Pharaoh that his refusal to heed God's word will result in a specific plague. The second of each set is identified by the instruction to "come" to Pharaoh, presumably to the palace,[21] and again warn Pharaoh that his refusal to heed God's word will result in a specific plague. The third in each set contains no warning to Pharaoh, only the information God tells Moses about the plague.

This pattern provides our first indication of God's approach to Pharaoh. Meeting Pharaoh by the river – the first in each set of three – was likely the least confrontational way to approach him. Early in the morning, Pharaoh is less likely to be surrounded by a significant entourage. Indeed, in their first riverside meeting, when Pharaoh wants his sorcerers, he needs to call them – they are not with him (7:11). The

18. While the acronym appears to have only three groups, 3-3-4 plagues in each, many understand them to be three groups of three followed by a tenth plague which stands alone. Rabbi Yitzhak Shmuel Reggio, a nineteenth-century Italian commentator, suggests (Ex. 7:3) that there are actually twelve plagues divided into four groups of three.

19. The root N-TZ-V is used frequently in the Torah to describe a purposeful standing, often in anticipation of or preparedness for an event. I thank Alan Shamah for noticing the significance of this word. Sam Stonefield reminded me that in the beginning of Exodus, it is Moses's older sister who is N-TZ-V at the side of the river watching over her baby brother in anticipation.

20. For the first two of these, God instructs him to stand before Pharaoh at the river. The second two mention that Moses is to go early in the morning; the first mentions only in the morning.

21. The phrase "come" to Pharaoh, as opposed to "go" to Pharaoh, is unusual. In the Bible the combination of *ba* (come) and *el* (to) often means to enter. See, for example, Gen. 6:4, 6:18, 16:2, 19:3, 29:21, 30:3, and many more.

riverside offers an opportunity for a less formal tone, affording Pharaoh the greatest opportunity for flexibility.[22] These riverside encounters always involve a request accompanied by a warning of what will happen should Pharaoh deny the request. The second meeting in each set takes place in the palace, where Pharaoh is sitting on his throne – with all that entails. Moses is told each time not to "go" to Pharaoh, but to "come" to Pharaoh, a language suggesting penetrating Pharaoh's palace, challenging him. In Pharaoh's royal court, witnessed by all those surrounding him, Moses delivers a demand with a warning of what will happen if Pharaoh refuses. For the third plague in each set there is no meeting, no encounter, no warning – Pharaoh is irrelevant as God exercises His will in Egypt, a blatant challenge to Pharaoh's authority.

When we turn our attention from the cyclical structure to the content of what Moses is to say, we notice that each set of plagues is introduced with an educational message. Before the first set, starting with blood, God identifies the purpose of that set – so that Pharaoh knows who God is. "Egypt will know that I am A-donai" (7:5) and "with this you will know that I am A-donai" (7:17). The same Pharaoh who initially indicated that he was unfamiliar with A-donai (5:2) would now know who He is. The second set of plagues, beginning with the animal swarm, takes the message one step further – not only does God exist, but He is very much present in the land – God is involved in the affairs of man. "So that you should know that I am A-donai in the midst of the land" (8:18). This was a new theological concept for most ancient cultures, that a god would be involved in human affairs not for his sake but for theirs. The lessons God wants Pharaoh to learn go one step further as the third set of plagues is introduced, in the warning prior to the plague of hail: "So that you should know that there is none like Me in all the land" (9:14). It is not enough to know who A-donai is or to know that He is involved in earthly matters; it is essential that Egypt – and by extension the rest

22. There are other plausible interpretations of this. One is that the riverside is where Pharaoh is most vulnerable, and therefore least likely to be amenable to the request. Another, following midrashic thinking, is that the riverside is the most confrontational, as Pharaoh's morning visit to the Nile was his way of demonstrating that he was the river God (see Ezek. 29:3).

of the world – knows that the God of Israel is unique, unlike any other deity the Egyptians knew.[23]

The structure of the sets of plagues and God's messages introducing them converge to paint a broad picture of their purpose: God is reintroducing Himself to humanity.

GOD RETURNS TO THE ARC OF HUMAN HISTORY[24]

To fully grasp the significance of this we need to take a step back. Genesis begins with Omnipotent God creating a world for humans, created in His "image." The very process of creating people capable of creativity and meaningful decision making necessitates that God relinquish some of His control – and possibly even some of His knowledge. Without relinquishing control, the *tzelem E-lohim* with which God endowed the people will never be able to be fully expressed, and the decisions and actions taken by those people will never be significant enough to warrant their very existence.

The question looming over this great experiment was whether people endowed with *tzelem E-lohim* would use it properly or abuse it. Would they intuitively discover ethical behavior just because they had a divine spark? Would they establish meaningful relationships with each other, and with God, without explicit instructions?

The stories of Cain and Abel and the generation leading up to the Great Confusion suggest that the initial attempt was less than successful. God reflects on the abuse of power among people: "It is insufficient that My spirit alone shall dwell within man, for he is also flesh" (Gen. 6:3). Noticing the general failure of the experiment, "God regretted that He had made the man in the land, and He became pained in His heart" (Gen. 6:6).

Despite the disappointment, God does not give up, as "Noah found favor in God's eyes" (Gen. 6:8). It was possible for humans to succeed, but maybe they needed a little guidance. Without changing the nature of

23. I thank Sam Stonefield for suggesting that the lack of warning for the final plague is God's ultimate demonstration that Pharaoh is a non-player – he has no capacity to influence or affect the plague.

24. This section is based on a more expansive explication found in *Genesis: From Creation to Covenant*, 3–124.

people, God retains Noah and his family as He re-creates the world and adds a few guidelines – based on the key mistakes He observed humans making in the first few generations. Murder is explicitly prohibited. The relationship between people and animals is recalibrated. According to rabbinic tradition,[25] there were seven universal rules God institutes – the seven Noahide laws – which He believes will help humanity achieve its potential.

Within a few generations, however, God needs to intervene again. The project is going awry again, this time not because of abuse of *tzelem E-lohim* but because of overzealous limitation of it. All humanity is concentrated in a single place, with a singular purpose and limited expression of ideas. That, too, prevents people from achieving their potential. So God introduces diversity of speech, and by extension diversity of thought, in the Dispersion from Babel.

Having learned that both the poles of limitless freedom and of excessive control are harmful to the success of His plan, God changes His approach yet again. He identifies an individual who intuitively understands core divine values and who also understands the need for transmitting and perpetuating them. It is with that individual that God elects to cultivate a relationship in the hope that he will become the conduit for those values to spread to the rest of humanity. Directing Abram to the crossroads of humanity where his impact will be greatest, God engages Abraham and Sarah as His covenantal partners. Their family will grow into a nation, and hopefully their influence will increase accordingly as they radiate God's message to humanity even as they endure hardships.

Jacob's descent to Egypt with his family, however, brings with it an unexpected surprise. The new Egyptian king has chosen to follow in the footsteps of the early tyrants in Babel. The same kind of arrogance of which only humans are capable has reared its head again. The attempt to dominate humanity and crush its spirit rears its ugly head yet again. And just as the project of Babel threatened to replace God with universal human control, the Egyptian project – replete with its pantheon of gods and belief in the Egyptian natural superiority – threatens to erase God's name from the planet, and end with the complete failure of the divine project in creating humans in the first place.

25. Sanhedrin 56a.

It is this threat – not the threat to Israel, but to God Himself – which demands that God return to the historical narrative. That return is not merely to prove a point; rather, it is the equivalent of another Genesis-like restart. The Pharaoh who did not know A-donai will learn. The all-powerful Egyptian Empire which tried supplanting God with its own supremacy will need to learn that God is the Creator of all and remains concerned about and involved with His creation, as He is committed to the success of the divine project. The success of that project will have repercussions far beyond Egypt. Israel will know who the Creator is; Israel will know with whom they have an immutable covenant and what their role in that covenant is; the world will recognize God as Creator and Israel as His emissary.

This return to history, interfering in the natural course of events, is actually quite problematic. After all, God created people with the freedom and power to choose, along with whatever consequences would result from those choices, and God would need to accept the fact that people can make choices with serious consequences.

What would appear from Exodus is that the latitude given to people to make decisions of consequence is certainly true on an individual level, on a communal level, and even on a national level. What God will not allow for, however, is when those choices pose an existential threat to the Creation itself. That is what God observed prior to the Great Confusion: "God saw that the evil of man was increasing, and that the products of the thoughts in his heart were only evil, all day" (Gen. 6:5). God is prepared to tolerate good and evil, but when the good is threatened and evil reigns supreme He must interfere to reset the world. Similarly, when God saw the leadership in Babel seeking to exercise total domination over humanity, destroying hope for the success of Creation, He felt it necessary to intervene to redirect the course of human history. "God said: Behold, they are a single people with a single language, and that is where their action began – now, nothing will prevent them from completing what they are plotting to do" (Gen. 11:6). It is not evil that God cannot tolerate but rather the total domination of evil over good. That threatens all of Creation itself, demanding divine intervention on rescue Creation.

The same is true in our present story. Pharaoh's domination of humanity was so overwhelming that it would have wreaked irreversible damage to God's hope for humanity. As the Rabbis write in the Haggada: "Had God not taken us out of Egypt, we and our children and our children's children would still be enslaved to Pharaoh in Egypt." God needs to reinsert Himself into history to bring about a critical course correction.

REESTABLISHING GOD AS CREATOR

This, I believe, is why God cannot simply airlift Israel out of Egypt and bring them to their promised land. That would miss the point God makes repeatedly as the plagues are introduced:

> Egypt will know that I am A-donai. (7:5)
>
> With this you will know that I am A-donai. (7:17)
>
> So that you should know that I am A-donai in the midst of the land. (8:18)
>
> So that you should know that there is none like Me in all the land. (9:14)
>
> However, it is for this reason that I have helped you to stand; so that I may show you My might and that My name should be told throughout the whole earth. (9:16)
>
> So that you should tell your children and your children's children how I mocked Egypt and the signs that I set among them, and you will know that I am A-donai. (10:2)

It is not just about humiliating the Egyptian gods, as Nahum Sarna suggests, but about reintroducing God as the One who created the world and its inhabitants with a purpose and who is determined to remain involved to ensure that the people can achieve that purpose. A survey of the symbolism of some of the signs and plagues will illustrate how they demonstrate that the Creator of the world is returning to assert His place in the world, challenging us to consider what the world might look like were the Creator to change any of the elements of that Creation.

Crocodile. This was intended as a sign, not a plague, but served as the introduction to the plagues (7:9–12). The crocodile was revered in Egypt as the god of water and a symbol of Pharaonic power, yet ironically, it is the only animal mentioned individually in the Creation (Gen. 1:21), emphasizing that it was God who created the crocodile and that the crocodile itself was not a god.[26] Introducing the plagues with a symbol in which God's crocodile devours Pharaoh's sets the tone for the message of the plagues.

Blood. Aside from the fact that the Nile was the source of Egyptian power and their belief in their natural supremacy[27] in addition to its being worshipped as a god, in the world God created, water and blood are the two liquids which sustain life – blood inside the body and water in the land. And while water dominates the Creation in Genesis 1, it is the blood of life which dominates God's instructions following the first re-creation (Gen. 9:1–7). Replacing one life-sustaining fluid with the other demonstrates the design of the Creator.

Frogs. A quick survey of Genesis 1 reveals the orderliness of the specific domains for all the living beings: the water creatures, the flying creatures, and the land animals. There is no mention of creatures which cross domains, yet that is precisely what frogs

26. Ezekiel 29:3 depicts Pharaoh describing himself as "the great crocodile" who created the Nile.

27. In the biblical world, there were three major civilizations, each of which featured a river which provided food security, enabling the civilization to flourish. Babel was founded on the Euphrates, Sodom was founded on the Jordan, and Egypt was founded on the Nile. The story in Genesis 19 describes the internal moral rot in Sodom which brought about divine intervention, essentially turning the source of life into a body of water which could sustain no life at all. Babel, as discussed above, was dispersed. Now it is the turn of the Egyptians.

On a different note, the Torah describes the blood as affecting "the wood and the stones" (7:19). In the Bible, this combination of terms is used to describe idols, made of wood and stone (Deut. 4:28, 28:36, 28:64, 29:16; II Kings 16:18; Is. 37:19; Jer. 2:27; and others). Hence this plague was intended to both highlight God as Creator and humiliate the Egyptian gods as helpless. See also the commentary of Cassuto on 7:19.

represent. They are water creatures who "violate" the boundaries, raising the question of what would have been had the Creator not established those boundaries.

Lice. Genesis 1 identifies life as the product of a divine act of creation. In fact, the verb *bara,* meaning creation *ex nihilo,* is reserved in Genesis 1 for only three creative acts, one of which is the emergence of life (Gen. 1:21). Life did not emerge spontaneously. This plague demonstrates the chaos which would be caused if spontaneous generation allowed life – even the smallest of creatures – to emerge willy-nilly.

Animal swarm. The water creatures and flying creatures were both blessed with fecundity – "Be fruitful and multiply" – as were humans. By contrast, the land animals were not blessed as such, lest they overrun the land and leave no room for the pinnacle of God's creation. This plague demonstrates what would have been if there had not been a Creator to limit the land animals.

Boils. This unusual plague, which was initiated by Moses throwing a handful of ash skyward, transforms matter which has been consumed by fire (ash) into a substance which can burn. This plague highlights that God can reverse the processes of nature, so that He is not only the Creator but the One who maintains control over His creation.

Hail. Throughout the Bible, God's explicit revelation is expressed in one of two ways – fire (e.g., the destruction of Sodom) and water (e.g., the Great Confusion). The rainbow after the Great Confusion is one of the rare examples of both revelations occurring simultaneously as the light is refracted through the water vapor. The hailstones mixed with fire are another example of the combined divine revelation.[28]

---

28. This may explain why the hail impels Pharaoh to finally acknowledge that he is in the wrong (9:27). The biblical text does not link directly to the Creation, but a

Locusts. The vegetation on earth was intended for all the land creatures, including humans, to eat (Gen. 1:29). Similar to the plague of the animal swarm, this plague highlights what would happen if the Creator allowed the other land creatures to consume that vegetation with no restraints.

Darkness. This plague brings us back to the opening scene of Creation, in which darkness is separated from light, and arouses the specter of what the world would look like were that separation not enforced by the Creator.

We noted earlier that the plagues were a direct attack on the Egyptian pantheon. While the details of that idea were first explicated in the twentieth century, in Exodus 12:12 God proclaims that He will exact retribution from the Egyptian gods.[29] Now that we understand that the plagues serve a dual purpose – humbling the Egyptian gods and reestablishing God as Creator – it is also clear why it was necessary for God to strengthen Pharaoh's heart. The plagues were not intended to apply pressure so that Pharaoh submit and set the people free; that freedom would be effected by God at the time of His choice. Rather, the plagues were there to demonstrate – to Israel, to Pharaoh, to Egypt, and to the rest of the world – that the Creator of the world was stepping back into the arc of human history to redirect that history and allow for humanity to achieve its potential. Pharaoh's quick submission to pressure would have subverted that goal; it was necessary for Pharaoh to resist so that the demonstration to all of humanity could be successful.

---

midrash offers to fill in that gap. Rav, in Genesis Rabba 4, suggests that the word *shamayim* (the heavens) is a contraction of *esh* (fire) and *mayim* (water), that is, that the essence of the heavens is where those two mutually destructive forces coexist. If so, then the hailstones mixed with the fire are essentially pieces of the sky falling, a demonstration of what the world might look like if the Creator did not retain the separation between the "upper" and "lower" waters (see Gen. 1:6–7).

29. Ex. 12:12. The idea is echoed in Numbers 33:4, appears in rabbinic literature, and is featured in the *Dayeinu* poem in the Haggada.

DEATH OF THE FIRSTBORN

This analysis draws our attention to the final plague, the death of the firstborn. After three sets of three plagues each, with their formulaic cycle of warnings, this one stands alone. While there is advance notice of the plague, there is no warning. Moses does not give Pharaoh a chance to release the people and avoid it. In fact, Moses informs Pharaoh of the plague while still standing in Pharaoh's presence after Pharaoh again reneged on the promise to let the people go worship.

This plague is also unique in that, unlike the other plagues which seem to be designed to demonstrate, instruct, and engender a sense of insecurity among the Egyptians,[30] this one seems explicitly designed to bring about death. It is hard to argue that it is intended as a punishment, as it affects the firstborn animals, the firstborn slaves, and even the firstborn prisoners, who ostensibly bear no responsibility for the plight of Israel. How are we to understand it?

Here, too, I believe that Genesis provides a conceptual backstory. One of the repeated themes throughout Genesis is the intrafamily struggle for dominance, and the consistent preempting of the firstborn by one of the younger siblings. Much is made of Cain being the firstborn, yet he and his line die out in the Great Confusion; it is Seth's line which survives via Noah. In Noah's family, too, Yefet is the eldest, but he is surpassed in the parental blessing and in the biblical history by the younger Shem, ancestor of Abraham. Among Abraham's children it is the younger Isaac who bears the covenant, and in the next generation the lengthy struggle for supremacy is settled as God identifies the younger Jacob to continue the covenantal line. Among Jacob's children Reuben is surpassed by both Judah and Joseph; within Judah's family the younger siblings (born from Tamar) take precedence over the much older Shela (from Judah's first wife); and Jacob – much to Joseph's chagrin – insists on preferring the younger Ephraim over his elder brother.

---

30. For example, blood challenges the sense of security brought by the regularity of the Nile (7:28); frogs challenge the sense of security in the home (7:28); lice shook the Egyptian foundations of reliance on magic (8:15); the animal swarm made the homes and cities unlivable (8:17).

The message seems clear – there is no such thing as natural superiority, and certainly not as a result of birth order. If supremacy in the family is going to happen, it must be earned.[31]

This core Genesis theme is challenged by Egypt. A powerful civilization built on the banks of the Nile with impressive achievements in mathematics, architecture, engineering, taxidermy, military prowess, and bureaucratic systems, the Egyptians believed that they were naturally superior to other peoples. They were blessed by the Nile, perhaps even chosen by it; they could not even bear to eat together with those whom they considered lesser peoples, like the Hebrews.

The clash between these two conceptions is highlighted in God's message to Moses as he is on his way to Egypt. God tells Moses to tell Pharaoh:

> Thus says God: Israel is My firstborn son. I told you, "Send out My son so that he will worship Me," yet you refused to send him out. Behold, I am going to kill your firstborn son. (4:22–23)

By no reasonable measure can Israel be described as God's firstborn, yet God has chosen to redefine that status from a biological one to one earned by merit. Pharaoh's refusal to accept that shift will necessitate his learning the hard way.

The death of the firstborns, whether human or animal and whether master or slave, was not a punishment, but a way of demonstrating that the entire notion of natural superiority is flawed. It was not the firstborns who were God's target but the entire notion of the supremacy of the one who exited the womb first. Destroying that notion

31. Deuteronomy 21:15–17 seems to maintain the supremacy of the firstborn. That, I believe, is a vestige of the ancient order which God tried to erase but with which He was not completely successful. The law of primogeniture in ancient cultures, still practiced today in some Middle Eastern societies, gave everything to the eldest son while the rest received nothing. It became the task of the heir to appease the other siblings by giving them from what he received. The double portion mentioned in Deuteronomy is the Torah's concession to the culture that refused to disappear, much like the law which precedes it in Deuteronomy related to the beautiful female captive of war.

was essential to destroying Egyptian dominance; when their firstborns died their entire claim to superiority died with them.[32]

WHO BRINGS THE PLAGUES?

Given the extraordinary significance of placing God at the center of the story, as we cycle once more through the plagues we discover that there is inconsistency in their implementation. Of course, neither Moses nor Aaron actually brings the plagues; only God can do that, and that is a key element of why they appear at all. Nonetheless, the biblical narrative – including their public presentation to Pharaoh and the Egyptians – recounts that sometimes it is Moses who initiates them, sometimes it is Aaron, and sometimes neither is involved. Even more, the way that the plagues are launched varies greatly, especially regarding the role of the staff. The following chart outlines the variations:

	Who does it?	How was it to be done?
Blood	Aaron	Take the staff and extend the hand
Frogs	Aaron	Extend the hand with the staff
Lice	Aaron	Extend the staff and hit the dust
Animal swarm	God	
Cattle death	God	
Boils	Moses	Throw soot skyward
Hail	Moses	Extend his hand skyward
Locusts	Moses	Extend his hand over Egypt
Darkness	Moses	Extend his hand skyward
Firstborn death	God	

32. This is likely the reason that, after the Exodus, God commands that all firstborns belong to Him (13:1–2 and 11–13). They are removed from any equation of superiority, as they are denied ownership of even themselves. Firstborn boys need to be redeemed to be allowed to have lives as independent individuals.

Aaron initiates three plagues,[33] Moses effects four, and God brings three, but God's three are not consecutive. The lack of a linear progression from Aaron to Moses to God challenges us to look for a different pattern, which emerges when we discover that the plagues can be divided into two groups of five. The first part of each group is done by a human agent, either Aaron or Moses, followed by plagues done by God without human agency. Note that the final plague in each group involves death, either of animals or of firstborns.

		Who does it?	
Group 1	Blood	Aaron	Human
	Frogs	Aaron	
	Lice	Aaron	
	Animal swarm	God	God
	Cattle death	God	
Group 2	Boils	Moses	Human
	Hail	Moses	
	Locusts	Moses	
	Darkness	Moses	
	Firstborn death	God	God

Further, this clustering into two groups suggests that we compare the two, and that comparison reveals that the instructions to Aaron explicitly require that he take the staff, while the instructions to Moses omit any mention of the staff at all.[34]

The introduction of the staff followed by its disappearance provides an important clue. Like in many ancient worlds, Egypt was steeped

33. If we include the sign of the crocodile, which is not a plague, then it turns out that both Moses and Aaron each initiate four signs.

34. In chapter 7 we will discuss the discrepancies between God's instructions and the way that they were implemented by Moses and Aaron. In chapter 8 we will explore the role of the staff.

in the belief and practice of magic. Pharaoh has a coterie of magicians who are martialed in our story to replicate – presumably through their wizarding talents – what Aaron does, as Pharaoh displays that he is unimpressed by Aaron's signs and unconvinced of God's supreme might. Hence, when Aaron turns his staff into a crocodile, the magicians counter by doing the same. Ultimately, Aaron's staff disappears after his final "performance," when the magicians themselves proclaim to Pharaoh that Aaron's signs are not magic at all: "It is the finger of God" (8:15).[35] The staff serves a critical role in that it creates the context for a "dialogue" between Aaron and the Egyptian sorcerers; it is the language which the Egyptians understand. The staff successfully draws the Egyptians into the contest. Once it has become clear that Aaron was, in fact, not a sorcerer himself but acting as God's representative, Aaron and the staff are removed from the story. It is then that God steps in and directly – without human agency – brings the next two plagues, highlighting their essential purpose of demonstrating God's full sovereignty on earth. Aaron's magic staff was not magic at all; in the contest between Israel's God and Egyptian magic there is an unambiguous victor.

Interestingly, while the commentators debate whether Israel was affected by the plagues or not, the Torah text seems clear that it is only in the fourth and fifth plagues – the ones done by God directly – that there is an intended distinction between Israel and the Egyptians.[36] Regarding the fourth plague, we read: "On that day I shall set aside the land of Goshen, upon which My people stand, that the animal swarm will not be there, so that you will know that I am God in the midst of the land" (8:18). And prior to the fifth Moses informs Pharaoh: "God will distinguish between the cattle of Israel and the cattle of Egypt; nothing of the Israelites will die" (9:4). This is not the invocation of magical forces

35. Ibn Ezra (7:9) understands that this is not Aaron's staff but that of Moses, and that it was used for all the plagues. Here, and in the subsequent chapter, I will present a different approach.

36. When we speak of an intended distinction, we mean that the separation between Israel and Egypt is part of the plan of the plague itself. Regarding the plague of darkness, the Torah records, post facto, that Israel had light (10:23), but there is no mention that the distinction between Israel and Egypt was part of the function of the plague.

which run amok and could affect Israelites as well, but direct divine intervention with a God who can highlight the distinctiveness of His people.

While upending Egyptian magic is the focus of the first five plagues, the second five challenge Pharaoh himself. The self-declared master of all will come to recognize that there is only one true God, the One who is returning to the historical stage to prevent another train wreck of human history and who is demanding the release of His people. In this cycle of plagues Moses is promoted as God's agent, and he is to perform his agency without the use of a staff. It is Moses's bare hands which are to take center stage.[37] Just as the first cycle ends with plagues done by God, this cycle closes with the final plague done by God alone. As the Midrash states: "I will pass through the land of Egypt in this night" (12:12) – I, not an angel; I, not a seraph; I, not a messenger. I am He, and there is no other."[38] And here, as before, regarding the plagues done by God Himself, there is an explicit plan to distinguish between Israel and Egypt.[39]

Given that the focus of this cycle of plagues is designed to demonstrate Pharaoh's powerlessness, it does not surprise us that it is precisely in these plagues that we hear of God interfering with Pharaoh's

37. See 9:8, 9:22, 10:12, and 10:22, where Moses's hands are mentioned explicitly but the staff is mysteriously absent. We will explore Moses's hands in greater depth when discussing the battle against Amalek.

38. *Yalkut Shimoni,* Exodus 199. This passage also appears prominently in the text of the Haggada.

39. In the plague of darkness, which was initiated by Moses, we also find that Israel is explicitly spared, yet the explicit intentionality of that distinction and the particular language of distinguishing Israel (H-F-L-H) are absent. Regarding the death of the firstborn and the distinction between Israel and Egypt, the Torah uses an unusual phrase to describe the contrast between the Egyptian terror and the Israelite feeling of safety – *lo yeḥeratz kelev leshono* (11:7). Rashi and others suggest that it means that no dog will bark; Ibn Ezra offers that it could mean that no dog will bite. A number of archaeological excavations have revealed an Egyptian practice of burying dogs with their owners. This might result from the belief that dogs, who lick their own wounds, have healing powers. Thus, the dogs brought to heal their masters were buried with them after their masters died. This suggests a novel reading of our text. While among the Egyptians there will be a great cry resulting from the deaths of the firstborns in every household, among the Israelites there will not even be a need for the healing dogs.

free will. Free will is the mark of humanity created in the divine image; it is what distinguishes humans from all other creatures. In trying to supplant God, Pharaoh abused that most fundamental human quality, using it to deny his subjects their own humanity. In response, Pharaoh is denied not only his godliness but his humanity as well. The consequences for Pharaoh's actions include God turning him into the instrument through which others will learn.

SHARING THE LIMELIGHT

As God reenters the human story, He brings along radical new ideas to a world which has forgotten Him. He, alone, is the Creator. There is no natural superiority of one human over another, and people do not have a right to deny others their humanity. There are ultimate consequences for our behavior, and the divine response is meant not only to punish, but to instruct people. God intervenes in the affairs of man only when absolutely necessary.

It is easy to interpret God's lengthy absence from the scene as abandonment or lack of interest in the affairs of people. In fact, it is the result of God's commitment to allow humans to self-correct, a commitment which He will abrogate only when without intervention the hope for humanity will be lost.

This is not the first time that God has intervened substantively in the arc of human history. When God brought the Great Confusion, He not only re-created the world but changed some of the parameters to allow for a greater chance of success. The distinction between humans and animals was emphasized, and basic rules were introduced to help delimit the exercise of free will. When He later brought about the dispersion of humanity, He introduced diversity of language and thought – leading to geographical diversity – to prevent individuals from crushing the free will of others. Here, too, God introduces some changes.

One unique feature of this intervention is the use of human agents. They are not only God's emissaries, but His partners. They seemingly perform wondrous deeds, even though they explicitly attribute those aberrations of nature to God. Both Aaron and Moses play essential roles in this process, and that is highlighted in their prominence in the plagues. In partnering with people God is taking a bold step. He would prefer not to have to get involved. He would prefer for people to take initiative, to make the appropriate course corrections in the vector of human history. And now, even as He intervenes, He insists on raising the profiles of His emissaries. He will redeem His people from Egypt, but wants His human partners to rise to prominence, so that they can lead.

Handing over the reins to people, however, will prove more complicated than anticipated.

Exodus 12:1–13:16

The Independent Partner

By now it should be clear that the Exodus is as much about reintroducing God to humanity as it is about freeing people from bondage. The design of the renewed encounter between God and people includes both short-term and long-term planning. In the short term, God will reveal Himself. He will engage and defeat Egyptian magic, He will confront the Pharaonic hubris, He will wondrously demonstrate His ultimate dominion with unambiguous revelation at the Splitting of the Sea and later at Mount Sinai. In the end, however, faith in God is rendered meaningless when His presence is overt and incontrovertibly apparent. Just as the statement "I believe that the sky is blue" is meaningless, as it is not a matter of belief but of knowledge, so too the statement "I believe that God is Master of the universe" is meaningless when standing before the dry path running through the middle of the sea. That is not faith; it is knowledge.

For faith to become meaningful it needs a context in which God's presence is not certain, in which God is not unquestionably involved in human affairs. Thus, in Genesis, it requires no great religious act for the first man and woman to acknowledge God's existence; there is no great act of belief involved when Noah's family exits the ark. God's direct involvement in the world precludes any possibility of faith. That switches when God tells Abram to leave his place and embark on an ambiguous mission. People may have told stories about the God of Creation or the God of the Great Confusion, but these were stories from a bygone era. The lack of explicit divine interaction was the context in which Abram needed to choose whether to act or not after hearing what he believed to be a divine instruction, and it was that choice which made Abram's move religiously significant. Eventually Abraham's task of being God's emissary to humanity was designed to fill the void left by God's receding into the background. For their religious beliefs and devotion to be meaningful they would have to come from a place of uncertainty, and it was the job of God's human ambassadors to ensure that that meaningful devotion could happen.

Exodus provides us with a new iteration of that model. As in Genesis, God makes His presence in Exodus readily apparent. He has a point to prove and will demonstrate it to but a single generation. After that, He will count on His nation, the scaled-up version of the Abrahamic model, to continue that work. The process of forging that nation, however, and charging it with that mission, is not an instantaneous one. Like raising children, it requires time, patience, and long vision to bring about the desired results – and even then, there are no guarantees.

The initial steps of that plan happen early on in Egypt. Pharaoh marks the Hebrews as different, other, and marks their destiny as slaves with endless demands made of them but according them no rights. However noxious his intent, it unwittingly begins to ignite an identity among the Hebrews as being a distinct people. That process moves forward incrementally when their champion, Moses, appears on the scene, and even more when it becomes clear that, for at least some of the plagues, they are being spared. In those early stages, however, that identity of otherness, perhaps even of belonging, is extremely limited, as the identity is one being imposed on them externally. It is what others – Pharaoh, Egypt, Moses, God – do which defines them. They are completely passive, and passive identity is weak, fragile. The instructions for them to prepare for their exit from Egypt begin to shift that national-identity building into an active one.

FORGING A NATIONAL IDENTITY

The first step in that process is subtle – the Israelites are to adopt a new calendar, and the first landmark of that calendar is their liberation. Embedding that event, which was then still only anticipated, into their psyche, functions on multiple levels which serve as important components of national-identity building.

On the most primitive level it begins the process of creating a shared language which both distinguishes them from the Egyptians and provides a symbol for the joint experience of the liberated people. Their counting of years will be referenced by the year of their freedom and their dates will be identified by the number of the month from the month of liberation. It was to become the standard frame of reference in the sphere of time.[1]

The role of the calendar in defining identity cannot be overemphasized, as the calendar helps shape the way we define ourselves and our year. The days of celebration and commemoration dotted throughout the year serve as emotional touchstones and generate a wave of definitional experiences. The calendar is one of the basic cultural institutions which mark the distinction between the insiders and outsiders of that culture.[2] Further, as Leon Kass notes, this represents a dramatic shift

1. Nahmanides (12:1) suggests that using this system is one of the 613 commandments. He struggles to justify its abandonment following the Babylonian exile, when the Babylonian names of the months became standard. Similarly, coins minted during the Bar Kokhba rebellion are dated referencing the year of the beginning of the rebellion as the first year and the second year. The same phenomena can be observed in the modern era, with many Jewish wedding announcements identifying the date as the X year from the founding of the State of Israel or the Y year of the liberation of Jerusalem (referring to the Six-Day War in 1967).
2. Imagine two Jewish friends living in the United States. One defines his year primarily by the holidays which affect his work schedule: Labor Day → Columbus Day → Halloween → Thanksgiving → Christmas → Martin Luther King Day → Presidents Day → Easter → Memorial Day → Independence Day. The other defines her year by the Jewish special days: Rosh HaShana → the Fast of Gedalia → Yom Kippur → Sukkot → Simḥat Torah → Hanukka→ the Tenth of Tevet → the Fast of Esther → Purim → Pesaḥ → the Counting of the Omer → Shavuot → the Seventeenth of Tamuz → Tisha BeAv → the month of Elul. Even in the Jewish calendar, minor variations change the entire annual experience. For Israeli Jews, there are additional days which both reflect and shape their identity and experience: Yitzhak Rabin Day,

from time being defined by the sun or the moon, which was the norm in the ancient word, to defining time by a historical event.[3]

In addition to identifying the month of liberation as the anniversary of the founding of the people, sharing this in advance generates an awareness that the event they are about to experience is truly a historical moment. It would be easy for an Israelite in Egypt to overlook that. They had experienced slavery, hope, frustration, and despair, followed by the surprise of the plagues, the gradual easing of their burdens, and the repeated cycle of Pharaonic promise only to be followed by disappointment. Simply being allowed to leave could have been experienced as one more event in their protracted, seemingly endless, experience. The instruction to mark the event on their new calendar puts the people on notice – they need to be aware that the moment they are about to experience is qualitatively different. It is a truly historical moment, a defining one which will prove to be the beginning of an entirely new phase of their lives.

One aspect of this is highlighted by Rabbi Joseph B. Soloveitchik, who notes that one of the defining features of slavery is that the slave has no control over his time.[4] It is for that reason that Canaanite slaves owned by Israelites, who are otherwise obligated to observe mitzvot, are exempt from positive, time-bound mitzvot – they have no ownership over their own time, or as Rabbi Soloveitchik would say, they even lack time consciousness. Handing the Israelites their own calendar, distinct

---

the Day of Universal Kaddish, Yom HaShoah, Yom HaZikaron, Yom HaAtzmaut, Yom Yerushalayim. For hasidic Jews there are days marking the anniversaries of the deaths of their rebbes. Every one of these changes affects affiliation, identity, community, and experience.

3. Kass, *Founding God's Nation,* 168. He formulates this as a rejection of the sun or the moon as determinators of the calendar. Rabbinic tradition perceives this differently, understanding that God insists that the holiday be celebrated in the month of *aviv* – which is an agricultural determination very much dependent of the seasonal cycle.

   This redefinition of time begins here, but will continue as each of the pilgrimage festivals will undergo a name change reflecting the shift from its agricultural origin to a unique Israelite, historical reference.

4. The articulation here is based on the writing of Rabbi Abraham Besdin in *Reflections of the Rav* (World Zionist Organization, 1979), 200. See also commentary of Sforno on Ex. 12:2.

from the Egyptian one, is a step in rebuilding their time consciousness even to the extent that they define time differently from their neighbors.

The second step in the process of forging a national identity is in the ceremony in which every family publicly displays their otherness from Egypt. Remember that Israel's otherness was initially imposed on it externally by Pharaoh (1:9–22) and was intended to separate and subjugate them. Later, God imposes His own version of otherness on Israel as He spares them from some of the plagues (8:18, 9:4, and 10:23). In those distinctions, however, Israel is passive; it is someone else who is defining their otherness. God's first instruction to Israel changes that; they will need to be active – preparing the sheep, organizing with other families, and most boldly, marking their homes with the blood of the slaughtered animal – declaring themselves to be distinct from their Egyptian neighbors.[5] That is the first declaration by the Israelites proudly proclaiming their otherness from Egypt.

The need for Israel to free themselves of Egypt before God redeems them becomes evident in the Torah's description of the Exodus, which is recorded twice, in two verses which are remarkably similar:

> It was at the end of four hundred and thirty years, it was on this very day, that all of God's forces left the land of Egypt. (12:41)

> It was on this very day that God took the Israelites out of Egypt, by their forces. (12:51)

One of the key differences between these two verses, which both use similar idiosyncratic phrases ("on this very day" and the Israelite "forces"), is that the first describes the Israelites as being active when leaving Egypt (God's forces left) while the second describes them as being passive (God took the Israelites out of Egypt, by their forces). It

5. Mekhilta (*Bo* 5) suggests the act of separating themselves by publicly setting aside the sheep was the action through which Israel merited their liberation. Similarly, Exodus Rabba (16:3) suggests that since the sheep was considered an Egyptian deity, the very act of preparing the sheep for slaughter was a public declaration of Israel's independence even before their actual liberation.

seems that the Torah is trying to indicate that the self-redemption of the Israelites was a prerequisite for God to redeem them.

It is also significant that this identity building happens at the core of the level of the family.[6] While the ultimate goal is fostering a sense of communal-national identity, there must be concentric circles of belonging which ultimately connect one to a much larger whole. The family, with its intimate relationships and the power of transmitted values inherent in those, provides the core unit for nation building. Indeed, it was the value of family which is what prompted God's choice of Abraham.[7]

The drama of the meal they are against eating on the night after the fourteenth of that month is palpable. As it is described, it is not a festive celebration but rather a fast-food meal in anticipation of a significant event. The meat is to be fire-broiled without a pot to ensure fast cooking; it is to be eaten in haste; the bread accompanying the meal should not be given a chance to rise; and the participants in the meal are to be prepared for immediate travel – shoes on (otherwise considered unacceptable in the Ancient Near East), belts fastened, and walking sticks in hand. Each family, isolated in their home, experiences the drama, fully aware that thousands of other homes are doing the same thing simultaneously. The bonds between the families are not visible, but there is a specialness in knowing that others are engaging in the same rebellious preparation, waiting in anticipation to join together with all the other families when the notice arrives.[8]

---

6. Notice that the word *bayit*, the home, appears four times in verses 3–4.
7. Genesis 18:19 highlights Abraham's understanding that family is the core unit for transmission of values as the justification for God's choosing him. By this point Ishmael is already thirteen years old, and Isaac's birth is less than a year away. In *Genesis: From Creation to Covenant*, 115–24, I demonstrate that in the Torah text, the one thing which stands out about Abraham prior to the *Lekh lekha* call is that he (and his brother) are the first men in twenty generations to be described as taking wives, and whose wives have names. Further, Abraham stays with his wife even though she is barren, and in all likelihood his wife is his orphaned niece. Finally, his dedication to his family is further highlighted in the excessive repetition of the already established familial relationships when mentioning his relatives. See, for example, Genesis 12:5.
8. For an exploration of the balance between the family-centered nature of this ritual and the community-centered focus, see Kass, *Founding God's Nation*, 170–71.

AN UNUSUAL COMMEMORATION

There is one other element that God shares with Moses in preparation for the Exodus, the plan for future commemoration of this momentous occasion, which seems to depart from the pattern of nation building evident in both establishing the calendar and the unique meal to be eaten on the night of redemption. One might imagine that God would instruct some form of reenactment of the event, whether the meal or the Exodus itself, but none of those are included. Instead, God instructs that Israel celebrate a seven-day holiday whose main features are no work on the first and the seventh days, and the requirement to banish all leavened products from the home before the onset of the holiday. Neither of those elements seem to capture any of what Israel is experiencing in the Exodus, leaving us somewhat perplexed.

To help understand this better it is worthwhile examining each of the components individually. The seven-day holiday with work prohibitions on both the first and seventh days would have sounded bizarre to the nation preparing to leave Egypt. These people would likely have known only slavery their entire lives. Even the idea of a three-day furlough was considered excessive by Pharaoh; the idea of a seven-day holiday was nigh inconceivable. When we add to that the prohibition of doing labor on the bookends of that holiday, for a nation of slaves that moves from unimaginable to absurd. Yet it is that absurdity which God introduces, as it represents the antithesis of slavery. It is not that work is optional on those days; it is forbidden, dramatically forcing the people to confront the reality that their slavery is a thing of the past. The rejection of slavery is an essential precursor to the self-definition of Israel as a nation which creates its own identity rather than having it imposed by others.

As for the requirement to banish leavened products and the prohibition against eating bread, the use of a sourdough starter – the ancient version of yeast, without which it would take days for the dough to rise – was discovered in Egypt.[9] Egyptian baking artisans designed bakeries to mass-produce this bread and bread became one of the

9. See H. E. Jacob, *Six Thousand Years of Bread: Its Holy and Unholy History* (Skyhorse, 2007), 25–38.

identifying markers of Egyptian culture. The command to celebrate a holiday in which leavened bread was forbidden, even to the point that it needed to be purged from the home prior to that holiday, was an ideal way to mark their liberation, as they purged Egyptian influence from their homes and declared their cultural independence from Egypt.[10] And it is precisely for this reason that, aside from the prohibition on leavened products, the prohibition on sourdough is mentioned twice in God's instruction[11] – banishing the sourdough from the home would require a new restart after the holiday.[12]

The bigger picture begins to become clear. Building their distinct national identity, God instructs the Israelites to physically mark their homes to separate themselves from their Egyptian neighbors and to establish a calendar with its time and cultural references which was distinct from that of Egypt. In addition, He commands them to participate in a ritual which celebrates their anticipated liberation and simultaneously binds them to family and all the others participating while marking them as distinct from the Egyptians. At the same time, the Israelites will imagine a future free of slavery in which work can actually be forbidden and in which they annually purge their homes of Egyptian bread and sourdough starter.

---

10. The need to separate from their Egyptian past, even to banish traces of its culture from the homes, is an important step in defining their identity as non-Egyptians. This is somewhat similar to Lot's exit from Sodom prior to its destruction, with the accompanying prohibition against looking back (Gen. 19:17). Looking back would be a sign of identifying with Sodom, and he had to leave it all behind; otherwise he would be liable to suffer the same fate as them. Indeed, when his wife turns back, she becomes a pillar of salt, like the rest of Sodom (Gen. 19:26). It is not surprising that a rabbinic tradition suggests that Lot's exit from Sodom took place on Pesaḥ (see the comment of Rashi on Gen. 19:3).
11. The biblical word for sourdough starter is *seor*, which is used in 12:15 and 12:19. The word *maḥmetzet*, meaning anything that causes leavening, appears twice in this passage and does not appear anywhere else in the entire Bible.
12. That restart reinforces the holiday, and the month in which it occurs, as a new beginning every year – which is how God's address begins. Later, after the entry into the Promised Land, this was further reinforced by the prohibition against eating from the new grain crop until after the Omer offering was brought on the second day of the holiday. See Lev. 23:10–14.

MOSES SURPRISES

With such a plan we expect Moses to deliver the message to the Israelites, with all its benefits, precisely as God instructed. We are surprised, then, when we discover that Moses modifies God's plan. We never hear Moses presenting the people with their new calendar.[13] He presents an abbreviated version of the command to slaughter the sheep and paint its blood on the doorposts, which will be a sign for God to not afflict their homes as He brings a plague on Egypt. Missing from the text but presumably included are the instructions for processing (roasted on a fire) and eating the sheep (accompanied by matza and bitter herbs, and eaten with all the preparations for immediate departure).[14] When it comes, however, to describing future commemoration of the event, Moses completely omits God's seven-day holiday and replaces it with a reenactment of the evening.

> When you come to the land which God will give you as He said, you shall keep this service. When your children say to you, "What is this service to you?" you shall say, "It is a *pesaḥ*-slaughter to God, who passed over the Israelite houses in Egypt as He smote Egypt and He saved our homes." (12:25–26)

---

13. Nahmanides (Ex. 10:2, Num. 16:5) notes that there are many instances in which the text doesn't record Moses speaking to the people despite God's instruction, and conversely, that there are times in which Moses tells things to the people seemingly without being instructed. I do not deny those possibilities, but where the omissions are particularly blatant, I believe that the Torah is intentionally trying to draw our attention to them. In this particular case, God eventually does command Israel to reenact the evening in future years, but only after Moses introduces it. Had this been a case of Moses simply explicating what God said but which the Torah chose not to record, there would have been no need to record it later. In his commentary to Numbers 16:5, Nahmanides himself is open to the possibility that the test of the fire pans in response to Korah's challenge was Moses's innovation. Similarly, Rashi on Numbers 17:11 suggests that the use of the *ketoret* to stop the plague was not a divine instruction but rather the product of Moses's creative analysis..
14. One interesting difference between God's description and that of Moses is that God speaks of Himself as passing through Egypt to bring the plague and recognizing the houses marked by the blood (12:12–13), while Moses speaks about a "destroyer" which will pass through Egypt whom God will instruct to pass by the marked houses.

Notice that there is no mention of the seven-day holiday bookended by prohibitions of labor, no mention of a requirement to eat matza, no prohibition against eating bread, and no requirement to banish sourdough. This absence of leaven consciousness is highlighted by the later narrative describing the Exodus, in which Israel had every intention of baking leavened bread that evening but were prevented from doing so because they were rushed out of Egypt and did not have time for their bread to rise (12:39)! Further, Moses describes reenacting a "service" so unusual that it will provoke questioning by the children – something which we expected to hear from God initially but was missing.

What is Moses thinking, omitting mention of the seven-day holiday and of the prohibition of leavened bread, which are so important in the divine plan to build a national consciousness? And what is he thinking when he initiates a commemorative reenactment instead?

The puzzle gets even more complex, as after the Exodus God seems to adopt Moses's plan and Moses finally conveys God's instruction. In 12:25, while Israel is still in Egypt, we hear Moses's idea to perform the service again in future years; in 12:43–49 – *after* the plague of the firstborns and *after* the Israelites rush out of Egypt – God commands Israel to do the *pesaḥ*[15] in future years, and He adds rules. Non-Israelites and non-circumcised Israelites may not partake; those who join the Israelites as full members may partake; circumcised slaves may partake. The meat of the *pesaḥ* may not be taken out of the house and no bones are to be broken. And it is only after that (13:3–10) that Moses instructs Israel about the seven-day holiday during which it is forbidden to eat or even possess leavened bread or sourdough starter.

It appears that Moses internalizes God's goals but given his understanding of the people, believes that there is a better way to accomplish those goals or that the timing to carry out God's instructions is not quite right. Let's take the idea of making sure that Israel appreciates the

15. The term *pesaḥ* appears in the Bible forty-nine times. With only one exception (Ex. 34:25), the term refers to the slaughtered animal or the day on which the *pesaḥ* is slaughtered. Only once is it referred to as a sacrifice (Num. 9:7), and that was by the people who missed doing it and before there was an institution of sacrifices in Israel.

moment of exodus as a historic one to be marked in the future, including the awareness of the significance of the event in the moment. God's plan was to have that commemorated through a seven-day holiday. Moses understands that while still in Egypt, the people still experience their lives as Pharaoh's subjects and would be incapable of even imagining a holiday celebration without work. As such, Moses waits until they are freed to convey that message, along with a veiled reference to their new calendar.[16] At the same time, he wants to make sure that they recognize the significance of the moment, and so he instructs them to be aware of it and to take mental notes on the evening as they will repeat it a year later. That, for them, is far more concrete than a holiday stripped of the labor which so defined their existence. It was only once they were no longer physically in Egypt that they could begin to see themselves as having an existence other than as slaves, and it is then that Moses shares that with them.

Perhaps even more surprising than Moses's emendation is God's reaction to it. Not only does God not rebuke Moses for deviating from His instruction, He actually adopts Moses's plan and codifies it with legal parameters.[17] Whether we understand this as God empowering Moses and his leadership or as God learning about the people from the man He charged with responsibility for Israel, it is extraordinary that even as God is grooming Moses for leadership, He is prepared to adjust His plan based on what Moses thinks is best.

PESAḤ AND THE HOLIDAY OF MATZOT

Throughout the rest of the Torah, Moses's innovative reenactment for the night of the fourteenth of the first month and God's seven-day holiday

16. In 13:4 Moses explicitly identifies the month using a blended metaphor of the month, referring to the lunar calendar, and the agricultural marker of the hollowing of the grain stalks (*aviv*), referring to the seasonal-solar one.
17. The power of this ritual is highlighted dramatically by some of the laws God attaches to it. People who did not start out as Israelites but joined them at a later time are to participate in the practice as well. While they cannot trace their biological ancestry to the Exodus from Egypt, the ritual incorporates them into the community to the extent that they can proclaim, "We were slaves to Pharaoh in Egypt, but God took us out of Egypt with a strong hand" (Deut. 6:21).

beginning on the night of the fifteenth live side by side and are given distinct names. The ceremony of the fourteenth at night, as well as the entire preceding day,[18] is called Pesaḥ, while the seven-day festival is called the Festival of Matzot.[19] For example:

> In the first month on the fourteenth of the month, in the afternoon, is Pesaḥ, for God. On the fifteenth day of this month is the Festival of Matzot for God, for seven days you shall eat matzot. (Lev. 23:5–6)

> In the first month of the fourteenth day is Pesaḥ, for God. And on the fifteenth day of this month is a festival – for seven days you shall eat matzot. (Num. 26:16–17)

Moses's innovation is adopted by God but is neither transformed into a holiday[20] nor is it absorbed into God's seven-day Festival of Matzot, which raises the questions of what it is and in what way is its nature different from the Festival of Matzot.

Perhaps it is best to begin by returning to our understanding of matza and the prohibition of leavened bread to define the nature of the Festival of Matzot. As leavened bread was the symbol of Egyptian culture, a seven-day holiday identified by separation from that leavened bread is Israel's declaration that it is purging itself of Egyptian culture and influence. That, of course, is not only a necessary step to independence but also functions as a precursor to Israel's ability to begin to create and foster

---

18. In the Sanctuary, unlike in the non-sacred space, the day begins in the morning and follows through until the next morning. Throughout the Mishna and the Talmud, the *pesaḥ* is referred to as a sacrifice and is treated as such halakhically. Hence the *pesaḥ* is slaughtered and processed during the day of the fourteenth and eaten the following evening, which is still considered the night of the fourteenth. We've already noted that in the Bible, only one of forty-nine references to *pesaḥ* identifies it as a sacrifice, and it is neither God nor a prophet who refers to it as such but laypeople.
19. While the distinction between Pesaḥ and the Festival of Matzot is clear throughout the Bible, that distinction is mostly blurred in talmudic literature. The first hints of that blurring can be seen in Deut. 16:1–8. For a somewhat different analysis of these two holidays, see M. Breuer, *Pirkei Mo'adot*, Vol. 1 (Horev, 1989), 94–162.
20. Only once in the entire Bible (Ex. 34:25) is Pesaḥ referred to as a holiday.

a new culture of its own. It is that culture which God will promote as He takes Israel as His nation, enters into a unique relationship with it, and will give it His unique direction and guidance. This is the essential meaning of the Festival of Matzot.

Quite different is the day/ceremony known as Pesaḥ, but before we can explore that we need to examine what the term *pesaḥ* actually means. Popular culture understands the word as meaning skipping or passing over, referring to God's pronouncement that He will "pass over" the houses of the Israelites who mark their doorways with the blood of the slaughtered sheep as He moves through Egypt smiting the first-borns (12:13 and 12:23). The name Passover is derived from this reading, although it is mistakenly used to identify the seven-day Festival of Matzot rather than the ceremony on the fourteenth.

There is, however, a problem with this reading. Even before God describes the events of the night following the fourteenth, as part of the description of the ceremony God tells Moses, "You shall eat it in haste; it is a *pesaḥ* to God" (12:11). That is, it is called a *pesaḥ* before God mentions anything about the plague, with the assumption that Moses already knows what a *pesaḥ* is.[21] This anomaly is repeated when Moses conveys God's message to the people, "Draw out and take for yourselves a sheep for your families and slaughter the *pesaḥ*" (12:21). Moses, too, tells them to take the *pesaḥ* before he describes the anticipated events of the night afterward (12:23). Again, it sounds like Moses assumed that they would know what *pesaḥ* meant even absent the context of the events that would follow.

It turns out that the word *pesaḥ* is rendered by the *Targum Yerushalmi* as compassion, to soothe, or to care for.[22] In our context that

---

21. Cassuto, in his comments to 12:5 and 12:11, also notes that the term *pesaḥ* was apparently known prior to this. He suggests that there was an ancient practice known as *pesaḥ* which predated the Exodus, and that God's instruction here is to dedicate that practice to Him.

22. See *Targum Yerushalmi* and Ibn Ezra on Ex. 12:11. See also Brown, Driver, Briggs dictionary (Hendrickson, 1979), 820, and Sarna, *Exploring Exodus*, 87 and n. 31. Sarna further suggests that the talmudic preference of lettuce for bitter herbs on Pesaḥ is based on the linguistic play between the Hebrew *ḥasa* (lettuce) and the verb *ḥus* (to have compassion).

would mean that on the night of the death of the firstborns, Israel is to paint their doorways with blood so that God will show His caring for them. Extending that, the animal which is slaughtered is called a *pesaḥ,* as it represents God's care for His people, and the day called Pesaḥ is the day on which God displays His caring for His people. In Egypt, even before Moses and Israel hear about being spared from the great plague which will rage around them, they understand that the day and the ceremony they perform will be acknowledgments of God's care for them. In the years following the Exodus, the fourteenth day will be celebrated with a ceremony reminding the people of God's love for them.

In Egypt this takes on special significance. Although the *pesaḥ* is not called a sacrifice, one element of the *pesaḥ* in Egypt does evoke the notion of sacrifice, and that is the application of the blood on the door frames. In the sacrificial order, the application of the blood to the altar is considered one of the two main processes.[23] In Egypt there was no altar, but applying the blood to the doorposts appears to be in lieu of its application to the altar, thus transforming every Israelite home into an altar. Thus, God's caring for Israel was contingent on their willingness to transform their homes into mini-sanctuaries dedicated to God.

Later in the Torah, the pair of Pesaḥ and the Festival of Matzot come to represent the mutuality of the relationship between God and Israel – Pesaḥ celebrates God's care for and dedication to Israel, and the Festival of Matzot celebrates Israel's rejection of Egypt and embrace of God. That mutuality was certainly unique in the ancient religious world and signifies a radical reorientation of the nature of the relationship between God and people.

We've already seen that the moment of exodus was recorded twice, once describing Israel's self-redemption and a second describing God as redeeming them. A similar pattern is observable in the Torah's

---

23. The other main process is what happens to the flesh of the animal, i.e., whether it is burned on the altar; is eaten by the *kohanim*; or consumed by the one bringing the offering (see *Mishneh Torah, Hilkhot Biat HaMikdash* 9:2). As slaughtering can be done by a non-*kohen* and the formal processes of the offering (*avoda*) are forbidden to be done by a non-*kohen,* the implication is that it is not considered part of the formal service (*Mishneh Torah, Hilkhot Biat HaMikdash* 9:6).

description of Abraham's circumcision, which is described in two similar verses using parallel idiosyncratic phrases.[24]

> Abraham took Ishmael, his son, and all the slaves born into his household, and those purchased with silver – all the males in Abraham's household – and circumcised the flesh of their foreskin on this very day, as God had spoken to him. (Gen. 17:23)

> On this very day, Abraham was circumcised, as was Ishmael his son. And all the males in Abraham's household, those born into his household and those purchased with silver, were circumcised with him. (Gen. 17:26–27)

The first describes Abraham's action, in which he commits to God's covenant; the second, which presents Abraham as passive, apparently indicates God's acceptance of Abraham's action. God's covenant with Abraham began a transition from people being passive in covenant to being active, if not full partners. That mutuality becomes evident as God redeems His future partners from Egypt, where they need to redeem themselves before God accepts their leap of faith and binds Himself to them. The initiatives taken by Moses are precisely what God is looking for in a leader for His covenantal partners.[25]

In fact, as the Torah reflects on the Exodus, there is another verse which indicates the dual nature of the event. "It is a night of keeping watch for God, to bring them out of Egypt; it is this night for God, a

---

24. Note that the phrase "on this very day" binds the two verses describing Abraham's covenant of circumcision, similar to the way it binds the two verses describing Israel's redemption.

25. The link between circumcision and the *pesaḥ* is anchored both in the text and in the halakha. When God instructs Israel regarding future reenactment of the *pesaḥ*, one of the requirements for participation is circumcision – an uncircumcised male may not participate. This is the only mitzva for which the Torah states explicitly that circumcision is a prerequisite. Even more, in general, there is no punishment for non-performance of a positive command. There are two exceptions – circumcision and *pesaḥ*. Even more astonishing, the punishment for both is identical – *karet*, excision from the community of Israel. See also Joshua 5, where the two mitzvot are clearly intertwined.

keeping watch for all Israelites, throughout their generations" (12:42). Once again we find an unusual phrase, in this case repeated within the same verse, used once to describe God keeping watch and a second to describe Israel's keeping watch. For Israel, this is an event they have eagerly anticipated and hoped for, a hope which they maintained for many years. For God too, the Exodus is an event which He has eagerly anticipated, waiting for when the people would be ready not only to leave Egypt but to assume their role as his covenantal partners.

MOSES THE TEACHER

Lest we think that this is the only time Moses exercises his independent judgment, consider the following passage in the beginning of Exodus 13, after the Exodus from Egypt:

> God spoke to Moses, saying: "Consecrate to me every firstborn, the one who breached the womb, whether human or beast; it is Mine."[26] Moses said to the people: "Remember this day, the one on which you left Egypt, the house of bondage, for God took you out of here with the strength of hand; do not eat any leavened products. Today you are leaving; in the month of *aviv*. When God brings you to the land of the Canaanite, the Hittite, the Emorite, and the Hivite which He swore to your ancestors that He would give to you, the land flowing with milk and honey, you are to perform this service in this month. For seven days you are to eat matzot, and on the seventh day – a festival to God." (13:1–6)

God opens by instructing Moses to inform the people about the command involving the firstborn.[27] We fully expect that Moses would do as

26. This command is the first time that God asks Israel to give something up for Him, ostensibly as acknowledgment of the central role He played in their liberation.

27. In the text, God omits any specifics regarding this command. When Moses conveys the instruction to the people he adds some details regarding the difference between human firstborn males, who must be redeemed, and animal firstborn males, some of which are to be "given to God" while donkey firstborns are to be exchanged with a sheep. Given that these instructions predate the existence of any sacrificial order, it is unclear what "given to God" means or how firstborn people are to be redeemed.

he was told but he surprises us when instead he elects to tell them about the seven-day holiday of matzot, the very one which God had told him about weeks before the Exodus and which Moses seemingly replaced with the commemoration that he innovated.

Lest we worry, Moses eventually does convey God's instruction about the firstborn (13:11–15), but he delays until after he finishes instructing them about the seven-day Festival of Matzot.

Apparently, as we saw earlier, Moses thinks that it is unwise to teach the people about the seven-day festival while they were still under the controlling arm of Egypt, since slaves would have a difficult time conceiving of a holiday with no work. Now that the people have left Egypt and begin to sense that the Egyptian yoke has been lifted from their shoulders, Moses determines that this is the right time to fill them in on God's earlier instruction.[28] It is this context that Moses adds an educational component to the seven-day holiday of matzot – "You shall tell your son on that day, 'It is for this that God did for me when I left Egypt'" (13:8).[29] Moses takes the holiday with its implicit message and adds an explicit one.

These specifics are first offered in Numbers 18:15–18. The relationship between this command of redemption and the descriptions of redemption in earlier passages in Numbers (3:11–13 and 8:15–19) needs to be explored.

28. It is unusual that Moses mentions only that the seventh day was a festive day whereas God had earlier indicated that both the first and the seventh would be considered festive days. It is also curious that Moses uses the word *ḥag* to describe the seventh day whereas God had earlier identified it as a day of "proclaimed holiness" upon which labor was forbidden (12:16), both of which are omitted by Moses.

29. The verse is translated as it is written and preserves the awkwardness of the expression. Commentators have debated the meaning of the statement. Rashi assumes that it relates to the *pesaḥ*, which is odd because this is discussing the Festival of Matzot, in which the *pesaḥ* is not featured. Rashbam suggests that the word *zeh* (this) be moved to the end of the statement, yielding, "because God did for me in Egypt, I am doing this," which reflects an awkward sentence construction. Ibn Ezra rejects this because it does violence to the text as written, suggesting that the verse should be read as, "it is for the purpose of our eating the matzot that God did wonders for me when I left Egypt." This reading preserves both the structure of the verse and its context, the Festival of Matzot. While Ibn Ezra uses the matzot as a paradigm for all God's commandments (perhaps playing on the fact that in the Torah the words "matzot" and "mitzvot" are written identically), I suggest that it refers specifically to the matzot, meaning the God took us out of Egypt so that we would reject its culture symbolized by the leavened bread, thus preparing Israel to become His people.

It is quite extraordinary that Moses feels confident enough to add to God's instruction and decide on both when and how to deliver it. Moses is not merely an oracle, receiving God's word and transmitting it, but an active and independent interpreter of the divine message, whose creativity is designed to ensure that God's message is not just transmitted authentically but received properly.[30] Even though the Torah will ultimately identify Moses's uniqueness as a function of his prophecy (Num. 12:6–8 and Deut. 34:10–12), the appellation attached to him in rabbinic literature and which sticks to this day is *Rabbeinu*, our Teacher.

---

30. Reflecting back on the plagues, it seems that already then Moses tried making changes, albeit subtle, to their implementation. The chart below outlines God's instructions as to how the plagues were to be implemented alongside the Torah's description of what Moses and Aaron actually did. Notice that in only two of the plagues (Boils and Darkness) does Moses actually follow God's instructions precisely.

	Who does it?	**How was it supposed to have been done?**	**How was it done?**
Blood	Aaron	Take the staff and extend the hand	Aaron strikes the water with the staff
Frogs	Aaron	Extend the hand with the staff	Aaron extends his hand
Lice	Aaron	Extend the staff and hit the dust	Aaron extends his hand with the staff and hits the dust
Animal swarm	God		
Animal death	God		
Boils	Moses	Throw soot skyward	Moses throws soot skyward
Hail	Moses	Wave his hand skyward	Moses waves his staff skyward
Locusts	Moses	Wave his hand over Egypt	Moses waves his staff over Egypt
Darkness	Moses	Wave his hand skyward	Moses waves his hand skyward
Firstborn death	God		

Moses plays out that role of teacher precisely in his innovations, emendations, adaptations, and educational choices.

Much attention has been given to the role of passing on the story of the Exodus to the next generation. The entire Pesaḥ Seder is built on that idea, and it has proven to be perhaps the single most impactful educational and psychological ritual in the Jewish tradition. The foundation of the parent-child dialogue at the core of the Seder is based on four passages in the Torah which discuss different aspects of that dialogue, three of which are in Exodus 12–13. A careful reading reveals that all of those are in passages born of Moses's initiative. The first (12:26–27) is in the passage where Moses innovates the reenactment of the *pesaḥ*; the second (13:8) is in the context of where Moses decides to teach the people about the seven-day Festival of Matzot; the third (13:14–15) is where Moses finally conveys God's message regarding the firstborn. Thus, Moses takes each of God's instructions with its implicit messages and transforms them into explicit educational tools with the requirement to use them as an opportunity to transmit Israelite historical memory to the next generation.

It is not surprising that rabbinic tradition embraced Moses's legislative and educational choices. It may be surprising that, extraordinarily, God does. Not only does He tolerate it – there is not even a hint of rebuke from God – He welcomes it, as we saw earlier with the institution of the day/ritual of *pesaḥ*. In fact, this is perhaps part of why He chose Moses in the first place.[31]

God learns to deal with the people, perhaps from Moses, and as we saw earlier in His recruiting of Moses, He learns how to deal with Moses himself. Moses's independent streak may be attractive to God, but it will come with a price.

31. The rabbinic story of the oven whose ritual status was debated by the Rabbis who ultimately overruled divine efforts to determine the law (Bava Metzia 59a) climaxes with God's joyful exclamation: "They have defeated Me; My children have defeated Me!" In the rabbinic conception, this perhaps represents the ultimate expression of God's partnership with His people, as He will accept being overruled by His human partners.

Exodus 13:17–14:31

The Bumpy Road

Pharaoh has been humbled. Having once vowed that Moses and Aaron would never appear before him again (10:25), he now summons them and gives them everything they asked for – the men, women, and children, the sheep – and he even asks them to pray for him too. The man who once declared that he did not recognize the God of Israel not only recognizes that God but seems to acknowledge that that God has bested him.

The Egyptians rally to send off the Israelites, or more likely, to chase them out of the land. In fact, they are in such a hurry to finally rid themselves of these pesky former slaves that the Israelites do not have time to let their bread rise before leaving. Even more, they bestow upon the Israelites gifts of silver and gold and clothes, perhaps out of guilt or shame or hope that the Israelites remember them well to their own God.[1] Regardless of the Egyptian motive, the net result is that the

1. The Torah thrice mentions that the Israelites will ask the Egyptians for goods prior to leaving (3:21–22, 11:2–3, 12:35–36). This is apparently in fulfillment of God's covenant with Abraham, "and afterward they will leave with great acquisitions" (Gen. 15:14). The verb indicating the request, *shaal,* is also used to refer to a question

Israelites can now be financially self-reliant, a critical element in shedding their mindset of dependence.

The Israelites have demonstrated their independence from Egypt by following Moses's commands rather than Pharaoh's. They have eaten their fast-food meal of freedom and are beginning the process of forging their chosen national identity through ritual eating, establishing their own calendar, and planning future celebrations. They have rejected core Egyptian cultural icons, the leavened bread[2] and the belief in natural superiority – the Egyptians are not inherently better than the Israelites and the firstborns are not naturally superior to any of the other siblings. They finally own their own time, can imagine celebrations in the future, can build intentional memories for their offspring by sharing their stories, and can wear both their history and their destiny proudly.[3] They leave

---

or a loan. Given that it sometimes means a loan, there is an extensive apologetic literature justifying what appears to be a deception. See Samet, *Iyunim BeFarashat HaShavua,* Series 1, Volume 1, 178–91, and Series 2, Volume 1, 263–85, for an extensive treatment of this literature. See also B. Gesundheit, "She'eilat Kelei Kesef UKhelei Zahav," *Megadim* 33:9–12. For other contemporary approaches, see Kass, *Founding God's Nation,* 180–83.

2. The Torah describes the Israelites leaving with their *misheret* wrapped in their cloaks. This word appears only four times in the entire Bible (Ex. 7:28, 12:34; Deut. 28:5, 28:17) and is clearly related to the bread-making process. Brown, Driver, Briggs dictionary understands it as the kneading trough. I suspect that it is more likely related to the sourdough starter that was saved from one baking to the next, given that the root of this word is likely SH-A-R, meaning "leftover." It is likely also related to the word for the leavening agent, *seor*. That is, that they did not successfully make bread but they did bring their leaven with them. This also highlights the first time the word is used, describing the plague of frogs which penetrated the Egyptian *misheret,* the symbol of Egyptian supremacy. It is not surprising that the Torah also describes the frogs as infiltrating the Egyptian ovens, also directly linked to their bread-making capabilities.

3. In rabbinic literature, the "sign on the hand and the memory between the eyes" (13:9) is understood as referring to the mitzva of tefillin. Similarly, the "sign on the hand and the *totafot* between the eyes" (13:16) also are understood in halakhic literature as a reference to tefillin. Ibn Ezra on 13:9, however, suggests that the sign on the hands is a metaphor, similar to "Write them on the tablet of your heart" (Prov. 3:3), meaning, as if it were engraved on your hand – that is, to be remembered constantly. Rashbam (13:9) writes similarly, citing instead the verse "Place me as a seal upon your heart" (Song. 8:6). Rashbam adds that the "sign between the eyes" means to be worn prominently, like an ornament worn on the forehead. While traditional

Egypt not as slaves fleeing their masters[4] but as free people, armed for battle[5] and laden with their newfound wealth, gifted to them by their former masters and neighbors, according them the ability to begin their lives anew with dignity.[6]

As for Moses, the man who couldn't speak and didn't want to get involved, he has come to stand confidently before Pharaoh, consistently raising the ante. He cares about God's mission and has successfully rallied Israel to follow him into defying the Egyptians. Moses understands the people and innovates based on what he believes is best; he has gotten creative both following God's directives and generating his own. He is respected by the Israelites and by Egyptians, both the nobility and the commonfolk (11:3).

But while dramatic transformations are impressive, they are rarely durable. They are significant in that they signal a meaningful will to make a very meaningful switch, but that shift needs to be accompanied by a long-term process in order for it to take root deep in the soul and become an integral part of the new self.[7] Hence Jacob, who struggled mightily with being forthright, makes a bold change when he finally confronts Laban (Gen. 31:36–42), but soon afterward is challenged to be honest with Esau when he assures his brother that he will follow him to Se'ir at his own pace (Gen. 33:14).[8] Similarly, when the prophet Elijah confronts Ahab and the prophets of the Baal at Mount Carmel and

---

commentators struggled to interpret the word *totafot* (13:16), archaeologists have discovered that Egyptian royals wore a diadem on their foreheads called a *totefet* (https://beinenu.com/lessons/הכרת-תרבות-מצרים-ותרומתה-לפרשנות-התורה), dovetailing with Rashbam's explanation that the stories the Israelites are to tell their children about God's redemption are to be worn proudly like royal ornaments. See also Shabbat 57b, the opinion of R. Yehuda citing Abaye that a *totefet* is an ornament.

4. Contrast this with Jacob's nocturnal flight from Laban (Gen. 31:17–20).
5. See Ibn Ezra on 13:18.
6. Later, the Torah will mandate gifting the indentured servant with enough sustenance to help him restart his life as free man (Deut. 15:13–14). Jeremiah (34:10–22) rails against those who freed their Hebrew slaves after his insistence, only to take them back again afterward. Those slaves were apparently released with no means of self-support and were forced back into servitude by financial exigencies.
7. See commentary of Rabbi Shmuel David Luzzatto to 13:17.
8. See Grumet, *Genesis: From Creation to Covenant*, 289–362.

defeats them in a dramatic showdown, he is gratified by the Israelites' thundering response, "A-donai is God! A-donai is God!" (I Kings 18:39). By the morning, however, he is disappointed and distressed when he is hunted again by Israelites following Jezebel's call to have him killed (I Kings 19:2–3).[9]

The morning after the Israelites leave, Pharaoh has a change of heart. "When Pharaoh was told that the people fled, his heart and that of his servants changed regarding the people. They said: 'What have we done that we sent Israel out from serving us?'" (14:5).[10] He harnesses his chariot and takes what appears to be the full military might of the Egyptian army – six hundred choice chariots and "all the [other] Egyptian chariots," not to mention the army and its military leaders – and heads out in pursuit. Pharaoh may have earlier felt pressured to release Israel, but his acknowledgment and acceptance of the Israelite God was not genuine, as evidenced by his eagerness the next day to undo his decision to send them free.

The Egyptian people are no less fickle. While their firstborns were dying, they did not hesitate to press Israel to leave (12:33), but when Pharaoh calls to pursue Israel there is no dissent, no subterfuge like that demonstrated by Shifrah and Puah, none of the willingness demonstrated by the people throughout the plagues to release Israel for their divine worship (10:7) or acknowledge the God of Israel (8:15, 9:20–21). These same people who gifted Israel with parting gifts were now encouraging Pharaoh to chase after them to bring them back.

---

9. For a full explication of this story, see Elhanan Samet, *Elijah: The Lonely Zealot* (Maggid Books, 2021), 96–133.
10. There has been critique of Moses's request of Pharaoh to go for a three-day work furlough as being disingenuous, when the real intent was to liberate Israel (see Samet, *Iyunim BeFarashat HaShavua,* Series. 1, Volume 1, 178–91, and Series 2, Volume 1, 263–85). The text here is unambiguous that regardless of the content of the initial request and subsequent negotiations, Pharaoh and Egypt had "sent Israel out from serving" them. It is interesting the reports Pharaoh receives are that the people "fled," suggesting there were others in his entourage who may have been unaware of or in disagreement with Pharaoh's decision to send them free.

The Israelites themselves do not fare much better. Unschooled at battle and chained to a slave mentality,[11] as soon as they see the Egyptians in pursuit they panic.

> When the Israelites raised their eyes and saw the Egyptians traveling after them, they became very fearful and cried out to God. They said to Moses, "Was it for the lack of graves in Egypt that you took us to die in the wilderness? What did you do to us by taking us out of Egypt? Isn't this what we said to you in Egypt, 'Leave us be so that can we can work for the Egyptians'? for we would rather serve Egypt than die in the wilderness." (14:9–12)

As for Moses, the leader who took so much initiative vis-à-vis both Pharaoh and God, he preaches passivity: "God will fight for you; you be silent" (14:14). Having been given advance notice that God had a plan, although unaware of the details (14:3–4), Moses proclaims his faith in God and hopes that Israel will follow suit, but beyond that he has no substantive response to Israel's cries. God's reaction to that passivity is quite telling: "Why are you crying out to Me? Tell the Israelites to move!" It appears that it is not just we readers who expected something more from the man leading the people out of bondage – God expects Moses to lead the people into action. In fact, Moses's proclamation of "As you see Egypt today you will not see them ever again" (14:13) echoes Pharaoh's earlier comment to Moses: "Take heed not to see my face again, for on the day that you see my face you will surely die" (10:28).[12] Given that there is no indication that Moses knew what was coming, the reader senses that Moses's promise may be as hollow as Pharaoh's threat.

Thus, it appears that God's intervention in Egypt was only temporarily successful in rebooting creation and redirecting humanity toward Him. It also appears that although Moses has made great strides forward,

11. See Ibn Ezra on 13:17 and 14:13. See also Rashbam on 14:8 and Maimonides, *Guide for the Perplexed*, III:32.
12. Pharaoh's threat itself is arrogantly similar to God's later comment to Moses, "You are unable to see My face, for no man may see My face and live" (33:20).

he still has a way to go in his leadership. And it looks like Israel's sense of feeling free is still far from being complete.

CONFUSION AND CLARITY

On some level, the sense of confusion demonstrated by the various characters in this story seems to be by design. As the Israelites leave, God chooses to send them on a less direct route, since the direct route would have them pass by the Philistines and God was concerned that the Israelites would be frightened by them and would want to return to Egypt. This is especially true in light of evidence that many of the Philistine cities were outposts of the Egyptian Empire,[13] and Israel would feel like they had left Egypt only to again encounter Egyptian forces on the way. Ironically, after the Israelites are distant enough from Egypt to be "on the edge of the wilderness" (13:20), God instructs them to backtrack and head back to Pi HaHirot.[14] It is that action which causes Pharaoh to conclude that Israel has lost its way, tempting him to pursue them to bring them back, and it is that illusion of confusion which actually brings Israel to contend with a real Egyptian military (not a Philistine one), which ultimately brings them to challenge Moses for taking them out of Egypt and to want to return there! Thus, while we, as omniscient readers who know how the story ends, understand that God has a plan, the reader encountering this for the first time would conclude that it is not only the Egyptians and the Israelites who are confused, but God Himself.[15]

Perhaps even more significant is the Torah's language describing God's action after the Egyptian chariots get stuck; *vayahom*, He confused the Egyptian camp (14:24). This word, used here for the first time, is used

13. See Sarna, *Exploring Exodus*, 103–6.
14. A midrash (Mekhilta, *Beshallaḥ* 1) identifies this as the same place as Pitom, one of the cities built by the Israelites (1:11). Pi-tom could be translated as "the beginning of the end," while Pi HaHirot could be read (as does the midrash) as "the beginning of freedom." Thus, God having them revisit the place that symbolized the beginning of their slavery transforms it into the gateway to their freedom.
15. This confusion is highlighted again later in the chapter. As the waters of the sea come crashing down upon the hapless Egyptians, the Torah uses a highly unusual phrase, "Egypt was fleeing toward it" (14:27). People usually flee from that which endangers them, not toward it. That description is used intentionally to highlight the Egyptian confusion.

throughout the Bible to describe divine disruption in the camp of the enemies of Israel, one which brings about defeat for Israel's enemies.[16] This confusion is reminiscent of the primordial state of creation, described as *tohu vavohu*, out of which God generates an orderly world.[17] In this scene, God takes the orderliness of Egypt and its organized army and transforms it into chaos, demonstrating that He, alone, is master of Creation.

The confusion of Egypt is starkly contrasted by the linearity of the path for Israel. Despite God's initial instruction to backtrack to Pi HaHirot, the Splitting of the Sea makes Israel's direction unambiguous. There is no way to turn to the right or the left, there is only the path through. This is highlighted dramatically by the repetition of the clause "The water was for them a wall to their right and to their left" (14:22 and 14:29).[18] Thus, the illusion of Israel's confusion brings the Egyptian army to the genuine chaos in the sea, marking their ultimate defeat, while the path God charts for Israel emerges as completely orderly. The Egyptians feel in control until their final moments while, conversely, Israel feels powerless until their final moment.

GOD'S PLAN

The apparent confusion and frustration on the part of the characters in this scene are contrasted with the clarity of God's plan which emerges from an analysis of the chapter.[19] God's plan to seduce Pharaoh to chase after Israel in the first half of chapter 14 is mirrored by His plan to draw the Egyptians into the sea in the second half, illustrated by the following chart:

---

16. See Ex. 23:27, Deut. 7:23, Josh. 10:10, Judges 4:15, I Sam. 7:10, and II Sam. 2:15. The glaring exception is Esther 9:24, which uses the word to describe Haman's plans for the Judeans. Apparently, the author of Esther was trying to describe Haman as attempting to usurp God's role.
17. See Grumet, *Genesis: From Creation to Covenant*, 3–17.
18. Later in the Torah the admonition to refrain from turning "to the right or the left" of God's path highlights the meaning of this phrase (Deut. 5:28, 17:11, and 28:14). Similarly, Israel's request for passage through Edom, promising not to veer from the main road (Num. 20:17), Moses's description of his overture to the Emorites (Deut. 2:27), and the description of Bilaam's donkey on a narrow path with no room to turn right or left (Num. 22:26).
19. Much of this analysis is based on Samet, *Iyunim BeFarashat HaShavua*, Series 1, Volume 1, 192–203.

14:2–4	14:15–17
Speak to the Israelites… that they should camp… next to the sea… so that Pharaoh should chase after them and I will be glorified through Pharaoh and his army and Egypt will know that I am A-donai	Speak to the Israelites that they should travel… into the sea… [Egypt] will come after them and I will be glorified through Pharaoh and his army and Egypt will know that I am A-donai

The two halves of the plan, getting Pharaoh to chase Israel and getting Egypt to follow Israel into the sea, use parallel language, demonstrating the unity of the plan. Those two plans are each followed by a description of what happens, which again mirror each other:

14:9	14:23
Egypt chased after them and caught them encamped by the sea	Egypt chased and came after them into the sea

The final element of this parallel builds on Moses's message to Israel as they panicked as they watched the Egyptians approach:

14:13	14:30–31
Stand in anticipation and see God's salvation which He will do for you today. For as you see Egypt today you will not see them ever again	Israel saw Egypt dying at the edge of the sea. God saved Israel…from the hands of Egypt on that day

God hears Moses's proclamation of faith in Him and translates that into action which mirrors Moses's prediction. Even more, Moses had promised that "God will fight for you" (14:14), which is exactly what the Egyptians proclaim as the walls of water crash on them: "Egypt said, I will flee from Israel because A-donai is fighting against Egypt on their behalf" (14:25).

God has been saying all along that the purpose of the plagues is so that Egypt would know God. They did acknowledge Him, but that turned out to be fleeting. Bringing them to the sea, God again declares that as His goal, "Egypt will know that I am A-donai" (14:4 and 14:18) – echoing His stated goal prior to the first set of plagues (7:17). It appears that regarding Egypt, God has all but given up on them going any further than that. In fact, their recognition of God is the last thing that they do before being engulfed by the sea.[20]

As for Israel, their panic was anticipated. In fact, God so expected their fearful reaction that He intentionally kept them from the short route to the Promised Land to avoid the Philistines. With the death of the Egyptians – and even more, their witnessing the destruction of the Egyptian army – God hoped to move them from their slave mentality. In fact, the waters crashing behind them served symbolically as a closing of a door. The return path to Egypt was sealed; there could be no going back.[21]

For Israel, however, sealing their past was not enough; it was essential that God now help them to build their future. That future would be dependent on their trust in both Him and His chosen leader, Moses. The scene at the sea served as an important step, although not the final one, in their building of that trust. In fact, the Torah's description of that is highlighted by a subtle play on the words for "to see" (*raa*) and for the description of the awe (*yira*) they experienced at that moment. "Israel saw (*vayar*) God's great hand that He did to Egypt, the people were in awe (*vayiru*) of God, they trusted in God and in Moses, His servant" (14:31).[22]

---

20. Ibn Ezra's commentary on 14:4 indicates his concern with this fleeting recognition of God by Egypt.

21. This echoes the blocking of the path back to Eden (Gen. 3:24). It also brings up the image of Lot, when fleeing Sodom, who is told not to look back, as there is no going back. Rashi (Gen. 19:4, s.v. *umatzot afa*) links Lot's flight from Sodom with the Exodus, suggesting that Lot fed his guests matzot because it was Pesaḥ.

22. Building this trust will turn out to be a lengthy project. The Covenant Between the Pieces, the foundation for the Exodus, is also prefaced by Abram's trust in God (Gen. 15:6).

God had plotted the seduction of Pharaoh to chase after Israel and anticipated Israel's panic.[23] He builds on Moses's response and weaves it into the second half of His plan which brings about the demise of Egypt and the hope for building Israel's trust. For God, there is no confusion. The clarity of His plan cuts through the clouds which obscured the vision of the actors in the scene. The Splitting of the Sea showed Israel an unambiguous path forward, in which there could be no mistake – the walls of water guide their path toward freeing themselves of the shackles of Egyptian servitude.

SYMBOLS OF EXODUS

The description of the Exodus is replete with symbols and imagery which add new dimensions to our understanding of the events. As the Israelites are busy with marching, fully armed, out of Egypt, and as God is busy ensuring that they don't turn back, Moses is busy gathering Joseph's bones. "Moses took Joseph's bones with him, for he had sworn the Israelites saying, 'God will account your destiny; bring my bones up from here with you'" (13:19). Joseph's words (Gen. 50:25) signal a dramatic shift in his own thinking. The same Joseph who had earlier told Jacob that the two sons Jacob wanted to take were his, and Egyptian ("which God gave me *here*" – *bazeh*), later recognizes that Egypt is not the future destiny of his people, and insists that his bones be taken up from *here* – *mizeh*.[24] Even more, Joseph's use of the root P-K-D to describe God's remembering indicates his understanding that their future would not consist simply of leaving Egypt but would signal the beginning of a fulfillment of their destiny. When Moses acts to uphold

---

23. A rabbinic tradition (Megilla 10b) tries to dispel any notion we might have that God took delight in bringing about Egypt's devastation. In the version recorded in the Talmud, when the sea was drowning the Egyptians, God prevented the heavenly angels from engaging in their daily song. "The creation of My hands is drowning in the sea, and you want to sing?" Variations on this appear in Sanhedrin 39b and Exodus Rabba 23:7. For a fuller explication of this approach, see Shalom Rosenberg, "Shirat HaMalakhim," *Akdamot* 5, and "VeShuv al Shirat HaMalakhim," *Akdamot* 7. For an alternative explanation, see David Henschke, "Al Shum Ma Ne'elmu HaMalakhim," *Akdamot* 6.
24. For more on this, see Grumet, *Genesis: From Creation to Covenant*, 433–47.

Joseph's vow he is proclaiming Joseph's message that their exodus is not merely a liberation from oppression but a gateway to the fulfillment of their national destiny.[25]

This point is made even stronger by Joseph's description of his remains. The closing verse of Genesis is quite explicit, describing the embalming of Joseph's body after he died, yet Joseph speaks not of his embalmed body nor even of his coffin, but of his bones. Embalming was a hallmark of aristocratic Egyptian burials, relating directly to Egyptian beliefs about the continuation of the body into the afterlife. That is one of the reasons that Jacob did not want an Egyptian burial, as he did not want to be associated in any way with that culture (Gen. 47:30 and 49:29). Joseph surely knew that he would be embalmed, yet he insists on highlighting to his brothers that he wanted to be remembered as the one whose flesh rotted, leaving only the bones. His final rest would be an Israelite one, not an Egyptian one. Moses's focus on those bones emphasizes not only the destiny of Israel, but that a prerequisite for the fulfillment of that destiny comprises rejecting the Egyptian culture and taking the Egypt out of Israel. Joseph's bones are the first significant symbol in the narrative of the Exodus.

The second symbol is the Egyptian chariot, representing Egyptian potency and Egypt's concept of power.[26] Rendering the chariots useless is God's way of signaling that the Egyptian concept of power is fallacious. That power, celebrating Egyptian innovation, was expressed specifically in the Egyptian chariots. When Joseph wanted to demonstrate to Jacob that he was still alive, he sent chariots (Gen. 45:21) – no one other than a royal could have done that – and it was those chariots which actually convinced Jacob that Joseph held a powerful Egyptian position (Gen.

---

25. There are many parallels between Moses and Joseph. Both are torn from their families at a young age, both are given Egyptian names, both are outsiders to their people who opt to rejoin, both sought out their brothers (Gen. 37:16 and Ex. 2:11), and both marry the daughters of foreign priests. The stark difference between them is that Joseph is the architect of the enslavement of his people, albeit unwittingly, while Moses is the architect of their redemption from that slavery. Moses removing Joseph's bones from Egypt may be understood as his effort to redeem Joseph.
26. Chariots were the ancient equivalent of tanks. Later, Canaanite chariots became the symbol of Canaanite power. See Judges 1:19 and 4:13.

45:27). As Pharaoh chases Israel, he prepares his own chariot, orders deployment of six hundred of the best chariots, and all the other Egyptian chariots (14:6–7) – all in a display of the full force of Egyptian power. Later, it is those chariots which get stuck in the once-dry seabed and which become the focus of the description of God's emasculation of Egyptian power.[27]

The technological superiority symbolized by chariots was the product of the Egyptian belief that they were above the gods. After all, they had improved upon the natural world and were able to create something that was superior to anything God created.[28] Similar to Babel, where the technology to fire bricks served as the catalyst for building the city and the tower and which God insisted would undermine His authority on earth (Gen. 11:1–9), Pharaoh's chariots needed to be humbled. Just a little bit of water mixed with the dry seabed – God's mastery over Creation – was enough to bring those chariots to a halt, rendering the Egyptians inside totally helpless.

The third symbol is the combination of the pillar of fire and the pillar of smoke. This symbol first appears as a guide, directing Israel's route as they leave Egypt (13:21–22) but quickly transforms into a protective shield for Israel when the Egyptians approach (14:19–20). This symbol accompanies Israel for the next forty years, until their arrival in the land, and becomes almost synonymous with divine revelation.[29] That symbol, however, has an antecedent in the Bible in the Covenant Between the Pieces. "The sun had set and there was darkness, and behold, a smoky oven and a flame of fire had passed through the cut

27. 14:23, 26, and 28. In the following chapter as well, 15:4 and 15:19. The description of what happens to Sisera's chariots (Judges 4–5) is remarkably similar. As the ground turned into mud, the wheels of the chariots got stuck, rendering the formidable fortresses on wheels into death traps.
28. This is similar to the Egyptian development of fermenting dough to a make bread. For an explication of bread as a symbol of human creativity, see Grumet, *Genesis: From Creation to Covenant*, 53–54.
29. The travels of the Israelites were all directed by the cloud (40:36; Num. 9 and 10). The association between the cloud and revelation emerges prominently in Ex. 19 as part of the preparations for the Revelation at Sinai and is repeated multiple times throughout the book of Numbers. It reappears prominently in I Kings 8:10–11 as Solomon inaugurates the Temple.

parts" (Gen. 15:17). As Israel sees the pillars of cloud and fire, they are moved back to the imagery of the covenant. Once again, their release from Egypt was not a mere act of divine kindness but an act of great historical and theological import – God is fulfilling the ancient covenant with the founding ancestors, and these people are the ones chosen for that fulfillment. It is for that reason that the symbol remains with them until they get to the land.

The fourth powerful symbol in this story is the water. The very walls of water which protected Israel and which guided its path were those which came crashing down on Israel's enemy. The Splitting of the Sea brings us back yet again to the story of Creation, where the waters were split into the upper waters and the lower ones. By extension, the crashing of the waters upon the Egyptians is reminiscent of the merging of the upper waters and the lower ones in the Great Confusion, leading up to the subsequent re-creation. Thus, the Splitting of the Sea serves as yet another reminder of Creation and the one and only Creator who is reasserting His presence in the world.

A fascinating midrash suggests that when the sea split all the waters throughout the world split as well.[30] The underlying idea the midrash is trying to illustrate is that God's reentry into human affairs is not localized. This is not about Egypt. God is reintroducing Himself, the Creator actively involved in His creation, to all humanity.

Even more, the symbol of splitting is the one which always accompanies covenant. The Covenant Between the Pieces is the clearest example, but even as Jacob and Laban sit to establish their covenant they "break bread." Later (Ex. 24), Moses will conduct a ceremony of covenant in which the blood is split. The recommitment to the covenant the Israelites enact upon entry into their land is done with the nation split on two facing mountains, Mount Gerizim and Mount Eval (Deut. 27:11–26). Even the verb used to describe covenant (K-R-T) means to cut. Israel's passage through the split sea has a great symbolic theological and profound educational significance – they are not only witnessing covenant but are experiencing it with their bodies.

30. Exodus Rabba 21:6.

When we broaden our vision of the use of the prominence of water in this scene,[31] we notice that, in the Bible, divine revelation usually takes one of two forms, fire or water. The Great Confusion in Genesis is revelation through water; the destruction of Sodom is through fire. The revelation at the sea is through water; the Revelation at Sinai is with fire.[32] What fire and water have in common is that they are both forces in nature which are necessary for human survival. Either of those elemental forces, however, when left unrestrained, can be the most destructive forces known to humanity. Hence the unleashing of those forces – whether through tsunamis or hurricanes or volcanoes – humbles man and serves as a powerful reminder of God's mastery of the fundamental forces of nature, in the face of which man is helpless.

THE MISSING SYMBOL

There is one additional symbol which appears in the scene of splitting the sea, and it is different from all the others. Moses's staff features prominently in God's instruction to Moses. "And you, raise your staff and extend your hand over the sea and split it" (14:16). This staff has featured in Exodus from Moses's first encounter with God at the burning bush, and it deserves closer attention.

At one point in that extended interchange with God, God has Moses turn the staff into a serpent as a sign.[33] In the closing moment of their encounter, God's parting instruction to Moses is to take his staff with which he will perform the signs. It is therefore quite puzzling that after this, God never instructs Moses in Egypt to use his staff.

---

31. The word for sea, *yam*, appears fourteen times in Ex. 14. R. Samet points out that seven of those refer to the Splitting of the Sea, enabling Israel's safe passage, while the other seven refer to the un-Splitting of the Sea, which guarantees that they will never again be pursued by Egypt.
32. These two typologies of revelation repeat throughout the Bible. One prominent revelation, in Elijah's confrontation with the prophets of the Baal (I Kings 18), involves an interplay between fire and water. We've already noted that the plague of hail was also a combination of fire and water.
33. In only one communication throughout the plagues does God refer to what He is doing to Egypt as *otot* (10:1–2).

The signs that God gave to Moses were ostensibly for Moses to perform in front of the Israelites in case they didn't believe that God had sent him. When they actually speak to Israel, however, it is Aaron who demonstrates the signs (4:30). Later, when Moses and Aaron go to Pharaoh, they do not demonstrate these signs and it is not Moses who is involved in the face-off with the Egyptian sorcerers; Aaron throws his staff to the ground and it becomes a crocodile – completely different from what Moses experienced at the burning bush. Even more puzzling is that throughout the plagues, only once does God instruct anyone to use the staff, and there it is in His instruction to Aaron, not to Moses (7:12).[34] In the instructions to Moses, however, he is to use his hands exclusively; the staff is not mentioned at all (9:8, 9:22, and 10:21). Here, as well, a careful reading reveals that Moses is to raise his staff, but to use his hand to split the sea.[35]

It appears that not only is the staff not central to God's wondrous deeds, it is being consciously deemphasized. Instead of the staff, God highlights Moses's hands as instrumental.

We've already seen that objects considered endowed with special properties were instrumental in performing magic. Pharaoh's sorcerers use them, Balak's sorcerers use them (Num. 22:7), and Joseph professes to use one (Gen. 44:5). As an important step in weaning Israel from their Egyptian upbringing, God wants to highlight that there are no magical objects; the staff is no magic wand.

The staff, however, did have another function, as a symbol of leadership. Shepherds use a staff to keep the sheep from straying, and ancient leaders used a staff to punish those who strayed.[36] That practical function led to the staff becoming a symbol of leadership, so much so that the biblical word for a tribe is the same as the word for staff. In fact, in Biblical Hebrew there are two words for staff which are used interchangeably,

34. There were two other times where God instructs Aaron to take the staff, but these are not accompanied by an instruction to use it (7:19 and 8:1).

35. We will discuss Moses's hands later in the context of the battle with Amalek.

36. Gen. 38:18, 49:10; II Sam. 7:14; Is. 10:24; Ps. 23:4; Prov. 13:24, 22:15; Job 9:34; and many more.

mateh and *shevet,* and both are also used for tribe – which follows the staff of its leader.

It was the function of leadership that God wants to highlight when He commands Moses to pick up the staff. God is trying to promote Moses's public image and self-image as a leader. We recall that the signs God gave to Moses at the burning bush were as much for Moses himself as they were for Israel; he needed to believe in his own leadership. The staff sets him apart; raising the staff is a sign for others to follow. We already saw God rebuke Moses for his passivity in this scene. "Why are you crying out to Me?" He says. The action that God commands immediately afterward is for Moses to demonstrate leadership. Take the staff – not as a magic wand with which to split the sea, but as a means to show the people who is at the helm.

It is not the hand with the raised staff which splits the sea; it is Moses's other hand, unadorned and without accoutrements. Just as God had earlier told Moses to invoke the plagues of boils, hail, locusts, and darkness, here, too, it is Moses's hand – Moses himself – who is being elevated. Indeed, by the end of the scene, the people trust in God and in Moses.

The path was not smooth, but God accomplishes His goals. The Egyptians die with God's name on their lips. The Israelites have renewed their trust in God and in Moses. And Moses has taken another step in believing in himself as he assumes the mantle of leadership.

Exodus 15:1–21

The Songs at the Sea

The Torah is comprised primarily of four types of literature: narratives, legal portions, prophecies/exhortations, and poetry/song.[1] One of the special features of the Torah is that they are interwoven in a single work, suggesting that are all interconnected, so that, for example, the legal sections and the narratives depend on each other. Poetry comprises the smallest portion of the three genres and is also linked to the narratives surrounding it. For example, Lemech's song (Gen. 4:23–24) is an integral part of the surrounding narrative, and each is incomprehensible without the other.

There are occasions, however, where the song is side by side with a narrative which seems complete on its own. The song of *Haazinu* (Deut. 32) is one example. The texts describing the covenant with God and the implications of adhering to it or departing from it are clearly explicated in Deut. 27–31; the song following it seems unnecessary. Similarly, the battle describing Sisera's defeat (Judges 4) seems complete, yet it is followed by an extended poetic version of those events (Judges 5).

1. One of the sections of the Bible, the Writings, adds philosophical explorations, also known as wisdom literature.

The story of the Exodus seems fairly complete, yet it is followed by a lengthy poetic version. These draw our attention, forcing us to explore the nature and value of the song.

To be sure, songs express emotion and can be used to generate emotion. Songs are powerful vehicles for creating moments of inspiration. Songs, both because of the attached music and because of the structure of writing, are often easier to commit to memory. In the Bible, especially when they are attached to what appears to be a complete narrative, songs often serve an additional function of adding perspective.

It is highly likely that the Israelites were filled with awe as they watched the sea split for them and then close behind them. It is fair to assume that there was a collective sigh of relief and gratitude when they understood that the mighty Egyptian army was no longer, and that they would never again be pursued by their former oppressors. We can even imagine a strange silence in the camp as the waters of the Reed Sea returned to themselves, and to be sure, the Song of the Sea would have rung out as a powerful expression of awe, relief, and gratitude all mixed together. Missing, however, is an understanding of the significance – or omni-significance – of the event beyond the immediate time and place in which it happened. What does the Splitting of the Sea mean for Israel beyond the completion of their exit from Egypt? What does it mean for the destiny of Israel? What does it mean for other nations which were neither present nor a party to the events? What are the implications of this event for God and His ultimate hopes and dreams for humanity? All of those served are by the song.

ABOUT THE SONG

Before we explore the macro message of the song, it is worthwhile making a few observations about the way it is written. First, we should notice what it includes and what it does not. Most victory songs highlight the hero, and this does not disappoint. The name A-donai, the One God revealed to Moses and whom Pharaoh said he did not recognize, appears eleven times and is the prominent word in the entire poem. Completely absent from the song is Moses's name. Normally, we would not necessarily be surprised by this, but in the context of the previous chapter, in which Moses and his hand are accorded superhuman status, his absence in this song makes a powerful statement that it is not he, but God, who is the hero of this story.

In a similar vein, we might have expected Pharaoh's name to be featured prominently in the song, as he is the prime villain in the story. Quite the opposite is true; Pharaoh appears once in the song and one additional time in the closing summary. Similarly, Egypt doesn't appear at all. By contrast, in Exodus 14, the previous chapter containing the narrative of the story, Pharaoh is mentioned eleven times and Egypt twenty-six! The emphasis in the song emerges clearly as not on the annihilation of the foe but on the glorification of God.[2]

The song includes many words which appear only once, including the word for strength (*koaḥ*), drown (*tubu*), song (*zimrat*), sword (*ḥerev*), war (*milḥama*), army (*ḥayil*), and fear/awe (*yira*). Some of these appear multiple times in the previous chapter, especially the ones related to the Egyptian military might, so that their de-emphasis in this chapter indicates that the demise of the Egyptians is not the primary focus of the song. Speaking more broadly, however, it seems like the song highlights the richness of the vocabulary of its author, who found synonyms for many of the words so that they did not have to be repeated.[3] One of the words in the opening, *ve'anvehu* (15:2), is unique – it appears nowhere else in the entire Bible. Its meaning, "I will glorify Him," is

2. It is interesting that in the narrative of the story Pharaoh appears eleven times, but in the song, it is A-donai who appears eleven times. It is also interesting that in the narrative, Egypt's name appears twenty-six times, which is the numerical equivalent of *YHVH* (A-donai). Aside from God's name, the most prominent word in the song is the word for sea, *yam*.
3. There are more than a dozen words which appear twice, including horse (*sus*), strength (*oz*), chariot (*rekhev*), like You (*kamokha*), stone (*even*), depths (*tehom*), wind/breath (*ruaḥ*), mighty (*ne'edar*), enemy (*oyev*). One of those, *gaa*, meaning to rise up or be exalted, and is used to describe God in the opening line (15:1), is used in Psalms (89:10) to describe the cresting tide, rendering our verse to be saying that the cresting tide which swamped the Egyptians was God's doing. The word for strength, *oz*, is attached in 15:13 to the word for to guide, or to lead (*nehalta*). The word *lenahel* is often used in the Bible to describe guiding sheep, or in metaphors for leadership in which the people being guided are compared to sheep (Gen. 33:14; Is. 40:11, 49:10; and Ps. 23:2). Its use here, with the adverb associated with strength, transforms God's guidance from the gentle guiding of sheep into a guiding of strength.

derived exclusively from the context and from its parallel phrase at the closing of that verse.[4]

What emerges is a beautiful artistry in the poem downplaying Egypt and Pharaoh while highlighting God as the sole mover in the story. With so much emphasis in the story about the battle with Pharaoh and the need to humble or teach him and the Egyptians, the poem represents a dramatic shift away from Pharaoh and Egypt. Pharaoh is a backstory. Egypt is irrelevant. From this point on God takes center stage.

FOUR-PHASED POEM

The relative lack of repetition of words in the song is contrasted with three verses which are recognizably repetitive, and it is those repeated verses which mark the division of the song into sections. The end of the first section highlights God's right hand – "Your right hand, God, is mighty in power; Your right hand smashes the enemy" (15:6). The end of the second section is marked by one of the rare instances in which a rhetorical question is not a form of rebuke – "Who is like You among the powerful, O God? Who is like You, mighty in holiness?" (15:10). The end of the third section focuses on Israel's ultimate entry into their land – "Until Your people cross over, O God; until the people You made Yours cross over" (15:16). The fourth section closes with the end of the song, which does not have a doublet but is a verse with three parts, each of which closes with the same word – *hayam* (the sea).[5]

---

4. This understanding of the word is influenced by the talmudic reading (Shabbat 133b) of it, which understands that it refers to beautifying the mitzvot. This is also the reading of Rashbam, Bekhor Shor, and Rabbi Luzzatto. Many of the traditional commentators, including Ibn Ezra and Nahmanides, understand it to mean "I will enshrine God."
5. The Song of the Sea is included in the daily prayers. In most siddurim, the penultimate verse is repeated (15:18), apparently to complete the pattern established by the first three stanzas. In the Torah scroll, poetry is written differently than prose and generally takes one of two forms:

   xxxxxxx   xxxxxxxx
   xxxxxxx   xxxxxxxx
   xxxxxxx   xxxxxxxx
   xxxxxxx   xxxxxxxx

With the parts of the song demarcated, we can now explore the theme of each stanza. In the first, the poet writes about himself in the first person and about God in the third. Thus, we have (italics are added to highlight the speaker and the reference to God):

> *My* strength and *my* power is God;
> *He* became *my* deliverance.
> This is *my* God and *I* glorify *Him*;
> God of my fathers and *I* exalt *Him*.
> God is a man of war; A-donai is *His* name.
> Pharaoh's chariots and his army;
> *He* flung into the sea. (15:2–4)

Notice that we repeatedly hear the poet's voice – he is the one who will be praising God (future tense) for what God did for him, namely, the destruction of Pharaoh and his forces. At the same time, he is not speaking *to* God but *about* God in the third person. God is still distant, and the poet is preparing himself to engage in song.

This shifts as we move into the second stanza. The first person of the poet disappears; it is replaced by the praises themselves. And those

---

or

xxxx xxxxxxxx xxxx
xxxxxxx xxxxxxxx
xxxx xxxxxxxx xxxx
xxxxxxx xxxxxxxx

The song of *Haazinu* is written in the first form; the Song of the Sea is written in the second. One fascinating feature of the Song of the Sea is that in lines written as xxxx xxxxxxxx xxxx, the middle section stands as a grammatically correct phrase which can stand on its own. That is true for every one of those lines with the exception of the final one, in which the middle section reads, "and the Israelites traveled on the dry land in the middle of," presenting a puzzle. If we broaden our vision, we notice that the first and last words of that final line are the same word, *hayam* (the sea), so that the line, in its totality, looks like this:

the sea   and the Israelites traveled on the dry land in the middle of   the sea.

Thus, the sea stands to their right and to their left as the Israelites traveled on the dry land between those two walls. It should be noted that the structure of the last line appears differently in the Leningrad Codex.

praises are not about God, but they address God directly, in the second person (again, italics added for illustration):

> In *Your* great rising *You* smash those who rise up against *You*; *You* send out *Your* wrath which consumed them like straw.
> And with the breath of *Your* nostrils the waters piled up; they stood like a pillar of liquid; the depths froze in the heart of the sea.
> The enemy had said: "I'll pursue, I'll catch, I'll divide up the spoils; I'll be filled by them; I'll unsheathe my sword; my hand will dispossess them.
> But *You* blew *Your* breath – the sea covered them; they sank like lead in the mighty waters. (15:7–10)

Notice that the poet's voice is gone. He already introduced himself, and now we just hear the praises; now they are spoken directly *to* God and not merely *about* Him. And the focus is not on this individual being saved by God, but on God's power to effortlessly bring down the arrogant, as Isaiah expresses it: "The eyes of human haughtiness are brought down and men's arrogance be lowered, and God alone will be raised high on that day" (Is. 2:11). Further, this second paragraph highlights that God suspended the laws of nature – waters stood tall or crashed down with only the slightest breath from God. The shift from the first stanza to the second is the shift from acknowledgment of God's help in a personal salvation to a broader recognition of God's unstoppable power over nature and man.

This movement continues into the third stanza. The focus is no longer on Pharaoh or Egypt or salvation. It is no longer on God's power over nature in some remote location. Rather, what impact does this have on the broader world? How does this affect humanity beyond the characters present in the scene? Here is the song's answer:

> In Your kindness You led this people that You redeemed; You guided them with Your strength to Your sacred abode. Nations heard and quaked; trembling seized those who live in Philistia.
> Then the chiefs of Edom were terrified; the mighty ones of Moab were seized by shuddering; all those who live in Canaan melted.

> Terror and fear fell over them; in facing the might of Your arm they fell silent as a stone. (15:13–16)

The perspective has changed dramatically. The events at the Reed Sea generated a virtual earthquake throughout the entire region. All the nations inhabiting lands that Israel was to pass through or settle into were filled with terror.

There are two implications to this new perspective. First, on a practical level, it will ease the passage of Israel into their land. As the song continues, "Until Your people cross over, O God; until the people You made Yours cross over" (15:16). No one would dare stand in the face of a people protected by such a God; no nation would want to bring upon itself the fate that befell Egypt. This, essentially, was the message that Rahab gave to the two Israelite spies in Jericho, forty years later:

> I know that God has given you the land, and that your terror has fallen upon us, and that all those who live in the land have melted before you. For we have heard how God dried up the Reed Sea before you when you came out of Egypt. (Josh. 2:9–10)

Beyond the practical level is the theological one. God entered this story not only to redeem Israel but to provide a restart to the world. It needed to be reintroduced to Him so that people could reclaim their path of morality, justice, and righteousness. This third stanza of the poem explicitly acknowledges the beginning of that restart on a scale far greater than the saving of Israel and defeat of their oppressor.

Which brings us to the final, climactic stanza, in which Moses moves from the global significance of the event to a historic – perhaps even cosmic – perspective. This event will not just ease Israel's passage and entry into their land and will not just bring about a broader acknowledgment of God, but will be an important step in establishing God's permanent dominion in the world as the uncontested King:

> You will bring them to and plant them in the mountain of Your heritage, the foundation of Your seat which You, God, have made – the sanctum,[6] God, which Your hands founded.
> God will reign for all eternity! (15:17–18)

The narrative story of the Exodus includes the difficulty of bringing Pharaoh and Egypt to recognizing God, the challenge of cultivating trust within Israel, and Moses's continuing struggle to believe in himself. It closes with Egypt proclaiming God's hand, with Israel's moment of faith, and with Moses's confident assumption of leadership – all within the context of the salvation of Israel and the end of Egypt as a meaningful force in the life of Israel. The song takes us much further. It begins with God's mighty hand at the sea and moves us to understand the broader implications, both in place and in history. Israel will arrive bloodlessly in their promised land[7] where it will settle and be planted firmly, and God is recognized universally and eternally as Sovereign.

A SECOND SONG

Moses's song is followed by a second, brief one, led by his sister, Miriam.

> Miriam, the prophetess, Aaron's sister, took the timbrel in her hand, and all the women went out and followed her with timbrels and dancing. Miriam led them responsively: "Sing to God for He has triumphed; the horse and its rider He flung into the sea." (15:20–21)

A simple reading of the Torah understands Miriam's song occurring in parallel to that of Moses; just as he leads the men and they respond, Miriam is doing the same for the women.[8] A closer reading, however, opens up some questions.

---

6. Most commentators understand this as referring to the Temple. I did not follow that route because it is unreasonable to suggest that at this point, Moses would have any foreknowledge about the Temple.
7. This idea is echoed in Numbers 10:35: "As the Ark journeyed, Moses would say, 'Rise, God; let Your enemies scatter and Your foes flee before You.'"
8. There are a number of variations on this. Rashi and Bekhor Shor understand that

First, why is there a need to have a separate "women's service"? Until this point there is no distinction in the entire book between the roles of men and women, with the exception of female heroism in the first two chapters. Had the Torah not mentioned Miriam, we would have no reason to believe that the women weren't part of the song alongside the men, just as they are indistinguishable from the men throughout the plagues, the night of the *pesaḥ*, the Exodus, and the salvation at the sea.[9]

Second, Miram's song appears to be slightly different from the men's song in two aspects. One is the accompaniment of musical instruments and dancing.[10] The second is a nuance in the opening line – where Moses says, "I will sing," Miriam calls to the women, "Sing!"[11]

Third, the introduction to Miriam's song indicates that the women "went out," but it is not clear what they went out of or why they went out.

Fourth, the description of Miriam is highly unusual. She is described first as a prophetess, something of which we were previously unaware, and second as Aaron's sister. Moses is the key figure throughout the scene at the sea – it is his arm with the staff that they all watch,

Miriam leads the women in parallel to Moses leading the men, so that they are each calling out the same song to their respondents. Rabbi Yitzhak Shmuel Reggio and Cassuto suggest that Miriam led the women in response to the men's response. All seem to agree that even though only the first line of the song is recorded, the women's recitation included the complete song as recorded for the men. As for what the respondents each said, this is debated in the Mishna (Sota 5:4). R. Akiva there suggests that the men repeated the refrain "I will sing to God for He has triumphed; the horse and its rider He flung into the sea" after each line of the song; R. Eliezer b. R. Yosi HaGelili understands that they repeated the entire song line by line after Moses; R. Neḥemya opines that, since this song was a product of divine inspiration, that divine spirit filled all of Israel who sang together with Moses.

9. The Talmud (Megilla 4a; Shabbat 23a; Pesaḥim 108a) establishes a principle that where women were involved in the same miracle as men, the halakhic requirements emanating from that miracle are equally incumbent on women as they are on men. The reference from Pesaḥim is especially relevant, because it is there that the Talmud establishes women's requirements for the Seder as indistinguishable from those for men.
10. Cassuto believe that the word *meḥolot* here does not refer to dancing but to a different musical instrument.
11. *Ho'il Moshe* suggests that the women were responding to the men's song, encouraging them to sing.

it is his unadorned arm which splits the sea, it is he who we are told that the people trust alongside God, and it is he who leads the nation in prayer. Why, then, is she identified as Aaron's sister and not Moses's?[12]

WHAT INSPIRES MIRIAM?

When we scan the Torah we find that Miriam is active in three contexts. In the first, where she is not mentioned by name, she is ensuring the safety of her baby brother after he is placed into the basket on the riverside (2:4–8). The Song of the Sea is the second, in which she is mirroring Moses's song. In the third (Numbers 12, where she is mentioned six times), she and Aaron are criticizing Moses's behavior and equating themselves to him.[13]

Her cameo appearance, albeit anonymous, paints her in an unquestionably positive light. She is patient, protective, creative, and wise as she masterfully negotiates the return of her baby brother to his mother to be nursed. The final time we hear from her she is painted in unambiguously negative terms. She speaks ill of her brother Moses, relates to him as fundamentally no different from herself, and is punished by God. Aaron, her older brother, is dragged in as well, and he suffers as he witnesses her awful punishment, the defiling *tzaraat* which requires her to be banished from the camp for a full seven days. All this raises the question of what the Torah is trying to say about her in this middle story. Is this a continuation of the Miriam we saw earlier, Moses's sister – caring, supportive, protective, and wise? Or is it a prelude to Miriam as Aaron's sister – seeing herself as a prophetess equal to Moses, just as Aaron is a prophet? We should note that Aaron was earlier identified by God as Moses's prophet (7:1), but Moses has not yet been identified as such.

12. Medieval commentaries offer a range of explanations to this question. Rashi offers two different explanations, which is often an indication that he is unhappy with each. Ibn Ezra also offers two possibilities. Rashbam and Bekhor Shor suggest that it was standard practice to identify a woman in relation to her older brother. Nahmanides offers that once the Torah mentions Moses and Miriam, it would be embarrassing for Aaron not to be mentioned as well.
13. She is mentioned two other times in the Torah, once when she dies (Num. 20:1) and again in the genealogical tree of Levi (Num. 26:59).

If we step back for a moment to consider what could justify viewing Miriam's actions suspiciously, we need to look no further than how the story might appear from her perspective. She doted on her baby brother, ensuring that he would be taken care of appropriately, both when he was floating in the water and after he was rescued by Pharaoh's daughter. But when he was finally weaned, he was brought to Pharaoh's daughter and was raised in royalty. There is no indication of subsequent contact between the birth family and the adoptive one, and she watched from a distance as her brother grew up as a stranger to her people. At one point rumors flew in the Israelite camp about an Egyptian prince who killed one of the taskmasters and then fled for his life. Before Moses returns, at the age of eighty (!), he has had no contact with Miriam for nearly her entire life – she probably has no clue as to what happened to her little brother. When he finally does return, it is likely difficult for Miriam to wrap her head around the idea that her long-lost brother, raised in the Egyptian palace and who later disappeared, is now a man of God returning to redeem his estranged people from Egyptian bondage. It sounds too unreal, too much like fantasy.

This same kind of perspective shift, looking from Miriam's vantage point, reveals a new understanding of her later reaction to Moses's Ethiopian wife when Miriam explicitly challenges Moses's uniqueness (Num. 12). That story is not the first time that people encounter a foreign woman married to Moses. Imagine that just a few weeks after the Exodus a Midianite priest arrives claiming to be Moses's father-in-law, bringing in tow a woman he claims to be Moses's wife and two children he fathered. At some point afterward there is an Ethiopian woman[14] also claiming to be Moses's wife. Miriam is challenged to understand who her brother is. Is he the man of God who humbled Pharaoh, split the sea, and brought the Torah to Israel after surviving forty days and nights on the mountain without food and water, or he is a man who has married at least two foreign woman and who knows how many more? Miriam's confusion about her brother only intensifies with time – as his status

14. Rashbam (Num. 12:1) cites "The Chronicles of Moses Our Teacher," a medieval midrashic work, which suggests that Moses spent forty years as a king in the Egyptian province of Ethiopia, and that the woman described is his wife from then.

as a man of God is confirmed it is accompanied by conflicting images, whether inspired by childhood memories or the revelations of suspicious marital relationships.

Is it possible that it is this Miriam, the one who is somewhat skeptical, who is leading the women in song? Could her song be an attempt to reclaim the heroic role that women played in the early phases of the Exodus, whether the brave midwives of chapter 1 who dared to defy Pharaoh or the cunning ones of chapter 2 who conspired to save a single Hebrew boy? Note that she sings differently than Moses does – he places himself as the song leader ("I will sing") while she leads the women to sing together collaboratively ("Sing!"). She leads the women "out" into a public display accompanied by instruments and dance, potentially outshining Moses's song.

Standing on the edge of the sea, she is reminded of the last time she stood at the edge of the water, guarding her infant brother, and of the righteous, rebellious women who conspired to save the baby who later turns out to be the hero of the story.[15] This might explain why her name is revealed to us here for the first time; Miriam could be read as *Meri yam*, "rebellious at the sea."[16] It is not a rebellion against Moses, but rather an attempt to reclaim the voices – literally and figuratively – of the forgotten heroines.

INSPIRATION MEETS REALITY

Movements, however noble, often take on a life of their own. Noble motives get mixed with darker ones, sometimes consciously and sometimes unconsciously. Consider the possibility that the intention of a noble rebellion of *Meri yam* becomes tinged by the bitterness of being eclipsed by a younger brother who defies understanding. Miriam could easily be rendered as *Mar yam*, the one who was bitter at the sea. In fact, the very next incident speaks of an entire people who encounter bitter waters, waters which are *marim*, ironically spelled identically to Miriam's name. Is it possible that Miriam's attempt to reclaim the voices

15. The Talmud (Sota 11b) records R. Avira as claiming the merit of the righteous women is what earned Israel its redemption from Egypt.
16. The word *miryam* meaning "their rebellion" is used in Neh. 9:17.

of the women saviors was somehow influenced by other, less noble, considerations? That would make Miriam very human, very much like the rest of us. From a literary perspective, Miriam's song functions as a transition between Moses's glorious Song of the Sea and a chapter filled with complaints – the water is bitter, there is no food, there is insufficient water. Those complaints may be justified, but considering what Israel just experienced they provide cause for reflection. It is amazing that wondrous, uplifting, exquisite moments like the exodus of an entire nation from slavery and the Splitting of the Sea can be undone by mundane concerns like "I'm thirsty" and "What's for lunch?" – and yet that is often the case. Certain individuals may be able to ignore the rumbling in their bellies, but for the masses to be able to soar, their basic needs need to be met. Perhaps Miriam's song is neither the harmony to Moses's nor a competing instrument, but an important reality check for those whose heads are in the clouds.

The songs at the sea provide a broader picture of the significance of the event. Pharaoh and Egypt, so dominant in the first fourteen chapters of Exodus, are no longer relevant to the story of Israel. They are part of Israel's past, but not its present or future. The songs reveal that the Splitting of the Sea has cosmic significance, not only for the story of the one nation which benefited from it directly but for all of humanity, which is reawakened to God's active presence in the affairs of humanity and willingness to exercise that presence. The events at the sea have the potential to be transformative in laying the groundwork for the ultimate restoration of God as Master of world, and the redemption of all people as they internalize the message of the return of the Creator. Miriam's song may be the counterpart to that, the grounding of a grand and cosmic vision in the reality of the everyday. Moses's song needs Miriam's to be able to translate a pristine ideal into a reality which works for real people, those with desires and needs, and who must contend with the range of emotions that make us who we are as humans. Indeed, the challenge of dealing with a people who live very much in the practicalities of this world will haunt Moses and God for a long time.

Exodus 15:22–17:7

What Do We Do Now?

There is a well-known phenomenon involving special events – weddings, formal ceremonies, big parties, trips, etc. We invest extraordinary effort and time planning, which generates considerable excitement in anticipation of the event. The event often speeds past us like a whirlwind, and then there is the day after. Having experienced the thrill of the moment, we feel an emotional letdown which accompanies the afterglow. Physically and emotionally spent, and used to being in the frenzy of preparation, the lack of a clearly defined mission or objective can lead us to a feeling of aimlessness accompanied by the question "What do we do now?"

The first eleven chapters of Exodus describe the descent into slavery and the seemingly endless battle to free the slaves. Chapters 12 and 13 describe the exacting preparations to leave and their march out of bondage, and are followed by the climactic events at the sea. As the sea returns to its normal self, the air is filled with the quiet lapping of the waves on the shore. Egypt is gone. Israel is free. The drama is over. What do we do now?

The tumult of the events at the sea is replaced by the creeping reality that there is no return accompanied by a rush of real and very practical questions. Where do we go next? What do we eat and drink? As individuals used to taking orders and working, what do we do? As a people whose identity has been defined by their masters as what they are not – not Egyptians, not free – they now ask, "Who are we?"

As recently freed slaves these people are used to having others make decisions for them and perhaps even to provide for their basic needs. The uneasy feeling of being uprooted from the only world they knew with no path back already puts them in a state of anxiety and is compounded by the reality of being stranded in the wilderness. The grand vision of liberation and restoring God's dominion in the world is inspiring, but it doesn't fill a hungry belly. The practical day-to-day problems of food and water catch the leaders of this newly born nation by surprise and repeatedly threaten to derail God's plan for Israel. Those problems are very real, and the complaints about them are quite reasonable. How will they survive without water, especially in the wilderness? How long can the food supply they brought from Egypt sustain them?

The grumbling frustrates Moses. After all, how can people be so small-minded when they've just witnessed God's hand? Add to that he has no prior experience feeding a mass of people, so that even Moses – with his vast experience in the wilderness – who may be able to take care of himself and his sheep, is ill-equipped to provide solutions to the problems at hand. And if God does not clue him in in advance, how is he to know how to respond?

Even more, while in Egypt, Moses had a clear game plan. He was to go to Pharaoh, make a request/demand, and God would respond when Pharaoh disappointed. Now that that cycle has ended, Moses has no direction. What will his next step be in bringing them into the land he promised them? With no leadership experience, he has little idea of even what is involved in leading the people, not to mention how to implement any of it. He has no clear picture of what he needs to do, either proactively or reactively.

These are the real challenges facing the nascent nation and its emerging leader. The Torah describes four incidents in rapid succession, each of which reflects grappling with these issues. We will investigate them individually, looking at reactions by the people, by Moses, and by God, before looking at the broader picture the Torah is painting.

BITTER WATER

The first incident focuses on water.

> Moses moved Israel from the Reed Sea; they went out to the Wilderness of Shur. They traveled for three days in the wilderness and found no water. When they arrived in Mara they were unable to drink the water from Mara because they were bitter (*mar*) – that's why they called it Mara. The people grumbled against Moses saying, "What shall we drink?" Moses cried out to God, and God taught[1] him a tree. When Moses cast it into the water, the water sweetened. It was there that God gave him a rule and justice and tested him. He said: "If you heed the voice of A-donai, your God, and you do what is proper in His eyes, and you hearken to His commands and keep all His rules, then all the sickness that I placed against Egypt I will not place upon you, for I am God, your healer." They came to Elim, and there were twelve springs of water and seventy palms, and they camped there by the water. (15:22–27)

This brief passage is unusually puzzling. The emphasis on bitterness, highlighted four times in a single verse (15:23); Moses's cry to God (reminiscent of his reaction after being challenged by Israel at the Reed Sea – 14:15); God "teaching" Moses a tree which, when cast into the water, magically cleanses it for drinking; the "rule and justice" that God gave; God's test; the proclamation about saving Israel from the illnesses God brought to Egypt; the subsequent trip to Elim – almost every sentence in this incident demands an explanation.

Indeed, the traditional commentators struggle greatly with each of these pieces, trying to figure out what they mean individually and how the disparate pieces fit together. For example, some[2] say that the tree was naturally bitter, compounding the miracle that a bitter tree could turn bitter waters into sweet; others[3] argue that the tree had

1. The Hebrew reads, *vayorehu*, literally meaning to teach. It sounds similar to and is apparently sometimes confused with *vayarehu*, which would mean to show.
2. *Midrash Lekaḥ Tov*.
3. Rabbi Yitzhak Shmuel Reggio, Rabbi Shmuel David Luzzatto, and Cassuto.

natural qualities of purification which God taught Moses; and others[4] suggest that the tree was irrelevant as God can sweeten bitter waters without sticks of wood. Regarding the rule and the justice, which some read as "the statute and the laws," the text is obscure. Some traditional commentators understand these as a sampling of the laws Israel will later receive, so that this is a testing ground for their ability to adhere to God's commands, and even offer suggestions as to which laws these are,[5] while others understand this as a general reference to God preparing Israel for their new existence in the wilderness.[6] The notion of the test and the comment about the illnesses in Egypt and God as their healer seem disconnected from the rest of the passage and lack context.

While I have no presumption to offer solutions to all these difficulties, I believe that the passage is nonetheless significant and instructive, especially as we explore other questions which it raises. Let's begin with the question of why God did not provide them with water to begin with. Should He not have tried to preempt the difficulties before they started? Moses was apparently troubled with this question as well. In one of his final orations, as he reflects on the Israelite experience in the wilderness, Moses says:

> He afflicted you and made you hunger and fed you the manna which neither you nor your fathers knew, so that you should know that man does not live by bread alone but man lives on everything which God speaks. (Deut. 8:3)

Later in that oration, describing God's leadership of Israel in the wilderness, he adds:

4. Bekhor Shor.
5. Conflating a number of rabbinic traditions, Rashi suggests that they were given the laws of Shabbat, the red heifer, and honoring parents – all for the purposes of study. In Mekhilta, one opinion understands that they were given the commands of Shabbat and honoring parents while a different one suggests that they were instructed regarding forbidden sexual encounters and various monetary punishments.
6. Rashbam and Nahmanides.

> [God] who brought you out of the land of Egypt, the house of slaves. Who leads you through the great and terrible wilderness – [filled with] fiery serpents and scorpions – and thirst, for there is no water. Who brings water out of the flint rock. Who feeds you manna in the wilderness which your fathers did not know, in order to afflict you and in order to test you, so that it should go well for you in your future. (Deut. 8:14–16)

In retrospect, Moses understands that the lack of water (and later, food) was intentional and purposeful. God wanted Israel to experience and fully understand the nature of the wilderness that they were in – that it was inherently unsurvivable for a large group without divine intervention. As a group of freed slaves who were used to being dependent on their Egyptian masters for their sustenance, it would have been nearly impossible for them to transition so quickly into self-reliance. As part of their transition, then, God shifted their dependence from a malevolent monarch interested in ensuring that his own needs are cared for to a benevolent king interested in caring for and nurturing His people as a step toward ultimately weaning them from that dependence.

That process, designed to prepare Israel for a future of independence, serves an additional function – it helps Israel to learn that all their toil, as necessary as it will be in order to achieve that independence, should not seduce them into believing that they, alone, are the source of their success. God hopes that their temporary but complete dependence on Him will begin the process of building a bond with Him, one which will survive long beyond their time in the wilderness. In that light, the word *nisayon,* usually translated as "test," should be understood instead as experience. God puts Israel through experiences which are designed to help them grow, "so that it should go well for you in the future."[7]

That is Moses's understanding looking back, with the benefit of forty years of experience. In the moment, however, he also needs to learn – not about depending on God but about his leadership of the people. We recall that prior to the Splitting of the Sea Moses cries out to God, and God rebukes him for that: "Why are you crying out to

7. Similarly, see Judges 3:1 and I Sam. 17:39.

Me?" Soon after their departure from the sea, as they hit their first sign of trouble, the people grumble against Moses, and his response, once again, is to cry out to God. Rather than rebuke him, God "teaches" him the tree. Whatever that tree might have been and however it may have worked, the key is recognizing that this is a learning moment for Moses. God teaches him to deal with challenging situations rather than simply taking care of them for him.

Perhaps this is connected to the puzzling verse which follows: "God gave him a rule and justice and tested him." While most commentators understand that it is referring to Israel, a simple reading of the text suggests that it is more likely referring to Moses himself. In fact, throughout this passage, Israel is referred to in the plural: "*They* went out to the Wilderness of Shur. *They* traveled for three days in the wilderness and found no water. When *they* arrived in Mara *they* were unable to drink the water from Mara because they were bitter (*mar*) – that's why *they* called it Mara. The *people grumbled* against Moses saying, 'What shall *we* drink?'" By contrast, the rule and the justice were given to *him*, not to *them*. In context, this would mean that "the rule and the justice" were part of the lesson God taught Moses about leading the people, and that this was a learning experience ("test") for Moses.[8]

After both Moses and Israel learned their respective lessons, they travel to Elim where there is plentiful water. Ironically, Israel's learning is one of dependence on God, while Moses's is one of independence from Him. Moses's lesson of independence is given opportunity for immediate expression as he finds the oasis from which the people can drink.

FOOD: THE COMPLAINT

Exactly one month after leaving Egypt, having left the oasis at Elim, the people's need for food takes center stage. Better to be well-fed slaves than starving free people, they argue, as they remember Egypt with its abundance. That reasonable argument is also quite revealing. People who were deeply committed to achieving their freedom and fought fiercely for it are less likely to be prepared to give it up quickly for food

8. Ibn Ezra was aware of this suggestion but rejected it.

security. While it is true that Israel cried out in anguish over their servitude and were willing to heed Moses's instructions preparing to leave Egypt, they were not actively engaged in the struggle to go free. In fact, when Moses's initial approach backfired, the home-grown leaders of the Hebrews challenged Moses and Aaron, charging them with worsening the lot of Israel, and while Moses battled Pharaoh for the people's release throughout the plagues, we hear little from the nation he is trying to free. The gift of freedom, handed to them on a silver platter, will be undervalued unless they fight for it.

This echoes a change that took place in Genesis. God created a world and entrusted its care and development to the humans He created: "Be fruitful and multiply, fill the earth and conquer it; dominate the fish of the sea, the birds of the sky, and all the animals which move on the land" (Gen. 1:28). Handed all of creation on a silver platter, humans abused it, so that in the span of ten generations God concluded that He had no choice but to undo the very creation He had handed over to people. "God saw the land, and behold, it was corrupted, because all flesh had corrupted its way on the land" (Gen. 6:12). As God re-creates the world, one of the core differences He makes is that Noah and his family are responsible for partnering with Him in that re-creation. It was they who preserved the plants and animals on the ark; it was they who cared for and tended to all living beings from the time the Great Confusion began until they left the ark and reintroduced their charges back into the world. God hoped that having them partner with Him in the re-creation would help them learn to care better for the world.

Israel's nonchalant approach to their freedom after the Exodus is similarly the product of their non-involvement in achieving it. This is not slave mentality, which they will ultimately need to shed to become truly free, but likely touches on something more subtle and yet more insidious. Complacency is the enemy of progress, as the famous quip goes, "Good enough" is the enemy of excellence. Missing from the people is the sense that freedom is important to them, that their lives are worth living for a purpose beyond their individual survival and continuity. People who are driven to accomplish a high goal – finishing a project, creating a work of art, caring for a loved one – will overlook or suppress their own physiological needs.[9] They can go for days or weeks on end barely eating and sleeping, driven by something that motivates them. But in the absence of inspiration to a greater goal, Abraham Maslow's hierarchy of needs takes over. We cannot begin to aspire toward higher ideals when we are consumed by insecurity and hunger.[10] Israel had not invested in their freedom; they were not driven by lofty spiritual or national goals. Until that is cultivated, Moses will need to deal with the nitty-gritty of daily life that occupies his people's minds.

BREAD AND MEAT[11]

Even before Moses can turn to God, God responds to Israel's complaint.

> God said to Moses: "I will shower you with bread from heaven; the people will go out and collect their daily portions, so that I can test to see if they will follow My instructions or not. But on the sixth day, they should prepare what they bring in; it will be double their regular daily collection. (16:4–5)

Several key ideas highlight God's initial response. First, God is not upset by the people's complaint, just as He showed no frustration with the people when they earlier complained about the pursuing Egyptians or about the bitter water. This is for the simple reason that, even though the people may have expressed themselves in unpleasant tones and used unfortunate language, their complaints are fundamentally legitimate. They are taken out of Egypt under the impression that they are going free; to their horror, they find themselves pursued by the full force of Pharaoh's military. They traverse the sea, which blocked any reasonable return path, only to discover that the wilderness is more dangerous than the Egyptians, as the wilderness has no capacity for compassion and

9. This idea is at the core of Viktor Frankl's *Man's Search for Meaning*.
10. See Abraham H. Maslow, "A Theory of Human Motivation," *Psychological Review* 50, no. 4: 370–96, and *Motivation and Personality* (Harper and Row, 1954).
11. My reading here is based on the way the text is written. Ibn Ezra (16:12) and Rashbam (16:11), and in their footsteps Rabbi David Zvi Hoffmann (16:12), reorganize the chronology of this story. Nahmanides (16:12) follows the chronology as written but offers a different interpretation.

there is no possibility of fighting it. They had camped in a place which provided food, but when they move from there they are justifiably hungry, and anxious about that hunger, as they experience profound food insecurity. Hence there is not even a hint of rancor in God's response.

Second, the daily portion is intended to not only build a sense of being able to trust God, but also to provide – once they get used to it – a sense of personal food security.[12] That personal security comes at the expense of communal bonding which often takes place over food, as their food cannot be shared, but the personal security it affords reduces wariness and builds a kind openness and acceptance which can help relationships to grow. Third, the daily per-person allotment also functions to level the economic playing field – everyone gets the same thing. Even more, as the text will later explicate, the inability to store it overnight is intended to remove any possibility of hoarding or transacting – it has no value beyond the immediate, and no one can use it as a tool for amassing wealth.[13] Fourth, while there is no explicit mention of Shabbat, God is preparing the foundation for the idea that every seventh day will be different, and that the sixth day should be used to prepare for the seventh. For a slave people, the notion of preparing for the future is a new experience, and God wants to begin to build that into their personal and cultural consciousness. Fifth, as in the incident of the bitter waters, God speaks of a "test" – and just as there we understood it as a form of providing for a growth experience, the same could be said here. This is God's preliminary foray into providing Israel with rules which will train them to follow directives that they do not as yet understand but which will ultimately prove to be incredibly valuable.

---

12. It should be noted that in God's plan, their trip to the Promised Land would have been short, so that the manna would have been a temporary fix until they could begin farming their new land. This supports my formulation of the desired goal as learning to trust God rather than a formulation which would focus on having them become dependent on God. There is little evidence to support that God wants Israel's dependence; in fact, when they arrive in the land, He wants them to produce their own food. Within that independence, however, God does desire a relationship with the people, which is quite different from dependence.
13. As Kass (*Founding God's Nation*, 237) points out, this prevents the concentration of wealth and power which marked Joseph's legacy in Egypt.

Sixth, Israel's experience of God until this point has been primarily one of destructive power – inflicting punishing plagues upon the Egyptians and crushing the Egyptians in the sea. The manna introduces them to God as a nurturer and provider.[14]

God's response is only one part of the initial reaction to Israel's complaint; the other parts are in the responses of Moses and Aaron, and there are three of them – one joint response, one response to the people by Moses, and one instruction Moses gives to Aaron.

The joint response of Moses and Aaron is filled with surprises. Whereas God had promised "bread from the heavens," Moses and Aaron speak of two responses by God, one in the evening in which Israel will "know" that it was God who took them out of Egypt, and a second one in the morning in which God's glory will be revealed to them. It is fascinating that Moses and Aaron do not even mention God's promise of food, and instead seem to be intent on deflecting the people's complaints from themselves to God. In fact, as they conclude their joint statement, they say this explicitly: "And as for us, what are we that you should be complaining to us?" (16:7).

It is this deflection of responsibility which also highlights Moses's individual response which follows. Even as he tells the people about the food, he concludes with an almost verbatim repetition of his concluding line: "And as for us, what are we? Your complaint is not upon us but upon God" (16:8). But Moses's response brings with it an addition, a surprise, as he tells them, the people – in an apparent clarification of his earlier joint statement with Aaron – that God will bring for them meat in the evening and bread in the morning. That meat was not mentioned at all in God's promise and appears to be something Moses added on his own in response to the people's earlier mentioning that when they were in Egypt they "sat on the fleshpots."[15]

14. I thank Sam Stonefield for this last insight.

15. This uncomfortable inconsistency is what led many of the traditional commentators to suggest that the chronology of the section needs to be rearranged; that God's later comment in which He promises meat (16:12) actually preceded Moses's communication to the people.

It seems that both in their joint statement and in the clarifying one Moses makes on his own, two elements are added by the leaders which are absent from God's initial message – the meat in the evening and the deflection of the people's complaints away from themselves to God. When we look at the instruction Moses gives Aaron afterward, it turns out that there is a third element which Moses has added, that there will be some kind of divine revelation to the people, perhaps to allow them to share grievances directly with God.

Perhaps the most surprising turn of events is what comes afterward. Despite never promising to appear before the people, God does in fact appear. "As Aaron spoke to the community of Israel they turned to the wilderness and behold, God's glory appeared in the cloud" (16:10). Even more, God then affirms to Moses that they will be provided with meat in the evening and bread in the morning, as Moses had earlier pronounced.

When we put the picture together, what emerges is that Israel's complaint sparks two parallel processes. In the first of those processes God addresses their very real and justified concern, promising to provide them with food, even without Moses turning to Him. The second process focuses on Moses and on his leadership. Having been rebuked by God once for crying out to Him, and a second time being "taught" to fix a problem, Moses chooses to not call out to God but to respond to the people. As he does so, however, he makes two bold moves. One, frustrated by being a middle manager who receives the complaints but is powerless to resolve them, he directs the people's ire away from himself and toward God. In fact, he encourages them to confront God directly, and in a second bold move he announces God's imminent appearance. In doing so he pushes back against God's demands of him and turns the tables by making a demand of God. That second move is even bolder than the first, as he forces God's hand by insisting that God reveal Himself to the people. It is that same boldness which allows Moses to take liberties with God's promise of food to expand it from bread to include meat.

It is here where it is God's turn to surprise. Not only does He not rebuke Moses for his brazenness, God actually does as Moses had declared – He reveals Himself in the cloud and He provides meat, exactly as Moses had announced. The net effect of this turn of events is startling. Moses had sought to relieve himself of the burden of leadership by placing responsibility on God's shoulders, but ironically, God's accession to Moses's demands actually empowers Moses and builds his leadership by demonstrating that he is more than God's mouthpiece. Of course, that leadership is fully dependent on God, but Moses becomes more emboldened than ever.

The crisis with Pharaoh established Moses as a leader in his own eyes and in the eyes of the people. The crisis at the sea reinforced both of those. The incident with the bitter water teaches Moses to take initiative rather than seek outside assistance, and the challenge of the food demonstrates to Moses himself and to the people that God will stand behind Moses's decisions as a leader. God is determined to transform Moses into the leader he needs to become, and all the crises along the way will-nilly serve as important stepping stones in Moses's path to that leadership, whether he welcomes them or not.

MANNA RULES

The manna came with a few basic rules. First, on a daily basis, they were to collect one omer per person in the family. Second, they were not permitted to leave it overnight. Third, on the sixth day they were to collect two omers per person and were to prepare on that day for the seventh day, on which the manna would not fall.

Regarding the first rule, the Torah states that the Israelites did as they were told (16:17). In fact, everyone – including those whose natural tendencies would have been to take more and those whose natural inclinations would have led them to skimp – overcame those leanings and followed Moses's instructions.[16] This, however, is contrasted by

16. The verse concludes with a mention of those who collect more and those who collect less, and the following verse continues that the ones who "collect more" did not have too much and that those who "collect less" did not have too little. This ambiguity led Rashi and Bekhor Shor to suggest that some intentionally collected more and others less, but when they got home, they discovered that, miraculously, they all had exactly one omer per capita. Ibn Ezra offers a more naturalistic explanation, that the reference to more and less relates to those with larger families who collected more and those with smaller families who collected less. According to our explanation, the Torah is emphasizing just how careful the people were to heed Moses's rules.

their response to the second rule: "They did not listen to Moses; some people left it over until the morning; it got wormy and reeked" (16:20). While people successfully controlled their instinct in collecting the manna, by the evening there were some who were still anxious – and not unreasonably – about their next meal. Perhaps even more significant than what the people do are the reactions by God and Moses to this first breach. God is silent, apparently understanding and tolerating the people's insecurity. By contrast, Moses becomes enraged. Blessed with a divine gift and the promise of a daily repetition, Moses cannot understand how anyone could be insecure.[17]

Which brings us to the third rule, to collect double on the sixth day. This is a bit deceptive, as Moses does not tell the people to do this until after they already do it;[18] they apparently find double the amount of manna and collect that, much to the surprise of their clan leaders, who report it to Moses. To be sure, Moses knows that there would be something special about the six and seventh days, as God had earlier shared that with him (16:5), yet he makes a conscious decision to not share this with the people in advance, waiting for them to first get used to the routine of the manna and then, when surprised by the deviation from that routine, they will be prepared to hear more about it. When he eventually does tell them, he doesn't say anything

17. On that first evening God provided meat, in the form of quail, for the hungry nation. According to Nahmanides (16:12), the quail also arrived daily from that point onward. Rabbi David Zvi Hoffmann rejects this opinion, asserting that it was a onetime event. If so, it would make sense that some people would be anxious when the quail did not arrive on the second night, and hence saved their manna for the next morning for fear that it, too, was a singular occurrence.

 The quintet of stories in this section – manna, meat, lack of water with the appearance of Moses's staff, a battle with an external enemy, and Miriam – is repeated in Numbers 11–12 and 20–21. There are other elements which they have in common as well, such as the appearance of God's glory in the cloud and the expression of a desire to return to Egypt. Bekhor Shor (Ex. 16:13) suggests that, at least with regard to the quail, the two stories are actually one which was repeated. A careful reading of the two stories reveals the difficulties in that approach, including the fact that God is not upset by the people's request for meat here but is not pleased when it is repeated in Numbers. Nonetheless, the parallels between the two sets of stories call for further exploration.

18. Rashbam, 16:22.

about the double portion, but tells them that they should bake and cook the manna as they usually do, and whatever is left over should be eaten on the following day.[19] It turns out, then, that there is no third rule regarding the sixth day. The people act instinctively, which is in accordance with the instruction Moses did not pass along. Even afterward, as the people awaken in the morning and discover that the leftover manna did not spoil, Moses informs them that they should eat it because they will not find any fresh manna to collect, but he does not issue any prohibition.

What happens afterward is fascinating. Despite Moses's assurance, there are some people who go out to look for manna. God expresses displeasure but acts as if it was expected, and He uses the opportunity to strengthen the message about the seventh day: "See, God has given you the Shabbat; that is the reason that He gives you on the sixth day bread for two days – each person should sit in his place; no one should leave their place on the seventh day" (16:29). Up until this point the root SH-B-T was used as a verb, describing a day of ceasing of the manna's fall, of desisting from collecting it. In God's follow-up, the seventh day gets a name, Shabbat.

This seamless transition from the manna to Shabbat opens a new window to understanding the purpose of the manna. True, the manna builds food security, builds a relationship with God, and functions as an economic equalizer. The cycle of the manna, however, adds a new dimension. On a concrete, tangible, experiential level, it forges for Israel the concept of a week, which has no parallel in nature.[20] Aside from the religious significance of the week, with its unmistakable bond to Creation, the cyclical rhythm – with its inherent day of desisting – is a dramatic break from the incessant labor of the slave. When our primary preoccupation is daily survival and making it to the next day, we become slaves to

19. Rashi assumes that implicit in Moses's instruction is the prohibition against cooking and baking on the seventh day, even though it is not mentioned explicitly. Ibn Ezra disagrees, asserting that no such implication can be drawn.

20. The sun and its cycle affecting the seasons is the foundation of the concept of a year. The moon, with its waxing and waning and influence on the tides, is the basis of the concept of the month. There is no natural equivalent for the week, which is a cycle not based in nature.

that survival.[21] The spirit-crushing relentless struggle robs us of the very essence which makes us distinct from all of the rest of creation. The built-in respite from searching for sustenance reminds the worker that there is a plane of living beyond that which we share with all the other creatures. It is precisely in the ability to temporarily suspend the accumulation of goods that we become elevated and ennobled as humans.

This is what Moses means in Deuteronomy (8:3) when he reflects on Israel's time in the wilderness:

> He afflicted you and made you hunger and fed you the manna which neither you nor your fathers knew, so that you should know that man does not live by bread alone but man lives on everything which God speaks.

The purpose of the manna, including its weekly cycle and the day on which the Israelites would not be preoccupied with feeding themselves, was to teach them that no less important than feeding their bodies is the necessity to preserve their human-divine spirit.

God certainly anticipated the need for food, and He chose to provide it in such a way that it would begin to shape the people's selves – religiously, politically, and economically. Moses is learning to take bolder leadership steps, shaping and timing God's messages to the people, even as he learns to grapple with the reality of people's needs and insecurities. And as for the people, for the most part they are willing to adhere to the rules given to them. They collect the manna without complaint, they learn not to leave it over, they approach their leadership for clarification when there is too much, and after God introduces the Shabbat, "the people desisted on the seventh day" (16:30).

THE MANNA LEGACY

The significance of the manna cannot be understated. It was designed to help build confidence, relationship with God, and economic and

21. I recall a conversation I had with a rice farmer in a third-world Asian country in which when I asked what his dreams were, he responded that his dream was to harvest enough rice to survive with his family until the next harvest.

social equity even as it introduces the flow of the Israelite week and the importance of ensuring that material pursuits are balanced by spiritual ones. The sheer volume of biblical real estate devoted to the story of the manna as it unfolds, thirty-four verses (as compared to the Songs at the Sea, which occupy twenty-one verses, or the Decalogue with fourteen), further highlights its significance. That is further emphasized in the coda to that story.

Moses instructs Aaron to fill a jar with a single omer of the manna, which will be housed "before God." To be sure, this section is somewhat anachronistic; it was clearly written toward the end of Moses's life and inserted here as a cap to the primary discussion of the manna in the Torah. This is evident because (a) the instruction is to place it "before God," which surely relates to the Sanctuary,[22] which does not exist yet, and (b) because the penultimate verse provides a retrospective about the manna at the end of forty years: "The Israelites ate the manna for forty years, until they reached the settled land; they ate the manna until they arrived in the land of Canaan" (16:35). Despite the anachronism, elevating the stature of the manna such that it shares the most sacred space alongside the Ark demonstrates just how significant it was.[23]

It is not unreasonable to suggest that Moses was looking beyond preserving a physical memento of their time in the wilderness. Rather, he, too, recognized the multifaceted message of the manna beyond its function as sustenance, and wanted to make sure that the principles God establishes for the foundation of the nation are preserved for all eternity as a benchmark, a reminder to the people of the core ideas and values God is trying to foster.

---

22. The fact that the manna was to be kept in the Sanctuary, into which non-*kohanim* do not enter, means that it was not visible to the people, which seems to conflict with the purpose Moses ascribes to that jar, that it is for the Israelites to see (16:32).
23. In Numbers 11:7 the manna is described as having the appearance of *bedolaḥ*. The only other time that word is used in the Bible is in the description of the Garden of Eden (Gen. 2:12), strengthening our sense of its uniqueness.

WATER, REDUX

After the incidents with the water and the food, we would think that the technical kinks of wilderness survival would have been worked out, but that is apparently not the case.

> The whole community of Israelites journeyed on their journeys, directed by God's word, and they camped in Refidim – but there was no water for the people to drink. They argued with Moses, saying, "Give us water so that we may drink." Moses said to them, "Why are you arguing with me and why are you testing God?" (17:1–2)

Two basic questions emerge immediately. First, why did God find it necessary to bring them to a place without water? After all, for the next thirty-eight years they had ample water until the incident in Numbers 20. Second, since their complaint is legitimate, why does Moses react so harshly?

Before we can address those questions, it is worthwhile making a few observations about the text.

1. The story happens in two phases. In the first, the people argue with Moses, who takes a combative tone in response (17:1–2). In the second, the people complain against Moses for bringing them to a place without water, and instead of responding to them, Moses turns to God (17:3–4).
2. This is the third story in succession in which we find the idea of *nisayon*, testing, but this one is considerably different from the other two. In the first, with the bitter waters (15:25), as well as in the second, with the food (16:4), it is God who is testing the people. By contrast, here Moses accuses Israel of testing God (17:2), so much so that he names the place Masa-Meriva, testing-arguing (17:7).
3. Third, the elders of Israel play no role in the previous two incidents but are mentioned twice in this one (17:5 and 17:6).
4. While Moses is clearly distressed by the people's complaint and arguing, God does not seem bothered by it at all.

5. While there are numerous times that God instructed Moses in the past to pick up his staff, this is the first time He explicitly tells him to use it.

As we've done in the previous two stories, it is worthwhile looking at this from three vantage points. What does this tell us about Israel? What does this tell us about Moses? What does this tell us about God?

It is easy to understand the people's frustration. As we noted earlier, they are completely dependent on their leaders, who don't seem to have a recognizable plan. They were supposed to be journeying to the land of their ancestors but seem to be wandering aimlessly. In fact, the opening verse of this incident contains an unusual phrase: They "journeyed on their journeys." That language is first used as Abram retraces his steps when leaving Egypt, apparently seeking the place that God was going to show him (Gen. 13:3),[24] and likely has similar implications here. They are retracing their steps, much like they did earlier to draw Pharaoh out to pursue them. What they do not understand is why, and that generates a sense of aimlessness and the fear of being trapped without sustenance. Perhaps that explains the name of the place in which they camp, Refidim. The root of that name is R-F-H, meaning to grow weak or soft, and echoes one of Pharaoh's early responses to Moses, that Israel was growing soft in their work habits (5:17).[25] While it was not true in Pharaoh's comments, the Torah seems to suggest that they are growing weak here, losing stamina for the journey,[26] and understandably so. They have been traveling for more than four weeks, seem no closer to their destination, and are subject to the whims of the wilderness. Whatever the goal of Moses's counterattack was, it does nothing to slake their thirst; "the people thirsted there for water," leading to an escalation of their

24. For a fuller explication of this, see Grumet, *Genesis: From Creation to Covenant*, 130–34.
25. A midrash (Sanhedrin 106a) suggests that Refidim is a contraction of *rafu yedeihem*, that their grip softened, but the discussion takes a different direction.
26. This is similar to the description in Numbers 21:4. Even in the fortieth year, as Israel is preparing their entry into the land, they take a circuitous route, circumnavigating Edom, Moab, and Amon. There, too, the fact that they were so close to the land and yet moving away again generated their loss of patience with the journey.

charge, using the rhetorical question "Why did you bring us up from Egypt? – to kill me and my children and my livestock by thirst?" (17:3).

We understand Moses's perspective as well. At every step along the way, God provided solutions to whatever problems arose, and Moses has a hard time understanding why the people don't yet trust that God will provide yet again. So deep was his sense of the people's lack of trust that he accuses them of testing God, reversing the pattern of *nisayon* established earlier and suggesting extraordinary arrogance on their part in that they are assuming God's role, that God is answerable to them. At the close of the scene Moses names the place Masa-Meriva, but that name does not seem to stick. The verse immediately afterward (17:8) describes the battle with Amalek taking place at Refidim, not at Masa-Meriva, and two chapters later we will hear that they traveled from Refidim to the Sinai Wilderness – not from Masa-Meriva, but from Refidim, the original name of the place. Moses's interpretation of their request for water seems to be rejected by the text of the Torah itself. In fact, there is a place which later will be called Meriva; however, it does not refer to Israel's testing of God but of Moses's moment of failure thirty-nine years later in a different incident involving a crisis around water. "*These* [emphasis added] are the waters of Meriva" (Num. 20:13), not the ones identified by Moses. Even more, in the previous incident, the one revolving around food, we saw considerable initiative by Moses and God following Moses's lead, doing as Moses declared would happen. In light of that we are surprised that Moses, too, seems to suffer a setback in his leadership, as he defers to God, seemingly abdicating responsibility and leadership. Perhaps this is why, for the first time, God instructs Moses to pick up and use his staff. Not as a magic wand with which to perform wonders, but as a staff of leadership. That staff will be used not to punish the wayward but to quench the people's thirst, establishing Moses as a provider.[27]

27. This is similar to the use of Aaron's flowering staff (Num. 17:16–24) as a demonstration of his unique election to the priesthood. Earlier, the priestly rites had brought about the fiery deaths of 250 of Korah's group; the flowering of the staff is God's way of communicating to the people that the priesthood is not about fear and power but about providing for the people. For more on this, see Grumet, *Moses and the Path to Leadership*, 220–22.

Which brings us to God's perspective. He seems to be gauging the progress of both Moses and the people. Are the people ready to trust God or do they still need the time to grow into that? Is Moses ready to assume a greater load of leadership or does he need more time to develop? It is for that reason that God doesn't get upset by either. The tests, both for Israel and for Moses, are not "pass-fail" tests but genuine assessments of their progress on their respective paths, and they provide valuable feedback for God about the steps He needs to take to help them along those paths. As such, He provides water for the people, and leadership for Moses. Perhaps it is for that very reason that we find God telling Moses to involve the elders of the camp. No leader can handle a nation on his own. Moses will need to capitalize on the existing elders, those respected by the people, and bring them into the circle of leadership.[28]

BATTLING AMALEK

The capstone event in the aftermath of the Splitting of the Sea is the unprovoked attack on Israel by Amalek. This brief story, which has been seared into the collective consciousness of Israel and later the Jewish nation, is marked by God's vow to obliterate the memory of Amalek from under the heavens (17:14) and by God's subsequent command to Israel to be the agent for executing that vow (Deut. 25:17–19). This incident, central as it may be, is pockmarked with multiple mysteries. Who is Amalek? Why did it attack? Compared to the treatment Israel received at the hands of their oppressors in Egypt over an extended period, why does God consider this attack so heinous? What was the nature of Moses's activity on the mountaintop? Where is God in this story?

Once again, there are a few observations within the text that can be helpful in building an understanding.

1. Moses acts, apparently on his own initiative, and deputizes Joshua – this is his first appearance in the Torah – to recruit the fighters and lead the battle.
2. Moses plans to ascend the mountain on the next day.

28. This, of course, serves as a precursor to the story of Yitro and foreshadows God's reaction to Moses's frustration in Numbers 11.

3. Moses takes the "staff of God" (or staff of power) to the mountaintop. This description of the staff appears only one other time in the Bible, as Moses embarks on his initial return to Egypt (4:20).
4. When Moses ascends the mountain, he takes two people who assist him, Aaron and the mysterious Hur.[29]
5. The narrative mentions Moses's hands six times in the span of four verses. The text (17:11) seems to suggest that it is Moses's hands which influence the course of the battle.[30] Moses mentions a hand in his closing proclamation.
6. While Moses's hands seem to influence the outcome of the battle, the Torah emphasizes that it was Joshua's efforts which ultimately swayed the battle to deflect Amalek's attack (17:13).
7. After the battle, God vows to avenge Amalek's attack and Moses proclaims this to be a battle for the generations.

One of the most fascinating aspects in this story is the focus on Moses's hands. It far eclipses the mentions of the "staff of God" which he brought up the mountain, and it is the featured element – appearing three times – in what Rabbi Elhanan Samet demonstrates[31] is the central, pivotal verse of the passage (17:12). The background to this begins in Moses's first encounter with God at the burning bush. In the passage describing the signs that God gives to Moses (4:1–9), the staff appears

29. Hur is mentioned in two places in the Torah, here and in 24:14, where Moses leaves him, together with Aaron, in charge of the people as he ascends Mount Sinai for an extended period. According to rabbinic tradition he was Miriam's son. According to I Chronicles 2:19, he was the son of Caleb. Later, we find that he was the grandfather of Betzalel, chief artisan of the Tabernacle. Josephus cites a tradition that he was Miriam's husband. Despite his potential prominence, he disappears after being appointed to an interim leadership position by Moses, prompting rabbinic speculation about his fate.
30. This point is noted explicitly in Mishna Rosh HaShana 3:8: "Could it be that Moses's hand make or break the battle?" Also note that Moses's name, as well as that of Amalek, are each mentioned seven times in this passage.
31. *Iyunim BeFarashat HaShavua,* Series 2, Volume 1, 288–306. He does not make special note of the word appearing three times in that verse but does convincingly demonstrate that verse 12 is the central verse of the passage.

but twice while Moses's hand is featured eight times,[32] and we have earlier explored the role that Moses's hand plays in the plagues and even in the Splitting of the Sea. Until the previous incident at Masa-Meriva, God had never instructed him to use the staff to do any of the wondrous things, lest people think that Moses was nothing more than a more advanced magician than the Egyptian sorcerers who possessed an especially powerful magic wand. The staff was to be the symbol of benevolent and directed leadership, not an instrument of supposed power with which to impress the people.

The emphasis on Moses's hands, aside from serving to de-emphasize the staff, was intended to build Moses's self-confidence as a leader. God had chosen Moses to be His human partner, but Moses needed to develop a range of skills before he could engage that role seriously. That is why throughout the plagues we see Moses growing bolder in his approaches to Pharaoh, raising the stakes whenever he senses a weakening of Pharaoh's position. That is also why, as we've noted, God rebukes Moses for crying out to Him at the Reed Sea. Moses needs to decide how to move forward, and God will ensure that it happens. That is what happens in response to the complaint about the food, and what fails to materialize at Masa-Meriva.

For now, it appears that Moses has learned his lesson. Without consulting God, he takes the initiative and deputizes Joshua as military leader. To help ensure God's backing[33] he prepares to climb the mountain, and there, too, he brings assistants – Aaron and Hur. This, too, he learns from Masa-Meriva, that leadership can and should be shared and distributed. In fact, in Moses's message to Joshua about his climbing the mountain and, presumably, for the counterattack against Amalek, he mentions that this will take place on the following day. The theme of significant events being delayed to the following days runs through the story of the plagues, appearing in six of them.[34] Many of these are

32. Yosef Zvi Rimon, in "Yedei Moshe," *Megadim* 22: 43–47, notes this as well, but draws conclusions which are diametrically opposite to mine.

33. This is in accordance with the second explanation of Ibn Ezra (17:11). Rashbam (17:11) understands that he brings the staff to the top of the mountain to provide moral support for the people as they look up to him and see their flag raised.

34. See 5:6, 8:19, 8:25, 9:5, 9:18, and 10:4.

at Moses's initiative as he flexes his leadership muscles vis-à-vis Pharaoh, so his invoking of the need to prepare for tomorrow's battle is yet another sign of Moses's stepping up to fill the role God chose for him.

With all that, it appears that Moses may have misread God's message. When charging Joshua with his mission it seems that Moses believes that overcoming this challenge will happen quickly, just as the previous crises were dealt with swiftly. "Moses said to Joshua, 'Choose for us men and go battle Amalek. Tomorrow I will stand on top of the hill'" (17:9). Moses believed that the battle would be short enough that he could stand through the entire event. It turns out, however, that he needs to sit. Even more than that, his hands grew heavy, so much so that when they began to "grow heavy" the battle turned against Israel, necessitating that Aaron and Hur prop up his arms. As Rabbi Samet elegantly writes, this battle took place at Refidim, the place of weakened hands – Moses's hands.[35]

It seems that God's vision of supporting a battle and Moses's vision of that support are not aligned. Moses believes that he must do his part, the people must do theirs, and God will miraculously make the problem disappear. That, however, is not God's vision. The people and their leaders must be prepared to do everything in their power to bring success to their efforts. God's role is not a miraculous swooping in and making the enemy disappear or drown, but to ensure that the human efforts are successful on a human scale. Thus, while Moses prepared for a divine appearance, such as the one at the Reed Sea, God's intention was that this would look like a battle like any other – the miracle would be that a ragtag band of militarily undisciplined men would be able to defeat a war-hardened adversary.[36] Moses thought that God would fight *for* the people, like He did at the sea, but God intended to fight *alongside* them. Ultimately, as the text attests unequivocally, it is Joshua with

35. *Iyunim BeFarashat HaShavua*, Series 2, 305.

36. Some of this approach is based on observations made by Mordechai Sabato in his very fine article, "Vekhi Yadav shel Moshe Osot Milḥama?" *Megadim* 50: 39–59. His conclusions are significantly different from mine. He believes that Moses intended to use the staff to magically win the battle, but that God thwarted that to remove any hint of Moses or the staff possessing special powers. Therefore, Moses was forced to resort to prayer.

his sword who repels Amalek (17:13). The battle must be fought on the human level with all that this entails. Only then will God intervene.[37]

THE EVER-PRESENT AMALEK

Who is Amalek, why does he attack, and why is God so incensed that He vows to erase his memory from under the heavens? In Genesis, Amalek is the grandson of Esau, the same Esau who was deceived by his brother Jacob, later Israel, and who ultimately reconciled with him. Is it possible that while the patriarch of that clan reconciled with Jacob-Israel one of his zealous grandchildren held onto the grudge? Of course that is possible, yet if that were true we might expect to find some hint that this is about that grudge, something about the stolen blessing, or even something about Jacob's unfulfilled promise to "catch up" to Esau in Se'ir (Gen. 14). Our text, however, is silent about any of those, leaving us to seek elsewhere.

A broad scan of the Bible reveals Amalek to be a nomadic, shepherding tribe whose origins predate Israel (Gen. 14:7) and who have tussled with Israel over shepherding land throughout the Bible (Judges 3:13, 6:3, and I Sam. 27:9). In the Torah, Amalek is a nation settled into the south of the Promised Land. The scouts that Moses sent who tried to dissuade Israel from entering the land insert into their report that "Amalek dwells in the dry south" (Num. 13:29). In the continuation of that story, after God's decree that Israel is to remain in the wilderness for forty years, we hear about a group which defies God's decree, insisting that they want to enter the land immediately. Moses warns them against trying, noting that they will fail because God is not with them, but they plow forth nonetheless. The result of that incident is tragic. "The Amalekites and the Canaanites, the hill dwellers there, came down; they struck them and crushed them until Hormah" (Num. 14:45). Four times in that

37. The counterpart to this declaration in the text is Moses's awareness that it is not he and his staff who led the people to victory, but that God was his flag bearer. That is what he names the altar he constructs (17:15).

This story provides our first exposure to the person who will ultimately succeed Moses. The very fact that he has a successor, as well as the reality that his hands grow heavy, highlight Moses's humanity: He is a person, not a God; he will die and move on.

story Amalek is mentioned as dwellers of the Land of Israel, suggesting that they had heard about Israel's exodus from Egypt and were launching a preemptive attack to prevent Israel's entry into the land.[38]

None of this, however, explains the intensity of God's reaction to the attack.

As we broaden our perspective, however, the picture becomes clearer. This attack comes just a few weeks after the splitting of the Reed Sea, in which God revealed Himself to all humanity and which Moses, in the song, reveals the universal significance of the event. God is restored as Creator and Director of humanity, Israel is acknowledged as His chosen ambassador, the entry into the land will be smooth and bloodless because everyone will be afraid to battle God, and God's dominion over humanity will be established and acknowledged by all. Amalek's attack not only threatens the unchallenged conquest of the land; it is a bold declaration that all the conclusions drawn from the Splitting of the Sea are false.[39]

Moses understands this all too well. After God's vow to erase the memory of Amalek, Moses responds with his own declaration, perhaps even a song:

> For the Hand is on *YH*'s throne,
> War for God against Amalek,
> For all generations. (17:16)

There are multiple interpretations of the opening of this song, including that Moses is declaring that this is God's oath, much the same way that people raise their right hand or that Abraham makes his servant place a hand beneath his thigh. This renders the short song as meaning that God swears by His throne that the battle with Amalek will be everlasting.[40] Rashi takes this one step further, noting that the word for throne,

38. This is the suggestion offered by Cassuto in his commentary on Exodus.
39. See *Midrash Tanḥuma Ki Tetzeh* 9 and the last lines of Nahmanides's commentary on 17:16.
40. This is the interpretation offered by Rashi, Rashbam, and Ibn Ezra.

kes, is an abbreviated version of *kisei*, missing the letter *alef* at the end. Rashi explains that God's throne is incomplete until Amalek is defeated.

Moses understood the universal significance of the Splitting of the Sea and celebrated that in his accompanying song. He also apparently understands the universal significance of Amalek's attack as well, as it threatens the Song of the Sea, and expresses that in his mini-song here.

Moses's understanding is influenced not only by his deep appreciation of God's design, but also by his initial encounter with God. We recall that at the burning bush, Moses asks God for a name he can pass on to Israel to verify that indeed it was their God who had sent him. God responds with a series of three cryptic responses, the third of which states:

> E-lohim further said to Moses: This is what you should say to the Israelites. "A-donai, the God of your ancestors – the God of Abraham, the God of Isaac, and the God of Jacob – sent me to you. This is My eternal name, the way I am mentioned for all generations." (3:15)

The closing phrase of that assertion, "for all generations" (*ledor dor*) is eerily echoed in the closing of Moses's mini-song (*midor dor*). Moses understands that God's very presence in the world is threatened by the existence of those would try to undermine it, like the ancient ones in Babel and the modern Pharaoh. It is for this reason that not only is God's throne truncated, God's name itself is truncated, as Moses's version of it in the opening line includes only the first two letters (*YH*, the first two letters of *YHVH*, A-donai). The very name by which God indicated to Moses that His presence will be felt in the world is now being threatened by a new threat, Amalek.

Moses's song reveals another layer as well: The threat is an everlasting one. Amalek is not only a nation; it is an ideology. Nations can be defeated in battle; ideologies live eternally. God's war against Amalek is an eternal one, for all generations, because in every generation there will be the forces which try to deny, hide, or challenge God. Those ideological attacks may take on a variety of forms and manifestations, but they all have a common core – supplanting God and all He stands for with something else, attempting to push God into the dustbins of history and humanity's ethics. Amalek is the eternal enemy of God and Godliness.

FIVE WEEKS AFTER THE SONGS AT THE SEA

The tumultuous period after the demise of the Egyptians presents challenges for the people, for Moses, and for God. During that period the people show the ability to move from being complainers to being good followers, and even to becoming fighters. That is quite impressive for people just beginning to taste freedom and the accompanying responsibilities and challenges associated with it. Moses demonstrates the shift from dealing with a single inflexible tyrant to trying to manage an entire nation. He learns to take initiative, to rely on God's backing, and to appreciate the importance of people doing everything humanly possible before turning to God for help.

The shifts that we witness are the baby steps in processes that will ultimately take much longer than anyone anticipates, but those baby steps are important because they demonstrate the capacity for growth. As for God, aside from shepherding the process for both the people (with His infinite patience) and for Moses, He too is learning the delicate balance between empowering His messenger and showing him the limitations of that empowerment. He is prepared to follow Moses's initiatives and even incorporate some of them into the broad framework of commandments, yet will nudge Moses so that he becomes better at what he does.

It has been a tumultuous but extraordinarily important five weeks. And now that Israel and Moses have begun to get used to the routine of life in the wilderness, little do they realize just how much things are going to change.

Exodus 18:1–27

The Sore Thumb

The story of Yitro sticks out like a sore thumb in Exodus. In the grand scheme of God's redemption of Israel and the upcoming divine revelation at Sinai (which only we, as readers, know about), the personal visit by Moses's father-in-law and the subsequent advice he offers feel like an interruption. We will not hear from Yitro again and there is no mention anywhere later in the Torah of the system he encourages Moses to implement – his appearance here seems to leave no lasting imprint. What would we be missing had the Torah omitted it altogether?

And yet, the story is here. Almost halfway through the book. The Sages were puzzled by its placement here since some of the details don't accord with this taking place prior to the Revelation at Sinai.[1] Here are some the chronological problems:

1. The Torah describes Yitro as arriving at God's mountain even though Israel doesn't arrive there until the following chapter (19:1–2).

1. Mekhilta, *Yitro* 18:1.

2. There is no reason to describe the place as "God's mountain" until after the Revelation, which hasn't occurred as yet.
3. On the day after his arrival, when he questions what Moses is doing, Moses responds that he is informing the people of God's statues and teachings, of which we are not aware until after the Revelation. All the language in that conversation has no context prior to the Revelation and God's instruction of the mitzvot which follows.
4. The story closes with Yitro returning to his land, and yet he seems to be around much later when Moses seems intent on convincing him to stay (Num. 10:29–32).[2]

The debate about the timing of Yitro's visit was later taken up by the commentators. Ibn Ezra champions the position that the story took place after the Revelation, while Nahmanides insists that the Torah be read chronologically, and each provides convincing arguments for their respective positions. And with all that, we are left wondering why it is important to be included at all, especially if it is an anachronistic interpolation.

It seems that the ambiguity of the text may be intentional – a literary device to draw our attention, demanding that we probe this much further.

The story of Yitro becomes even more intriguing when we realize that there are actually two stories here with a clear chronological demarcation between them. The first (18:1–12) takes place on the day of his arrival. It describes his motivation, his arrival, and his personal interactions with Moses, and is capped by his sacrificial offering which is shared by Aaron and the elders. In this story, Moses's interaction with Yitro seems personal, and Yitro's name is prominent, appearing seven times. The second story (18:13–27) happens on the following day. It describes his observation of Moses being overwhelmed by dealing with

---

2. The commentators debate if Hobab mentioned in Numbers 10 is Moses's father-in-law (Rashi) or brother-in-law (Ibn Ezra). This is not the only instance of him being described with multiple names. According to a rabbinic tradition (*Midrash Tanḥuma Shemot* 11) he had seven names.

the people's questions, his advice to establish a bureaucratic system to relieve the pressure, Moses's acceptance and implementation of that advice, and Moses sending his father-in-law back home. In this story, Moses's interaction with his father-in-law seems professional, and his father-in-law's name is not mentioned even once. This division provides the beginning of a road map for exploring further.

THE FIRST STORY

As we begin studying the first story there are a number of important observations to make about the text.

1. Yitro is introduced here as he was when he was first presented to the reader (2:16), as a Midianite priest. That appellation disappears after it is used once in the opening verse.
2. Although his name appears seven times, it is never used in the context of Moses's speaking or relating to him. For example, 18:7 describes Moses going out to greet his father-in-law and 18:8 speaks about what Moses tells his father-in-law, but his name is absent from any interaction initiated by Moses.
3. His decision to come is apparently inspired by what he heard about what "God did for Moses and His people, Israel, that God took Israel out of Egypt." When he speaks with Moses, Moses tells him "all that God did to Pharaoh and Egypt on behalf of Israel," about the travails from which God saved Israel on their journey. Yet when Yitro afterward blesses God, he does so "because God saved them from Egypt and from Pharaoh, that He saved the people from under Pharaoh's hand."
4. Yitro is very conscious of the wife and sons that he is bringing to Moses; they are mentioned three times in the opening of the story (with variations). By contrast, while Moses greets his father-in-law warmly, the absence in the text of any reference to Moses's welcoming of his nuclear family is startling and disturbing.

Perhaps it is worthwhile to try to construct the story from Yitro's perspective. To backtrack a little, he is a Midianite priest who gave his daughter to the heroic Egyptian man who rescued (*hitzil*) them from the nasty Midianite shepherds. That heroic Egyptian man turned out to be more complex than anyone suspected, and eventually took his wife and sons back to Egypt to check on his family. Much to his surprise, not long after Moses leaves, his wife and the two boys return to Midian, having been sent away (SH-L-Ḥ) by their husband and father. Let it be clear – in ancient times, including in the Bible, there was no formal legal procedure for divorce; the man sent his wife away and that was understood as divorce. That is certainly the way Hagar understood it when Abraham sent (SH-L-Ḥ) her away (Gen. 21:14) and certainly the way the Torah uses the term multiple times in Deuteronomy (21:14, 22:19, 22:29) until the formal process of divorce is introduced (Deut. 24:1). From Yitro's perspective, then, the mysterious and complex visitor who married his daughter returned to his homeland and divorced his wife by sending her back to hers.

Much to his surprise, he later hears that the God responsible for taking his son-in-law away was responsible for extraordinary wonders. Whether for reasons of personal benefit, for the welfare of his daughter and her children, or perhaps to learn more about this mighty God who could do such wondrous things,[3] he journeys to Moses and brings with him Moses's (former?) wife and sons[4] to rekindle those relationships.

When he arrives, he is repeatedly surprised. Moses personally comes to greet him, bowing to and kissing him and inviting him into his tent. The word used to describe going into the tent is *ha'ohela* and is used only eight times in the Bible. Abraham rushes *ha'ohela* (Gen. 18:6) to tell Sarah to prepare bread for their three guests; Isaac's union with Rebecca is marked by his bringing her *ha'ohela*, the place formerly occupied by his mother (Gen. 24:67); the place where Moses will later commune privately with God is *ha'ohela* (33:8–9); Yael entertains the Canaanite general Sisera *ha'ohela* (Judges 4:18). It is a place of privacy,

3. After all, he does come to meet Moses at the place identified as God's mountain.
4. When describing Yitro's actions and words, the Torah twice refers to the two boys as *her* children (18:3 and 18:6). When simply narrating their arrival, the boys are referred to as *his* sons (18:5).

of intimacy, and it is where Moses brings his father-in-law. This is the first surprise.

The second surprise is in the realm of relationships. Within that respect and intimacy, Moses looks past him as Yitro, seeing him only the father-in-law.[5] Even more, while Moses shows warmth for his father-in-law, he completely ignores his wife and sons – whether they are presented as her sons or his.

The third surprise is that while Yitro has been moved by what God has done *for* Moses and his people, Moses seems focused on what God did *to* Pharaoh and Egypt. In fact, even after Moses shares that with him, the Torah troubles to reiterate that what delighted Yitro is that God saved (*hitzil*) Israel from Pharaoh and Egypt. Aside from the focus on the helpful rather than the punitive aspect of God's intervention, Yitro seems moved that the God of Israel acted much in the same way that Moses himself did when he saved (*hitzil*) his daughters from the Midianite shepherds.[6]

The combined effect of Yitro's experience is apparently transformative. Whatever brought him to Moses, he is no longer a Midianite priest, but a believer in the truth of Israel's God. "Now I know that A-donai is greater than all the other gods, for [He struck the Egyptians] with the same thing that they conspired against Israel." That is, the Egyptians conspired against Israel to drown all the baby boys in the water, but in the end it was they who drowned in the water. Thus, even though Yitro remained focused on what God did *for* Israel, reading through the lines of Moses's description of what God did *to* Egypt revealed to him a God of justice, one whose sense of justice results in His meting out consequences measure for measure rather than randomly wielding force to afflict or crush those who violate His rules.[7] It was in response

5. That description dominates the entire chapter, appearing thirteen times.
6. The word *hitzil*, in various forms, appears four times in this narrative (18:8–10) and seems to be central to what moves Yitro. It appears a fifth time when explaining how Moses's son Eliezer receives his name, as God saved him from Pharaoh (18:4). It stands in contrast to *nitzel*, which is used to describe what God told Israel to do to the Egyptian (3:22 and 12:36).
7. In this first story there are numerous references to the family relationships – the father-in-law, the wife, the sons. This is reminiscent of Abram's journey from Haran,

to that that he initiates a covenantal meal with God, replete with an altar, a burnt offering, and offerings to be eaten.[8]

It is also quite telling that Aaron and the elders join Yitro's meal, but Moses is absent (18:12). They rejoice in Yitro's transformation, while Moses seems to be as unmoved by that as he is by the arrival of his wife and children. As far as Moses is concerned, when Yitro's advice is done, he is happy to send (SH-L-Ḥ) his father-in-law back to where he came from (18:27), just as he once did with his wife and sons.

This first story, then, is primarily about Yitro and his transformation. That is why his name is so prominent. He comes inspired by what he hears and becomes even more inspired when he hears even more about the positive things that God did for Israel. Regardless of whether Yitro undergoes a formal conversion, if such a thing existed yet,[9] or whether he remains a Midianite inspired by the God of Israel, he stands as a paradigm of how God's intervention in the affairs of humanity is affecting positively those beyond Israel.

THE SECOND STORY

If the first story details what Yitro received from his encounter with Moses, the second describes what he gives to Moses. The discussion here is not philosophical or theological but practical. Yitro witnesses a dedicated man being overwhelmed by his desire to help everyone and asks a rhetorical question: "What are you doing to these people?" Rhetorical questions are usually not meant to be answered; they are intended as rebuke. When Avimelekh confronts Abraham after discovering that Abraham had misled him into thinking that Sarah was his sister, he says: "What did you do to us?" (Gen. 20:9). He is not expecting a response, as that is not a question waiting for a response but an attack, and indeed, Abraham is silent as there is no justified response. Similarly,

suggesting that Yitro's trip to Moses is his equivalent of Abram's *lekh lekha* journey. The other parallel to Abraham is that both are attracted to God because of a commitment to justice.

8. The language is nearly identical to that later used in the covenantal ceremony arranged by Moses in 24:5.
9. Similarly with Ruth, whose "conversion" is captured by her adopting her mother-in-law's people, God, and land (Ruth 1:16).

when Laban challenges Jacob who had recently snuck out of his house and says, "Why did you steal my gods?" (Gen: 31:30), he is not expecting a response from Jacob as there cannot be a meaningful response to such an attack. Here, too, Yitro's challenge to Moses does not expect a response. Ironically, Moses does respond: "Because the people come to me to inquire of God" (18:15).[10]

Moses's response is a prime example of what Yitro is advising him to cease doing: answering every question that is posed. Not every request can or should be answered, and certainly not by him alone. Yitro's rhetorical question and Moses's straightforward response demonstrate that there has been an inversion in Moses's concept of leadership – he is no longer leading the people but is being led by them. He is being reactive when he should be proactive. He is managing their requests but is not projecting a vision or a way to move forward. If earlier Moses was less than sympathetic to the people and their petty concerns, he is now being overly careful to listen to them and is losing his own direction.

Yitro's suggestion is not merely one of good management, which is important but not to be confused with genuine leadership, but it is one which allows Moses to assert his leadership. Once he is freed from personally dealing with everyone and all the problems, his time and his head can begin to prioritize and imagine how to move the nation forward. Moses can assume the role that only he can fulfill, while others take on the tasks that they can do. To be sure, Yitro's suggestion of distributing responsibility is not new – it had already been introduced when God instructs Moses to take the elders with him to bring water from the rock and was employed by Moses when he deputizes Joshua to lead the battle against Amalek. But those were ad hoc responses to episodic challenges; Yitro is suggesting a fundamental change in the system, one which will free Moses to focus on leading.[11]

10. The Hebrew, *lidrosh E-lohim,* lends itself to multiple translations-interpretations, including "to seek justice" (Bekhor Shor), "that I shall inquire of God" (Rashi and Rashbam), or "that I shall beseech God" (Nahmanides).
11. It is puzzling that although the text here records that "Moses listened to his father-in-law and did all that he had said," nowhere in the any of the Torah narratives do we

It is quite telling that, in this second story, Yitro and his personal transformation fade into the background, as does his name. Put into a broader context, the two stories together describe not only how God's intervention impacts the world beyond Israel, but how that reverberates back to impact Israel as well. We have here the representative of a nation who brings wisdom from his world to assist Israel. The teaching is bilateral – Israel shares with the world about God and His ethical system, while they share with Israel their accumulated wisdom.

THE CLUES FROM CONTEXT

Aside from examining the story of Yitro as a standalone, it is important to understand how it connects to what comes before and after. Ibn Ezra (18:1) was one of the first to be aware of this, and he suggests that the purpose of the story's placement here is to contrast it with that of Amalek – that not all nations of the world are evil like Amalek; there are good non-Israelites like Yitro. Cassuto broadens this idea, pointing to long-standing traditions in Israel which contrasted the relationship of Amalek-Israel to that of the Kenite tribes (identified with Yitro) and Israel.[12] He strengthens this contention by noticing the linguistic links between the story of Yitro and the battle with Amalek and the contrasts which emerge. Here is a summary of his analysis:

The story of Amalek	The story of Yitro
Amalek came (*vayavo*) (17:18)	Yitro came (*vayavo*) (18:1)
and battled (17:18)	and they inquired of each other's peace (18:7)
Choose (B-Ḥ-R) for us men (17:9)	Moses chose (B-Ḥ-R) valiant men (18:25)

find this bureaucratic system in function. Was it set up but never really implemented, implemented but not maintained, dismantled after the great leadership failures at the Golden Calf?

12. This contrast climaxes in the story of Saul's battle with Amalek, in which the Kenites are asked to separate from Amalek so that Saul can do what he needs to without harming them (I Sam. 15:6).

(for the sake of war)	(for the sake of instituting justice)
Moses sat (*vayeshev*) (17:12)	Moses sat (*vayeshev*) (18:13)
(because he was weak)	To judge the people
Moses's hands were heavy (*kaved*) (17:12)	Yitro tells Moses that the task was too heavy (*kaved*) (18:18)
Moses plans to stand (*nitzav*) on the mountain (17:9)	The people stand (*nitzav*) over Moses (18:14)
Until the sun set (17:12)	Until evening (18:13)

Beyond that, the story of Yitro is the last in a series – perhaps even the climax of that series – focusing on Moses's leadership, and specifically, on distributed leadership. We move from capitalizing on the people already there to carefully selecting people with specific qualities, and from episodic distribution of leadership to a systematic one. It could even be argued that the Yitro story is so important that the earlier incidents are designed to prepare Moses for Yitro's arrival.[13]

On the other end, perhaps this is linked not to what came before but to what will follow. Assuming that the story is inserted here before its time, the "laws and statutes" that Yitro refers to are likely those included in the Decalogue and in the list which immediately follows in Exodus 21–23. With an overwhelming set of rules and regulations being delivered in a single tranche we understand why Moses would be overwhelmed with questions, so that it is critical to introduce the system he proposes.

Beyond that, there are many who see Yitro as the quintessential (male) convert to the religion of Israel.[14] His entry into the covenant is marked by his acknowledgment of God and a sacrificial offering, which are about to be mirrored on a national scale as Israel establishes

13. See Sabato, "Vekhi Yadav shel Moshe Osot Milḥama?" 57.

14. Zevaḥim 116a. For a longer discussion on this, see my "Within and Without Our Encampment in the Desert: The Ambivalent Acceptance of a Biblical Convert," *Tradition* 27, no. 3 (Spring 1994). The female counterpart to Yitro is Ruth.

its covenant with God.[15] The story of Yitro thus becomes the introduction to the Revelation at Sinai.

WHY IS THIS HERE?

We return now to our opening question: What critical information or insight does the story of Yitro add to our understanding of Exodus that justifies its being included, and placed here? To be sure, it cannot be about Yitro himself. He is but a supporting character in the Torah's narrative; as harsh as it is to say, the Torah is not really interested in him per se, just as the Torah is not really interested in Avimelekh, Laban, or Pharaoh's baker. In light of our analysis in this chapter, it seems that the story of Yitro represents the nexus of three critical ideas, without which it would be difficult to understand the continuation of Exodus.

1. Leadership needs to shift

The adjustments made by Moses to his leadership until this point were sporadic, improvised, and do not seem to have stamina. Even with God at his back, for him – and anyone who follows him – to succeed, there needs to be a system; leadership cannot be dependent on the whim or the momentary inspiration of the leader. That is untenable for the survival and health of any people or institution. The previous stories demonstrate how tenuous and fragile such leadership is, and the religious-legal framework God is about to share demands that the human implementation of that structure be systematized. As Leon Kass writes: "Jethro's visit shows us why what happens at Sinai is indispensable: we must move from anarchy and seat-of-the-pants justice to given law, and from precarious charismatic leadership to authorized hierarchy."[16] In other words, without the system, the Giving of the Torah cannot be successful.

---

15. Israel's sacrificial offering will be delayed until 24:5. Ironically, while Yitro's conversion serves as the model for Israel, Maimonides (*Hilkhot Issurei Bia* 13:1–4) sees Israel's entry into the covenant as the model for all future converts.
16. *Founding God's Nation*, 264–65.

2. Moses is *sui generis*

Our understanding of Moses up until now has been based on the assumption that he is like other people. He eats and drinks, he has personal relationships, he experiences the regular emotional strains and joys just like everyone else. All that is about to change. Moses is about to enter realms unlike anything known to others. He will go forty days and nights without food or water, he will have encounters with God that even the Torah seems to say are impossible. The story of Yitro introduces that Moses to us.

Yitro visits but Moses does not relate to him on a personal level. He remains, in Moses's eyes, the father-in-law, the Midianite priest who needs to be brought out of his silly religious beliefs. His discussions are theological, not personal. Moreover, he completely ignores his wife and children. Kass believes that it is his position as leader which is responsible,[17] but I am convinced that it is because he has transformed, and that transformation affects both his story and ours. It is ironic that the man who introduced education of children into the Israelite experience,[18] which later becomes embedded as one of its cornerstones, does not include his own in the experience of the fulfillment of the covenant,[19] the Exodus from Egypt, or the Revelation at Sinai. Only the man who can't imagine greeting his wife upon their reunion could decree, in the very next chapter, that the preparation for the Revelation include the restriction of "Don't approach a woman" (19:15).[20] The story of Yitro and Moses's missing reunion with his wife and children demonstrates that Moses has crossed over; his personal transformation into something else, not just someone else, has begun. The man who did not belong with the Egyptians or the Israelites in Egypt, who tried to settle into Midian but was wrenched away from that as well, seems to be a better partner with God than with any people.[21]

---

17. *Founding God's Nation*, 266–67.
18. See 13:8 and 13:14–15.
19. It is his wife, Tzippora, who tends to that.
20. This was not one of the preparations mentioned earlier by God and seems to be Moses's addition.
21. Indeed, we will soon see that he spends forty days and forty nights on the mountain with God without food or water. It seems like Moses is moved by the idea of help-

3. The message of the Exodus is being heard

Yitro's personal transformation, including the words he utters, stand as a testimony of a reaction to the events of the first fifteen chapters of Exodus that God would consider a success. A foreigner, with only a tangential connection to the people being saved, proclaims, "Now I know that A-donai is greater than all the other gods." The Midianite priest has become a devotee of A-donai – and so could and should every other nation on the face of the planet.

God entered the fray in Egypt to reset the direction of humanity, to reintroduce Himself as the Creator, to reestablish Himself as the God of justice and righteousness. Amalek fought to undermine that; Yitro affirms and proclaims it. According to one midrash, he went back to Midian to spread his discovery of God among the rest of his clan and his people.[22] His story is the paradigm of what God has been seeking to accomplish and stands as a testimony that it could and should have happened.

In the beginning of the next chapter, as God introduces His covenant to Israel, He begins with a brief description of what they have seen Him do for them, and based on that how He hopes they will respond to His offer. The echoes of Yitro still echo for Israel as they make their decision.

---

ing people, especially those suffering injustice, but not by the personal engagement with them. For more on this, see Grumet, *Moses and the Path to Leadership*, 63–98. It is quite telling that in the entire Torah there is no dialogue between Moses and his wife or children. Even in their initial encounter at the well, especially when contrasted with Jacob's initial encounter with Rachel at the well, Moses shows no interest in any of the women; it is Yitro who initiates the encounter and who gives his daughter Tzippora to Moses. Moses is passive throughout the entire scene.

22. Mekhilta, *Yitro* 18:27.

Exodus 19:1–25, 24:1–18

The Elusive Covenant

It's not clear that Moses knew what was coming. In their first meeting God had mentioned something about worshipping on this mountain at some point in the future (3:12), but it is not clear that Moses understood what that meant. Later, God mentioned that "He would take [Israel] as His people" (6:7), but again it is not clear that anyone understood the full implications of what God intended. And if it was not clear to Moses what any of this meant, then it was certainly not clear to Israel. In fact, there is no indication that Moses shared any of this with the people.

The arrival at Sinai some six weeks after the Exodus was a surprise stop, a detour, from what everyone understood was their primary objective – their ancestral homeland, the one promised by God. This is what God had told Moses and what Moses repeatedly shared with the people.

> I am descending to save [the people] from Egypt and to bring [them] up from that land to a good and broad land, and land flowing with milk and honey (3:8)

> I will bring you up from the oppression in Egypt to the land of the Canaanite, the Hittite, the Emorite … to a land flowing with milk and honey (3:17)
>
> I will bring you to the land which I swore to give to Abraham, to Isaac, and to Jacob, and I will give it to you as a legacy (6:8)
>
> When you come to the land which God will give you as He said (12:25)
>
> When God brings you to the land of the Canaanite, the Hittite, the Emorite … which He promised your ancestors, the land flowing with milk and honey (13:5)
>
> When God brings you to the land of the Canaanite as He swore to you and to your ancestors, and He gives it to you (13:11)

Even though no one knew what the purpose of coming to this place was, Moses knew that this place was special. He had been there before. This was where it all started for him – the burning bush, the lengthy dialogue with God, learning about his own past and about who God is, the mission which he so did not want to accept and which he ultimately embraced with his whole self. In a moment of incredible intimacy he goes up the mountain, even without being invited,[1] in a moment which brings back for him a flood of life-transforming memories.

Moses's personal experience, no matter how moving, is not the purpose of Israel's arrival at Sinai. God is about to propose an idea unheard of in the annals of human history – a covenant binding God to a people.

BIBLICAL COVENANTS

Before delving into the text, it is worthwhile to briefly explore the notion of covenant in the Bible and in the ancient world. Covenants in the

1. The verse describing Moses's ascent to the mountain is written in the past perfect, Moses had already gone up to God.

ancient world were well known. They usually involved two kings, one superior, called the suzerain, and the other less powerful, called the vassal. Covenants were sometimes imposed by the suzerain but were often mutually beneficial – the suzerain would offer protection to the vassal in return for which the vassal would pay tribute and demonstrate loyalty to the suzerain. Those covenants would often begin with the suzerain declaring what he has already done for the vassal, followed by an enumeration of what he expects in return. The agreement would be sealed by a ceremony and "guaranteed" by invoking curses on the one who betrayed the covenant.[2]

Covenants between God and people are rare in ancient literature, but are the primary ones discussed in the Bible. This anomaly of the Bible should not surprise us, given the unique core story described in the Torah – God creates people and seeks to have a relationship with them. Thus, the first explicit covenant in the Torah appears early on in Genesis, in which God affirms His solemn oath to Noah and his family that the creation will never again be undone (9:8–17).[3] When it becomes clear that God's goal of having a relationship with humanity needs tweaking in order for it to become a realistic possibility, He establishes the Covenant Between the Pieces with Abram (15:1–21).

Those first two covenants are themselves quite radical in two ways. First, that God makes commitments to people and second, that He demands nothing in return. This sets them apart from the pagan world in which gods make demands of people and guarantee nothing in return. Yet despite that radical departure, in the biblical view these covenants represent baby steps in the relationship between God and humanity, as they are lacking mutuality – God commits Himself but makes no explicit demands of the people. Noah has no obligations in his

2. For a more complete description of the nature of covenants in the ancient world, their parallels to biblical covenants, and the uniqueness of the biblical covenants, see Joshua Berman, *Created Equal* (Oxford, 2008), 15–39.
3. As we will later discuss, the root used throughout the Bible to describe establishing a covenant is K-R-T. The verb used in the Noahide covenant is *lehakim* (Gen. 6:18, 9:1, 9:9, 19:17), meaning to uphold, suggesting that the Noahide covenant was actually not a new one but a reaffirmation of a preexisting one, which is never specified explicitly in the Torah.

covenant with God and all Abram needs to do is endure and be patient. The covenant of circumcision (17:1–27) adds demands of Abraham and his descendants, but also intensifies God's involvement. Abraham must commit himself, his children, and his children's children for all eternity to the bond. Newborn males are inducted into the covenant eight days after birth and have their very reproductive organs committed to the covenant for future generations. God's commitment is also intensified:

> I will establish My covenant between Me and you and your offspring for their generations, an eternal covenant, to be a God to you and to your offspring following you. I will give to you and to your offspring following you the land in which you dwelled, the land of Canaan, for an eternal holding, and I will be for them a God. (17:7–8)

Not only is God's commitment increased, but Abraham's role shifts as he is now tasked with being a "father to a multitude of nations" (17:4–5). Not surprisingly, soon after we find Abraham negotiating with God to save the region of Sodom, which God wants to destroy, and soon after that we find that Abraham's encounters with Avimelekh leave him and his people with a fear of God.

This sets biblical covenants even further apart from any others in the ancient world. God establishes these covenants with people so that they can be His partners, not His servants or His vassals. It is in this light that we read God's approach to Israel.

AN OFFER LIKE NO OTHER

As Moses stands on the mountain[4] God calls to him with His message.

> You saw what I did to Egypt; I carried you on eagle's wings and brought you to Me. So now, if you will obey My voice and guard My covenant, you will be for Me a unique treasure from among

4. Throughout the narrative of the Revelation Moses speaks to God while standing on the mountain and speaks to the people after descending from it.

> all the nations – for all the land is Mine. You will be for me a kingdom of priests and a nation set apart. (19:4–6)

The parallels to ancient suzerain treaties are clear – God begins by identifying what He has done for them followed by a brief summary of what He expects from them. The difference between this and suzerain treaties is also clear – God is not looking for tributes; He is seeking Israel's partnership. Nowhere is this clearer than in His proposal to elevate them to become a nation of priests.[5] Priests serve as intermediaries between people and God; a nation of priests is to serve as intermediaries between the rest of humanity and God. God is interested in Israel serving a unique role, but that role is to help God reconnect with all humanity as He declares, "For all the land is Mine."[6]

This represents a transformational upgrade to the covenant of circumcision in two ways.[7] There, too, God was interested in human partnership, but that was with an individual, Abraham. As an individual Abraham serves as a prototype of the relationship and what God is

---

5. Later in this chapter (19:22) we find God canceling the status of those who until this point were considered priests. They are to remain off the mountain like everyone else.
6. God's formulation generates a dynamic tension for His chosen nation. The word for sanctity, *kedusha*, means to be set apart; to sanctify something is to set it apart, to distinguish it from the ordinary. At the same time that God wants Israel to serve as a bridge to the rest of humanity, it must become separated from the rest of humanity. That sets up a tension between those two elements, one which seeks to ensure their uniqueness while demanding that they interact with others. That same tension is evident as God identifies Abraham as His partner. On the one hand, Abraham's mission is to become more universal, the father of a multitude of nations. On the other hand, that election is accompanied by the requirement for Abaham and his descendants to mark their bodies with circumcision, distinguishing themselves from the rest of humanity.
7. It appears that this covenant is built on the foundations of the covenant of circumcision, in which Abraham was promised that God would maintain a relationship with His descendants. Both are what Rabbi Soloveitchik would call covenants of destiny, pointing to a mission or purpose, rather than a covenant of fate like the Covenant Between the Pieces, which does not identify a purpose to Israel's suffering but does identify their predestined fate. See "Kol Dodi Dofek" in *Besod HaYaḥid VeHaYaḥad*, ed. Pinchas Peli (Orot, 1976), 331–400.

hoping to accomplish, but for God to reach all humanity He needs more than an individual; He needs an entire nation committed and devoted to His mission. The land He gives them will serve not only as a national homeland but as God's embassy, the place from which His message to the world can radiate. This is the vision which Moses earlier expresses in his song: the establishment of God's sanctuary in His promised land populated by His emissaries, yielding a universal declaration of "A-donai reigns forever and ever." It is also the message echoed by later prophets. Isaiah, for example, declares: "For from Zion shall go forth the Teaching and God's word from Jerusalem" (Is. 2:3).

The uniqueness of this message is not only in what it says – its universality and the fact that God is seeking the partnership of an entire nation[8] – but in what it is missing. There are numerous other messages in the Torah which open with a phrase such as "If you listen…" They are all followed by enumeration of a reward, after which there is the "If you don't listen…" followed by the punishment. Thus Leviticus 26:3 opens with "If you follow My statutes" and the ensuing blessing, followed by "If you do not listen to Me…" and the resulting calamities. Similarly in Deuteronomy 6:10–15, 7:12–8:20, 11:13–21, and 28:1–68, the formula of blessings and punishments seems standard.

Here, however, as God presents His covenant to the people, that formula is absent. There are no promises of bounty if they observe God's word and no threats of punishment if they do not. In fact, there isn't even an "If not" clause; there is only an "If yes" opening – and that opening is followed not by a promise but with the natural result: If Israel accepts God's covenant then they will become His special people.

The absence of promise and threat, of reward and punishment, transforms this into a truly voluntary decision by the people.[9] If they

---

8. Joshua Berman (*Created Equal*, 40–46) argues that the approach to nation rather to its leader stands out as unique in the ancient world.
9. The talmudic statement of R. Avdimi (Shabbat 88a), that God held the mountain over the nation's head and threatened them if they do not accept His Torah seems to be diametrically opposed to the meaning of the biblical text. A broad, theological reading of the text, however, could suggest that the redemption of Israel was the precursor to God's last hope for humanity, Israel's acceptance of the mission to become God's emissary to humanity. Should they decline that offer, all hope would

do not accept this upgrade to the covenant then they remain with the covenant to which God is still committed, the one He made with Abram to return his descendants as a wealthy people to their ancestral land and give that land to them. The significance of this covenant being voluntary cannot be overstated. We earlier briefly reviewed the history of biblical covenants, noting how they start from being one-sided promises from God and develop into relationships with mutual commitments. The common thread in those Genesis covenants is that they are all imposed – God never asks for Abraham's agreement, He simply informs or commands him. By contrast, the covenant at Sinai takes the concept a step further. In the bid toward establishing a genuine bilateral relationship with people, the next step is for people to willingly enter that relationship with God.[10]

CROSSED MESSAGES

Moses descends the mountain and lays out God's proposal. In light of the people's behavior during the prior six weeks we are not sure what their response will be. Will they react like they did just before the Splitting of the Sea or just after? Will they be skeptical like some were surrounding the manna, fearful like they were at Masa-Meriva, or confident as they were following Joshua into battle with Amalek? Will they even understand what God is suggesting? In light of the uncertainty displayed earlier, their response to the offer is nothing less than stunning: "The people responded, in unison, saying: 'All that God said we shall do'" (19:8).

Moses's delight in their response is evident. Though he knows that God is aware of what they said, he immediately turns to God to tell Him. "Moses brought the people's words to God" (19:8). It is at this moment that we find an unusual interaction between God and Moses.

---

be lost, necessitating that God restart Creation as He did in the days of Noah. That theological understanding of the text, however, was likely unknown to Israel at that time, so that their decision was a free one intentionally designed by God to be a free one.

10. Jeremiah (31:30–33 and 50:5) hints that the next step of the covenant with God requires Israel to initiate that covenant after they completely internalized God's message and their mission as His partners.

God does not react to the people's acceptance or to Moses's excitement, and instead seems to be interested in pursuing a different agenda.

> God said to Moses: Behold, I will come to you in the thickness of the cloud so that the people will overhear as I speak with you and thereby permanently believe in you too. (19:9)

Whatever God is interested in (which we will explore later), He does not seem to be reacting at all to Israel's acceptance of His offer. Moses, aware of this, turns back to God and repeats what he told Him earlier, as if to reiterate how significant this is: "Moses told God the people's words" (19:9). It seems like Moses and God are pursuing two different agendas, each talking past the other but not to each other.

As unusual as the dialogue is, it is only the first in a series of interactions between Moses and God in which they seem to not be in sync.

God instructs Moses to prepare Israel for two days – they are to clean their clothes and "sanctify" themselves.[11] On the third day God will "descend" upon the mountain and reveal Himself to the people, and they are to be careful not to touch the mountain lest they be stoned or shot – even animals will suffer that. Indeed, Moses "sanctifies" the people, has them clean their clothes, and tells them to prepare themselves for three days. Moses seems to have omitted mention of keeping away from the mountain and, strangely, changes the two-day preparatory period into a three-day one.[12] In light of that switch it is no wonder that,

---

11. The nature of this sanctification is unclear, but likely relates to God's opening message to the people: You will be for me a kingdom of priests and a sanctified nation. Moses, following God's instruction, is preparing the people to be distinct from other nations.

12. The Sages in Shabbat 88a note the switch from a two-day preparation to a three-day one.

    Moses adds an additional restriction to "keep away from women" (19:15). We discussed this in the previous chapter as possibly emerging from Moses's own personal intensity and related to his non-attention to the return of his wife. Moses's added requirement seems to imply that the event at Mount Sinai is intended only for males, which seems to be contraindicated by the description in the narrative. All this is particularly surprising given Tzippora's central role in the scene of the bloody bridegroom on the way to Egypt.

when the people rise on the third morning and find that the mountain is covered in a thick cloud accompanied by thunder and lightning, they are truly frightened: "The entire people in the camp trembled" (19:16). They were expecting an event after three days of preparation, and they are surprised when after only two days they are caught unprepared.

Moses's omission of telling the people to stay away from the mountain does not go unnoticed. In the midst of the storm brewing on the mountain, God "descends" onto the mountain and calls Moses up. The first words God says after Moses climbs the mountain are "Go down," and the instruction which follows is for Moses to warn the people not to approach the mountain. When Moses argues with God about the necessity to tell the people, God repeats His command, "Go, go down" (19:24).

What is happening?

ONE RESPONSE, TWO REACTIONS

It would seem that Moses and God each have different reactions to the people's initial response of "All that God said we shall do." Moses is excited about what they say – they agree to God's request and will do as He instructs. He is so excited that he tells God, and when God seems to ignore him, he repeats it. He doesn't feel that it is necessary to warn them not to go up onto the mountain, because whatever signs he made indicate that it is off-limits, and these are a people who – after generations of servitude – know their place and how to follow instructions. So confident is Moses, that even after God tells him a second time to go tell them Moses insists that it is unnecessary.

God, however, has a different agenda. He is not as interested in whether the people will listen to His instructions as He is in whether they will be good covenantal partners. The difference between being obedient and being a partner is huge. Being obedient means that they will do whatever God tells them. Being a partner means that they will be active in pursuing God's agenda, not simply obedient workers. Obedient workers are not necessarily committed to the company's mission; they want to follow the rules and collect their pay. They will not take their work home with them. Partners, however, will constantly be thinking about how to further the mission of the institution they work for; they will need to identify with that mission and actively seek out ways to bring it to fruition.

Moses is a primary model of that kind of partner. He began by following God's instructions, sometimes not even so carefully, but eventually bought into the mission, seeking actively and creatively to fulfill it. It is for that reason that God's initial reaction to the people's response is to ignore it, focusing instead on how to increase Moses's stature in their eyes, so that the people permanently trust him as well.[13]

When God hears the people say that they will "do" whatever He tells them, He hears servant people willing to trade their servitude to the wicked Pharaoh for their servitude to the benevolent God. But it is not servitude He seeks; it is partnership. He wants not only "If you will obey My voice" but also "Guard My covenant" – and He has not as yet heard that from the people.[14]

It is that distinction which is at the core of what happens on the third and fourth days. On the third day God descends on the mountain; He is preparing to meet His covenantal partners. It is not necessarily a day of instruction; that will come later. Rather, it is a day when the two partners meet. God had told Moses to prepare them for the third day, the day of Revelation, of the meeting of the partners.[15] Moses, on the

---

13. Remember that Moses's believability was a key concern at the burning bush, where Moses expressed fear that the people would not believe him (4:1) and God provided him with signs to ensure that they do (4:5, 4:8, and 4:9). When Moses first goes to the people, his initial success is marked by their believing in him (4:31). That faith is enhanced as they witness him splitting the sea (14:31), and God wants to firm that up so that his commitment to God's mission is maintained as a living model of what they should be aspiring toward. In all the above, the same root for belief (A-M-N) is used.
14. At Masa-Meriva Moses had accused the people of challenging whether God's presence was within them or not (17:7). While it is not clear if they were actually challenging that or not, it appears that God's offer takes that challenge and presents it back to Israel. If they want God's presence among them, then they need to enter into a covenant with Him. The answer to their query is in their own hands.
15. Evan Wolkenstein (personal communication) notes that there are two tremblings related in this scene – one of the mountain (19:18), representing God, and the other of the people (19:16). (Note: The same root, Ḥ-R-D, is used to describe both.) Those tremblings are the anxiousness of a first encounter in which both sides are aware that this might be a long-term relationship, with all the associated pitfalls. This is very different from the presentation in Psalms 114, where the trembling of the mountain is similar to that of Israel in that both tremble in the face of the presence of the

other hand, doesn't think that the people are prepared for that. He hears their response and understands that they, as recently freed slaves, have no concept of covenant, of mission, of partnership. They are, however, capable of obedience, and given that the instructions are not necessarily the essence of the Revelation, he prepares them for the instructions they will receive – on the following day.

Moses hears the people's preparedness to obey God and is thrilled; but God is not interested. Moses knows that if he marked the mountain, they will not approach it; but God wants them to understand that it is His presence on that mountain which they may not approach,[16] that they understand that in this partnership He is the senior partner. Moses is satisfied with obedience; God wants covenant.

When we read the narrative through these eyes we are left with a huge, lingering question. If Moses dd not prepare the people for covenant because he didn't think that they were ready for it, did Israel actually enter a covenant with God at Sinai?

COVENANT, DELAYED

A search for the covenant prior to the Decalogue yields no results. When we extend our search to afterward, we encounter a strange sequence of events in Exodus 24 – five chapters later, after the Decalogue (Ex. 20) – and a long list of laws (Ex. 21–23).[17] Here is the text:

> Moses came and told the people "all the words of God" and the *mishpatim* (laws); the entire nation responded, in unison, saying, "All the things that God said we will do." Moses wrote *all the words*

Almighty. "Why do you dance?" asks the psalmist figuratively of the mountains. Their answer: "Before the master the earth shakes, before the God of Jacob, who turns rock into a pool of water."

16. Yoel Bin-Nun (personal communication) reads the description of the mountain during the Revelation as resembling an active volcano. Thunder and lightning, ground tremors, rocks spewing forth. The presence of God on the mountain brings even the dead rock to life – it becomes a living, breathing being. That same presence is what Israel is to meet on that day.

17. We are reading the text according to the chronology as it is presented in the Torah text, as does Nahmanides. Rashi uses a chronology for the entire second half of Exodus that veers dramatically from the text multiple times.

> *of God,* arose early in the morning, and built an altar at the foot of the mountain, as well as twelve *matzeva* (monument) stones for the twelve tribes of Israel. He sent the young Israelite men who brought burnt *ola* offerings; and they slaughtered cows to God, *shelamim.* Moses took half of the blood and placed it in the collecting pans, and half the blood he sprinkled onto the altar. He took the Book of the Covenant and read it aloud to the people; they said, "*All that God said* we will do and we will listen." Moses took the blood and sprinkled it on the people and he said, "Behold, the blood of the covenant which God established with you over *all these things.*" (24:3–8)

Before we continue, it is valuable to explore some background material regarding sacrifices and covenants. When it comes to the sacrificial order (which is laid out in great detail in Leviticus), one of the two most important elements of any sacrifice is the sprinkling of the blood. From a halakhic perspective, the core service of the sacrifice – the parts which must be done by a *kohen* – is that involving collecting, transporting, and sprinkling the blood.[18] The number and placement of the blood sprinklings varies greatly from one sacrifice to another and carries great significance. According to the description in the Mishna, it is the most significant identifier of the level of sanctity of the sacrifice and how the flesh of the animal is to be processed.[19]

We have already noted that regarding biblical covenants, the ceremonies often contain an element of taking something and splitting it. The paradigm for this is the Covenant Between the Pieces, in which Abraham was instructed to split the animals. Other examples include the covenant Jacob makes with Laban, in which they "break bread," literally, splitting the bread between them. In fact, the verb used in the Bible for establishing covenant is K-R-T, "splitting." This verb and the associated symbolism of splitting are used because covenant involves

18. Talmud Zevaḥim 7a.
19. Regarding the placement of the blood see 29:12, 30:10; Lev. 1:5, 3:2; and many others. For a systematic description of the placement of the blood, see Mishna Zevaḥim ch. 5.

two entities choosing to share a common fate or destiny; the item split between them represents that they are each one half of that whole and that the two halves are interdependent.

With that background we are prepared to return to our text. The scene opens with Moses relating two things to the people, "all the words of God" and the *mishpatim*. Identifying the *mishpatim* as the laws enumerated in Exodus 21–23 is easy, as Exodus 21 opens with the introduction "These are the *mishpatim* which you shall place before them."[20] What is less clear is what the Torah identifies as "all the words of God," and we will return to this soon. Regardless, Israel's response to Moses's presentation is the same as their response to his initial presentation of God's offer in Exodus 19: "We will do." We recall that the first time Israel responded Moses was excited, so much so that he shared their response with God, twice, while God didn't seem moved by it. Here, it seems that Moses's enthusiasm for their response has disappeared; he was apparently hoping for something else, or something more.

Early the next day he writes what is described as "all the words of God," which is still undefined, and prepares a ceremony featuring two items he constructs and the blood of freshly slaughtered offerings. One of the items he constructs is an installment of twelve *matzeva* stones representing the tribes of Israel; the other is an altar, presumably representing God. Moses takes the blood from the offerings and divides it – half he sprinkles on the altar and the other half he retains in the vessels he used to collect it. It is at that point that Moses picks up the "Book of the Covenant" and reads it aloud to the people. When they respond, "All that God said we will do and we will listen," Moses sprinkles the rest of the blood on them and declares, "Behold, the blood of the covenant which God established with you over all these things."

It is now easy to recognize this as a covenant ceremony – Moses says so explicitly and it is accompanied by an act of splitting, half of the blood on the representative of God and the other half on the people.[21]

20. See Ibn Ezra, 24:3.
21. It is difficult to imagine Moses sprinkling the blood on the hundreds of thousands of Israelites. It is possible that he sprinkled it instead on the twelve *matzeva* stones representing Israel.

Even more, the "Book of the Covenant," which appears mysteriously, is likely what Moses wrote earlier that day, containing what the Torah describes as "all the words of God." When we look back at the story we discover what is in this "book" as the full picture begins to emerge.

Prior to the Revelation, God had offered Israel to join Him in covenant, to become His partner. As recently freed slaves, that was something that they could not fathom; hence their response to God was concrete and pragmatic, that they were prepared to do whatever He would instruct them to do. For Moses that sufficed at the time, but not for God, which is why God looks past their response. Following the Revelation, and following the long list of mitzvot which follows, Moses understands that the people need to be moved to a greater commitment than merely obeying God's commands. As such, he tells them about the *mishpatim* but also about "all the words of God" – referring to the covenant God wishes to establish with them. Their response, however, did not change from their earlier one; they are prepared to do whatever God tells them to do. Now it is Moses's turn to realize that this is insufficient, and so he creates a ceremony that will feature a single element – the covenant. He writes the Book of the Covenant with a single element – the covenant with God, otherwise identified as "all the words of God." The animals are slaughtered and the blood is sprinkled on the altar, indicating God's preparedness to enter the covenant. He then reads the Book of the Covenant aloud so that the meaning of this event is unambiguous. When the people understand the substance of this event they finally respond, "All that God said we will do and we will listen," indicating their acceptance of the covenant. It is only then that Moses sprinkles the blood on them as well, completing the sharing of the blood, and declares it to be the blood of the covenant.

THE YOUTH AND THE ELDERS

Within this climactic scene orchestrated by Moses, there are two groups of individuals who stand out. First are the youth, whom Moses charges with bringing the sacrifices whose blood will be used in the ceremony (24:5). This is not the first time that Moses has introduced youth as essential persons – at the Exodus it was Moses who twice instructed the people to be prepared to tell their children in the future about what God had done for them. Moses understands that for covenant to be long-lasting it is necessary to induct the next generation from an early stage, and here he does that by including them physically in the covenantal ceremony.

This focus on the transmission of covenant to the next generation, even at an early age, has precedent. The initial covenant of circumcision required Abraham to circumcise his children, from infancy, inducting them into the covenant long before they have any consciousness of what that could mean. In fact, the circumcision itself is done to the reproductive organ, essentially committing the newborn child to not only receive the covenant but to transmit it as well.

While Moses brings the youth into the covenant, God invites the elders (24:1 and 24:9) – not only as representatives of the people but as those whose are charged, both then and in future generations, to transmit the covenant further. Regarding these elders, however, the Torah records a most unusual scene:

> They saw the God of Israel, and under His feet was like sapphire brickwork and the pure essence of the heavens. God did not send for His hand against the nobles of Israel, and they ate and drank. (24:10–11)

I will not even attempt to explain what the elders saw, but the description of them in this scene illuminates the story in two ways. First, we recall Israel's reaction to the sights and sounds at Sinai – they recoiled in fear and stood at a distance. By contrast, in this scene the elders are partway up the mountain where they have a visual experience of God, and they are not struck down. It is an experience which they, as the elders, will likely retell to their children, and their children to their children, to know that the encounter with God need not consume the individual.

Second, the description of the elders eating and drinking is likely connected to the offerings brought by the youth. Those offerings were of two types – *olot* (burnt offerings) and *shelamim* (peace offerings). The *olot* represent complete submission to God, as they are completely consumed on the altar, while the *shelamim* represent partnership with God, as both the altar and those who bring the offering share in the consumption of the animal. The two offerings in combination serve as an extraordinary metaphor for the relationship between Israel and God. On the one hand, the covenantal people are in partnership with God. On the other hand, God is clearly the senior partner in this special relationship.[22] If the elders were eating, it was not a Sunday picnic; rather, they were consuming the very *shelamim* which represented Israel's new partnership.

Introducing the youth and the elders together into the covenantal scene highlights a path for transmitting the covenant across multiple generations. The elders bear the memories and traditions of the past and are charged with passing them on to future generations.

MOSES, THE HERO OF THE COVENANT

The events at Sinai did not necessarily go as God had planned or hoped. The people did not enter the covenant prior to the Revelation; they were simply unprepared for that. Nonetheless, despite the disappointment, God continues with the Revelation and the giving of the *mishpatim*. Moses, however, enables God's vision to come to fruition. Before the story can continue, he – as God's chosen leader and as the one who has accepted his partnership with God – designs and facilitates the people's entry into covenant with God. Moses's initiative saves Israel from missing their opportunity and saves God's roadmap for the future of His involvement with humanity.[23]

God had intended to elevate Moses by having the people witness His speaking with Moses: "Behold, I will come to you in the thickness of the cloud so that the people will overhear as I speak with you and thereby permanently believe in you too" (19:9). Moses ultimately does become elevated, not because God did so but because of his own leadership in negotiating between God and the people – it is his own success which propels him to a new status. He ascends the mountain and enters the fiery cloud representing God's presence, where he will remain for as long as God wants him there.

22. This mirrors the Decalogue, which we will soon explore, which opens with the declaration that Israel will have no other god.
23. Since Moses's first encounter with God at the burning bush, he has demonstrated independence and gumption. Perhaps it is these qualities which God so welcomes in His chosen leader, as He seeks a genuine partner, not just an obedient mouthpiece.

Exodus 20:1–18

The Decalogue

Maimonides describes the encounter with God as a dance between intense love and yearning on the one hand and terrifying awe on the other.[1] Like a moth attracted to a fire, it can't resist approaching the fire but if it gets too close it will be overwhelmed and incinerated. Love of God and the desire to apprehend as much as possible draws people close until that love is replaced by overwhelming awe of being in God's presence, accompanied by a profound feeling of insignificance, which generate an instinctive pulling back.

God's appearance on the mountain – with the attendant full-immersion experience of thunder, lightning, smoke, sound, and ground tremors – is so terrifying that the people pull back; Moses needs to "take them out" so that they greet God. At the same time, God is concerned that their curiosity, their desire to see, will draw them to encroach upon the mountain and thus perish.

Indeed, the experience defies description in human terms, so much so that the Torah records:

1. *Hilkhot Yesodei HaTorah* 2:2.

> All the people are seeing the sounds and the flames and the sound of the shofar and the smoking mountain; the people saw and recoiled and stood at a distance. They said to Moses: "You speak with us and we will listen; let God not speak with us lest we die." (20:14–15)

"Seeing the sounds" is the Torah's way of describing an experience which the senses cannot capture, so that sight and sound become blurred, as neither is an adequate description.[2] The intensity of that experience was so extreme that it generated Israel's recoil and led to their insisting that Moses approach the dark cloud of God as they keep their distance.[3]

While the text records these events after the giving of the Decalogue, prompting some commentators to understand the chronology as written,[4] some of the classic commentaries suggest that this scene takes place in the middle of the theophany, interrupting the Decalogue.[5] They ground their suggestion in the observation that only the first two statements of the Decalogue are written with God speaking in the first person: "I am A-donai, your God.... You shall have no other gods in My Presence...for I am A-donai your God...who does kindness for thousands of generations for those who love Me and guard My commands" (20:2–5). Afterward, the language switches to speaking about God in the third person: "You shall not take the name of A-donai your God in vain...the seventh day is Shabbat for A-donai your God...for in six days God created the heavens and the earth" (20:9–11).

2. See Ibn Ezra on 20:14.
3. A careful reading of the Torah text reveals that, contrary to the way this scene has been portrayed artistically, Moses is at the foot of the mountain together with the rest of the people during God's pronouncement of the Decalogue. This has profound symbolic meaning in that despite God's efforts to ensure that Moses's status becomes elevated, when it comes to entering the covenant with God all are equal – no individual member of Israel can claim a greater position or access to it than any other, not even Moses.
4. Nahmanides, 20:14.
5. Rashi on 19:19 based on Mekhilta. This could be supported by the grammatical formulation of the opening of 20:14, which can be interpreted as describing an event that is already in progress.

Regardless of whether this takes place before, during, or after the pronouncement of the Decalogue, it is clear that the experience of the meeting between the two partners of the covenant shakes the Israelites to their core. It is perhaps for this reason that immediately afterward God forbids the attempt to capture any image of that experience (20:19–20). When we have profoundly moving experiences, whether as a result of witnessing the grandeur of the world or an extraordinary display of human achievement or spirit, we yearn to take some of that experience with us – in the form of photographs or recordings or souvenirs. While those remind us of the experience, they can never quite capture it. It is precisely for that reason that God forbids creating "souvenirs" or visual reminders of the experience at Sinai. Any such reminders will fall short of the authentic experience and will, by definition, portray the event as a shallow – and false – representation of what it was.

With the passage of time Moses himself becomes acutely aware of the danger of the temptation to re-create the visual experience. Reading through the Torah's presentation of the event here, the sense which dominates is that of sight. Prior to the Decalogue God warns Moses to warn the people against approaching the mountain, "lest they break through to God to see" (19:21), and afterward the Torah describes that they "saw the sounds" (20:15). Forty years later, as Moses retells the story, he recasts the experience as one exclusively of sound:

> God spoke with you from the fire; you heard the sound of words but saw no image. (Deut. 4:12)

> You did not see any images on the day that God spoke with you at Horeb from the fire. (Deut. 4:15)

One of the distinguishing features of hearing as opposed to seeing is that hearing is about understanding. Transmission of the spoken word involves taking the message and internalizing it in a way that the message can then be retransmitted; it is about retaining the content, not the form. As Moses shares the message with the new generation, that is precisely what he does; he takes the words and reshapes them so that the message can be shared anew. It is that content, and not the experience, which he understands must be the focus.

WHAT IS THE DECALOGUE?

Before we examine the specifics of the substance of the Decalogue, two notes are in order. First, despite the popular terminology, the Decalogue is not ten commandments; it is ten statements.[6] There are debates in the Jewish tradition of how many commandments are included and little agreement about which statements are included in the commandments. There are, however, ten clearly identifiable statements, each separated from its neighbor by a Masoretic break in the text. For that reason I choose to use the term "Decalogue," which best describes it.

Second, the Decalogue does not emerge from a vacuum. We've already looked at the sweep of the biblical story until this point. God created humans and endowed them with His image, hoping that would be enough for them to figure out how to conduct themselves appropriately. That initial effort failed when people ignored or abused that divine spark, necessitating a restart. After the Great Confusion, when God restarts the Creation, He introduces a few rules, hoping that these will help guide humanity on its path. The relationship between humans and animals is restructured – humans are permitted to kill and eat animals, but not live animal flesh, and are forbidden from killing other humans precisely because people are created in the divine image (Gen. 9:6). As that effort falters, however, God elects to follow a different path to reach humanity. Starting with Abraham and eventually climaxing with the covenant He establishes with Israel at Sinai, God will find a nation – a sanctified people – to represent Him. An essential part of that process, just like God's renewal of the world with Noah, is God's making explicit the things He thought people would have figured out for themselves. At each stage there is more which is made explicit, so that the Decalogue represents the core ideas that God would have hoped humanity would have intuited and which He now needs to make explicit. To be God's partner requires embracing these foundational principles about which God wants to make sure there will be no misunderstanding. They are

6. See 34:28; Deut. 4:13 and 10:4.

the expanded version of what Abraham intuited – God's way, founded on justice and righteousness (Gen. 18:19) – the core values which qualify a people to become God's covenantal partner, His special people.

It is no wonder, then, that rabbinic tradition identifies seven Noahide laws[7] introduced after the Great Confusion.

1. The requirement to establish a justice system
2. The prohibition of profaning God's name
3. The prohibition of idolatry
4. The prohibition of illicit sexual relationships
5. The prohibition of murder
6. The prohibition of theft
7. The prohibition of eating the flesh of a live animal

A quick survey of the seven reveals that five of those are included in the Decalogue; the Sages understood that these are fundamental for leading lives as beings created in the divine image.

The idea that the Decalogue reflects the fundamental principles of humanity is sharpened as we reflect on it in light of Genesis, where we find multiple examples of human failure precisely in the areas spelled out in the Decalogue.

Genesis	Decalogue
Jacob's family carries idols with them (Gen. 35:4)	You shall not make any idol
Jacob's four oldest sons each mount rebellions against him	Honor your mother and father
Ham disgraces Noah (9:22)	Honor your mother and father
Cain kills Abel	You shall not murder
Reuben lays with his father's wife	You shall not commit adultery

7. Sanhedrin 56b. Later authorities suggest that many of these were forbidden to the first people God created as well, even though the Torah text is silent about them.

Theft is rampant prior to the Great Confusion (6:13)[8]	You shall not steal
Joseph's brothers kidnap him	You shall not steal[9]
Jacob lies to his father	You shall not bear false witness against your fellow
Jacob is repeatedly deceived by Laban	You shall not bear false witness against your fellow
Jacob's sons deceive him	You shall not bear false witness against your fellow
Judah deceives Tamar	You shall not bear false witness against your fellow
Potiphar's wife lies to her servants and her husband	You shall not bear false witness against your fellow
The woman in the Garden sees the tree as desirable (Ḥ-M-D)	You shall not covet (Ḥ-M-D)

The Decalogue seems to be God's declaration that if we didn't figure out from the stories in Genesis what the basic expectations of humanity are, He is now making them explicit.[10]

The connection between the Decalogue and Genesis goes beyond being a corrective for the human failures in Genesis; they bring us back to God's decision to change course and choose to connect to humanity through the choice of an ambassador, whether the individual Abram or the people Israel. Perhaps nothing expresses this better than seeing the

8. The Torah describes what was happening as *ḥamas*. Most commentaries understand that to mean theft.
9. The Talmud (Sanhedrin 86a) interprets this as a prohibition against kidnapping.
10. A similar idea emerges from a careful reading of Deuteronomy 21:10–25:16. The subtext of that extended section of legal material are the stories of Jacob's family, including a man with a favored and a less favored wife, preferential treatment of children, choosing the younger son over the elder, rebellious children, spreading false rumors about a betrothed woman, adultery, rape, seduction, *yibum* (levirate marriage), and *ḥalitza* (the refusal to perform levirate marriage). The composite message of that entire section is that the Torah is making explicit the many messages it had hoped that people would learn from the mistakes made in Genesis.

parallel between the opening statement in Abram's Covenant Between the Pieces and the opening of the Decalogue.

> I am A-donai who took you out of Ur Kasdim. (Gen. 15:7)

> I am A-donai, your God, who took you out of the land of Egypt. (Ex. 20:2)

The near-identical formulation used in both opening statements highlights their function as the beginning of a new kind of relationship – a special mutual bond between God and His select people.

STRUCTURING THE DECALOGUE

Just as there is little agreement on how many commandments are included in the Decalogue, it is far from clear what the ten statements are. Is 20:2, "I am A-donai, your God," to be considered a separate statement, an introduction to the prohibition against worshipping other gods, or a general introduction to the Decalogue? Similarly, there are two statements at the end which both start with "You shall not covet," and they are separated by a Masoretic break in the text. Are those part of the same statement or are they to be considered two distinct statements? What makes these questions valuable is that organizing the Decalogue into groups helps us to analyze it and direct exploration of the meaning of each of those and the relationship between them. For centuries, artistic renderings of the Decalogue typically show two tablets, each engraved with five of the statements. Those artists were well aware of the imbalance between the two, the first containing nearly 150 words and the second only 15; they abbreviated those first statements, typically including only the first one or two words of each statement on the first tablet, but what drove those artists was the need for meaningful structure. Many commentators typically see the first five statements as dealing with the relationship between man and God while the second five relate to the relationships between people. That neat breakdown is challenged by what they see as the fifth statement, "Honor your father and mother," necessitating creative interpretations of that statement to rework it so that it fits into the category of between man and God.

When we read statements using a literary lens, we notice that from the beginning through the statement about Shabbat (20:11), the statements are relatively lengthy and are accompanied by an explanation of why (*ki*) Israel should adhere to the injunction. In this section, which we will call the opening section, the name A-donai is featured seven times, five of which are in the formula of "A-donai, your God."[11] These stand in dramatic contrast to the final statements, beginning with "You shall not murder," which are terse – three of them consist of two words each, not enough to even constitute a complete verse – and they have neither an explanation nor God's name. We will call these the closing section.

In that lens, the statement about honoring parents is transitionary. It is shorter than any of the opening statements yet longer than any of the closing ones. It includes reference to "A-donai, your God," even though it is not about relationship with God, and it includes a reward for observance but is missing the *ki* word of explanation.

THE OPENING SECTION

The opening section is God's introduction of Himself to Israel. While Israel has witnessed what God can do, they know little else about Him other than that He is the God of their ancestors.[12] As God introduces Himself to Israel He emphasizes three things: (a) His name, the one which He earlier revealed to Moses (6:2–8) and now repeats seven times; (b) that although He is the Creator of all, He has selected Israel exclusively;[13] and (c) that Israel is to worship Him exclusively. These three core ideas form the foundation of the mutually exclusive covenant He is establishing with Israel, a relationship that the zealous God will protect and enforce.

Within their understanding of the nature of God, as opposed to the gods to which they were exposed to in Egypt, A-donai, the God of past, present, and future, the God who will be what He will be, who cannot be manipulated – only He will choose what He will be and what He will do. Other Near Eastern gods could be bought, bribed, or

11. See Ibn Ezra's commentary on 20:2 and 20:12.
12. Presumably, Moses shared this with them when he first came to them.
13. This is the meaning of "A-donai, your God," that is, your God and no one else's.

cajoled through gifts, sacrifices, or other theurgic practices designed to empower people to sway them. This God cannot be controlled by human practices; invoking God's name to affect the outcome of some human endeavor is in vain and will not be tolerated.[14]

The climax of the opening section charges Israel to distinguish Shabbat from other days of the week by being in a constant state of awareness that their God is not only the One who performed wonders for them but is, in fact, the Creator of the world – the very idea that God has been trying to reignite since He decided to upend Pharaoh and his reign. The subtext of the first half of Exodus now becomes explicit as part of the foundation of God's relationship with Israel.

One meaning of Shabbat emerges when we consider it in the context of Israel's exodus from Egypt. When Pharaoh first heard Moses's request for a three-day furlough to serve God, he not only rejected the request but intensified their work so that they would be too busy to think about anything other than their service to Pharaoh. Shabbat demands the break from physical labor precisely to allow for the kind of reflection and contemplation which ennobles the human spirit and which Pharaoh sought to prevent. The constant awareness of that respite prevents daily drudgery from dominating the human spirit, so that even the animals and the household need to desist from that labor to create an environment which is free of doing in the physical world.

An entirely different dimension of Shabbat becomes clear when we examine it in the context of covenant. A careful reading of the closing verse of the statement regarding Shabbat reveals that Israel does not commemorate Shabbat because God desisted from work on the seventh day, but that God desisted from creating on the seventh in order that Israel should do the same. *Al ken berakh A-donai et yom haShabbat vayekadeshehu* – it is for this reason (i.e., that Israel should be aware of and distinguish the Shabbat) that God blessed the Shabbat and sanctified

14. The expression to "bear God's name" appears only five times in the Bible. Two of them are in the Decalogue here (20:7) and two are in the Decalogue in Deuteronomy (5:11). The final time it appears is in the Psalms (16:4), where the psalmist declares that, as opposed to the idolaters, he will neither bring libations to their gods nor bear their names on his lips – both of which were practices intended to influence those gods to do their bidding.

it (20:11). The potential with which God initially endowed Shabbat, to allow humans to express their divine spark beyond creation in the physical space, lay unfulfilled from the days of Creation. It is here, at Sinai, with Israel entering the covenant, that the potential can finally be expressed.[15]

In the framework of the Decalogue, this analysis takes on a special meaning. Shabbat should have belonged to all humanity – it celebrates Creation, which is universal, and provides opportunities for developing the human spirit, also universal. Paradoxically, by demanding that only Israel observe Shabbat, God has transformed the universal idea into one which celebrates Israel's uniqueness. This is what the Torah later makes explicit:

> Israel is to observe the Shabbat, to do the Shabbat for all generations as an eternal covenant. Between Me and Israel it is an eternal sign that God created the heavens and the earth in six days but on the seventh He desisted and inspired. (31:16–17)

With Shabbat, the opening section of the Decalogue – the foundational definitions of the covenant – is complete. Israel has been introduced to God, Israel accepts A-donai as their only God, and God elevates Israel as His exclusive chosen nation.

THE CLOSING SECTION

If the opening section lays out the core building blocks of the covenant, the closing section outlines a definition of being a holy nation, or a nation set apart.

---

15. The two roots B-R-KH (bless, to endow with potential) and K-D-SH (sanctify, to set aside and distinguish) appear together in only two places in the Bible. One is in the Creation when describing the seventh day (Gen. 2:3) and the other is here in the discussion of Shabbat in the Decalogue. See Grumet, *Genesis: From Creation to Covenant*, 29–38.

The idea of the Decalogue as the completion of a phase of Creation may be linked to the statement of the Mishna (Avot 5:1) which notes that God created the world through ten sayings (identified by the word *vayomer*). If the Decalogue marks God's reentry into the world, a revitalization of the Creation, then it would make sense that there be a parallel between the ten "sayings" of Creation and the ten "statements" of the Decalogue.

The first three statements are self-explanatory, as attested to by their brevity. These are the most basic requirements of what it means to be a human living with other humans. They capture most succinctly the errors of the early generations of humanity and the values which the Sages described as belonging to the Noahide laws. They have nothing to do with God or our relationship with Him; they have everything to do with being people endowed with a divine spirit. And they are essential for establishing a civil society – including the need for an incorruptible justice system.

In the close of that section, however, the brevity disappears as we begin to see clarification, in significant detail, in the final instruction.

> You shall not covet your neighbor's home.
> You shall not covet your neighbor's wife or his male servant or his female servant or his ox or his donkey or anything that is your neighbor's. (20:14)

The repetition of the opening "You shall not covet" is particularly startling. In a set of statements marked by brevity we would have expected that phrase to have been written just once. Alternatively, we might even have expected a much simpler formulation. "You shall not covet." Period. Just like, "You shall not murder," "You shall not commit adultery," and "You shall not steal." Yet instead of brevity, the Torah chose to state the instruction twice, once as a general statement and a second time with the specifics spelled out.[16]

It would appear, then, that these statements take us beyond the core of what it means to be a human living with other humans. In fact, as a person living with other people, jealousy of what the other has is expected. Taking this a step further, because jealousy is a normal human reaction, that is precisely why the Torah needs to spell out the details – it can't rely on basic human judgment to suppress all the different things that drive people to want to have what others do.[17]

---

16. The expanded list partially overlaps with the list of those who must desist from work on Shabbat (20:10). The overlap is emphasized even more in the version of the Decalogue in Deuteronomy.
17. The prohibition against coveting is the subject of considerable discussion among

The prohibition against coveting takes us beyond the Noahide laws, the things we expect people to intuit – it brings us to a much greater demand, the kind that is not expected of all people but is expected of those God elects to be His partners. God expects more of those who represent Him, whom He can call a people, a people set apart from others. If the preceding statements are the basic requirements for being civil people in a civil society, the prohibition against coveting pushes Israel to go a huge step beyond as they are charged with being God's people, set apart. This is what will set them apart.

THE CENTER OF THE DECALOGUE

In between the opening, which defines the foundation of the covenant, and the close, which lays out the outline of a distinguished civil society, is but a single statement: "Honor your father and your mother, so that your days on the earth which A-donai, your God, gives you, may be long" (20:12). It is shorter than the opening statements but longer than the closing ones. Literarily it seems to belong to the first group, as it references God explicitly and offers a reward, but it is different in that there is no *ki* explanation offered. And its content, human relationships, seems to suggest that it would be more comfortable in the second group. Despite the many attempts to justify the inclusion of this in the first group,[18] it seems that this statement stands alone, and that demands our attention.

The relationship between parents and children is perhaps the most fraught, and most dynamic of all. When children are first born, they are completely dependent on their parents. Every step beyond that involves the child taking small steps toward independence. Mastering the toys in the crib, exploring the various stages of locomotion followed by transportation, learning to self-feed, gaining facility in speech – every one of these is a stage in the child's slow march toward independence. That process continues through adolescence and emerging adulthood, and

---

the commentators. After all, how can God forbid an emotion? Mekhilta, and later Maimonides (*Sefer HaMitzvot* 265–66), were so bothered by this that they reinterpreted the prohibition as planning to take what the other has. Ibn Ezra (Ex. 20:14) offers a creative, actionable, cognitive suggestion for controlling this emotion.

18. See Bekhor Shor, Nahmanides, Rabbeinu Baḥya, Abrabanel, *Kli Yakar*, Rabbi David Zvi Hoffmann, and Cassuto.

for many continues well into their advanced years. It is not for naught that already in the Garden the Torah proclaims, "Therefore a man shall leave his father and his mother and will cleave to his wife" (Gen. 2:24). Learning to cut the umbilical cord is an essential step in the child's development into healthy adulthood.

Parents are well aware of this and want it too, even though relinquishing control of their children is never easy. Every step of the child's independence brings a mixture of joy and trepidation for the parents, whether it is the first time that the parents drop the child off at school or let them walk to a friend's house by themselves or take the car. Despite the fear and anxiety, parents want their children to grow into independent people.

Even with grown, adult children, however, the relationship continues; independence does not require estrangement. So that while the relationship will hopefully not be one of need or dependence, it can include a mixture of gratitude, care, respect, reverence, valuing, and more.

The parent-child relationship is an extraordinary metaphor for the relationship between God and Israel. In the nation's infancy it needs constant care – food, water, protection, guidance. As the nation matures God hopes that it begins to learn independence, grow its own crops, fight its own battles, chart its relationships with other nations. To be sure, there are times when some corrective measure is necessary, but God's ultimate vision is one in which the nation chooses to include God in its life rather than needing to do so out of crisis.

This, I believe, explains the placement of honoring parents in the center of the Decalogue. Not because it belongs to both the opening and the closing, and not because it can serve as a bridge between the first and last parts of the Decalogue, but because it is the core, the paradigm, for the long-lasting, time-tested, enduring covenantal relationship God seeks with Israel[19] – a relationship which grows as the people grow, which

19. This completes the circle begun with God's choice of Abraham. Genesis 18:19 explains the choice because Abraham is committed to transmitting God's values to his children. Here the Torah completes the cycle: That process is truly completed when the children honor their parents for successfully following through on Abraham's mantra.

shifts dynamically, and which encourages the people to become God's true partner in the world. That partnership rests not on their following His instructions but on their internalization of His mission to humanity along with a determination to bring that vision to fruition.

Exodus 20:19–23:33

Beyond the Decalogue

One of the distinguishing features of the Torah is that, as literature, it deems to defy categorization. On the one hand, approximately half of it is narrative. From the creation and the prehistory of the world through the period of the patriarchs, from the slavery in Egypt to God's glorious salvation and Revelation at Sinai, and through forty years of travel and travails in the wilderness, the Torah is filled with stories. On the other hand, approximately half of the Torah is legal in nature. Beginning with the laws surrounding the night of the Exodus and its commemoration, there are multiple collections of legal material in every book of the Torah except Genesis. In fact, Rashi's first comment in his commentary on the Torah presumes that the legal material is primary, and he questions the necessity for the narratives at all.

A different perspective would suggest that the primary function of the Torah is its sweeping narrative about God's relationship to humanity in general, and His relationship to Israel in particular. According to this view, the legal sections are an integral part of the narrative. The laws also tell a story – why these laws were chosen to be taught at this point, why they are grouped as they are, how they are structured, and what ideas they are trying to convey, all enhance our understanding of God's expectations and hopes for humanity and for Israel. That is the approach we saw in our exploration of the Decalogue. Rather than looking to understanding specific details and requirements, we sought to understand why these statements were considered essential in the context of the covenant God is establishing with His people.

The collection of mitzvot following the Decalogue is particularly enigmatic. While it mostly focuses on interpersonal matters, there is a smattering of other laws, seemingly randomly inserted, including laws about cursing judges, slaughtering for worshipping other gods, witchcraft, forbidden food, and holidays. The style of writing is also inconsistent, so that the first set of laws is formulated as case law ("If X happens then the consequence should be Y") but it is followed by a set of laws which mostly are expressed as that X is forbidden or that X is obligatory. Finding a pattern, a progression, or an organizing principle has proven elusive, despite many efforts to do so.[1]

Another challenge posed by the collection is that many of the laws included offend the sensibilities of contemporary Western thinking. These include laws about slavery, selling daughters into servitude, incurring the death penalty for witchcraft or cursing parents, and the requirement that a rapist who rapes an unmarried woman must marry his victim.

I will not attempt to provide an overarching solution to all the problems posed nor will I engage in apologetics. I will, however, suggest a framework based on the internal context of the Torah to help – in a most general sense – provide a conceptual framing for many of the mitzvot included. I will also briefly explore external, historical context to gain a better understanding of what the Torah might be trying to convey through these mitzvot.

---

1. Ibn Ezra's comment on 21:1 (first commentary) indicates his acceptance that each of the mitzvot needs to be understood as a standalone. In the twentieth and twenty-first centuries, see, for example, Menachem Leibtag's educational approach at https://tanach.org/shmot/mish/mishs1.htm, Yoel Bin-Nun's structural approach in *Bina BaTorah*, vol. 1 (Herzog, 2022), and Leon Kass's analysis in *Founding God's Nation*, 339–425.

THE BOOK OF THE COVENANT

Perhaps the first commentary to address this extended section of mitzvot as a unit is Ibn Ezra's. While he explicitly acknowledges that he will limit himself to commenting on each mitzva independently, he sees them as a unit which he calls the Book of the Covenant, that is, that they are the content of the covenant that Moses will later forge in Exodus 24.[2] One of the striking features of Ibn Ezra's comment is that he sees the section as framed by two references to the prohibition of idolatry – the opening of that frame in 20:19 and the closing of that frame in 23:33.[3] Indeed, Ibn Ezra breaks from most of the other commentators who view the section of mitzvot as beginning with "And these are the laws which you shall place before them" (21:1), which is the traditional beginning of the Torah portion known as *Mishpatim*.

While Ibn Ezra's framing of the section is intriguing, he himself readily acknowledges that it is insufficient to explain how the collection of mitzvot hangs together meaningfully as a unit. That step is provided by Nahmanides.

Nahmanides (21:1) understands that the list of mitzvot is actually an expanded version of the Decalogue. We remember that the Decalogue itself has discrete components – introducing God, establishing God's uniqueness in Israel's relationship to Him, the prohibition against "using" God's name for purposes of witchcraft or manipulation, sanctified time as a reminder that God is Creator, the relationship with parents as a paradigm for the relationship with God, the basic rules of civil society – including an incorruptible justice system – to protect the life and property of others, and the charge for Israel to become a people apart (i.e., a holy nation) by controlling their desire. These elements are

2. Ibn Ezra addresses this in 21:1 and 23:24. His understanding is that God had earlier instructed Moses to establish this covenant.
3. Although he does not comment on this, there is an unmistakable parallel between the introduction to this covenant (20:19) and God's earlier introductory comment when preparing Israel for the covenant at Sinai (19:3–4).

> God said to Moses, "Thus shall you say to the Israelites. 'You saw that I spoke to you from the heavens.'" (20:19)
>
> God called to him from the mountain saying, "Thus shall you … tell the Israelites, 'You saw what I did to Egypt.'" (19:3–4)

not necessarily sequential, but they are all essential for establishing the norms befitting God's earthly ambassadors. The expanded version of the Decalogue begins to flesh out those different categories. Here is an approximation of what the collection of mitzvot looks like organized along the lines of the Decalogue:

- *The uniqueness of God in Israel's relationship to Him*
  The prohibition of gold or silver representations of the Divine (20:19–20)
  The prohibition against slaughtering to any other gods (22:19)
  The prohibition against worshipping other gods (23:24)
  The requirement to destroy places of idolatrous worship in the Promised Land (23:24–25)
  The prohibition against establishing a covenant with any other god (23:32–33)

- *The prohibition against "using" God's name manipulatively*
  The requirement to put a sorceress to death (22:17)
  The prohibition against mentioning the names of other gods (23:13)

- *Sanctified time as a reminder that God is Creator*
  The seventh year as sanctified (23:10–11)
  The seventh day as sanctified (23:12)
  The three key agricultural festivals are dedicated to God (23:14–19)

- *The relationship with parents as a paradigm for the relationship with God*
  Death penalty for striking parents (21:15)
  Death penalty for cursing parents (21:16)

- *Laws of civil society (respecting justice and the life and property of others)*
  Laws related to Hebrew servants (21:1–11)
  Death penalty for intentional murder (21:12, 21:14)

Exile for accidental manslaughter (21:13)
Death penalty for kidnapping (21:16)
Payment and penalty for wounding another person (21:18–19)
Death penalty for killing a servant (21:20)
Penalty for causing miscarriage (21:22)
Death penalty for accidental death of a pregnant woman (21:23)
Freedom for the servant whose owner caused significant bodily damage (21:26–27)
Responsibility for damage done to another's property by one's animals or through negligence (21:28–36, 22:4–5)
Augmented penalties for depriving another of his livelihood (21:37)
Under certain circumstances, thieves' lives may be forfeited (22:1–2)
Augmented penalty for theft (22:3)
Responsibility for other people's property in one's care (22:6–14)
Responsibility for deflowering an unmarried woman (22:15–16)
Prohibition against oppressing widows, orphans, and outsiders (22:19–23, 23:9)
Prohibition against taking advantage of the impoverished (22:24–26)
Prohibition against demeaning communal leaders (22:27)
Prohibition against distorting justice (23:1–3, 23:6–8)

- *Israel as a nation set apart (holy)*
  The prohibition of bestiality (22:18)
  The requirements to give firstborns to God (22:29–30)
  The prohibition against eating animals torn by other animals (23:30)
  The requirement to help one's adversary (23:4–5)

While the order of the mitzvot still presents a puzzle, it certainly appears that Nahmanides's conceptual understanding of the passage – especially given its context – is credible.[4]

4. The collection of mitzvot in Lev. 19–20, sometimes referred to as the Holiness Code,

THE LAWS IN THEIR HISTORICAL CONTEXT

Organizing the laws is but a first step. Understanding them, especially through the eyes of contemporary readers, presents a significant challenge. For many, the very idea of trying to interpret God's law in light of the norms of the Ancient Near East is anathema. For them, God's law is absolute, and while there might be debates about whether they reflect God's wisdom, God's justice, or God's kindness, the fact that they are divine mitzvot means that they are ideals. Any discomfort modern readers may have with them is the result of flaws in the readers; the readers must reshape their values so that they are aligned with God's. In addition, reducing the laws to God's reaction to various ancient practices suggests a level of subjectivity, implying that human judgment could play a role in determining whether this or that injunction is still applicable today – a dangerous and slippery slope for religious commitment.

Throughout the ages, however, there has also been a parallel approach. The Talmud already records an opinion that the law of the beautiful female war captive was God's concession to the reigning sexual impulse which He understood was not yet prepared to be completely suppressed but could be moderated with limitations.[5] Maimonides's discussion of the sacrifices and a variety of other practices understands them as tools introduced by God to wean Israel away from idolatry.[6] Indeed, the halakhic principle that things which are considered immoral in the general society become forbidden halakhically as well[7] has brought about changes to the law such as the prohibition of polygamy,[8] and various rabbinic enactments have reshaped a number of biblical laws to render

---

rounds out the collection here, focusing heavily on those practices which distinguish Israelite society as distinct from those in Egypt (from which they left) and Canaan (to which they are going). Those two Hamite nations were known for their sexual impropriety and are contrasted with the strict rules established for God's people. *Sifra* (*Kedoshim* 1:1) understands that the section there is also an amplification of the Decalogue, identifying it as a passage containing "the majority of the body of the Torah."

5. Kiddushin 21b.
6. *Guide for the Perplexed,* III:32.
7. See *Turei Zahav* on *Yoreh De'ah* 27:1.
8. See *She'eilat Yaavetz* 2:15.

them almost unrecognizable.[9] In that spirit we will examine some of the laws in the context of Near Eastern practices and legal systems, so that we can better understand God's agenda in legislating these laws.

A classic example in our text relates to the regulations regarding the Hebrew servant. In principle, the Torah does not favor the institution of servitude. God did not free Israel from slavery so that they could reenter servitude. As the Talmud (Bava Metzia 10a) records, God claims Israel to be His servants (Lev. 25:55), not servants to servants. That being said, there are a few circumstances under which servitude was permitted.

One is when a thief gets caught and has to not only return what he stole but must pay the owner double. If the thief is unable to pay, rather than being incarcerated, which helps nobody, the thief must sell himself into servitude to pay off his debt. A second is when someone has fallen on hard times and cannot support himself, he is permitted to sell himself into servitude to restart his economic path. A third is when a destitute father wants to ensure that his daughter can marry out of poverty he may sell her into servitude with the explicit intention of that sale turning into a marriage.

What stands out in all of these is that the period of servitude may not exceed six years, except when the servant decides that after the six years he wishes to stay permanently.[10] That rule stands in stark contrast to the rules of slavery in other Near Eastern texts, which speak of freedom for the slave as the exception rather than as the rule. Beyond that, it becomes clear from the various examples that servitude is intended as a pathway out of poverty rather than as an eternal dead end. The Torah wants to provide that option as a last resort for those who were stuck in permanent debt. Finally, it also becomes clear that the owner does not own the body of the slave but only his services. If the servant is abused

9. Prominent among these in the Talmud is Hillel's institution of the *prozbul* to allow for loans to be collected following the Sabbatical year. Later innovations include *heter iska*, permitting paying and taking interest on loans; and the sale of *ḥametz* before Pesaḥ. For more on this, see Eliezer Berkovits, *Not in Heaven: The Nature and Function of Halakha* (Ktav, 1983), 8–32.

10. The phrasing in the Torah portrays this as reflecting deep relationships the slave built with his new family. "Should the servant say, 'I love my master, my wife, and my sons – I will not go free'" (21:5).

to the extent that he loses a limb, even a tooth, then he is set free; if the slave is killed in the process of the owner's attempt to discipline him then the owner faces a death penalty. A servant is a human being, not property, and he retains his human dignity despite his status.

Even the extreme example the father selling his daughter as a servant, which sounds unconscionable to the contemporary reader, is designed to find ways out of the cycle of poverty – not just for the father but for his daughter. Absent that outlet, it was unlikely that the young woman would have access to families from a different socioeconomic class, and once she was married, she was accorded all the same benefits and protections as any other wife. Further, if the "purchaser" decides that he does not want to marry her and does not want his son to marry her, she is to be set free without delay.

The law of the young woman sold into servitude for the purpose of marriage may be linked to another regulation which offends the contemporary ear. If a man seduces an unmarried woman and sleeps with her, he must pay the father the standard bride-price and marry the woman, unless the father (or, presumably, the woman) refuses the marriage. While it seems to make little sense to the modern reader, to the ancient reader this was revolutionary. A young woman who had a sexual encounter outside of marriage was deemed unmarriageable and would have been subject to a life of destitution. Obligating the seducer to marry her provides a safety net for the woman and generates significant responsibility for the seducer. The serious consequence for the man thus also serves as a deterrent against unrestrained sexual activity, especially the kind which takes a toll on others, and helps to foster the kind of relationships which would be appropriate for God's representatives.

Understanding the social context in which these laws are given opens a window into how God intends to move the needle of human and societal behavior for His people.

LAWS FOR CIVIL SOCIETY

It is not only the social-historical context which sheds light on God's moral code, but the legal context. In the ancient world there were a number of legal texts which predate the Torah, most famous among them is the Code of Hammurabi,[11] a Babylonian legal text composed in the eighteenth century BCE. Despite the similarities between Hammurabi and the code presented in Exodus, the differences between them reflect dramatically different ethical and moral value systems.

The longest section of laws in Exodus (21:18–22:16) deals with damages, whether done by a person or by their animal and whether done actively or as a result of negligence (for example, uncovering a pit in the public sphere, leaving a fire unattended, or not being careful with an object left in one's care). Rabbi Elhanan Samet[12] has demonstrated that the order of those laws is significant – the primary consideration in grouping these laws focuses on the victim rather than on the perpetrator. Thus, situations in which a person is killed are accorded primary importance[13] and are followed by situations in which a person is wounded. Only afterward does the Torah discuss cases in which animals are damaged, and the section concludes with loss incurred to a person's property. This hierarchy of legal material focuses the reader's attention on the primacy of human life, echoing God's instructions to Noah: "One who spills the blood of a human, by humans will his blood be spilled – for the human was created in the image of God" (Gen. 9:6). By contrast, the Code of Hammurabi opens with a lengthy list of laws dealing with the loss of property, highlighting financial loss as the ultimate crime.

A similar contrast emerges when we look at criminal law and the penalties imposed for various offenses. The Torah distinguishes between intentional murder and unintentional manslaughter, with the perpetrator of the former incurring the death penalty but of the latter being sentenced to exile, while Hammurabi condemns both to death. The differences between God's code and Hammurabi's are sharpened when dealing with damage to or loss of property. In God's code, loss of value to an individual's property is always redressed by financial payment. Those payments may vary, depending on whether the damage

11. In James Pritchard, *Ancient Near Eastern Texts Relating to the Old Testament* (Princeton University Press, 1969), 166–80.

12. *Iyunim BeFarashat HaShavua*, Series 1, Volume 1, 217–23.

13. The one exception is that the law of the person who is killed by an animal is presented only after the law of the Hebrew servant who goes free if he or she loses a limb as a result of a blow by the master.

is done by the person or by their property (e.g., an unsupervised animal), if there is a fine imposed to de-incentivize theft, or a penalty for harming a farmer's livelihood (as in stealing his sheep or his ox), but monetary loss is always responded to in the Torah by monetary compensation. By contrast, many of Hammurabi's laws demand the death penalty for financial offenses, placing a primacy of value on possessions over human life. In fact, Hammurabi's code does not demand the death penalty for murder, allowing the murderer in some cases to pay for his offense. With Hammurabi's code providing context, the value of human life is dramatically distinguished in the Torah.[14]

Finally, where a person's animal does damage, God's law contains an extensive discussion of the consequences. If the damage is to crops, the animal's owner must pay; if the damage is to another animal, the animal is to be sold and the proceeds split between the owners of the victim and the perpetrator; if a person is killed, whether an adult or a child, the animal is to be killed. If somehow the animal is not killed and it kills again, the animal is to be put to death and the owner is deserving of the death penalty – although the owner can pay to redeem his life.[15] Once again, the distinctions between human life and property are sharp,[16] and the requirement to forfeit (in the case animal damage) or kill the animal (in the case of human death) demonstrates the Torah's commitment to ensuring that communities are safe. Strikingly, parallel laws to these are completely absent from Hammurabi.

A PUZZLING COLLECTION

The end of the code of mitzvot veers from the primary focus on civil laws. In a segue from a series focused on the need to protect the outsider and the poor (23:6–9), the Torah introduces the seventh year, during

14. For a more extensive treatment of the differences, see Kass, *Founding God's Nation*, 358–73. See also David Arnovitz, ed., *The Koren Tanakh of the Land of Israel, Exodus* (Koren Publishers, 2019), 112–26.
15. The presentation here is based on a literal reading of the Torah text. The extensive talmudic discussions in Bava Kama render the laws somewhat differently, adding extraordinary nuances not reflected here.
16. The one anomaly is if a non-Hebrew slave is killed by the ox. The animal must be killed, and the owner must pay a fine, but is not deemed to be deserving of death.

which no agricultural work is permitted and the produce must be left for collection by the poor. The mention of the seventh year opens the door for a brief mention of the seventh day, on which the underprivileged in society (the servant-child and the outsider) must also be given an opportunity to reinvigorate.[17] These two laws about the sanctified seventh (year and day) are followed by an expanded discussion about sanctified time in the form of three primary festivals:

> Three annual pilgrimage festivals you are to celebrate to Me. Keep the holiday of matzot; for seven days you will eat matzot, as I commanded you, in the month of the hollow stalks, for in that month you left Egypt; they may not appear before My presence empty-handed. And the holiday of the harvest, the first fruits of your labor which you sowed; and the holiday of the gathering as the year leaves, as you gather your produce from the field. Three times a year all your males are to appear before the Master, God. (23:14–17)

This flow seems to make sense. The problem is that between the sanctified sevens and the discussion about the holidays there is an interruption with the injunction against invoking the names of other gods. Adding to the puzzle are the two verses which conclude this section.

> You shall not slaughter the blood of My slaughter with leavened bread, nor shall you leave the fats of My holiday festival until the morning. The first fruits of your land shall be brought to God's house; do not cook a kid in its mother's milk. (23:18–19)

The closing of this unit (23:20–33) is surprising as well. It discusses Israel's eventual arrival in their promised land, the dangers presented by the local idolatry, and the warning not to establish covenants with the local peoples or their gods. This is significantly different from all the preceding material, which is essentially a dense collection of mitzvot initiated after the Decalogue.

---

17. The verb used to describe their resting, *veyinafesh* (23:12), is the same as the one which describes God's behavior on the seventh day of Creation (Gen. 2:3).

How are we to understand the flow of the last mitzvot discussed and the surprising closing of this section?

A PARALLEL COLLECTION

It turns that there is a similar passage later in Exodus, so similar that there are verses which are identical.[18] Following the giving of the second set of tablets (Ex. 34), there is a section which includes the prohibition of idolatry, the sanctified seventh, the three annual holidays, the unusual collection of injunctions following the holidays (including the prohibition against cooking a kid in its mother's milk), and a warning about building bonds with the Canaanite nations lest those relationships lead to idolatry. And while the order is somewhat different, the chart below demonstrates the clear parallels between the two passages.

Exodus 23	Exodus 34
Six days you shall do your work but on the seventh day you shall desist (v. 12)	Six days you shall do your work but on the seventh day you shall desist (v. 19)
You shall not invoke the names of other gods; they should not be heard on your mouth (v. 13)	You should not for yourself make mask-gods (v. 17)
Three annual pilgrimage festivals you are to celebrate to Me (v. 14)	
Keep the holiday of matzot, for seven days you will eat matzot, as I commanded you, in the month of the hollow stalks (v. 15)	Keep the holiday of matzot, for seven days you will eat matzot, as I commanded you, in the month of the hollow stalks (v. 18)
They may not appear before My presence empty-handed (v. 15)	They may not appear before My presence empty-handed (v. 19)
And the holiday of the harvest, the first fruits of your labor which you sowed (16)	You shall make for yourself the holiday of weeks, at the beginning of the wheat harvest (22)

18. This parallel was first observed by Ibn Ezra in his comment on 30:12.

and the holiday of the gathering as the year leaves, as you gather your produce from the field (16)	and the holiday of the gathering at the close of the annual seasonal cycle (22)
Three times a year all your males are to appear before the Master, God (17)	Three times a year all your males are to appear before the Master, God (23)
You shall not slaughter the blood of My slaughter with leavened bread (18)	You shall not slaughter the blood of My slaughter with leavened bread (25)
nor shall you leave the fats of My holiday festival until the morning (18)	nor shall you leave the slaughter of the Pesaḥ holiday until morning (25)
The first fruits of your land shall be brought to God's house (19)	The first fruits of your land shall be brought to God's house (19)
Do not cook a kid in its mother's milk (19)	Do not cook a kid in its mother's milk (19)
When My messenger goes before you and brings you to the land of the Emorite, the Perizzite (23)	I am banishing from before you the Emorite, the Canaanite (11)
Do not bow down to their gods nor worship them nor do their practices (24)	Do not bow down to any other god (14)
You should certainly tear them down and certainly smash their *matzeva* stone-monuments (24)	You should shatter their altars, smash their *matzeva* stone-monuments (13)
Do not establish a covenant with them or with their gods (32)	Lest you establish a covenant with the residents of the land; when they whore after their gods and slaughter offerings to them, they will invite you and you will partake of their slaughter (15)

While there are minor differences, including the change of the identity of the second annual festival from the festival of the harvest to the festival of weeks, the similarities between the two passages are overwhelming.

THE COVENANTAL FORMULA

While we will explore the need for the repetition when we study the story of the Golden Calf, there is a clue from that later passage as to what this collection represents. Immediately prior to this repetition God tells Moses, "Behold, I am establishing a covenant" (34:10), suggesting that this group of mitzvot is a formula for covenant.

Let us try to understand why.

The opening to this collection is the prohibition of and warning regarding idolatry.[19] This echoes the opening of the Decalogue as it sets the foundational understanding of the relationship with God – it is an exclusive one. To the contemporary reader benefiting from thousands of years of tradition and exposure to what is called the Judeo-Christian ethic, this is no surprise. Our culture is suffused with monotheism. To the ancient Israelites, however, this is truly revolutionary. The culture in which they lived worshipped multiple gods, and that was fairly universal. That is why the Decalogue and its expanded version both open with an explicit iteration of the idea, and it is for that same reason that the close of the section, the covenantal formula, opens with a reiteration of that core assumption.

That opening is followed by two parallel tracks. On the one hand, we have Shabbat. In our discussion of the Decalogue we pointed out that Shabbat, as a celebration of Creation, should have been celebrated universally – all people are beneficiaries of Creation and should be celebrating it. What God does by focusing the Shabbat on Israel, in essence limiting Shabbat to Israel, is that He takes a universal gift and dedicates it to His people, highlighting their uniqueness in this relationship. This idea is celebrated in the morning Shabbat prayers:

> You, O Lord, did not give it to the other nations of the world, nor did You, our King, give it as a heritage to those who worship idols. In its rest the uncircumcised do not dwell, for You gave it in love to Israel Your people, to the descendants of Jacob whom You chose.[20]

---

19. In our passage it is also the closing.
20. Translation by Rabbi Jonathan Sacks, *The Koren Siddur* (Koren Publishers, 2009), 486.

On the other hand, the festivals represent the parallel to Shabbat. Throughout the Ancient Near East, peoples celebrated annual agricultural festivals – the beginning of the barley harvest, the beginning of the wheat harvest, and the ingathering of the produce at the close of the agricultural year. These celebrations included a variety of pagan practices, as the ancient world understood that the various natural powers, from sun and moon to the seasons and fertility, were all intimately linked to the gods who controlled them. What God asks of Israel is to take those universal, pagan, agricultural festivals and dedicate them to Him. "Three annual pilgrimage festivals you are to celebrate to Me" (23:14). When Israel takes its universal festivals and transforms them into worship of their One God, they are mirroring God's dedication of Shabbat to them, declaring His exclusivity.[21]

The shift from the focus on the universal agricultural aspect of the festival to their unique Israelite, historical dimension is an essential part of the dedication of those festivals to God. The agricultural element of the first of those festivals was the first to disappear. Already at the Exodus, the holiday was named the Festival of Matzot, celebrating Israel's liberation rather than the barley harvest.[22] The other holidays, however, retain their agricultural identification when they are first introduced here in Exodus 23. That, however, begins to change already in Exodus 34; the holiday of the wheat harvest (as it is called earlier) is now called the holiday of weeks (Shavuot), likely in anticipation of the counting of weeks which will link the two.[23] The transformation of the third holiday, from the ingathering of the harvest to the holiday of booths (Sukkot), completes the cycle, but doesn't happen until Leviticus 23:34.[24]

This brings us to the final two verses of the mitzvot. A second look reveals that the initial mitzvot are clearly related to the dedication

21. It is possible that the halakhic obligation to recite Kiddush on the festivals, which sanctifies all the meals eaten, is an expression of the dedication of the festival to God.

22. To be sure, elements of the barley harvest remain, as evidenced by laws later introduced regarding the Omer offering (Lev. 23:9–14).

23. Lev. 23:15.

24. Because there is no clear historical event in the Torah associated with Sukkot, it is precisely there, in Leviticus 23:43, where the holiday gets renamed as Sukkot, that the Torah offers a historical framing.

of the festivals to God. The prohibition against having leavened bread and leaving the slaughtered animals until the morning are restrictions related to the *pesaḥ*; accepting God's restrictions indicates their dedication to God. The same can be said for the requirement to dedicate the first fruits to God, as Shavuot is when those first fruits are harvested.[25] The final mitzva, however – the prohibition against cooking a baby goat in its mother's milk – seems harder to explain.

If the previous restrictions related to the first two of the three holidays, it is logical to assume that this final injunction is related to the third holiday. Indeed, Rashbam and Ibn Ezra already point out that there was a practice in the ancient world to do precisely what the Torah forbids, and Maimonides[26] suggests that the practice was connected to idolatry, so that the injunction is designed to distance us from idolatry. None of that, however, explains the connection to Sukkot. Cassuto completes the picture, having learned from Ugaritic documents this was a pagan practice performed at the harvest festival, dedicating the new life and the milk it was designed to drink to the pagan gods. Thus, the Torah's command specifically in this context is not necessarily about *kashrut* but about ensuring that the harvest festival be refocused away from its pagan origins and dedicated exclusively to God.

PREPARATION FOR COVENANT

The three key elements work together to highlight the covenant's essence – mutual declarations by God and Israel of exclusivity in the relationship between them. The prohibition of idolatry highlights Israel's acceptance to worship only God; dedicating Shabbat to Israel is God's gift demonstrating Israel's exclusivity in His eyes; dedicating the festivals to God is Israel's gift demonstrating God's exclusivity in theirs.

The tripartite formula is capped by God's reassurance that He will bring Israel to their promised land. In the context of the new covenant, that destination now takes on a new dimension. Their arrival there is not only so that God can fulfill the promise He made to the patriarchs – it

25. Similarly, when the Torah discusses this holiday in Leviticus, it includes the requirement to leave a corner of the field unharvested for the poor to collect (Lev. 23:22).
26. *Guide for the Perplexed,* III:48.

provides Israel with the opportunity to fulfill its mission as God's covenantal partner. The land will serve as the capital, the embassy, for God's people to share His message with the rest of humanity. That potential can only be actualized if the land is purged of idolatry, which is anathema to God's mission.

This close to the lengthy discussion of mitzvot refocuses the mitzvot themselves. We began by exploring Nahmanides's idea that the collection of mitzvot is an expanded version of the Decalogue, but we also recall that in the preparation for the encounter at Sinai God had hoped for Israel to be prepared to enter in covenant, but they were not. The return to that now thus serves an extraordinary function – it refocuses the mitzvot back to the Decalogue, and in the process, brings the topic of covenant sharply back into focus.

Moses hears this and understands that God will not be satisfied with anything less than a covenant with Israel. It is at this point that he again turns to the people and presents them with all that he has heard, including this closing. Israel, still unable to grapple with the grand idea of covenantal partnership with God, reiterate their preparedness to do whatever God tells them. Moses, having heard the expansion of the Decalogue, understands that he needs to highlight only the covenant. When he does, the people accept. "We will do and we will listen." *Naaseh venishma*. They are prepared to establish their covenant with God.

Exodus 24:12–27:21

Designing the *Mishkan*

With Moses's facilitation, God and Israel have entered into a covenant. This extraordinary event is not marked by parties or celebrations, but they do need to set up a work plan, an office space, or even just a system of regular communication. God summons Moses up the mountain for exactly that purpose. He will ultimately present Moses with two stone tablets, engraved personally by God with the essential covenantal code.[1] Until then, for as long as it will take,[2] He teaches Moses the plans for constructing the Tabernacle, the *Mishkan*.

Nahmanides[3] powerfully describes this as something much more significant than a joint workspace.

> Now that they are His people and He is their God … and now that they are a sanctified people, it is only fitting that there should be a sanctified place where His presence can dwell among them. For

1. See Deut. 5:19.
2. Moses ends up being there for forty days and nights, but the initial intention of the duration of his stay is never indicated (24:12-18).
3. Comment to 25:1. His description is much more extensive than I cited here.

> that reason He first instructs them about the *Mishkan*... and there He will speak with Moses and instruct the Israelites.

This sanctified place, a *mikdash*, is described by Nahmanides as nothing less than a re-creation of Mount Sinai, or perhaps, a portable version of it which Israel can take with them so that the dialogue begun with God at Sinai can continue. He strikingly parallels the description of Sinai with parallel images from the *Mishkan*. Here is a sample of the parallels he draws:

Sinai	***Mishkan***
God's glory dwelt on the mountain (24:16)	God's glory filled the *Mishkan* (40:34)
From the heavens He made His voice heard to you (Deut. 4:36)	Moses heard the voice speaking to him from above the *Kaporet* (Num. 7:89)
He showed you the great fire (Deut. 4:36)	From between the two [golden] *keruvim* (which looked like fire) (Num. 7:89)

PREPARING THE PROJECT

One might have thought that God would have opened His discussion of the *Mishkan* with an introduction like that of Nahmanides. "Here is the project, this is its purpose, and this is how you will go about doing it." Instead, God begins by clarifying that the materials for the *Mishkan* are to be voluntarily donated, not imposed. Following that He provides the list of materials necessary, much like we would expect to find in a recipe or a do-it-yourself guide.[4] Only afterward does God say what the project and its purpose are: "They will make for Me a sanctified place so that I can dwell among them."

4. One of the unusual features of the list is that it includes both materials used for the construction and some of the consumables used regularly, specifically the oils for the Menora and the spices used for anointing the vessels and for the daily incense offering.

A closer reading reveals something even more startling – the final line, the goal of the project, is not part of what Moses is to tell the people. Rather, it is part of God's message to Moses, so that he understands.

Clearly, at some point, the people would need to be informed of the nature of the project. Even had he wanted to keep it a secret it is unlikely that Moses would have been able to do so given the number of craftspeople who would eventually be required to fabricate it. That being said, it is curious that that information was not part of what God necessarily wanted Moses to share.

It would seem that God listened carefully to Israel's multiple responses when offered the covenant, when they said, "We will do," and only on Moses's insistence did they add, "We will listen." God understood that the people were not yet able to comprehend the implication or scope of covenant, and so rather than try to explain to them what these donations were for He simply instructs Moses to collect the donations. Given the people's preparedness to do as they were told, that would have made the collection a fairly simple process. Indeed, when Moses presents the project, he mentions the materials needed and their technical purposes, that is, what vessels they would be used for, but at no point does he mention that the purpose of the *Mishkan* was to provide a place for God's presence to dwell among them. Later, during the extended period of the actual construction, they would slowly begin to grasp the nature and purpose of the project.

In this light it is quite telling that the donation needed to be voluntary. Had Moses imposed a tax, he would surely have been able to generate the materials necessary. Apparently, however, just like the *Mishkan* was intended to continue the Sinaitic experience, Israel's part in it needed to mirror their acceptance of God's offer at Sinai. Their acceptance in both had to genuinely come from them – God would impose neither His covenant nor His presence upon them.

INTRODUCTION TO THE *MISHKAN*

To gain a better understanding of how the goals of the *Mishkan* were to be accomplished, it will be valuable to explore both some of the details of its construction, including some of its individual parts, as well as to take a step back to get a macro view. The combination of both views will demonstrate remarkable symmetry and consistency, which are part of God's way of communicating with Israel. It will also reveal the unique features of the different components and how they work together to support God's message.

The complex in which the *Mishkan* is located consists of two primary areas – the outer courtyard, which, in theory, was accessible to anyone who was ritually pure, and the portable edifice of the *Mishkan* itself. The outer courtyard is delineated by a curtain with a single entrance in the east, and it contains two vessels distinguished by the copper in their construction – the altar for sacrifices and the washing basin.

While the outer courtyard is identified by the use of copper, the building of the *Mishkan* itself is marked by the use of gold – even the walls are made of gold-plated acacia wood. The building is separated into two rooms, the larger room known as the *Kodesh* (Holy) and the smaller as the *Kodesh HaKodashim* (Holy of Holies). In the *Kodesh* are three vessels: the *Shulḥan* (Table) for the showbread, the Menora (Lamp), and the small altar for incense. The *Kodesh HaKodashim* has a single item, the *Aron* (Ark).

It is not only the metals which mark the different domains but also the fabrics. The fabrics in the outer courtyard consist of unadorned white linen, while the innermost layer of fabric covering the building features a complex weave of undyed linen and blue, purple, and red wools. The inner curtain, separating the *Kodesh* from the *Kodesh HaKodashim*, is similar to the innermost layer of covering, while the screens for the entrance to the courtyard and to the building itself are a modified version of those specialized fabrics.

THE INTERIOR VESSELS

As we just noted, there are four items inside the *Mishkan* building: the Ark, the Table, the Menora, and the incense altar. These are echoed by a similar list of furnishings in the guest room prepared for the prophet Elisha on his visits to the Shunamite family: "Let us make for him a small upper chamber. We will place there for him a bed, a table, a chair and a lamp" (II Kings 4:10). To be sure, God does not need these items, and there is no parallel in the *Mishkan* for the bed; nonetheless the parallel suggests that, at a minimum, the *Mishkan* is to serve as a "guest room" for the Divine Presence when it dwells among the people.

The interior vessels of the *Mishkan* share the following features:

- Excepting the Menora, the body of each is made of acacia wood coated in what is called *zahav tahor*, a purified gold.
- Excepting the Menora, each has rings attached to the body to accommodate poles which will be used for carrying it.
- Excepting the Menora, each is capped by a golden "crown" around the top.
- Each is covered with its own special cover during transportation.

In light of the parallel to Elisha's guest room, the golden crown on each of the vessels functions much like a royal seal on the crockery and cutlery found in a palace; it marks the items as set aside exclusively for the King, enhancing the sense of the distinctiveness – the *kedusha* – of the place.

Ark and *Kaporet*

The Ark is the first of the items discussed in the Torah. Its dimensions are 2.5 cubits (approximately four feet) long, 1.5 cubits (approximately two feet) wide, and 1.5 cubits high – shaped somewhat like a shoebox. It is gold-plated both on the inside and out, has a golden crown, and apparently has two sets of rings for the poles: one for a set of poles which are never to be removed and a second set of removable poles – all of which were made of gold-plated acacia wood – which are to be used for carrying.[5] Capping the Ark is the cover, called the *Kaporet*, which is to be made of a solid block of purified gold and features two

5. See Ibn Ezra's long commentary on 25:12. He deduces this from the verse which says, "You shall cast for it four golden rings and set them on its four feet, and two rings on its one side and two rings on its other side" (25:12). He adds that the legs must have been part of a stand for the Ark, as it would have been improper for the Ark to be resting directly on the ground. See also Numbers 4:6, which describes the poles being placed to carry the Ark, despite the Torah's insistence here that the poles are never to be removed. This is one the places where Ibn Ezra's long commentary directly contradicts his short one.

three-dimensional angelic figures, *keruvim,* whose wings cover the *Kaporet* and who face both each other and the *Kaporet.*[6] It should be noted that the Ark and its *Kaporet* are two distinct items which are designed to become a single unit.

The Ark-*Kaporet* serves a double function. On the technical level, it is to house the tablets, the "testimony" which God will give to Moses. On the substantive level, the Ark-*Kaporet* is designed as the place from which the dialogue between God and Moses will be continued.

> You shall place the *Kaporet* on top of the Ark after you will have placed into the Ark the testimony which I will give you. I will meet with you there and I will speak with you from above the *Kaporet,* from between the two *keruvim* which are above the Ark of Testimony. (25:21–22)

We now understand why the Ark is discussed first – it facilitates the primary function of the *Mishkan,* the continued communication between God and Moses.

At this point we should step back and revisit some of the details of the Ark to explore their significance.

1. The tablets are the symbol of the covenant, and it is their presence in the Ark which enables the Ark to fulfill its function.
2. The Ark is never actually intended to be viewed by anyone. It is housed in the *Kodesh HaKodashim,* which has no source of light, either natural or artificial (the Menora is in a separate chamber separated by a curtain). When the *Mishkan* is packed or unpacked for traveling, the Levites responsible for transporting the Ark use the curtain which separates the two parts of the *Mishkan* to cover it so that it is not viewed by anyone, and add an additional two coverings on top of it.[7] This is apparently to

6. The importance of these *keruvim* is emphasized by the fact that they are mentioned seven times in this passage.
7. See Num. 4:5.

ensure that the Ark – with its *Kaporet* and *keruvim* – does not become an object of or an inspiration for improper worship.[8]

3. One of the dangers of God's presence among the people is the people's sense that God "belongs" there, that is, that they can expect God's presence among them regardless of what they do. This opens the door to ethical and religious corruption, given the assumption that they can always count on God to be there. Indeed, this is apparently God's concern when Solomon builds the Temple and asks God to bring His presence there.[9] In order to prevent that abuse, God adds two design features to the Ark. First, the poles are never to be removed, indicating that the Ark and all that it represents can depart the *Mishkan* at any moment. God's presence must be earned; it is not guaranteed. Following that same theme, the *Kaporet* features *keruvim* with their wings spread, ready to ascend and "carry" God's presence back to heaven at a moment's notice.[10]

When we put the picture together, the Ark is the seat of God's presence, God's throne,[11] as it were. It is from there, built on the foundation of the covenant that it houses, that God continues His dialogue with Israel through Moses. But God's presence, and the conversation with Him, can never be taken for granted. It is not only for practical reasons that the *Mishkan* was designed as a temporary structure. God wants to ensure that His people know that His presence must never be taken for granted.

---

8. Later this became a problem as Israel began to assign magical powers to the Ark to defeat their enemies. The earliest hint of this can be found already in Numbers 10:35, but it is expressed more powerfully in the story of the capture of the Ark by the Philistines after Israel brought it into battle (I Sam. 4).
9. I Kings 9:2–9. This was apparently Jeremiah's concern when he addressed the people in the Temple courtyard, having witnessed precisely the kind of abuse God mentioned to Solomon. See Jer. 7:1–15.
10. This is apparently the scene described in Isaiah's vision (Is. 6:1–4).
11. Psalms 80:2 and 99:1 describe God as the One who dwells upon the *keruvim*, while Psalms 18:11 describes Him as the One who rides the *keruvim*.

Table

The Table, also made of acacia wood plated in purified gold, is 2 cubits (approx. 3 feet) long, 1 cubit (approx. 1.5 feet) wide, and 1.5 cubits high. It, too, has a golden crown. Its most distinguishing feature, however, is an elaborate set of racks and shelves for the twelve loaves of bread placed there each week. Those loaves, apparently representing the tribes of Israel, were to be eaten at the end of each week by Aaron and his sons. The racks, also made of purified gold, were organized as two parallel stacks of six shelves in each. The Table also had a set of golden rings into which gold-plated poles of acacia wood were inserted for carrying.

From early Genesis, bread takes on a special symbolic meaning in the Torah. Upon being banished from the Garden, the man is told by God that he will eat bread produced with great labor – which is both a curse and a blessing. On the one hand, it means that Man's food will no longer come easily, as it was in the Garden. On the other hand, that food will be the result of human creativity, which takes God's natural creation, grain, and dramatically transforms it into what will become the staple of the human diet. As such, bread not only becomes the symbol of the distinction between humans and animals – as no animals can produce it – it becomes the symbol of human creativity which can transform and improve upon God's natural world.

While the *keruvim* atop the Ark may have represented some celestial being,[12] the Table with its racks and shelves looks like nothing in the natural or supernal worlds described by the prophets. It is the most artificial looking artifact in the *Mishkan*, because it is meant to represent human endeavor, creativity, and productivity.

Menora

In contrast to all the other internal vessels, the entire Menora is hewn from a single block of purified gold. It lacks rings for carrying, has no acacia wood, and has no crown. Including the central stem, there are seven branches on this candelabra, with three pairs of two branches each extending from the center stem, one on each side of the stem. The

12. See Gen. 3:24. They are mentioned more than thirty times in Ezekiel's visions.

Menora is adorned by knobs where the branches meet the stems, as well as almond-like cups and flowers along the branches and stem.

Even more striking is the absence of any dimensions. While the Torah was meticulous in detailing the dimensions of the Ark and the Table, and it will be as precise in describing the sizes of the other appurtenances of the *Mishkan*, the absence of those dimensions demands our attention.[13] When we consider that the description of the Menora sounds like that of a plant – stems, branches, almonds, flowers – what emerges is that the Menora is meant to be a golden representation of a purely natural object, one unimpacted by human activity.[14] Precisely because the Menora is meant to represent an organic being, the Torah omits its dimensions, because organic beings by their nature are dynamic and grow. It is not the size which is primary but its organic nature which is being highlighted.

The essence of the Menora as representing the natural is also evident in the oil which is used. The Torah specifies that the oil is to be pure, of the initial pressing of the olives (27:20). That pressing was done mostly by the weight of the olives upon themselves and involved the least amount of human intervention. Thus both the Menora and that which goes into it represent the natural world, or the world which is God's handiwork rather than a human production.

All this is further highlighted by the adjective "pure," used to describe the Menora, which is not used for any other vessel.[15] While this might be because the Menora is the only vessel which is pure gold throughout, even that suggests that the untarnished purity of the Menora, unaffected by human intervention, stands out in its uniqueness.

One final note regarding the Menora. The discussion of the oil for the Menora in the context of the construction of the *Mishkan* is quite unusual, as is the Torah's instructions to Aaron and his sons to light it

13. The Sages in the Talmud (Menaḥot 29a) debate the height of the Menora.
14. Nogah Hareuveini, *Nature in Our Biblical Heritage* (Neot Kedumin, 1980), 127–35, notes the similarity between the description of the Menora and the *moriah* (*Salvia palaestinae*) plant. See especially the photographs on pp. 135–36 with the branches, knobs, flowers, and cups of the plant.
15. 31:8, 39:37; Lev. 24:4. It should be noted that II Chronicles 13:11 puzzlingly describes the Table as pure.

daily (27:21). The Torah does not describe the preparation or lighting of the incense, nor does it describe the bread-making in this context. Here again the Menora stands out. It would seem that the Torah is communicating that the lighting of the Menora is part of its construction, that is, that the Menora is reconstructed daily with the kindling of its lights. Visually, the lights burning on the top of the Menora seem to serve as its crown.[16] The Menora does not need a golden crown, as it receives a new one daily.

Table-Menora duo

One of the fascinating things about the Menora is that its lights were to illuminate what was facing it (25:37 and Num. 8:2), and facing the Menora in the *Mishkan* was the Table. In fact, throughout the Torah the Table and the Menora are presented together,[17] usually as a duo facing each other.

> You shall place the Table outside of the *Parokhet* and the Menora facing it on the eastern wall; the Table you will place on the western wall. (26:35)

> You should bring the Table and arrange its arrangement; and you should bring the Menora and light its lamps. (40:4)

> He placed the Menora in the Tent of Meeting facing the Table. (40:24)

In light of what we just learned about the Table and the Menora, the pairing of the two not only makes sense, but highlights a core value of the *Mishkan* as they function as counterparts to each other. While the Menora represents God's unmodified handiwork, the Table

16. The Torah does say to place the bread on the Table weekly (25:30), as this apparently completes the Table. It does not, however, have the same visual effect as the lights on top of the Menora, and cannot be considered as its golden crown.
17. Leviticus 24:1–4 discusses lighting of the Menora, while 24:5–8 deals with preparing the bread and placing it in the Table.

represents human creativity. If the *Mishkan* is to represent the partnership between God and humanity, or between God and His human partners, Israel, then the Table and the Menora as a pair reflect the two partners working synergetically. Illuminating the human endeavor by the light of the Menora facing it indicates the ideal in that relationship, in which human creativity is guided by the divine light rather than trying to undermine it. Thus the Table-Menora partnership functions as a symbolic contrast to what the Torah earlier portrays as the approaches taken in Babel and Egypt.

The golden ratio

Missing in the Torah's presentation of the internal vessels is the golden incense altar, for reasons which we will discuss later in the context of where the Torah does discuss it. Suffice it to say for now that like most of its neighbors inside the *Mishkan,* it was constructed from acacia wood coated in purified gold. It was one cubit (approx. 1.5 feet) long, one cubit wide, and two cubits tall.

The details of the dimensions of the vessels lead us to question whether they are significant or not. The chart below lays out these details for further exploration.

	Length	**Width**	**Height**
Ark	2.5 cubits	1.5 cubits	1.5 cubits
Table	2 cubits	1 cubit	1.5 cubits
Altar	1 cubit	1 cubit	2 cubits

A quick look at the chart reveals that if we remove the halves from the various dimensions, all three vessels have the same dimensions, with the altar standing on its short side while the Ark and the Table lay on their long sides. Removing the halves makes sense when we consider the thickness of the walls.[18] The Ark has walls on all sides, so that halves

18. See Ibn Ezra's long commentary on 25:10 where he suggests that the half cubit represents the thickness of the walls of the Ark.

may be the thickness of those walls. The Table only has thickness in its upper surface, which is where the thickness appears. The altar has no internal space at all, leaving its dimensions as 1x1x2.

This remarkable symmetry, which we will later see reflected in the floor plans of both the *Mishkan* and the courtyard, may again represent the *Mishkan*'s essence as the meeting place between God and Israel. If we imagine God represented by a perfect 1x1x1 cube and Israel by another, then the 1x1x2 ratio symbolically represents the meeting of God and Israel..

What we have seen, then, is that the internal vessels, both in their form and their function, represent the partnership between God and Israel. In terms of their functions, the Ark is where the communication happens while the Table-Menora duo represent the joint work of God and His people. In terms of form, the 1x1x2 theme running throughout makes the statement about this being a meeting place for God and Israel, even as the golden crowns on the vessels mark this clearly as being God's domain in which people are His visitors.

THE WALLS

The walls of the *Mishkan* are designed to be assembled and disassembled so that the *Mishkan* can be transported in pieces as the Israelites travel. Made of gold-plated acacia wood, twenty identical interlocking panels (10 cubits tall and 1.5 cubits wide) comprise each of the north and south walls, and another eight comprise the west wall.[19] The panels are held together by a series of rings at the top as well as a set of beams made of gold-plated acacia wood for additional support. Two corner pieces complete the western wall with the northern and southern walls. At the base of each panel is a pair of silver "feet" which slide on and off, perhaps to allow the *Mishkan* to stand firm on uneven ground and prevent sand entering though the bottom.

The floor plan of the *Mishkan* with its walls appears like this:

---

19. The Torah does not specify the thickness of the walls.

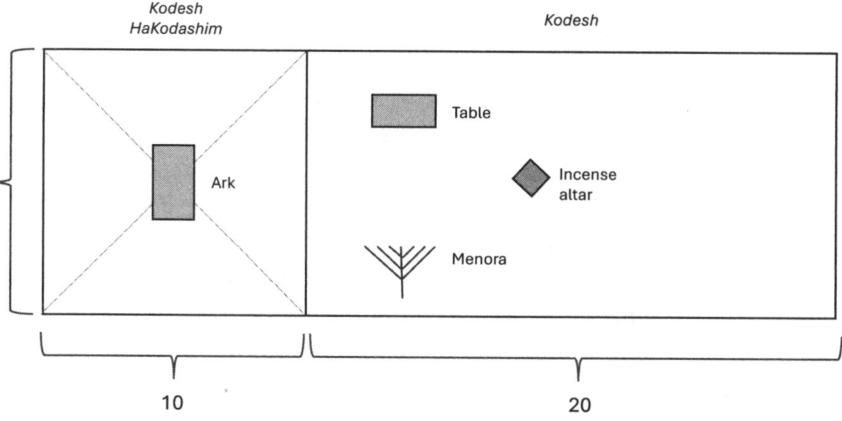

This diagram helps to visualize the *Mishkan* with its inner vessels and invites two significant observations. First, since the height of the *Mishkan* is also ten cubits, the area identified as the *Kodesh* is 20x10x10, a 2x1x1 ratio – the same ratio as we observed in the individual inner vessels – identifying it as a meeting place between Israel and God. This area saw activity by Aaron and his sons on a daily basis as they burned the incense and lit the Menora, and on a weekly basis when they removed the bread from the Table and replaced it with a fresh set of loaves. We also notice that the vessels are clustered in the inner portion of the *Kodesh*, closer to the *Kodesh HaKodashim*, suggesting that the area, with its crowned vessels, is God's domain rather than man's.

The second observation it that the *Kodesh HaKodashim*, God's inner sanctum, is a perfect 10x10x10 cube, a 1x1x1 ratio. This departure from the ratio we've observed marks it as the inner sanctum, God's private place which people cannot enter unless specifically invited. One such invitation is explicit in God's initial instruction to Moses about the *Mishkan*, in that this is the place to which Moses will go to hear God's further instruction for Israel. Another invitation is to be found in Leviticus 16, where God issues instructions for how and when Aaron is to enter.

THE CLOTHS

Three sets of cloth covers are described. The innermost set is woven of undyed linen and blue, purple, and red wools, with a design of *keruvim* woven integrally into the fabric. This woven design involved an advanced weaving process identified by the Torah as *maaseh ḥoshev.* Ten panels, each measuring 28x4 cubits, are woven, and the panels are then sewn together to yield two sets of five panels each. Those panels are connected by fifty loops made of blue wool on either side and golden hooks to link them together. This cloth, when completed, is draped over the walls, and it is what the Torah calls the *mishkan* (26:1 and 26:6).

The materials used for this cloth are particularly rare. The blue color, for example, called *tekhelet,* was produced from the gland of an underwater creature found almost exclusively in the Mediterranean Sea. It was usually worn by royalty, and later the Romans forbade its use by anyone who was not a royal.[20] It is theorized that the purple dye was similarly produced, either from the same creature, using a slightly different process, or from a similar one, and was also reserved for royalty. Thus, this cloth known as the *mishkan* was not only expensive to produce, but clearly marked the building as fit for the King.

Like the rest of the inner *Mishkan,* this cloth was never seen by anyone other than Aaron and his sons, as it was covered by a second cloth, slightly larger both in length and width, made of undyed goat hair. Third and fourth coverings, likely for weather protection, were made of red-dyed ram skins and skins of an animal known as a *taḥash.*[21]

Two more cloths complete the *Mishkan.* One was identical in construction to the *mishkan* cloth – same material, same design, and same *maaseh ḥoshev* weaving process. It was called the *Parokhet,* and it separated between the two chambers in the *Mishkan.* The *Parokhet* is held up by upright pillars similar in materials (but not in size) to the panels of the *Mishkan.* The second cloth, known as the *masakh* (the screen) covered the entrance to the *Mishkan.* It is made of the same materials as the *mishkan* and *Parokhet* but does not specifically include the *keruvim* design, nor was it made using *maaseh ḥoshev,* so that any design that it

20. For the history of *tekhelet,* see Baruch Sterman's *The Rarest Blue* (Ptil Tekhelet, 2017).
21. Although there is debate about whether these are a single covering or two separate ones, in multiple places the text seems unambiguous in its presentation of them as two distinct coverings. See 26:14, 36:19, and Num. 4:25. The identity of the *taḥash* is unclear. Many opinions understand it as some kind of sea creature.

did have was embroidered onto it, not woven into it integrally. It, too, was held up by pillars, but since this was on the outside border of the *Mishkan* its "feet" were made of copper rather than of silver.

The *keruvim* design, essential for all the inner cloths, obviously hints at the *keruvim,* which were never seen by anyone. It was those *keruvim* which were the source of the communication between God and Moses, the continuation of the Sinaitic Revelation, the ongoing relationship between God and Israel.

THE EXTERNAL VESSELS

As we move outside of the building into the courtyard, there are two items. One is a copper washing basin and the other is the central sacrificial altar. As the Torah does not discuss the washbasin here, we will save our discussion of it for where it is described; we will focus here on the one item which is described, the altar. This was a hollow box made of acacia wood plated in copper, befitting an external vessel. This altar was also a square, five cubits (approx. 7.5 feet) long and five cubits wide, but it was three cubits tall. It had copper rings for transportation, and copper-plated poles with which it would be carried. It does not have a crown, just as it is not made of gold, as it is not part of "God's chamber."

The altar has four protrusions, one on each corner, called the horns of the altar. While horns on altars were common throughout the Near East and can be found on many altars dug up in archaeological excavations, these take on specific significance in the Torah, as much of the processing of sacrifices focuses on placing the blood on the corner. It should also be noted that these horns are referenced earlier in the list of mitzvot regarding sanctuary from a vengeance: "Should a man intentionally conspire against his fellow to kill him by cunning, from My altar you shall take him to die" (21:14).

Two things stand out about this altar. First, given the golden (2x1x1) ratio found through the *Mishkan,* we would have expected that it would be ten cubits high, twice the other dimensions. In fact, there is a talmudic opinion which suggests that it was, obviously necessitating an explanation of why the Torah described its height as three cubits.[22]

22. Zevaḥim 59b. R. Yehuda reads the text as written; R. Yosi argues – apparently based

There are a number of possible explanations for why this altar stands out as different.

1. An altar ten cubits high (approx. 15 feet) would have made bringing the animal sacrifices unwieldy.
2. An altar ten cubits high would make it as tall as the *Mishkan* itself. Anyone processing the sacrificing standing on top would in effect be looking down at the adjacent *Mishkan*, which would have been wholly inappropriate.
3. A height of ten cubits for the altar would have made it virtually impossible for anyone to seek sanctuary under any circumstances, unless they actually climbed up onto the altar itself.

The second thing which stands out about this altar is that it seems too small for the purpose it is to serve. If this is to function as the sole altar for the entire nation, then given the number of sacrifices we expect to be brought, there is no way that it can accommodate the number of animals which would be brought on a daily basis. This technical issue will be discussed in greater length in the first epilogue, where we will address the relationship between Exodus and Leviticus.

THE COURTYARD

The courtyard of the *Mishkan* was fairly simple. It was demarcated with a plain linen cloth held up by wooden poles with bases of copper and hooks at the top made of silver. It was five cubits tall and extended around the courtyard area, which was one hundred cubits long and fifty cubits wide. The curtain had an opening of twenty cubits on the eastern side for an entrance, which was covered by a screen similar to the screen at the entrance to the *Mishkan* – undyed linen and blue, purple, and red wools with embroidery work for the designs. The diagram below presents a schematic overview of the entire *Mishkan* complex, including the courtyard surrounding the *Mishkan*.

---

on the *Mishkan* ratio – that it was ten cubits high.

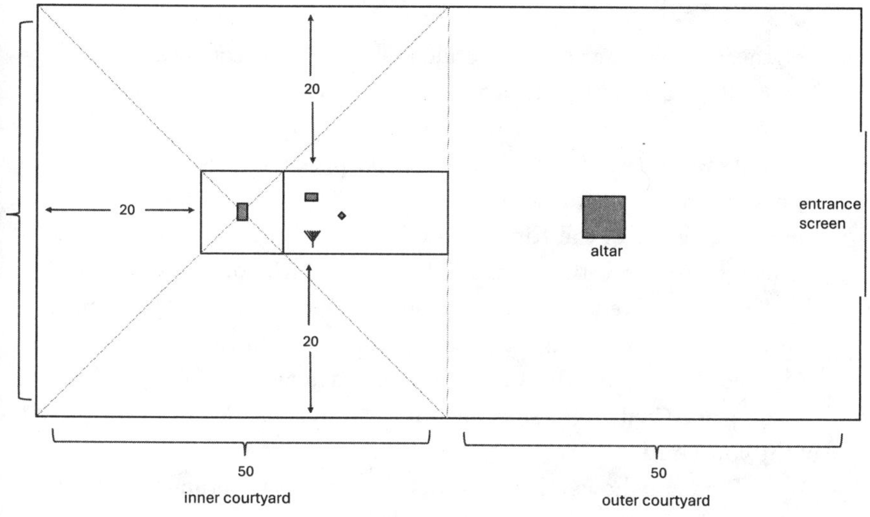

Perhaps the most significant feature of the courtyard is that it preserves the 2x1 *Mishkan* ratio, but this time in two dimensions only. From a bird's-eye view, the shape of the courtyard mirrors precisely the shape of *Kodesh* area of the *Mishkan*. Further, just as the *Kodesh* area splits into two equally sized areas, one marked by the royal vessels and the other left for access by Aaron and his sons, the rectangular courtyard also divides into two equal areas of 50x50 cubits each. The outer, eastern area is distinguished primarily by the altar and permitted access to all visitors to the *Mishkan*, while the inner, western area is distinguished by the *Mishkan* itself, to which access was limited to Aaron and his sons.

Three other features stand out. One is that the Ark, the locus of God's direct communication with Moses, is located not only in the center of the *Kodesh HaKodashim*, but in the center of the inner courtyard. This highlights its centrality as the most significant component of the entire enterprise. Second, the location of the *Mishkan* in the inner courtyard creates a beautiful symmetry of space surrounding it, with twenty cubits on the northern, southern, and western sides. While it is not clear if this has any meaning, it accentuates the aesthetic beauty of the place. Third, it should be noted that there is a direct line between the

Ark, the incense altar, and the sacrificial altar.[23] Aside from the aesthetic beauty of the arrangement, we will later explore the significance of this alignment.

As we've seen, the *Mishkan*'s core purpose is reflected in many of its details. The pure gold and crowns of the inner vessels indicate that this is the palace of the King, as do the royal threads of the *mishkan* cloths. The juxtaposition of the Table and the Menora represent the essence of the covenant – a partnership between God and His people. The *Mishkan*'s function as the meeting place between God and Israel is indicated through the *Mishkan* ratio, reflected in nearly every one of the objects placed in it, in the structure of the building, and in the structure of the courtyard.

There are, however, a few questions still outstanding. Why did God omit the incense altar from the *Mishkan* and the washing basin from the courtyard, only to reveal them later? How could such a small altar service the multitude of sacrifices required by an entire nation? What is the significance of the alignment of the Ark and the two altars? For these, we will need some patience, for the Torah will first address the preparation of those who serve in this *Mishkan*.

23. This is in line with R. Yehuda's opinion that the external altar was indeed three cubits high. According to R. Yosi, who posited that the altar was ten cubits high, a long ramp was needed to access the altar, necessitating that it be skewed off-center in the courtyard.

Exodus 28:1–29:46

Aaron and Sons

On the mountain, Moses hears all about the *Mishkan* – not only its construction but its service. We will soon learn that there is at least one critical service that he will need to perform; according to rabbinic tradition he served temporarily as the high priest.[1] There was no reason for him to suspect that as Israel's primary religious guide, as the one who is currently standing on Mount Sinai with God and who served as the intermediary between God and the people in the theophany at Sinai, and as the one who is to be invited into God's inner sanctum to continue the dialogue begun at Sinai, that he would not be the one performing the regular services in the *Mishkan*. He is likely, therefor, surprised when he earlier hears God describing one of his roles:

1. See Ps. 99:6. Zevaḥim 101b–102a describes Moses as a full, albeit temporary, *kohen gadol* (high priest). See also *Sifra, Tzav* 14 and Numbers Rabba, *Naso* 9. Zohar, *Teruma* 56:597 describes Moses as watching one of the ministering angels perform the service in a celestial *Mishkan* to learn how it is to be done. Moses performs all the priestly tasks in Exodus 29 in the process of installing Aaron and his sons into their positions. Tellingly, the description of the washbasin (30:17–21) refers to it as serving Aaron and his sons, yet we find in practice that it serves Moses as well (40:31).

> You shall command the people to take for you clear, beaten olive oil for lighting, to light a constant light. In the Tent of Meeting, outside of the *Parokhet* covering the [Ark of] Testimony, Aaron and his sons will arrange it before God from morning until evening. (27:20–21)

For the first time Moses learns that his job is to command, but not to perform. This may not have been too bothersome, as it is limited to only service in the *Mishkan*. What Moses hears next, however, changes the picture completely, when God tells him to bring Aaron and his sons forward to induct them into the *Mishkan* service. While Moses is the commander-in-chief responsible for constructing the *Mishkan*, his name is never really associated with it. Betzalel is the chief architect and artisan; Aaron is responsible for the service. All this might be part of God's continued plan to diversify the leadership, distribute the sources of power and authority, and teach Moses to delegate – all important things for Moses to learn on his path to leadership. But it could also signal something else which gives us cause for reflection as well, regarding both Moses and Aaron.

According to a midrashic tradition, passing over Moses as the primary minister in the *Mishkan* was punishment for his repeated refusal to accept God's mission.[2] Along similar lines, there was a more recent event which is more thematically linked, which may be responsible. At Masa-Meriva, Moses interpreted the people's complaints about water as challenging God: "Is God in our midst or not?" (17:7). There is little indication that the people were asking that, and God doesn't indicate that He saw it that way. And while God does not react to Moses's accusation there, perhaps the *Mishkan* is an appropriate place for that reaction. God opens with, "They shall make for Me a Sanctuary and I will dwell among them" (25:8). This almost sounds like God's reaction to Moses's suspicion, as if to say, "If you think that the people are in doubt, then don't accuse them – help them. If you build it then I will come, and there will be no more doubts." Moses's skepticism about his people disqualifies him from being the one responsible for maintaining the Divine

2. Exodus Rabba 3:17.

Presence.[3] To be sure, he would be the one with whom God spoke in the *Mishkan* to continue the dialogue at Sinai, but he could not be the one to bring and maintain God's presence among them. That function would have to go to someone else.

Of course, Aaron is already known as a significant figure. God had singled him out as Moses's partner in dealing with Pharaoh, we've seen him bear the load of leadership together with Moses in Israel's early stations in the wilderness, he was one of the two people who held up Moses's hands in the battle with Amalek, and he was one of the two people left in charge of the camp when Moses ascended the mountain for an indeterminate tine. What we do not know is why that qualifies him for service in the *Mishkan,* and that is a question for which the Torah does not even seem to provide an answer.

The other question raised for us is that of Aaron's sons. Certainly the elder sons were featured briefly, as they were part of the nobles of Israel who partially ascended the mountain and ate and drank while they witnessed God's revelation after sealing the covenant (24:9–11). Aaron, however, has two other sons, and we will later learn that they, too, are inducted into the *Mishkan* service. Does this imply that the job of serving in the *Mishkan* is hereditary? Why would that job be passed from father to son but not Moses's position? After all, we earlier hear about Moses's two sons, but there is never a suggestion that they will inherit his office. These questions, too, are ones we are left to ponder on our own, as the Torah never addresses them.

What then, does God share with us about them? The clothes they wear and the process of their formal induction into service.

Here's one more observation before we begin studying about their clothes and their induction. The title *kohen,* usually translated as "priest," but whose origin suggests something more akin to one who serves,[4] is used six times earlier in Exodus. Yitro is identified as the *kohen* of

3. *Midrash Tanḥuma* 23 criticizes Moses's skepticism regarding Israel at a much earlier stage in his career.
4. II Samuel 8:18 describes David's sons as *kohanim* although they are clearly not from Aaron's family. Deuteronomy is careful to describe priestly *kohanim* and *kohanim* who are Levites. See Deut. 17:9, 18:18, 18:1, 21:5, 24:8, 27:9, and 31:9.

Midian; there were some kinds of *kohanim* (plural of *kohen*) who had an unclarified, preexisting position (19:22 and 19:24); and God's offer to Israel included that they will become a kingdom of *kohanim*. We would expect that the section dealing with the special vestments for Aaron and his sons, as well their induction, would feature the *kohen* identifier multiple times. It is surprising then that the title *kohen* appears at most twice.[5] What does appear multiple times is the root K-H-N used as a verb, meaning to induct into service or to serve.

What does this suggest? I believe that the Torah is making a profound statement here about the position of the *kohen*. Perhaps the reason that we are told nothing about their qualification for this position is because there was no way to qualify. That means that God did not choose them because they were special, but that they become special because God chose them. Their induction is more important than who they were prior to that induction. Why God chose Aaron seems irrelevant; the only thing which is relevant is the fact that God chose him. As for the clothes, here it seems clear that they are what make Aaron the man he becomes.[6] As the text says: They should make Aaron's clothes to set him aside (i.e., sanctify him) and induct him into My service (28:3).

THE CLOTHES

Aaron's sons wear four items of clothing, all fabricated from plain, unadorned linen. The pants, whose function is to prevent indignity of exposure (28:42), extend from the hips to the thighs. Tunics cover the upper body, and a sash is wrapped around the waist. Completing their uniform is a linen hat.

---

5. 29:9 and 29:30. It is unclear if this is a title or an adjective meaning "the one who serves."
6. This point was the crux of one debate between Moses and Korah (Num. 16). Korah argued that all of Israel was equally qualified, and according to a talmudic interpretation, he was more qualified than Aaron because he was the descendant of a more senior branch of the Levite family. Moses's counterargument is that there is no qualification other than what God chooses. God had earlier chosen Aaron, and Moses wants to demonstrate that He will again choose Aaron through the contest with the fire pans.

As for Aaron, he has two sets of clothes, which – except for the pants[7] – are for honor and splendor (28:2). The pants, whose function is simply to cover the nakedness, are identical to those of his sons. He, too, has a linen tunic, but his has a checkered pattern woven in. Aaron's linen sash is adorned with embroidery work, and his linen headgear is wrapped like a turban.[8] These clothes are what the Sages call the white clothes.[9]

There is a second set of clothes – which the Sages call the gold clothes[10] – which are worn on top of the white clothes. There are three of these – the *efod,* the *ḥoshen,* and the *me'il* – plus one additional item, the golden *tzitz.*[11]

The *efod*

The first of the garments discussed, the *efod,* catches our attention as it sounds somewhat familiar. It is made of the same threads as the innermost *mishkan* cloths and the *Parokhet,* but in addition has strands of gold thread as part of the weave, which those other fabrics do not. In terms of its look, the *efod* is an apron-like garment worn from the waist down with a band which ties around the waist. From that band, in the back, are two straps which extend vertically and reach just over the shoulders. On each of those shoulder straps, on the part that reaches the top of the shoulder, is a gold setting into which is embedded a stone engraved with the names of six tribes, so that there are six tribes engraved in the stone on the right shoulder and six on the left. The Torah describes the purpose of these stones, called *avnei shoham*: "stones of memory of the Israelites; Aaron will carry their names before God on his shoulders as a memory" (28:12).

7. It is telling that the pants are not included in the list of clothes the Torah introduces in 28:4 and are mentioned only after all the clothes are discussed (28:42) in what feels like an afterthought.
8. Aaron's turban is called a *mitznefet,* while their headgear was called a *migbaat.*
9. Mishna Yoma 3:6 and 7:4.
10. Mishna Yoma 3:4 and 7:3–4.
11. When the Torah introduces the clothes in 28:4, the *tzitz* is not mentioned. It apparently has a different status, which we will discuss later.

Aside from that fabric seeming like an upgraded version of the holiest cloths we've seen until now, there are other elements in the *efod* which evoke items in the *Mishkan*. The two *avnei shoham*, each bearing a stack of six names, is strikingly reminiscent of the Table with its two sets of six shelves each. Further, the two stones echo the two stone tablets which are housed in the Ark. This parallel also reveals the dramatic difference between the tablets and the *avnei shoham*. The tablets are engraved with God's message to Israel, the testimony to the covenant, their commitment to Him; the *avnei shoham* are engraved with the names of the tribes of Israel, bringing before God a constant reminder of His commitment to them. The *efod* thus not only parallels the Ark but is its counterpart in the array of *Mishkan* symbolism reflecting the ongoing relationship between God and His people.

The *ḥoshen*

The *ḥoshen*, also called the *ḥoshen mishpat* (the *ḥoshen* of justice), is made to match the *efod*, and is made of the same fabric as the *efod*, including the gold threads woven in. It is the only garment whose dimensions are given, and those dimensions are unusual: "It should be a double square, one half-cubit long and one half-cubit wide." That means that the fabric itself should be a double square, otherwise known as a rectangle whose length is double its width, so that when folded in half it yields a single, two-layer square. On the upper edge of the garment are two golden rings, onto which are affixed cords woven of purified gold which are then attached to the shoulder straps of the *efod*, specifically onto the gold settings for the *avnei shoham*. On the lower edge of the *hoshen* are two more golden rings, onto which are affixed strands of *tekhelet*-colored wool which are affixed to corresponding golden rings on the front of the waistband of the *efod*. The *ḥoshen* thus not only perfectly matches the *efod* but is affixed to it both on the top and the bottom, so that "the *ḥoshen* shall not slip from the *efod*" (28:28), effectively making the two garments seem like one.

Two features mark the uniqueness of the *ḥoshen*. The more prominent feature is the array of stones. Attached to the outward-facing side of the fabric are twelve golden settings into which are embedded twelve precious stones, called the *avnei miluim*, arranged in four rows of three stones each. On each stone is engraved the name of one of the tribes of Israel, so that "Aaron will carry on his heart the names of the twelve tribes of Israel as he enters the Holy, as a constant reminder before God" (28:29). The less prominent but not less significant feature are the *Urim* and the *Tummim*,[12] which are placed into the pocket created when the garment is folded in half, so that "they will be on Aaron's heart as he enters before God, and Aaron will carry the judgment of the Israelites on his heart before God constantly" (28:30).

Speaking broadly, the *ḥoshen* is rich with symbols linking it to the inner vessels of the *Mishkan*. Like the *efod*, the fabric, including the gold, demonstrates that it shares an affinity with them. Strengthening that link are the golden rings, which are present on the inner vessels, and the cords of purified gold reinforce that bond further.

When we examine some of the specifics we notice parallels to individual vessels. When describing the attachment of the golden cords to the shoulder straps of the *efod* the Torah uses an unusual phrase, "*el mul panav*," meaning "on its front side." This phrase appears only seven times in the Torah, all in the context of the *Mishkan*, five of which refer to the Menora lighting up the Table facing it. Furthering the bond with the Menora are the *Urim*; while we may not know what these are, their name means "lights."

Finally, a comment about the dimensions of the *ḥoshen*. We already noted that this is the only garment for which a size is specified, and that it is an unusual description – a double-square half-cubit. When unfolded, the fabric of the *ḥoshen* is a cubit long and a half-cubit wide; when folded, it is a square of a half-cubit on each side. We recognize these

12. The Torah never identifies what these are, but their appearance in the text, especially with the definitive "the," indicates that they are two distinct items (see Ibn Ezra on 28:30) and that they are well known to Moses (see Nahmanides on 28:30). Rabbinic tradition understands that these somehow contain God's ineffable name which mysteriously powered the stones of the *ḥoshen* to light up and reveal God's response to questions posed by the high priest (see Rashi and Nahmanides on 28:30). The precise nature of what they are remains a mystery, and as Robert Alter, in *The Hebrew Bible: Translation and Commentary* (Norton, 2019), 327, writes, "It is probably not coincidental that these two words begin respective with the first and last letter of the Hebrew alphabet."

ratios. The unfolded *ḥoshen* is a 2x1 garment, reflecting yet again the golden ratio running throughout the *Mishkan*, representing the meeting place between God and Israel. When folded, it is a perfect square, like the floor plan of the *Kodesh HaKodashim*. As such, the *ḥoshen* reflects both the meeting of the covenantal partners as well as God's inner sanctum into which, with rare exception, people are not invited.

When we step back and look at the *ḥoshen* in its context, we notice that it is an individual item of clothing which is attached to another, the *efod*, so that the two seem like a single unit. In the *Mishkan*, the Ark and its covering, the *Kaporet*, are similar. That *Kaporet* is a separate entity yet never intended to be removed. Even more, the Ark-*Kaporet* houses the tablets while the *efod-ḥoshen* unit is where the *Urim* and the *Tummim* reside.

It seems that like the *efod*, the *ḥoshen* serves a similar role as empowering Aaron to regularly bring the memory of Israel before God (28:29) and to bring their case before God as God sits in judgment of them (28:30). The *efod-ḥoshen* unit mirrors the Ark in form and serves as a counterbalance to the demands of the covenant in function, as it brings the memory of Israel before God.

The *me'il*

The *me'il* is a sleeveless, neck-to-ankle tunic worn over the linen *ketonet* but under the *efod-ḥoshen*. It is made entirely of *tekhelet*-colored wool and is adorned at the bottom with golden bells and pomegranates made of *tekhelet*, purple, and red-dyed wool.[13] The purity of the garment appears to indicate a single-minded dedication by Aaron to the divine service – while wearing the vestments he is not to be distracted by anything else.[14] This idea is later amplified (Lev. 21:10–14), as the one invested in these garments is forbidden from engaging in any non-sanctified activities and is even prohibited from leaving the sanctified

13. The nature of these pomegranates is unclear. It is also unclear whether the bells and pomegranates alternate along the bottom hem (Rashi, 28:33) or if the bells are embedded inside the pomegranates (Nahmanides, 28:31).
14. The purity of the garment also echoes the Menora, which is described as the pure Menora. This parallel is enhanced by pomegranates which adorn both.

precinct of the *Mishkan*. The bells at the bottom are to announce his presence, either as a warning to others that they should not be present in the Sanctuary at that time or as a means of announcing his approach to God, as a sign of respect.[15]

It is possible that the *me'il* serves an additional function as an intermediate garment between the more ordinary white garments and the ultra-sanctified *efod-ḥoshen*. If so, then this three-layered hierarchy of clothing echoes the three stages of sanctified spaces in the *Mishkan* – the courtyard, the *Kodesh*, and the *Kodesh HaKodashim*. As we saw before, the similarity invites an exploration of the differences, the most significant of which is the order. While in the *Mishkan*, the white linen courtyard is on the outside and the most sanctified *Kodesh HaKodashim* is on the inside, in Aaron's clothing that is reversed, so that the white linen is on the inside and the most sanctified *efod-ḥoshen* are on the outside.

The golden *tzitz*

Completing the picture is the *tzitz*. While it is not listed initially as a garment (38:4), it is appended at the end. The *tzitz* consists of a band made of purified gold engraved with the words *Kodesh lAdonai*, "Dedicated to God." It is worn on Aaron's forehead, constantly, tied on by strings of *tekhelet* and "facing" the front of the turban and serves an explicit purpose: "So that Aaron will bear the sins of the sanctified (K-D-SH) things which the Israelites will sanctify (K-D-SH) for all of their sanctified (K-D-SH) gifts" (28:38). This tripled focus on the sacred things which Israel consecrates with the repeating K-D-SH calls for attention and suggests that there is a concern about the very materials that Israel will be donating to the *Mishkan*. What is the provenance of those materials? How were they obtained? Are they fit to be an integral part of the Sanctuary?[16] The Torah seems to recognize that it is impossible to root out all impropriety in financial dealings, and that some of those proceeds may end up in the *Mishkan*. As such, it becomes necessary to bear that stain, and that appears to be the function of the *tzitz*.

15. The first opinion is that of Rashbam (28:35); the second is expressed by Nahmanides (28:35).
16. Deuteronomy 23:19 explicitly lists two items which are forbidden for donation.

While the *tzitz* bears no apparent resemblance to any of the vessels of the *Mishkan*, it actually echoes them all. Each of the vessels was capped by a golden crown; the *tzitz* is the golden crown of Aaron's head. In fact, the crown on those internal vessels is called a *zer*, and the *tzitz* is referred to later (39:30 and Lev. 8:9) as a *nezer*, meaning a crown.

Aaron's full dress

We've already noted the theme of the *keruvim* in the *Mishkan* and how they hint at a more pure, perfect world represented by the Garden of Eden, whose access was blocked by the *keruvim*. Aaron's clothes push that hint one step further. The mix of the wool and the linen, which is prominent in the *efod-ḥoshen*, is later prohibited by the Torah (Lev. 19:19). While many commentators consider that prohibition to be in the category of those things which defy rational explanation, others point out that it carries echoes of the inability of farmers (who produce the source of linen) and shepherds (whose flocks provide wool) to coexist in the same space, as the sheep would consume the flax plants from which the linen is made. This incompatibility can be traced back to the first siblings, Cain and Abel, the farmer and the shepherd, whose conflict over the land[17] brought about the first killing, a fratricide. The counter to that tension is the Garden, where there is no enmity or competition, where the lion and the lamb lie together. The *Mishkan*, and the priestly garments, maintain a dream of a world in which the incompatible can coexist, in which the word of God is ubiquitous and His message apparent to all.[18]

When we put the picture of Aaron's vestments together, the composite image which emerges is that Aaron's vestments generate an inside-out rendition of the *Mishkan*. In the *Mishkan* the white cloths were the outermost and viewable by everyone; on Aaron the white cloths were the innermost and were mostly hidden from view. In the *Mishkan* the multicolored cloths were kept on the inside and were hidden from view; on Aaron the multicolored garments were worn on the outside

17. Note that the killing happened in the field (Gen. 4:8), where Cain was growing crops as a farmer and to where Abel apparently wanted to bring his flocks. See Genesis Rabba 4:5.
18. See the image in Isaiah 11:6–9.

and were viewable by all. Aaron has a golden crown in the form of *tzitz*, mirroring the crowns on the internal vessels.

On the level of the vessels themselves, the Ark-*Kaporet* model is re-created in the *efod-ḥoshen*; the stone Tablets of Covenant are mirrored by the stones of memory Aaron carries on his shoulders; the twelve loaves of bread in two parallel stacks are reworked as the names of the twelve tribes engraved on the *avnei shoham*; the lights of the Menora are echoed in the *Urim*; even the symbolic *Mishkan* 2 x 1 ratio is found in Aaron's clothing in the foldable *ḥoshen*. When fully clothed, Aaron is effectively transformed into one of the vessels of the *Mishkan*, complete with the golden crown, or perhaps even into a living replica of the *Mishkan* which is accessible to the people. Whereas the *Mishkan* brings God's presence to the people, Aaron brings the people to God.

INDUCTING AARON AND HIS SONS

The inauguration of Aaron and his sons is comprised primarily of three steps – donning the vestments, the preparatory sacrifices, and the transformation of Aaron and his sons into sanctified "vessels." Moses plays a central role in each of those steps, and this is the only time he will perform functionary duties in the *Mishkan*.

Clothing Aaron and his sons is fairly straightforward. For modesty, they are to don their pants by themselves, after which Moses formally dresses them. For Aaron's sons, Moses begins with the tunic, followed by the belt, and concluding with the hat. For Aaron himself, the tunic is followed by the *me'il* and then the *efod* and the *ḥoshen*. The process is completed with wrapping the turban, placing the *tzitz* on top, and anointing Aaron with anointing oil. The pattern for both is clear – the direction of dress is upward.

The preparatory sacrifices are somewhat complex, and also unique. Three types of sacrifices are brought – a bull as a *ḥatat*, which is essentially a purification offering (sometimes called a sin offering); a ram as an *ola*, which is an offering completely burned on the altar; another ram as a *shelamim*, of which part is consumed on the altar, part is eaten by Moses (as the functional *kohen*), and part is eaten by Aaron and his sons. These three types of offerings are found throughout Leviticus and are almost always in this order, since as a unit they function to symbolize the renewal of the covenant. The *ḥatat* serves to purify the one bringing it in preparation for reengaging with God, much like God instructed Moses to have the Israelites sanctified and cleansed before their encounter at Sinai (19:10). The completely burned *ola* signals subordination and complete acceptance of God as the senior partner in the relationship. The process is completed with the *shelamim,* whose flesh is shared between the altar, the functioning *kohen,* and the one renewing his bond with God, symbolizing the shared covenantal commitment.[19]

These standard offerings, however, deviate from the standards we will later learn about. In general, there are two kinds of *ḥatat* – in broad terms they break down into the ones for individuals and the ones for public figures (or for the public). In the ones for individuals, the blood is sprinkled on the external, bronze altar and the animal is offered on that same altar. In the one for public figures, the blood is sprinkled on the inner, golden altar and the animal is burned outside the camp. This *ḥatat* is unique in that the blood is sprinkled on the outer altar but the animal is burned outside the camp.

	Blood	**Flesh**
Individual *ḥatat*	External, bronze altar	External, bronze altar
Public *ḥatat*	Internal, golden altar	Outside the camp
Inaugural *ḥatat*	External, bronze altar	Outside the camp

There are a number of possible explanations for this aberration. It could be as simple as the reality that Moses has not as yet been informed of the existence of the internal, golden altar, which begs the question of why that was delayed.[20] It is also possible that the inauguration of Aaron and his sons is different in that the process functions both on the

19. Yitro brought the last two offerings, in the proper order, but not the first (18:12). Similarly, in the covenantal ceremony Moses directs, the Israelite youth bring *ola* and *shelamim,* but not the *ḥatat* (24:5); perhaps the purification was already effected in their earlier sanctification and cleansing of clothes.
20. This is also questionable as the inaugural process takes place long after Moses learns about the golden altar.

personal and on the public levels. On the public level, they are being inaugurated into public service as they will function in the *Mishkan*. On the personal level, they are not yet those public servants until after the inauguration – the inaugural process is what transforms them into that. That tension is reflected in the uniqueness of their *ḥatat* offering.

The unique situation of this inaugural process is reflected in a phrase which is repeated multiple times, in various forms, and which throughout the Bible only appears in the context of being inducted into divine service. The phrase "*lemalei yadayim*" (literally, "to fill one's hands") is an unusual one which commentators have struggled to decipher throughout the centuries.[21] In fact, a related term, "*miluim*," also appears in this context to describe not only some of the sacrifices (29:22) but even the entire process (Lev. 8:33).[22] Regardless of the origin of the idiom, in its context the meaning seems clear – it refers to a transformative process in which an individual becomes sanctified, perhaps transformed into a vessel of the *Mishkan*, and inducted into divine service. As Aaron and his sons go through that process, their offerings retain some elements of them as individuals and take on new dimensions of them as public people.[23]

The idea of Aaron and his sons being transformed into vessels of the *Mishkan* is reflected in another unique practice. When processing the *ola* ram, identified as the ram of *miluim*, Moses is to take some of the blood and place it on the right earlobes, the right thumbs, and the right big toes. This highly unusual practice becomes more intelligible

21. Multiple opinions have been expressed regarding this phrase throughout the ages and there is no consensus about what it means. Rabbi Shmuel David Luzzatto (29:9) sums it up best when he concludes his explanation with the comment that this requires further investigation. While the phrase is used primarily here, it appears throughout the Bible in similar contexts. See, for example, Judges 17:15, I Kings 13:33, Ezek. 33:26, II Chr. 13:9. It is used ironically in Isaiah 1:15, where he accuses the priests of filling their hands with blood (not sacrificial blood) instead of filling their hands in the ways that *kohanim* are expected to.

22. The term "*lemalei yadayim*" appears four times in this passage. The term "*miluim*" appears five times. In addition, the stones on the shoulder straps of the *efod* are called "*avnei miluim*." The term "*lemalei yadayim*" also appears in 32:29. We will discuss it in context there.

23. Pesaḥim 59b.

when we recognize that these small parts of the body are being paralleled to the horns of the altar, which stick out and onto which blood is usually placed. This ceremony effectively transforms Aaron and sons into *kohanim* – portable, living altars. It is not surprising to later discover that the consumption of the meat of certain sacrifices by the *kohanim* is not simply a benefit of the work they do but an essential step in the atonement process.

The induction of the *kohanim* thus is not merely a training process nor an inaugural ceremony, but a transformative one in which the *kohanim* become extensions of the *Mishkan* itself and Aaron is transformed into a walking version of the *Mishkan* accessible to the people.

THE DAILY OFFERING AND THE DIVINE PRESENCE

Capping the process of constructing the *Mishkan* and inducting Aaron and his sons is the instruction for what happens in that *Mishkan* and its purpose. Two daily *ola* offerings, one in the morning and the other in the evening, are the only sacrifices God commands for the regular functioning of the *Mishkan*. While we later learn of an annual purification for maintenance of the *Mishkan*, it seems that God envisions it as a place that is silent for the bulk of the day, enabling it to serve its primary purpose as enabling the Divine Presence to dwell in the camp so that He can continue His communication with Israel through Moses.

> It is a perpetual *ola*, for all generations, at the entrance to the Tent of Meeting before God; where I will meet with you there to speak to you there. I will there meet the Israelites, and it will be sanctified by My glory. (29:42–43)

Two things stand out in this declaration. One is the is word "perpetual" or "constant" – in Hebrew, *tamid* A number of items in the *Mishkan* have been marked with this word: the weekly showbread, the flames on the Menora, the *ḥoshen* on Aaron's heart, this daily *ola*, and the daily incense offering (which we will hear about in the next chapter). This is the stuff of the daily service, and it is their regularity and constancy which accords them their power to bring the Divine Presence. The Bible repeatedly makes the point that while the occasional flashy events can be very powerful and moving, their effect is transitory at best. We earlier saw that in the plagues and at the Reed Sea, we will soon witness that in the sin of the Golden Calf, and that will become evident in events such as Elijah's dramatic showdown on Mount Carmel (I Kings 18). By contrast, the daily service – whether as a result of or despite its monotony – builds a routine which becomes ingrained over time. It is routines like those where meaning and lasting change happens, and it is in that context that the Divine Presence dwells among the people.

The second aspect of this is the fact that the daily offering is an *ola*, completely burned on the altar. Like the individual *ola*, which symbolizes subservience to God and recognition that He is the senior partner in this relationship, the public *ola* represents the same subservience, but on a national level rather than a personal one.[24] That daily declaration by the people allows for God to bring His presence among the people, and it is what makes their offering "sweet smelling" to God, as it reflects their understanding that they are God's emissaries.[25]

With the introduction of the twice-daily *ola*, the *Mishkan* and its purpose are complete. Circling back to His introduction of the *Mishkan*, "They shall make for Me a Sanctuary and I will dwell among them," God reaffirms that goal, adding a surprise – that this was His intention from the time He elected to take them out of Egypt. It was not their liberation from Pharaoh, reaching the land of their ancestors, or even the giving of the Torah which was the primary purpose – it was Israel's partnering with God so that He could dwell among them.

> I have set aside the Tent of Meeting and the altar, and I will set aside Aaron and his sons to serve Me. I will dwell among the Israelites, and I will be for them a God. They will know that I am A-donai, their God, who took them out of the land of Egypt to dwell among them; I am A-donai their God.

---

24. It should be noted that at this point there is mention in the Torah of personal offerings. We will discuss this later in the first epilogue.
25. The first "sweet-smelling" offering was Noah's, whose sacrifice indicated his profound discovery of the difference between humans and animals, which was especially pleasing to God. See Grumet, *Genesis: From Creation to Covenant,* 89.

Exodus 29:1–31:17

Appendices to the *Mishkan*

The plans for the *Mishkan* are completed. Everything necessary to bring God's presence into the Israelite camp has been designed and presented to Moses. There are a few additional issues which need to be addressed which are related to the *Mishkan* but not essential for its primary function, some of which are surprising for a variety of reasons. There are seven of these appendices:[1]

1. The golden incense altar
2. The half-shekel
3. The copper washbasin
4. The unique anointing oil
5. The unique incense
6. The artisans who will fabricate the objects
7. Shabbat

1. Rabbi Elhanan Samet (*Iyunim BeFarashat HaShavua*, Series 1, Volume 1, 252–65) demonstrates that all these passages are linked to the *Mishkan*. Nahum Sarna (*Exploring Exodus*, 213) argues that these are not appendices, but that from the introduction of the *Mishkan* (25:1) through the close of this section (31:17) there are seven passages opening with the words "God spoke to Moses," all of which are integral to the *Mishkan*.

THE INCENSE ALTAR

Technically, the golden incense altar seems like an integral member of the inner vessels of the *Mishkan*. Like the Ark and the Table, it is a rectangular box made of acacia wood plated in purified gold, with a golden crown around the top and golden rings to accommodate the gold-plated acacia poles which will carry it. Also like the Ark and the Table, its dimensions reflect the *Mishkan* ratio of 1x1x2, and it is perhaps the most perfect example of that ratio as there are no half-cubits – the length and width are both one cubit and it stands two cubits tall. It is located in the *Kodesh* of the *Mishkan* along with the Table and the Menora, aligned directly on the same centerline as the Ark and the external, copper altar.[2] All this highlights the glaring question: Why is it not included together with its siblings, left until after the plans for the *Mishkan* are complete?

Traditional commentators grapple with this. Nahmanides, for example, offers a mystical response suggesting that its function is not to bring God's presence but to provide a buffer for Israel to protect it from that presence.[3] Sforno suggests a more rationalist explanation that once the Divine Presence has arrived it is incumbent on Israel to be hospitable; hence the altar for the incense which is pleasing to God. The common thread in many of the approaches reflects the core idea, grounded in the text, that the incense altar does not serve the function of drawing in the Divine Presence.[4] Understanding what the altar is *not* – not essential for inviting God's presence into the *Mishkan* – does not explain what it is for.

In attempting to understand the function of the incense altar we need to take note of its distinctive features. First, its placement seems to link it with the Ark.

---

2. See Ibn Ezra on 30:18.
3. Associating the incense offering with placating divine wrath is based on Numbers 17:9–12, where Aaron uses it to stop a divine plague.
4. Rabbi Meir Simha HaKohen of Dvinsk, in his *Meshekh Ḥokhma*, goes so far as to suggest that this vessel was not essential even for bringing the incense, as it could be offered in the absence of the altar.

> You shall place it before the *Parokhet* which is over the Ark of Testimony, before the *Kaporet* which covers the Testimony, the place where I will meet you. (30:6)

Second, its technical function links it chronologically with the Menora.

> Aaron shall burn upon it the incense; morning after morning, when he arranges the lamps, he shall burn it. And when he kindles the lamps in the afternoon he should burn it; the perpetual incense before God for your generations. (30:8–9)

Third, this is the only one of the vessels for which the Torah imposes explicit limitations of its usage. It is to be used exclusively for this twice-daily incense offering; it is forbidden to bring any other incense upon it, to use it for animal or grain sacrifices, and no libation of wine or water is to go upon it. Finally, once a year, Aaron is to place the blood of the purification-atonement sacrifice onto its horns as an atonement.[5] Presumably, the purification-atonement offering mentioned is the one explicated in Leviticus 16:

> He will atone for the sacred place from the impurities of the Israelites and from their offenses, for all their errors; he shall do similarly for the Tent of Meeting which dwells with them among all their impurities. (Lev. 16:16)

> He will go out to the altar which is before God and atone for it; he should take from the blood of the bull and the blood of the goat and place it on the horns of the altar all around. (Lev. 16:18)

When we put the details together it appears that there are two distinct functions for this altar. There is its daily function, in which it somehow adds to the service of the Menora even though that addition is not essential. Then there is its annual function, in which it is used as part of the purification of the entire *Mishkan*, cleansing it of the sins of Israel

5. In this verse, the root K-P-R, meaning to atone, appears three times.

which have somewhat defiled the *Mishkan,* threatening to cause God's presence to withdraw. Presumably, that withdrawal means that God is no longer accessible at the external altar or even in the *Kodesh,* as He will pull back behind the *Parokhet* to the *Ark* in the inner sanctum. The annual purification draws that presence out so that Israel can encounter Him in the *Mishkan* courtyard. While this is an essential function, so much so that the altar may not be used for anything else, ever, and without which there is the threat of the retreat of God's presence, it is not an integral part of the daily service which invites God's presence in.

THE HALF-SHEKEL

An initial reading of the instructions regarding the half-shekel leaves the reader perplexed as to why it is here at all. The primary focus seems to be on a procedure for taking a census, and it is only tangentially connected to the *Mishkan.* A later passage, however, reveals that it is the census which is tangential, and that the silver collection is an integral part of the construction of the *Mishkan.*

Exodus 38 begins with an accounting of the gold, silver, and copper donated for the *Mishkan.* While the gold and copper are described using the term *hatenufa* (literally, for the waving), that description is missing for the silver. Instead, the silver is described as the silver of the *pekudim* (see next paragraph), and the other descriptions of the donations of silver match the language used here:

Exodus 30:13–16	**Exodus 38:25–26**
Half a shekel of the sanctified shekel	Half a shekel of the sanctified shekel
Everyone included in the *pekudim*	Everyone included in the *pekudim*
From the age of twenty years and up	From the age of twenty years and up

That silver was used for the sockets at the base of the planks forming the walls of the *Mishkan,* and for the hooks at the tops of the pillars used for holding up the *Parokhet* and the entrance screen (38:27–28). When we read our passage more carefully, we discover a number of other clues binding this silver collection to the *Mishkan* in multiple ways.

- The silver collected is called the silver of atonement (*kippurim*), which echoes the purification-atonement process described in the prior passage of the incense altar.
- The root K-P-R, meaning to atone, appears four times in this passage.
- The root P-K-D, meaning to count, to remember, or to appoint, appears five times.
- The silver of atonement collected from the people serves Israel as a "reminder before God," the same term used earlier for the *ḥoshen*.
- The word *teruma*, colloquially meaning a donation, appears five times in this passage, echoing the opening of the entire *Mishkan*: "Let them take for Me a *teruma*" (25:2 – the word *teruma* appears three times in that opening passage, 25:2–3).

Exploring the link of *teruma*, there is an interesting shift which takes place from the opening passage to this one. In the opening passage, although the donations are completely voluntary, the verb used repeatedly (three times) is to "take" the *teruma*. By contrast, the *teruma* discussed regarding the half-shekel is a mandatory one – every male who reached the age of twenty is obligated in that half-shekel, yet the operative word is to "give" the *teruma* (which appears five times).

The multiple ironies of the give and take reveal that the two passages are directed at different audiences. The opening passage is apparently directed at the public figures responsible for collecting the donations. As the *Mishkan* is a public project, the focus there is on those who will play active roles in moving that project forward. By contrast, the passage of the half-shekel focuses on the individual responsibilities of each adult Israelite male, and that responsibility is to give.

This subtle shift uncovers a hidden tension regarding the very notion of a relationship between God and a nation. The relationship is between God and a corporate entity known as Israel, yet that entity is comprised of a multitude of individuals. How many individuals need to be in fulfillment of that covenant for it to be considered successful? How many need to be in breach of it for God to withdraw His presence from the *Mishkan*? How many individuals need to be fulfilling the covenant for God to reward the corporate entity, or how many need to be violating it for God to impose sanctions on the nation? These are difficult questions, and we certainly have no concept of what the calculus is, and yet these will be some of the questions which will be tested as Israel struggles through its first years of relationship with God and which will emerge repeatedly through their long and complex relationship throughout the Bible and beyond. What is clear, however, is that God understands the need for the relationship to be personalized with the individuals, and not only generalized through the corporate Israel, in order for it to be successful.

When we broaden our view to some of the other links between this passage and the rest of the *Mishkan*, we see this issue of the individual and the communal emerging repeatedly. For example, the notion that every individual needs to be represented and that all are represented equally through the half-shekel – no one is permitted to give more or less – highlights the individual commitments, yet the fact that these were joined together to produce the sockets at the base of the planks of the *Mishkan* and the clips to hold up the curtains (38:27–28) emphasizes that which binds them together rather than that which marks them as individuals. Perhaps it is for this reason that, like the *ḥoshen*, the half-shekel collection serves as a "reminder of the Israelite people before God" (30:16), as the Israelite collective is forged by the commitments of multiple individuals. This core idea serves as the underpinning of the Torah's repeated assertion that the half-shekel is a source of atonement.[6]

6. Another association with this collection of silver is built on the word *pekudim*, which is prominent in the beginning of Numbers in the context of counting the number of soldiers (it appears there forty-five times in the first three chapters), who are counted from the age of twenty. As the soldiers bind themselves to God, presumably as they continue to the conquest of the Promised Land, recognizing that their battle is in the service of God – to establish His headquarters on earth – is what will bring God to protect them in battle. It is for that reason that the Torah here uses the phrase "that there be no *negef* as they are called to their *pekudim*," that is, that they will not be defeated by their enemies. The term *negef*, understood by many to refer to some

THE COPPER WASHBASIN

Strategically placed in the courtyard between the *Mishkan* and the copper altar is the washbasin. It is not so much a vessel of the *Mishkan*, even though it is made of copper and is permanently stationed, appropriately, in the courtyard, but is rather a tool which enables the work in the *Mishkan* to happen. Aaron and his sons are to wash their hands and feet when either entering the *Mishkan* or proceeding to deal with the sacrifices on the altar. Because it serves only a preparatory purpose, enabling Aaron and his sons to do their work, it is not included in the primary discussion of the *Mishkan* among the parts which serve to invite the Divine Presence into the camp.

One of the fascinating aspects of this is that the washing needed to take place even when moving from the altar to the *Mishkan* or from the *Mishkan* to the altar. This is somewhat surprising because we might have expected that a *kohen* who was already prepared to enter the *Mishkan* would surely be prepared to approach the altar, whose sanctity is considerably less. What this suggests is that the nature of the altar and that of the *Mishkan* are completely different, so that preparing for one does not automatically imply being prepared for the other.

THE UNIQUE ANOINTING OIL AND INCENSE

These two items, each discussed in its own passage, share a number of qualities. They are each introduced by God instructing Moses to "take," followed by the recipe involving specific spices, and the demand that they be produced using a special perfume maker's artisanry. Both are identified as *kodesh kadashim*.[7] Both are distinguished by the prohibition against creating this mixture for any purpose other than their specific functions in the *Mishkan*, with violations being punished by being "cut off from the nation."

---

sort of plague (see, for example, Nahmanides's comment here), is used throughout the Bible to refer to defeat in battle. See Lev. 26:17; Num. 14:42; Deut. 1:42, 28:25; Judges 20:32–36; I Sam. 4:2; I Kings 8:33; II Kings 14:12; Zech. 14:12; and many others.

7. There are two different, albeit similar, phrases in the Torah which are often confused as being the same. One is *Kodesh HaKodashim*, the other is *kodesh kadashim*. This is an example of the latter.

Despite the similarities in content – that they are made with special spices using the same special process and that it is forbidden to make or use these compounds for anything other than their respective purposes in the *Mishkan* – and even in the language the Torah uses to describe these two items and their restrictions, which is frequently nearly identical, there is a substantive difference between them. The restriction of the anointing oil makes sense, as God wants to ensure that there will be no competing sacred places. Historically, the very existence of alternative places of worship was a slippery slope which repeatedly and inevitably led to idolatry.[8] If there is going to be an intimate relationship between God and Israel, there must be a single locus for that, and the prohibition against anointing or even manufacturing anointing oil for anything other than the singular *Mishkan* is a significant precautionary measure.

The prohibition regarding the incense, however, is less clear. There is no parallel explicit prohibition to make a facsimile of the Menora or even an altar for private use, and there were periods when it was even permitted to offer sacrifices on alternative altars.[9] It is possible that this is linked to the uniqueness of the incense altar, for which we earlier find the explicit prohibition of "You shall not offer on it a foreign incense offering" (30:9) and it is now being expanded to any non-*Mishkan* use of the recipe. It is also possible that this is due to the nature of the incense and the incense altar. We've already seen that the incense altar does not serve to facilitate the divine-human encounter (as does the rest of the *Mishkan*), but functions as an extension of the Menora and as a vehicle for purifying the place of the encounter. While there were periods when private sacrifices were permitted, the altars on which those sacrifices were brought did not generate "sacred spaces" set aside for God's presence – they were simply places on which to bring sacrifices. As such, they were never accompanied by an incense altar, since the incense altar implies a sacred space.[10] The prohibition against making

8. The most significant examples of this are the altars established by Yerovam in Beit El and Dan (I Kings 12:28–33), which were later transformed into centers of idolatry.
9. This is based on multiple incidents in the books of Joshua, Judges, and Samuel where we find sacrifices being offered in a variety of locales. I Kings 3:2 explicitly describes the practice as accepted prior to the establishment of the Temple in Jerusalem.
10. I Kings 3:2, which describes the use of private altars, discusses only sacrifices, not

or using the incense outside of the *Mishkan* highlights that the goal of "I will dwell among them" is exclusive to the *Mishkan* – no other place of worship can claim that.

THE ARTISANS WHO WILL FABRICATE THE OBJECTS

It is hard to know how a nation of slave laborers is expected to possess any of the skills necessary for all the fine craftsmanship necessary to manufacture everything necessary for the *Mishkan*. It is even more extraordinary that God identifies two individuals, who between them possess all the required skills – from metalwork to weaving and embroidery, to work with precious stones and perfuming. Nahmanides is so moved by this that he declares it nothing less than wondrous. It is perhaps for this reason that God clarifies that He filled them with

> the spirit of God in wisdom and in understanding and in knowledge and in every task, to devise plans, to work in gold and in silver and in bronze, and in stonecutting for settings and in wood carving, to do every task. (31:4–5)[11]

Who are these artisans? The first is identified as Betzalel, son of Uri, son of Hur, of the tribe of Judah. The fact that we are told three generations of ancestry rather than the standard two suggests that there is something important in that extra generation in his background. Indeed, his grandfather's name is Hur, leading the reader to link him with the one who stood at Moses's side on the mountain during the battle with Amalek and one of the two people Moses left in charge of the camp as he ascended the mountain where he would learn about the *Mishkan*. When we consider his name, Betzalel, it sounds like a contraction of two Hebrew words,

---

incense offerings. The following verse, however, which is critical of Solomon, includes the verbs used to describe both sacrifices (Z-V-H) and incense offerings (K-T-R). See also I Kings 11:8, 22:44; II Kings 12:4, 14:4, 15:4, 15:35, 16:4; and Isaiah 65:3, which use both verbs to describe practices abominable to God.

11. The text says that God gave wisdom to those who had wisdom in their hearts (31:6). Kass (*Founding God's Nation*, 518) suggests that this is analogous to God toughening the heart – in both, God strengthens those qualities which are innately at the individual's core.

betzel (in the shadow of) and *El* (God). This chief artisan carries himself in God's shadow, or perhaps, *betzelem El*, in God's image, echoing the creation of humanity itself (Gen. 1:26 and 9:6) and God's creative spirit.

Assisting Betzalel is Oholiav son of Aḥisamakh, of the tribe of Dan. Here, too, the name is quite expressive. Oholiav is also a contraction – *oholi* (my tent) and *av* (father), rendering the name as meaning the tent (the *Mishkan*) is his father, his guide. His father's name, Aḥisamakh, is also a contraction – *aḥi* (my brother) and *samakh* (the one on which I lean). His name brings together his father and his brother, the *Mishkan* which became the center of his focus, and his reliance on his brother, suggesting that he is not doing this alone but builds on the strength of his brethren.[12]

The names of the artisans thus highlight two key ideas which are to guide the attitude toward the *Mishkan*.

- Understanding that the *Mishkan* and what it represents, the partnership with God, is to help Israel, as a people, to achieve the highest level of humanity – being guided by their innate image of God.
- Understanding that the *Mishkan* is not a place for individual spiritual seeking but is a place which binds the people together, as their covenant with God is communal, not personal.

This last point, that the *Mishkan* not only binds people to God but to each other is driven home by the tribes from which Betzalel and Oholiav hail. Betzalel is from Judah, whom Jacob had blessed with royalty and who will ultimately lead the camp as they travel through the wilderness and even into the battles for the conquest of the Promised Land.[13] By contrast, Dan was the leader of only the children of Jacob's maidservants, traveling last in

---

12. Oholiav's name is later echoed in Psalms 122. "For the sake of my brothers and friends, I shall say, 'Peace be with you.' For the sake of the House of A-donai our God, I will seek your good."
13. For the travels in the wilderness, see Numbers 2:3–9 and 10:14. Judah's prince was also the first to bring his gifts at the inauguration of the *Mishkan* in Numbers 7:12–17. Regarding the battles in the Promised Land, see Judges 1:1–2. In Joshua 12, Judah is the first of the tribes to receive their allotment in the land.

the camp, and eventually abandoning their portion in the Promised Land.[14] The artisans of the *Mishkan* thus represented the entire camp, from the front to the back, from the most noble to the most humble.[15]

SHABBAT

We must wonder why Shabbat is included in these appendices. This question vexed many of the medieval commentators, who concluded that the purpose of the juxtaposition of these two completely unrelated topics is to convey the message that as important as the *Mishkan* is, its construction is suspended on Shabbat.[16] Despite Heschel's beautiful sermonic reading of Shabbat as a sanctuary in time,[17] in the context of the other items discussed in the appendices Shabbat still stands out as unusual. And yet, although it seems out of place, this passage is clearly the final one – fittingly, the seventh appendix[18] – in the string of instructions God gives Moses on the mountain, for immediately afterward God gives him the tablets as He just completed His words with him (31:18).

Two new explicit elements distinguish this passage of Shabbat from the three previous ones.[19] One is that violations of the prohibitions of Shabbat render one liable for the death penalty. The other is that Shabbat, for the first time, is identified as a triple sign for Israel – a

14. Num. 2:25–31 and 9:25. Regarding their portion in the land, see Joshua 19:47 and, in greater sordid detail, Judges 18:1–31.
15. Ironically, their connection to the sanctuaries ultimately led them in dramatically different directions. Judah's descendants establish the Temple in Jerusalem while Dan's host a competing one in their territory (I Kings 12:29–30).
16. See, for example, Rashi and Nahmanides on 31:13. Ironically, while the construction of the *Mishkan* is suspended on Shabbat, the daily *tamid* sacrifices (and later the additional *musaf* sacrifice) are not suspended on Shabbat. Kass (*Founding God's Nation*, 520) points out that this building project is contrasted with those of the Egyptians. In the Egyptian model, nothing interferes with the work, not human need or divine demand. By contrast, in relation to the *Mishkan*, God insists that human dignity be preserved and that the people never be turned back into slaves, even to God.
17. Abraham J. Heschel, *The Sabbath* (Farrar, Straus and Giroux, 1951).
18. Nahum Sarna (*Exploring Exodus*, 213) notes that this is the seventh passage beginning with "God spoke to Moses" since Moses ascended the mountain at the end of Exodus 24.
19. It was first introduced with the manna, later legislated in the Decalogue, and mentioned again as part of the covenantal formula in Exodus 24.

sign for Israel to know that God is the One who distinguished (i.e., sanctified) them (31:13), a sign of the covenant between God and Israel (31:16), and a sign that God created the world in six days but desisted on the seventh (31:17).

This passage of Shabbat is similar to the one in the Decalogue in emphasizing the prohibition of *melakha*. In fact, Yonatan Grossman[20] has pointed out that both passages are written chiastically, with the prohibition against working at the center of each. Here are both laid out to highlight those parallel structures.

The Decalogue:
A. *Sanctify* the Shabbat
  B. *Six days* you shall *work* and do all of your *melakha*; the *seventh* is Shabbat for A-donai, your God
    C. You shall not do any *melakha*
  B'. For in *six days* God *made*...but rested on the *seventh*
A'. For that reason God *sanctified* Shabbat

The *Mishkan*:
A. However, keep My *Shabbatot*
  B. For it is *a sign* between Me and you for your generations
    C. To know that I, A-donai, distinguish you
      D. *Keep the Shabbat* for it is dedicated to you
        E. Those who *violate* it *shall die*
          F. For six days your *melakha* may be done but the seventh day is dedicated to God
        E'. Anyone *doing melakha* on the Shabbat day *shall die*
      D'. The Israelites shall *keep the Shabbat*
    C'. To do the Shabbat for their generations as an eternal covenant
  B'. Between Me and the Israelites it is *an eternal sign*
A'. That in six days God made the heavens.... But on the seventh day *He desisted* (SH-B-T)

20. https://etzion.org.il/he/tanakh/torah/sefer-shemot/parashat-vayakhel/shabbat-sinai-and-shabbat-mishkan.

With all this, however, it is still unclear as to why it belongs here, as the final coda to the instructions for the *Mishkan*.

A careful reading of both passages highlights a Hebrew word which I did not translate – *melakha*. In the context of Shabbat, that word is often translated as creative work, as that is how halakha defines the nature of the prohibition. In fact, the word *melakha* is first introduced at the conclusion of the Creation story (Gen. 2:1–3), where it is used thrice in the span of two verses to describe God's work in Creation, and how God desisted from that creative work on the seventh day. When we broaden our scan of the Torah we will find that *melakha* is identified with Shabbat/Creation fourteen times. The other context in which the term *melakha* is used frequently is the *Mishkan*, where we find it twenty-three times.[21]

Aside from the *melakha* link, Sarna notes multiple literary links between Shabbat – especially its description in the Creation – and the *Mishkan*.[22]

Shabbat-Creation	*Mishkan*
God saw all that He had made and, behold (Gen. 1:31)	Moses saw the *melakha*, and behold (Ex. 39:43)
The heaven and the earth and all that is in them were completed (*vayekhulu*) (Gen. 2:1)	The work of the *Mishkan*, the Tent of Meeting, was completed (*vateikhel*) (Ex. 39:32)
God completed (*vayekhal*) (Gen. 2:2)	Moses completed (*vayekhal*) the work (Ex. 40:33)
God blessed the seventh day (Gen. 2:3)	Moses blessed them (Ex. 39:43)

In the process of exploring Shabbat we discover another link, that of *Mishkan* and Creation. That link, however, carries beyond the initial

21. By contrast, the word appears in contexts that have nothing to do with Shabbat, holidays, or the *Mishkan* only eight times in the Bible and distributed over four disparate contexts.

22. 213–14.

chapter of Creation into the Garden of Eden. We've already noted that the *keruvim* in the *Mishkan* broadcast the *keruvim* which guarded the entrance to the Garden of Eden. The "good gold" described in Genesis 2:12 is echoed in the purified gold used for the internal vessels of the *Mishkan*, and the *bedolaḥ* appears in the Bible only in the contexts of the Garden and the manna, of which a jar was permanently placed in the *Mishkan*. Similarly, the *shoham* stones on the shoulder pieces of the *efod* are also first mentioned in the description of the Garden (Gen. 2:12).[23]

Rabbi Jonathan Sacks describes Creation as the space God created for humans while the *Mishkan* is the space people create for God,[24] but that elegant symmetry is only part of the bigger picture. The *Mishkan*-Creation link completes the interlinked circle of Shabbat-Creation-Israel-*Mishkan*. Creation presents a model for an ideal world within the God-human relationship. Israel's observance of Shabbat both brings Shabbat's potential to fruition, completing that Creation, and functions as a sign of the bond between God and Israel. *Mishkan* on the one hand is linked back to that ideal world of Creation and on the other is the expression of the God-Israel (and, by extension, the God-human) relationship. Shabbat and *Mishkan* complement each other; it is befitting that the sanctified seventh day of the week complete the presentation of the sanctified space of the *Mishkan* as its seventh and closing appendix.

Leon Kass's concluding thought on the *Mishkan* in his work *Founding God's Nation* captures this idea beautifully. He writes:

> The project of Creation through which the Lord brought the natural world and the human race into being is here to be completed in a joint building project through which human beings, following the Lord's instructions, create a place where the Lord and His "image" may meet and know each other. (p. 528)

---

23. There are only two other places in the Bible where these stones are mentioned. Ez. 28:13 mentions them in the context of the Garden of Eden while I Chr. 29:2 mentions them in the context of the Temple in Jerusalem.
24. *Covenant and Conversation: Exodus* (Jerusalem: Maggid Books, 2010), 205.

As God reenters human history, engages with Israel, and launches Israel into their role as His representatives, the *Mishkan* and Shabbat bring together God and Israel alongside Creation and God's hope for all humanity.

The appendices to the *Mishkan* – from the golden incense altar and the silver of the counting, through the artisans who bind Israel together as they construct the symbol of the covenant, and to Shabbat which reminds Israel that their election is to further God's purpose and not their own – complete the picture of the *Mishkan*. It is a beautiful, idealized vision whose fulfillment will be elusive.

Exodus 31:18–32:35

Crisis

Israel's experience with God has been nothing less than spectacular. They observed God demonstrate His mastery over nature in Egypt, with a climax at the Reed Sea. They watched Him turn bitter water into sweet and bring water from a rock. They ate, and are still eating, the miraculous heavenly food which arrives fresh every morning. They experienced a multisensory divine revelation at Sinai and even entered into a covenant with Him which transformed their status into His treasured nation and a kingdom of His ambassadors. Their roller-coaster-like ride with God has been breathtaking, although the eerie quiet since the covenantal ceremony is becoming disconcerting.

Their experience with Moses has been no less eye-opening. The man who did not seem to belong cares about them more than anyone they've ever known. In the depths of Egyptian slavery he gave them hope in the form of God's promise. He brought relief from their crushing servitude and retribution to their Egyptian oppressors. He galvanized the people to rise up against their taskmasters and led them out of Egypt. He split the sea for Israel to pass through and brought it crashing down on the pursuing Egyptians to deliver the final blow. They observe him sweetening the bitter waters and bringing water from the rock, and with

God's help, arrange for their daily sustenance in an inhospitable wilderness. He communes with God almost at will and when he enters the divine cloud on the mountain he emerges unscathed. They still don't know if he is a man, an uber-wizard, or some kind of demi-god himself.

When he last went up the mountain it was in the afterglow of the covenantal ceremony, and he was to receive stone tablets and other instructions from God. It was clear that this was to be a longer trip than the others, as he left Aaron and Hur in charge during his absence, but nobody knew how long it was going to be.[1] With each passing day the anxiety of the people grows. Could any human survive for that long without eating or drinking? And if he is not a human, did he rejoin God in heaven and intend to stay there? How could they survive without his leadership? How would they know where to go or what to do when they got there? Who would intercede with God or use his magic staff the next time a crisis arose? With tensions rising, a group rises up against Aaron.[2]

> Rise up! Make for us a leader/gods[3] who will go before us, because this man Moses who took us up from Egypt, we do not know what happened to him. (32:1)

Given their experiences of the past year, many readers are shocked at this demand. Did the people not witness God's miracles or experience His presence? Did they not agree to His terms? We, however, should not be so surprised. Throughout the Bible we hear of individuals or groups who

1. The end of ch. 24 (v. 18) says that he ended up staying there for forty days and nights, but there is no indication that he or anyone else knew that in advance.
2. The root K-H-L means an assembly of people. When used as a verb coupled with the modifier *al* (upon), it refers to a challenge, an uprising. See also Num. 16:3, 17:7; Josh. 22:12; Ezek. 38:7.
3. The Hebrew word they use is *elohim,* and the verb they ascribe to it going before them is plural. The word *elohim* means mighty, and is often used in the Bible to describe God as the Almighty, or the capitalized *E-lohim.* If their intention is to replace God, then their words to Aaron are to be understood as requesting gods who will walk before them and fits with the plural verb which follows. There are, however, numerous places where *elohim* refers to people in positions of power or leadership. If that is its meaning here, then their intention is to ask Aaron for a replacement for Moses, which would fit well with the close of the verse.

seem to undergo radical transformations that do not seem to have lasting power. Singular, dramatic experiences can make an impression, but for any change to endure it needs time to sink in and regular reinforcement. In addition, while a superficial reading would lead us to believe that the entire nation was involved in ganging up on Aaron, that is probably far from reality. We later hear that three thousand people were punished by the Levites for their involvement. For sure, three thousand people is a formidable crowd for Aaron to deal with, yet they represent only half a percent of the entire population. Even if ten times more than that join in afterward, and God does send out a plague which affects many whom the Levites did not slay, that is still only five percent of the population. It is therefore likely that a relatively small group of anxious people approach Aaron, a larger group gathers as followers, and many more wait and see what happens, perhaps donating to the cause.

The fact that the restiveness is understandable and the numbers of the actively involved are not overwhelming does not make the uprising excusable. From God's perspective this is a massive public violation of the foundation of the Decalogue: "I am A-donai, your God, who took you out of Egypt, the house of bondage. You shall not have any other gods." Even more, considering that God has been planning with Moses to build a sanctuary so that His presence can dwell among the people, the notion that any significant portion of His covenanted people could be planning to have another god in their midst is a vile betrayal. As Rabbi Aharon Lichtenstein once described, imagine a newlywed couple on their honeymoon, and when the groom returns from buying a bottle of champagne for their intimate celebration, he discovers his bride in bed with the bellhop.

Up on the mountain, while God had apparently finished teaching Moses about the *Mishkan*, it is not clear that He was ready yet for Moses to return to the people. The incident with the calf, however, ended that tête-à-tête. "God said to Moses: 'Go, go down! For your people, whom you brought up from Egypt, has wrought ruin'" (32:7). The time for intimacy, even with Moses, was over. Moses, however, does not move, even after God describes to him the scene down below,[4] opening with

4. We here have another example of God speaking twice consecutively, each instance

God's threat: "So now, allow My anger to flare at them and I will finish them – I will make you into a great nation" (32:10). For us readers of the Bible this is not an empty threat. In Genesis, God destroyed all of humanity and began again with the one family he deemed worthy. And while God vowed not to repeat that with all of humanity, He seems prepared to do the same with His chosen nation – He will wipe them out and start again with the lone survivor He deems worthy.[5]

Moses's defense of the people draws from one of the core themes of Exodus. If a significant component of God's involvement in Israel's plight, the humiliation of Pharaonic Egypt, and the covenant with His chosen people was to inaugurate God's reentry into the affairs of humanity and sanctify His name, then destroying Israel now would thwart that plan. In other words, why would God do something which would result in a desecration of His name?

> Why should the Egyptians [be given an opportunity to] say, "With evil intention He took to kill them in the mountains and put an end to their presence on the face of the earth." (32:12)

Moses seems to be successful, as God pulls back from the response He threatened.

This story raises many questions. Did God not know Moses's argument, so that He needed to hear Moses say it? How are we to understand Aaron's role in this story? If God already retracted His decree, why does the story continue for another two chapters?

Let us examine each of the characters involved and their roles as we try to get a better understanding of the events and their implications.

---

introduced with its own *"Vayomer,"* "And God said," one in 32:7 and the second in 32:9. Moses did not descend the mountain as God had instructed, necessitating that God speak again.

5. The root of the verb used to describe what the people did, SH-H-T, is the same one used to repeatedly describe what the people did in the days of Noah (Gen. 6:11–12).

AARON

An initial reading of the story reveals a picture of Aaron which is quite problematic. He is clearly both the architect and the artisan in charge of making the calf. Later he shirks responsibility, but the text is clear in assigning that responsibility directly to him. Here are three relevant texts.

> Aaron said to them: "Remove the golden earrings from your wives, sons, and daughters, and bring them to me." The entire people removed their golden earrings and brought them to Aaron. He took it from their hands and fashioned it with an engraving tool; he made it into a mask of a calf. They said, "These are your gods, Israel, who took you up from the land of Egypt." Aaron saw and built an altar before it; he called out, "A festival for God tomorrow." They awoke early the next morning, they offered *ola* (burnt) offerings and *shelamim* (peace) offerings; the people sat to eat and drink and rose up to play. (32:2–6)

> Moses said to Aaron: "What did these people do to you that you brought upon them this great sin?" Aaron said: "Don't let your anger flare, my master, you know this people, that they are in an evil way. They said to me: 'Make for us a god which will go before us for this man, Moses, who took us out of Egypt – we do not know what happened to him.' So I said to them: 'Who has gold? Remove it!' and they gave it to me; I threw it into the fire and out came this this calf!" (32:21–24)

> God brought a plague upon the people because they made the calf which Aaron made. (32:35)

The first and third passages seem unequivocal in how the Torah text sees Aaron. He makes the calf, which brings ruin and disaster upon the people. The middle paragraph, Aaron's version of the event, is different in that he takes no responsibility at all. It is the people who are evil, and the calf just jumped out of the fire. Both Aaron's role in making the calf and his seeming unwillingness to take responsibility are deeply troubling.

Ironically, neither Aaron nor the people are as yet aware of the role God had intended for him. Moses was told by God on the mountain that Aaron was to be the prime functionary in the *Mishkan,* but no one else has heard it. This, of course, opens a number of very difficult questions. Why does God never reconsider His choice of Aaron? How can the man responsible for creating the calf be the one entrusted with the atonement for Israel? How will Moses relate to Aaron in that position? How will the people be able to accept Aaron in that position? And finally, how will Aaron's role in the Golden Calf affect him as he functions in the *Mishkan*?

Let us first reexamine the core narrative. Aaron faces an anxious and distressed mob feeling vulnerable and lost. They were promised to be brought to the land of their ancestors but that seems to have gotten waylaid as they wait for Moses to return and believe that he never will. They want some kind of leadership figure, perhaps even a god-like figure, to move them from their twilight zone in the wilderness onto their path to their promised land. It is certainly difficult to negotiate with a mob like that and so Aaron decides to get creative. He will make for them a figurine that will be a mask (*masekha*), so that it will be obvious to them all that this is just a mask.[6] It is neither a god nor a representation of one, just the hollow shell to remind the people that it is insignificant. It will not lead them anywhere but will at least be a concrete image toward which they can direct their energies of frustration. By taking charge of the entire process Aaron is attempting to control it, ensuring that they don't take up the project on their own.[7]

The problem is that the fine philosophical distinctions Aaron is navigating may work in an intellectual discussion, but not with a mass of people raised in an idolatrous culture. It is hard, really hard, to

---

6. The same root, M-S-KH, is used in the *Mishkan* (26:36) to refer to the curtains masking the *Mishkan* from viewing by outsiders. Later, God will repeat the prohibition of idolatry but will specifically add the prohibition against making a god which is just a mask (34:17), apparently to make sure that errors like this do not recur.
7. *Midrash Tanḥuma* 19 suggests that Aaron is trying a delaying tactic, convinced that Moses will return momentarily. This is based on the understanding that the people knew that Moses's trip up the mountain would last for forty days, an assumption not supported in the Torah text.

undo the underlying models ingrained in people's heads. When they see Aaron's handiwork they declare it to be the God who took them out of Egypt. Aaron misjudges his clientele; his plan backfires. Sensing this, Aaron continues to try to work with them while attempting to gain control of the masses, like a captain trying to regain control of a massive ship tossed by a storm, so he declares a holiday for God, for A-donai, on the following day. Once again, however, he is outdone by the crowd, as they arise early and transform the holiday for God into something completely different.

When we split the verses into two columns, one for Aaron's actions and the other for the people's, the picture becomes clearer.

What Aaron does	What the people do
He took it from their hands and fashioned it with an engraving tool; he made it into a mask of a calf.	
	They said, "These are your gods, Israel, who took you up from the land of Egypt."
Aaron saw and built an altar before it; he called out, "A festival for God tomorrow."	
	They awoke early the next morning, they offered *ola* (burnt) offerings and *shelamim* (peace) offerings; the people sat to eat and drink and rose up to play.

Aaron's failure is not that he committed idolatry, but that he misjudged the people – a leadership error. The text does not hide this, and later holds him responsible for it. When Moses confronts him, he is still grappling with how this could have gone so wrong. "The people hijacked my plan to redirect," he says. That is the meaning of his claim that "you know this people, that they are in an evil way." As he continues and claims that he did not make this calf, it just happened – he really believes that! – he did not intend for this to become an idol, but it did anyway.

Perhaps it is precisely for this reason that God ultimately sticks with him.[8] An error in leadership requires that the leader ultimately take responsibility, and that is exactly what he does when he atones for Israel. More than anyone else, Aaron brings himself into that atonement. In fact, on the Day of Atonement, prior to processing any offerings for the people Aaron must bring a personal offering of atonement and cleansing (Lev. 16:6). One can imagine Aaron on the Day of Atonement seeing the golden horns on the incense altar and being reminded of a different set of golden horns for which he is atoning.[9] Indeed, it could be argued that there is no one more appropriate to be conducting the ceremony of cleansing than one who so deeply understands its necessity.

As for how Moses and Israel will relate to Aaron in this position, I will discuss those later.

MOSES

From one perspective, this story paints an entirely new picture of Moses. Far from being the one transmitting God's message to the people, Moses gets up and stands as the one challenging God's decision, like Abraham confronting God to defend Sodom. In this, Moses demonstrates a great measure of independence and courage, much as he did when he killed the Egyptian hitting the Hebrew. Not only is Moses reinventing his role vis-à-vis God, he is redefining his role vis-à-vis the people. Until now, Moses brought them God's message of hope, God's direction, and God's commands. He turned to God for assistance when they became unruly. Now, however, he is taking on a new role as their defender and advocate.

---

8. We will later explore other angles of this.
9. See Nahmanides, Lev. 9:3. *Sifra* (on Lev. 9:7) describes Aaron's hesitation to approach the altar on the day following his inauguration because the horns on the altar evoke images of the Golden Calf. *Sifra* (on Lev. 9:2) directly links the calf of the sin with the calf of atonement. This is apparently grounded in a subtle textual clue. The word *egel*, calf, appears eleven times in the Torah in only two contexts – eight times in the context of the Golden Calf and the other three in the context of the offerings on the eighth day of inauguration – thus linking the two stories and suggesting that they are related.

Drawing from what he has learned about God's broad agenda, he uses that to mitigate against God's plan to destroy the people and start again with him. Even more, Moses will later (32:32) strong-arm God, tendering his resignation to make God's plan impossible to fulfill.

With Aaron, as well, Moses takes on an entirely new position. It is hard to really know how Moses related to his older brother until now. Kass suggests that there is an inevitable, hidden fraternal tension.[10] It is possible, but until now there is certainly no evidence for it. Moses brought him into the project at God's insistence and turned him into a partner. Together they went to Pharaoh and Israel, and they were partners in bringing the plagues upon the Egyptians. When the people complain they include Aaron in those complaints, and Moses tries to shield his brother from that.[11] When it is time for Moses to ascend the mountain, he leaves Aaron and Hur – the two who supported his hands in the battle with Amalek – in charge of the people below. And while Moses is on the mountain he learns that the *Mishkan* which he is learning to construct and operate will become Aaron's unique domain. This fraternal pleasantness – atypical for biblical brothers – however, takes an abrupt turn when Moses confronts Aaron upon his descent from the mountain. Without even knowing about Aaron's role, just by the sheer fact that Aaron was left in charge while the travesty happened, Moses challenges: "How could you bring this great sin upon the people?"

> Moses saw the people, that it was wild, for Aaron unleashed its wildness making them shameful in the face of those looking to rise against them. (32:25)

It is unclear whether Moses's internal attitude toward his brother, and especially his brother's role in the *Mishkan*, has changed, and Aaron's response does little to restore Moses's confidence in him. But it is hard to imagine that his frustration does not play a role later in his rebuke immediately after the deaths of Aaron's two sons. Moses turns to Aaron's surviving sons and charges:

10. *Founding God's Nation*, 478–480.
11. See 16:7–8.

> Why did you not eat the purification offering in a holy place? For it is Holy of Holies! This He gave you to carry the sin of the community to atone for them before God! Behold! Its blood was not brought inside the *Kodesh*; eat it in a sanctified place as I commanded. (Lev. 10:17–18)

We don't know for sure, but it is certainly plausible that Moses's anger with Aaron's sons is a redirected, underlying, long-term frustration with Aaron's role in this incident.

Regarding the people, Moses is unequivocal. He burns and grinds up the Golden Calf, sprinkles what's left into the water, and makes them drink it. A midrash already sees in this a precursor to the processing of the *sota*, the wife accused of infidelity, who must drink water infused with the letters of the scroll pronouncing a curse if she is guilty.[12] Israel, the unfaithful partner, drinks the remnants of their sin; it becomes an integral part of who they are.[13]

There is no popular resistance. The people know that they have badly erred. Even more striking, however, is that there is no resistance to Moses's next act in which he asks for volunteers, "Whoever is for God – to me!"[14] When the Levites answer the call, Moses issues his instructions:

> Let every man gird his thigh with his sword. Go back and forth, from gate to gate through the camp; and each man kill [even] his brother and each man kill [even] his friend and each man kill [even] his relative. (32:27)

It is hard to imagine. Like Simeon and Levi rampaging through Shechem, the Levites move through the camp and slaughter three thousand people.

---

12. Avoda Zara 44a.
13. I thank Sam Stonefield for suggesting that forcing them to drink the water peppered with the gold is Moses's way of dispelling any notion of divinity of the calf.
14. In his charge to the Levites, Moses tells them that their actions will "fill their hands" – *milu yedkhem* – the same language God used to describe the induction of Aaron and his sons. His understanding is that fulfilling this instruction will earn them a special status, although it is not at all clear to anyone what that status might be.

Was Moses's a carefully thought-out decision or a reflex, echoing an impulsive act of his youth from which he later fled and which distanced him from his people? Traditional Jewish sources debate if Moses's action is seriously praiseworthy or significantly problematic – some midrashim praise him[15] while others criticize him severely, even suggesting that his order was a sin worse than that of the Golden Calf itself.[16] Regardless of how Moses's action is judged, it reflects a boldness we have never seen before and will never see again.

Finally, Moses confronts the covenant itself. We don't know what Moses understands regarding the status of the covenant, but the tablets are the one item which symbolize it. In fact, they are later called the Tablets of Testimony, in that they stand as witness – like a marriage contract – to the unique bond between God and Israel. A couple remains married even in the absence of the document testifying to that fact, but actively destroying the document carries great significance. Furthermore, the tablets are to serve a practical function – they are supposed to be the seat of continued communication between God and the people. "And into the Ark you shall place the tablets which I will give you.... I will meet you there, and I will speak to you from above the *Kaporet*" (25:21–22). Smashing the tablets is Moses's way of signaling his understanding that the continued communication between Israel and God is not assured.

In fact, were we to want to look generously at the motivation for creating the Golden Calf, it could be argued that the people's intent was not idolatrous at all. Their link to God, Moses, was lost; they needed

15. See Mekhilta, *Bo* 12 and Exodus Rabba 43:1. Steven Marx, "Moses and Machiavellism," *Journal of the American Academy of Religion* 65, no. 3, and Michael Walzer, in *Exodus and Revolution* (Basic Books, 1986) see in Moses's action a supreme act of leadership.
16. *Pesikta DeRav Kahana* (*Ki Tissa*) holds Moses accountable for the deaths of three thousand people, and *Pitron Torah* (*Pinḥas* 215) proclaims that the zealotry of Moses and the Levites here is a sin even worse than that of the Golden Calf itself. John Geerken, "Machiavelli's Moses and Renaissance Politics," *Journal of the History of Ideas* 60, no. 4, suggests that this action is a more extreme version of what Moses did in killing the Egyptian, and Ai Zivotofsky in "The Leadership Qualities of Moses," *Judaism* 43, no. 3, opines that the Sages sought to limit presenting Moses as a role model to discourage this extreme kind of behavior.

to find a replacement. Of course, their choice of replacement was prohibited at Mount Sinai, but the desire was to find an alternative link to the God who took them out of Egypt. In that light, Moses smashing the tablets and destroying the calf are similar, as each was a symbol of the desire for communication – the tablets were God's symbol, the calf was the people's. Moses's actions broadcast his reading of the situation – the lines of communication are no longer functioning.

In all four spheres – with God, with Aaron, with the people, and with the covenant – Moses acts alone. While we earlier saw minor innovations or modifications on his part, we are now witness to a man who independently takes charge, without direction or instruction from above. The unfolding drama catapults him into completely new modes of leadership.

GOD

Of all the players in this story, God is the most difficult to understand. Is He really planning to destroy the people? If yes, does Moses "change God's mind" by actually telling God something He doesn't know? Does Moses's defense of the people teach God something about people, or perhaps about Moses himself, of which He was not aware earlier? This sounds so strange to the religious ear. Yet if we believe that God really did intend to follow the Noah model and begin again with someone He trusts, then something must have changed as a result of Moses's intercession.

Then again, is the alternative possibility that God hadn't changed at all. His threat to destroy the people was never a real one; it was there to provoke Moses into action,[17] to help Moses transform himself in all the ways discussed above. For this, too, there is a model. In the beginning of Exodus, when Pharaoh intensifies the servitude as a result of Moses's request and Moses is faced with the suffering of the people to which he was a partner, Moses becomes committed to a mission he was initially reluctant to take on. God's orchestration of the scene is what changed Moses's approach.

---

17. Much like God's invitation to Abraham prior to the destruction of Sodom (Gen. 18:17–21).

And perhaps Moses's actions with Aaron, the people, and the tablets allow God to follow Moses's lead. If Moses plays a more active leadership role, perhaps that is a significant step enabling God to play less of an active role in managing the people and their foibles.

Is God playing the ultimate learner or the ultimate leadership coach?

WHAT HAPPENS NEXT?

The story of the Golden Calf leaves us with many questions – about God, Moses, Aaron, and the covenant. Perhaps most perplexing is Moses's statement to the people after dealing with Aaron, the calf, and the people. "Moses said to the people: 'You have sinned a great sin; now I will go up to God, perhaps I can atone for your sin'" (32:31). If God already drew back from His threat to destroy the people, what is left for Moses to do?

The Torah's response to that question is complex, riddled with mystery and surprises.

Exodus 33:1–34:35

Covenant Affirmed?

After God sends a plague to punish the people for what they had done, He instructs Moses to take the Israelites to their promised destination, adding that He will send His messenger[1] to chase away the nations currently dwelling there. While one might think that this is a positive sign, that notion is quickly dispelled as God adds that He will not be present: "I will not go up in your midst for you are a stiff-necked people, lest I consume you on the way" (33:3). Only now is the impact of the sin beginning to emerge; God will not accompany the people.

A closer reading reveals that the damage is even worse than we understand. As we review the story, and particularly the communication

1. The implication in the text is that the divine messenger is a substitute for God's direct presence, and is thus God's way of informing Moses that he will not accompany Israel. Rashi (23:20) clearly understands it that way as well, but Nahmanides (23:20) disagrees and argues that this is not the same divine messenger God had promised earlier, as that earlier angel represented a positive promise to Israel while this present one is a negative consequence of Israel's betrayal. According to Nahmanides's understanding, Moses was earlier prepared to accept the angel as part of God's promise to deliver His people to the land, but here he rejects it as it will be perceived as a rejection of Israel by God.

between God and Moses, we discover a discomfiting pattern which plays off the people's own words. Notice words which have been italicized to emphasize the pattern. In the background we have the opening of the Decalogue in which God introduces Himself to Israel:

> "I am *A-donai,* your God, *who took you out of the land of Egypt.* (20:2)

That identification is built not on some abstract concept of God as Creator or as the Omnipotent or as the All-Knowing, but on Israel's concrete experience with Him as their redeemer. When we fast-forward to the Golden Calf, the people's approach to Aaron is notable in that they identify Moses as the one who took them out of Egypt, and when the calf is finally crafted, they identify *it* as the god who took them out of Egypt.

> They said to [Aaron]: Rise up! Make for us a leader/gods who will go before us, because this man *Moses who took us up from Egypt,* we do not know what happened to him. (32:1)

> They said, "These are *your gods,* Israel, *who took you up from the land of Egypt.*"

The replacement of God by Moses and then the calf provides the background for God's response.

> God said to Moses: "Go, go down! For *your people,* whom *you brought up from Egypt,* has wrought ruin." (32:7)

We can almost hear cynicism in God's words – if the people believe that it is Moses who took them out of Egypt, then so be it. A second look at that verse uncovers yet another twist, as God identifies Israel as Moses's people, not His own. It is this point that concerns Moses perhaps even more than the threat to destroy them. Is this simply a power play, like two parents saying to each other about their child, "Look at what your child did!" or is God distancing Himself from Israel? Moses hears God's words and responds to both the question of who took them out of Egypt and the issue of whether God still considers Israel His people.

> "Why, God, should Your anger flare at *Your people* whom *You took out of Egypt*?" (32:11)

While the narration of the text hints at God's ultimate intention, "God relented on the evil He spoke about doing to *His people*" (32:14), Moses is unaware of this so that this question becomes one of the core issues about which he persists on getting clarification. Will God restore Israel's status as His people? In the continuation of the narrative Moses presents a series of requests-demands of God. To be sure, the core requests are obscure, yet there is much to be learned from that which surrounds them. At the close of the first one Moses adds:

> And see that *this nation is Your people.* (33:13)

After a mysterious response from God, Moses comes back again and clarifies:

> How will it be known that I and *Your people* have found favor in Your eyes? Is it not when You travel with us? Only then will I and *Your people* be distinguished[2] from all the other nations on the face of the land! (33:16)

The multiple issues here are all linked. Who has responsibility for Israel (i.e., "took them out of Egypt")? Does God still consider Israel His people? Will God's presence dwell amidst Israel? These questions are at the core of the restorative work Moses is trying to carry out. The implications are immense, as they are all expressions of whether the covenant has been broken, and if so, can it be restored. As we will continue to see,

2. The language used here is the same as that used to describe when God distinguished Israel from Egypt and shielded them from the plagues. See 8:18, 9:4, and 11:7. Those three references plus this one are the only places in the Torah where this root (P-L-H) appears.

rebuilding the relationship with God is far more challenging than preventing the elimination of Israel, and will persist until the end of Exodus.

REESTABLISHING CONTACT

While the people have not as yet heard even a word about the *Mishkan,* they clearly expected some kind of divine presence among them in the wake of the covenant at Sinai. When they hear that God will not be going with them to the land, they are gripped by sadness, mourning the loss. "When the people heard the bad thing they mourned and did not put on their ornaments" (33:4), and when God confirms that they should keep those ornaments off, "the Israelites stripped themselves of their ornaments from Mount Horeb" (33:6). While we don't know what these ornaments are, they are clearly something linked to their covenantal experience at Sinai-Horeb.[3] Removing those indicates their understanding that the covenant they entered at Sinai was endangered.[4]

It is at this point that we hear of an alternative plan, apparently another initiative of Moses. The description is powerful and moving – Moses leaves the camp to go to a Tent of Meeting he pitches and where he will meet with God, people look longingly at him as he makes the trek out to the camp, people bowing as they observe the cloud-pillar signifying God's presence standing at the front of the tent.[5] There is no *Mishkan,* no Divine Presence within the camp, but God will commune privately with Moses outside the camp, far from the camp with the people. The communication with Moses will continue, even

---

3. According to a midrash, these were "crowns" bestowed upon them when they declared, "We will do and we will listen."
4. The precise nature of the endangerment is a matter of debate. Ibn Ezra (33:1) suggests that they are in danger of losing the Divine Presence, but that the covenant itself is unaffected. Bekhor Shor (33:15) proposes that at stake is Israel's unique status as God's chosen people; Sforno (33:16) opines that at stake is the way Israel is viewed by the other nations. Contrasting with all those is Rabbi Shmuel David Luzzatto (32:19), who understands that the covenant itself is broken, as signified by Moses's smashing of the tablets.
5. The word *ohel,* tent, appears eleven times in the span of five verses (7–11), and contrasts the Tent of Meeting, (*Ohel Moed*) where God *will* appear, with the private tents of the Israelites, where God's presence will be longed for but will not be present.

intensify – God will speak with Moses "face-to-face" – but it is a private one. God's presence will not enter the camp of Israel.

It is here, in the Tent of Meeting, that Moses enters into a series of negotiations about the nature of God's relationship with Moses and with the people. Here is the first round of discussion:

> Moses said to God: "Look, You are telling me to bring this people up but You have not informed me who You will send with me; and You said that "I know you by name and you have also found favor in My eyes." So now, if I have found favor in Your eyes, please inform me of Your ways so that I can know You, so that I can find favor in Your eyes; and see that this nation is Your people."
>
> He [God] said: "My face will go with you and I will put you at ease."
>
> He [Moses] said to Him: "If Your face doesn't go with us then do not bring us up from here. How will it be known that I and Your people have found favor in Your eyes? Is it not when You travel with us? Only then will I and Your people be distinguished from all the other nations on the face of the land!" (33:12–16)

This unusual exchange characterizes some of the difficulties in unraveling what Moses is trying to accomplish and God's response. Here are some of the puzzling questions:

- Why does Moses need to find favor in God's eyes if he was already favorable in God's eyes?
- What does God mean when He says that "His face" will go with them?
- What does God mean when He says that He will put Moses at ease?
- Why does Moses seem to ignore the fact that God had just told him that "His face" would go with them?

Despite the mystery, three observations can point us to some kind of understanding.

1. Moses wants the relationship between himself and God to be more reciprocal, so that just as God "knows Moses by name," Moses wants to "know God's ways."
2. Moses wants to build on his existing relationship with God ("I know you by name" and "you also found favor in My eyes") and deepen it by "knowing God's ways," so that the relationship can be extended to include all of Israel.
3. Moses is unsatisfied with "God's face" going with them to put him at ease – for him, if "God's face" does not accompany them then he will not budge from Mount Sinai! Rather, Moses wants to ensure that God's presence will reaffirm the unique status of both himself and the people of Israel.

God had wanted to start anew with Moses. Moses refused, insisting that he was not an independent operator but the representative of the people. If God wants Moses then He must be prepared to accept the people as well. Nothing will put Moses at ease if it does not include Israel as well. At the same time that Moses states his condition, he understands that his own responsibility will grow considerably. The people are still undisciplined and troublesome, and there will be a need for additional intervention on their behalf. As such, he wants the relationship with God to be more reciprocal; he wants to know God better, so that he can intervene on their behalf more effectively. Moses wants God to be prepared to bear the burden of Israel and offers himself as a partner in helping to ease that load.

God seems amenable to this:

> God said to Moses: "This, too, of which you spoke, I will do, for you have found favor in My eyes, and I have known you by name." (33:17)

Moses's success encourages him to make yet another request, to see God's glory. Again, we don't know what that means, especially for someone who spent forty days on the mountain with God and who, in the Tent of Meeting, speaks with God "face-to-face." Nonetheless, this request sparks three responses from God.

1. All of My goodness will pass over your face and I will call before you the name of A-donai, but I will show favor to whom I show favor, and I will show mercy to whom I show mercy.
2. You may not see My face, for no man may see My face and live.
3. There is a place with Me; you will station yourself on the rock. When My glory passes I will place you in the cleft of the rock and cover you with My palm until I pass. Then I will remove My palm and you will see My back, but My face will not be seen.

One can imagine many different interpretations of this scene, but what appears is that whatever it is that Moses is asking for is partially granted and partially rejected. Moses asks to see God's glory, and God says that is not possible. God reserves the right to be gracious and merciful to whom He chooses and when He chooses; Moses may not anticipate or invoke it at will, but he will learn something about God's goodness which will pass by his face. And while he may be able to understand God's actions after they happen, neither he nor any human can predict or forestall them – God's face may not be seen.

What was it that Moses asked for? We can only conjecture, and perhaps God's responses provide the clues. Why does Moses want that? Again, conjecture, but the context of God's response enlightens. Moses apparently wants to understand God to the extent that he can predict God's response and guarantee that he can moderate it. God informs him that what he asks for is not possible, that there are things that are beyond the realm of human understanding.

These dialogues point to three very significant observations. First, it appears that Moses has made considerable progress in restoring God's relationship with Israel. That being said, a precise identification of that progress is elusive, and whatever progress there is seems to be very much dependent personally on Moses. While that may be helpful in the short term, it is incredibly limited and poses grave risks for a long-term relationship. Second, it marks an entirely new kind of relationship between man and God. In another major departure from ancient religions, man does not control God in any way. Neither offerings nor prayers nor mystical acts can force God to do anything. The best way to try to influence God's behavior toward us is to seek greater understanding of God and demonstrate that we are acting in godly ways ourselves. And third, that no human, not even one who speaks to God "face-to-face," can claim genuine knowledge of God. With all that God seeks partnership with people, no relationship is possible without human humility of recognizing their own limitations vis-à-vis God.

ANOTHER SET OF TABLETS

With Moses's entreaties and God's red lines, the scene is now set for the next step toward rapprochement. In the context of God "passing by Moses's face," showing him "His back," and sharing what are known as His thirteen attributes of mercy,[6] God gives Moses a new set of tablets to replace the ones which he had earlier shattered. These, however, as well as the staging of the event, are completely different from the original ones. Even though the words inscribed on them are the same, the tablets themselves are different. The initial tablets are purely divine: "The tablets were of God's making, and the writing was God's writing, engraved on the tablets" (32:16). The second tablets, however, were hewn[7] by Moses who brought them up the mountain where God inscribed them.

---

6. This list receives considerable attention in rabbinic literature. One tradition goes as far as to suggest that they constitute a guaranteed formula for allaying God's anger (Rosh HaShana 17b). The formula is repeated by Moses, with minor modification, in his defense of Israel after the "sin of the spies" (Num. 14:18), and it is referenced disdainfully by Jonah in his complaint against God's leniency for sinners (Jonah 4:2). In Jewish liturgy, this formula is the central pillar of *seliḥot* and plays a very prominent role in the Yom Kippur prayers. For a theological exploration of the formula, see Ezra Bick, *Thirteen Attributes of Mercy* (Maggid Books, 2010) [Hebrew].
7. Ironically, the root of the verb used to describe this hewing is P-S-L, the same root which the Torah uses repeatedly to describe forbidden idolatry. See, for example, the prohibition in the Decalogue, 20:4. I thank Sam Stonefield for pointing out the glaring difference between the two – in one it is the aesthetic form which is accentuated while in the other the form simply functions as the canvas for the substance of what is inscribed on it.

I have argued elsewhere[8] that the first set of tablets, which were entirely divine, represent a divine ideal. In a perfect world inhabited by perfect beings, the tablets of perfection would serve as the ultimate guide for sanctified human behavior. Those tablets, however, never made it to earth intact, and probably could not have, because people are not perfect. A divine ideal can gain no footing in a world inhabited by imperfect beings. Seeing the Israelites prostrating themselves and dancing before the Golden Calf, Moses becomes acutely aware of that reality and hence smashes the tablets even before they reach the Israelites. The second set of tablets, hewn by Moses but inscribed by God, represent a different model of relationship. They are a partnership between man and God, in which the divine ideal is adjusted by the reality of the human condition, and it is precisely because the divine ideal is tempered by human input that it has the capacity to be transformative for humanity. And while it may have been important for God to initially present an ideal, God's ability to adjust that to accommodate for human imperfection is what allows His vision to achieve fruition.

A second distinction focuses not on the tablets themselves but on the staging of the event. The initial Revelation at Sinai was public – witnessed by all of Israel and accompanied by an overwhelming theatrical display of sound and light and trembling. By contrast, this second revelation is quiet and private – Israel sees and hears nothing as God reveals Himself in a private encounter with Moses on the mountain. There are many possible interpretations of the significance of this event, including the educational one – that a single, overwhelming event may have powerful impact but that impact is likely to be short-lived in comparison to a sustained but more low-key set of interactions.[9] Perhaps even

8. See my article "The Ideal and the Real," *Tradition*. Rabbi Joseph D. Soloveitchik, in his work *Beit HaLevi* (*derush* 18), similarly suggests that the first tablets included not only the Written Torah but also a fixed version of the Oral Torah, leaving no room for human interpretation, while the second ones left the Oral Torah for people to interact with and continually generate new insights.

9. This distinction is powerfully evidenced in the distinction between the prophet Elijah and his protégé Elisha. Elijah preferred flashy, impressive displays, especially the showdown at Mount Carmel (I Kings 18) after which the masses enthusiastically proclaim, "A-donai is the God," but which is followed by them turning on Elijah

more significant, however, is that it appears that this revelation and its content are directed at Moses himself, not toward Israel.

The implications of this cannot be overstated. This revelation is more than a response to Moses's entreaties; it appears to be a complete reshaping of the covenant. While God will not destroy Israel and will even fulfill His patriarchal promise to bring them to their promised land, the covenant which accompanies this revelation is intended for Moses and Moses alone. I do not make this claim lightly, but a close reading of the text indicates that this, indeed, appears to be the case.

After God shares with Moses His thirteen attributes of mercy, Moses turns to God and repeats his long-standing request that God retract His threat to send a messenger with Israel instead of personally accompanying them.

> [Moses] said: If, please, I find favor in Your eyes, let please, A-donai, travel in our midst. (34:9)

Read carefully God's response, especially the italicized words.

> Behold, I will establish a covenant. Before *your people* I will perform wonders which have not been created in all the earth and in any of the nations; the people *in whose midst you are* will see God's wonders which are awe-filled, which I do *with you.*[10]

Moses had asked for God's presence to travel within the people, as he had done many times before, hoping that God will reaffirm His covenant with them. Indeed, God does promise a covenant, and the

---

himself. Those events precipitate God's dismissal of Elijah as a prophet, deeming him worthy of being carried up to the heavens but not belonging on earth. Elisha, by contrast, prefers multiple small and mostly private acts of providing assistance to people. For more on Elijah, see Elhanan Samet, *Elijah: The Lonely Zealot* (Maggid Books, 2021).

10. Many of the commentators were aware of the challenge posed by the text but were apparently uncomfortable drawing the conclusion I do. Ibn Ezra, Bekhor Shor, and Sforno (34:10) all argue that the covenant is with Israel but in Moses's merit.

collection of mitzvot which follows – the prohibition of idolatry,[11] the sanctified seventh day, and the pilgrimage holidays – is essentially the same as in the covenantal formula just prior to the covenantal ceremony Moses conducts in Exodus 24. The reaffirmation of the covenant, however reassuring, turns out to be quite troubling, as God still insists on referring to the people as Moses's people and not as His people, that it is Moses who is in the midst of those people and not God, and that the wonders God promises will be for Moses, with the people as witnesses.

Is it possible that, despite Moses's efforts, God is sticking with His plan to replace Israel with Moses as His covenantal partner?

While it certainly appears that way, the continuation of God's message suggests that that formulation may be a little extreme. As He continues and speaks about the dangers of idolatry in the land to which He is bringing them and the covenantal formula, He switches between the singular and the plural when referring to His audience, suggesting that the covenant may be expanded to include Israel as well. That ambiguity serves God well and continues even after He completes the covenantal formula.

> God said to Moses: You write these words, for based on these words I have established a covenant with you and with Israel. (34:27)[12]

Notice that God affirms the covenant – with Moses, then with Israel. This is different from the initial covenant at Sinai, which was directly with Israel. It now seems that the covenant is with Moses, and by extension with Israel. Without Moses there is no covenant with Israel. In their extended dialogue in the Tent of Meeting Moses had offered to take on personal responsibility for navigating that relationship, and it appears

11. Notice that here the prohibition of making idols is expanded to making gods which are masks, *elohei masekha*, a clear reference to the violation which just happened with the *egel masekha* which Aaron had fabricated.

12. Moses is instructed to write the covenantal formula. This is strikingly similar to what Moses had initiated in Exodus 24, in which he writes down "all of God's words" and later calls it the Book of the Covenant.

that God is taking him up on that offer. Thus, despite the fact that the covenant between God and Israel has been reaffirmed, it is now conditioned on Moses as mediator.

On one level, the uncertainty of God's presence has already been anticipated, long before the Israelites' great error. Recall that the design of the Ark includes two poles which are not to be removed, symbolizing the idea that God's presence could not be taken for granted and that the Ark and all that it symbolizes could leave at any moment. Recall also that the *keruvim* atop the Ark had their wings outspread, ready for lift-off at a moment's notice, and that the image of those *keruvim* and the tentative nature of God's presence are woven into the fabrics which greet all those who entered the *Mishkan*.

And still, there is a huge difference between having the Divine Presence in one's midst while knowing that it could depart, and not knowing if God even wants His presence to dwell among the people.

The relief that Moses expected to experience in the reaffirmation is considerably moderated and generates great uncertainty. Does this mean that God's presence will or will not accompany the people? Is the intimacy established at Sinai recoverable? What will be of God's covenant after Moses passes?

ALIENATION OF MOSES

God seems to be in no rush to answer those questions. Perhaps this is His way of conveying the magnitude of their violation. Perhaps He will only restore the bond when the people, not Moses, long for it. With no resolution in sight it seems that God has an interest in prolonging and escalating the uncertainty.

At the close of the final[13] set of forty days, Moses receives the new tablets. Unbeknownst to him, Moses's face has become unusually radiant,

---

13. Two sets of forty days are described in Exodus, each culminating with God giving Moses a pair of stone tablets. Rabbinic tradition understands that there was an intermediary forty days during which Moses pleaded on the people's behalf. According to that tradition, the end of the first set of forty days concluded on the Seventeenth of Tamuz, so that the day of mourning is associated first with the breaking of the

so much so that the people are fearful of him. If they were earlier uncertain as to whether Moses was a man or a god, his new radiance gives him a completely otherworldly appearance. And just as Joseph's brothers are afraid to approach him when he first reveals himself until he summons them to come close, the people are afraid to approach Moses until he calls to them to approach him. The similarities between these fraternal reunion type-scenes are not accidental. Joseph's brothers are afraid to approach him because of shame for what they had done in the past and by what he, as an Egyptian viceroy (i.e., an alien to them), might do to them in retribution. The same factors are present in the people's reaction to Moses's return from the mountain – shame for what they had done and fear of Moses, who is very much alien to them.

Perhaps nothing symbolizes the chasm between Moses and the people more than the mask he dons.

> Moses commanded them all which God had spoken to him on Mount Sinai. When Moses finished speaking with them he placed a veil on his face. When Moses would come before God he would remove the veil until he left; he would then exit and speak to the Israelites that which he had been commanded. The Israelites would see Moses's face, that the skin on Moses's face was radiant; Moses would then replace the veil on his face until he came to speak with Him. (34:34–35)

The mask is off when Moses speaks with God and when he transmits God's commands to the people. The rest of the time, however, Moses's face is covered. In the context of the story of the Golden Calf, Moses has become the demi-God sought by the people – he can go for multiple forty-day periods without eating or drinking and his face is aglow. He is the mask which Aaron tried to create when he forged that calf-mask, the *egel masekha*. In the context of the lengthy negotiations Moses conducts

---

tablets; the second set concluded on the last day of Av, and the final forty days were completed on Yom Kippur, the Day Atonement, with the second set of tablets representing the first atonement for Israel's sins.

with God, in which God's face cannot be seen, Moses has become to the people what God was to him.[14] They cannot speak with him face-to-face just as he could not speak with God that way. God needed to cover Moses as He passed so that Moses does not see His face, and Moses needs to cover his face.

Moses's transformation into a man of God, or perhaps a man-God, is complete. He achieves what no one else is capable of. But that achievement comes at a great price. The leader the people so desperately sought is inaccessible; he is behind a mask. And just as he is inaccessible to them, they become inaccessible to him. As the leader draws closer to God, a wedge is driven between him and his people, with significant implications we have yet to explore.

---

14. Moses's face is mentioned six times in this passage (34:29–35). The Torah uses an unusual verb form, *midaber,* to describe Moses's speaking with the people. The only other place where this form is used in the Torah describes God's communication with Moses from above the *keruvim* (Num. 7:89).

Exodus 35:1–40:38

If We Build It, Will He Come?

The last six chapters of Exodus have flummoxed readers for centuries. They contain Moses's instructions to the people regarding the *Mishkan*, mirroring those given by God to him, with the same level of detail. They also contain an itemized description of all that was fabricated and how Moses took all the components and put them together to form the *Mishkan*. The nearly verbatim repetition is highly unusual – the Torah would usually state something akin to, "Moses did all that God had instructed him." The level of detail and length of the repetition demands our attention.

The methodology for approaching repetitions in the Bible usually begins with a close reading to reveal the differences – additions, deletions, and changes. We will do this in two parts, one relating to the instructions to build the *Mishkan* and a second regarding the description of the construction of the vessels and components of the *Mishkan*. Indeed, doing that reading reveals a number of differences.

INSTRUCTIONS FOR BUILDING THE *MISHKAN*

The chart below highlights the most significant differences between God's teaching Moses about the *Mishkan* and Moses's corresponding instructions to Israel.

	God's instruction	Moses's instruction
Shabbat	The mitzva of Shabbat is the final instruction.	The mitzva of Shabbat is the opening instruction.
		Moses adds the specific prohibition of igniting fire.
	Shabbat is a sign of the covenant between God and Israel.	
Purpose	Construction of a *Mishkan*.	
	Create a place for God's presence to dwell among the people.	
Artisans	Identified as an appendix to the instructions for the *Mishkan*.	Identified at the beginning of the instructions to build the *Mishkan*.
Details of the contents	Given to Moses one item at a time.	Listed by Moses even before collecting the raw materials

There are two main areas which categorize the changes Moses makes. The first of those could be described as the limitations on the process, such as the injunction to preserve the sanctity of Shabbat and the exclusive identification of Betzalel and Oholiav as the ones who will direct the manufacturing. Whereas God had saved these items for the appendices to the *Mishkan*, for Moses it is essential that these be delineated clearly from the start. A corollary to this category is Moses's attention to details which were not spelled out earlier – the prohibition against lighting a fire on Shabbat and the specific listing in advance of every item which will be constructed for the *Mishkan*.

Given the catastrophe of the Golden Calf, these changes are understandable. A passionate and unruly mob intimidated Aaron, resulting in the Golden Calf. Moses is cautious to ensure that the building of the *Mishkan* will not fall prey to those same untamed passions. Thus, the first thing he announces is that whatever project he will present will be limited. There will be no work on Shabbat; the passionate fire must be controlled. Only those authorized to do the construction can do the work or direct it; there will be no repeat of religious zeal running amok. There is a prescribed list of what is to be made and who will be making it. And later, when we hear that the donations driven by religious fervor exceed the need, Moses issues instructions that the donations must stop. This construction project, contrasted with the Golden Calf, will be regulated.

The second area in which Moses makes changes is his omission of the purpose of the project. There is no mention of Divine Presence or of God dwelling among the people. When discussing Shabbat, Moses even omits any mention of the covenant, which was one of the defining features of God's presentation of Shabbat to Moses. And perhaps most surprisingly, the *Mishkan* itself is never referred to.[1]

It seems that, aside from trying to preempt any possibility for a repeat of the sin of the Golden Calf, Moses does not want to raise the people's hopes for the possibility of the Divine Presence dwelling among them – perhaps because he himself is not sure if the *Mishkan* will be able to facilitate that. Even more, Moses does not yet know if God's covenant with the people has been restored. Yes, there was a second set of tablets. But God's promise to reaffirm the covenant has so far been only to Moses or through Moses. God has not committed to anything more than that.

It is for that reason that Moses frames this entire project as simply another one of God's commands. "All the wise-hearted among you

1. The references in 35:11 and later in Ex. 36 are to the inner set of curtains which are called the *mishkan*, not to the building.

should come and do what God has commanded" (35:10). It is a command, not a promise or a hope.

CONSTRUCTING THE VESSELS AND COMPONENTS

The second part of the apparently repetitive narrative describes what Betzalel and Oholiav craft. Here, too, there are slight but significant differences between this telling and the earlier one. The chart below highlights these differences.

	God's instruction	**Moses's instruction**
The order	The inner vessels are discussed first, followed by the covering cloths, the walls, the screens, the altar, and the courtyard.	The covering cloths are discussed first, followed by the walls, the screens, the inner vessels, the altar, and the courtyard.
The golden altar	Discussed as the first of the appendices.	Discussed alongside the other golden vessels.
The washing basin	Discussed as an appendix.	Discussed next to the external altar.
The function of the Ark	The seat of God's ongoing communication with Moses.	

The differences here are related to those we saw in the previous section, and they deepen the sense of God's vision for the *Mishkan* contrasted to the project that Moses is directing. God's presentation begins with the conceptual heart of the *Mishkan*, the Ark, which will serve as the seat of the ongoing communication between God and Israel. From there He continues to the inner, golden vessels, the ones which mark this as God's royal-divine abode, and only afterward does the focus expand to the building and the courtyard. In that vision, since the golden altar does not serve to invite the Divine Presence it is presented as an appendix, and the wash basin is also an appendix, as its function is to enable the service but is not an integral part of it.

By contrast, Moses's project follows a practical, logical order. First erect the building, then furnish it, and afterward deal with the courtyard. The golden altar is presented alongside all the other golden vessels, as we are not interested in its function but in its placement. Similarly, the washing basin is presented alongside the external altar, as they are both external vessels made of copper. Moses's presentation holds no expectations for what the *Mishkan* can accomplish, as he is unsure of whether God's presence will dwell there, and is thus limited to doing precisely as God says.

In fact, precise adherence to God's instructions becomes a central focus when the Torah describes fabrication of the garments for Aaron and his sons (39:1–31) and afterward in the summary of the work (39:32–43) and in the description of Moses assembling all the components (40:1–33). The theme phrase, which appears twenty times, is "as God had commanded Moses" (with slight variation). It is here that we recognize that the two threads which are woven through the actual construction of the *Mishkan* – the strict adherence to God's instructions and the doubt regarding the appearance of God's presence in the camp – are two halves of the same coin. The strict adherence is a reaction to the deviation from God's instructions in the story of the Golden Calf, a way of ensuring that nothing goes awry with this construction project. The anxiety about the Divine Presence relates not to the sin of the Golden Calf but to what it precipitated, the departure of God's presence. Moses is deeply concerned about both, and the text conveys his apprehension.

THE CLIMAX?

Of course, the question of whether the *Mishkan* will function as God's abode within the people has implications way beyond whether the intimate relationship between God and Israel will be restored, as that relationship is not an end unto itself but a means to a greater end. The broader question is whether Israel will be restored to its position as God's partner and whether God will have to try yet a different path to His interactions with all humanity. After everything is made according to God's instructions, and after Moses completes the assembly of the *Mishkan,* the Torah records God's reaction.

> The cloud covered the Tent of Meeting, and God's glory filled the *Mishkan.* Moses could not enter the Tent of Meeting because the cloud rested upon it and God's glory filled the *Mishkan.* (40:34–35)

We can imagine Moses's elation at recognizing that God's presence had filled the *Mishkan.* It seems that his efforts bore fruit, and that the relationship between God and Israel has been restored. As Nahmanides[2] notes, the parallels between the description here and of the Revelation on Mount Sinai point to the idea that the *Mishkan* is actually functioning as a portable facsimile of that mountain. The chart below highlights those parallels:

Exodus 24	**Exodus 40**
The cloud covered the mountain. (24:15)	The cloud covered the Tent of Meeting. (40:34)
God's glory dwelt on Mount Sinai. (24:16)	God's glory filled the *Mishkan.* (40:35)

Indeed, the author of Kings must have understood it the same way, as the description of Solomon's inauguration of the Temple is apparently inspired by this account.

> When the *kohanim* exited the Sanctuary the cloud filled God's house. The *kohanim* could not stand to serve because of the cloud, as God's glory filled God's house. (I Kings 8:10–11)

Despite the apparently glorious moment, our text leaves us with questions. We earlier saw that the Tent of Meeting is distinct from the *Mishkan.* The Tent is a private meeting place between God and Moses situated

2. Ex. 25:1.

far outside the camp, and the cloud hovering over it signified God's presence speaking with Moses. By contrast, the *Mishkan* is inside the camp, and signifies God's presence dwelling among the people. Are both going to function? Will Moses continue to have his private meeting place with God distinct from God's presence in the camp? If so, then what are the implications for God's presence in the *Mishkan* if it does not serve as a means of communication? What is the meaning of God's presence if He will not be in communication with Israel? How will He conduct His partnership with Israel without the ability to communicate with them?

The fact that Moses cannot be in the Tent of Meeting because the cloud hovered over it is puzzling. Could it be that Moses, who spent forty days and nights on the mountain speaking with God face-to-face and whose face radiated when he descended, is now unable to be in God's presence? Further, we earlier saw that the presence of the cloud was a signal that God was speaking with Moses. Why now does the cloud signal to Moses that he is unwelcome in the Tent of Meeting?[3]

The closing verses of the book foreshadow the travels of Israel through the wilderness as described in Numbers.

> When the cloud would rise from above the *Mishkan*, Israel would travel on all of their journeys. But if the cloud would not rise, then they would not travel until the day that it would rise. For the cloud of God was on the *Mishkan* by day while the fire would be upon it at night; in the eyes of the entire House of Israel for all of their travels.

What is interesting is that there is no command for them to remain in place until the cloud lifts; they chose to do so themselves. On the one hand this can easily be read as depicting intimacy between Israel and God. Israel does not grow impatient and waits, moving instantly when

3. Jonathan Grossman, *Torat HaKorbanot* (Maggid Books, 2021), 27–36, cites a suggestion by D. K. Stuart that the inaugural moment of the House of God demands exclusivity as a demonstration that this is God's home alone. He does not, however, note the distinction between the Tent of Meeting and the *Mishkan*. See also Rashbam on 40:35.

the cloud representing God's presence lifts from above the *Mishkan*. In light of the aftermath of the Golden Calf, however, it seems likely that what we have is not a description of intimacy but one of panic, even terror. Imagine a child who got separated from its mother in a large shopping mall. Those moments of feeling abandoned are so terrifying that on subsequent trips to similar places that child will be holding on to its mother, remembering the fear of being helpless. Israel, having lost God's presence, entered into mourning which, at its core, is an experience of profound loneliness. Regardless of communication with God, the sense of terror of being lost or abandoned in the wilderness without God is terrifying. They do not need to be commanded to follow the cloud; they anxiously watch it to make sure that they are never far from God's presence.

Exodus presents a vision: God's dream of reasserting His place in the world and reentering the affairs of humanity accompanied by His partner, Israel. Indeed, He confronts Pharaoh, the anti-God, and humbles the dangerous Egyptian Empire, much as He ensured that the arrogance of Babel was deflated and its plans thwarted. He saves Israel from Egyptian servitude and makes them free people, enlisting them – with Moses's help – to be His partners. He established His new covenant with them and charged them to be a nation set apart, sanctified into His service. All that is threatened by the Golden Calf.

Moses toils to restore the relationship. He makes gains for himself and for the people, and there is hope with God's presence dwelling in the *Mishkan*, but the book ends with ambiguity regarding his success – we are left with more questions than answers. Thankfully the story doesn't end with the close of the book. There is a sequel, in fact, two of them. One is called Leviticus, the other Numbers. In the following two chapters we will see how each, in its own way, completes our saga.

Epilogue 1

Leviticus

The opening line of Leviticus is somewhat awkward. "He called to Moses, then God spoke to him from the Tent of Meeting, saying." Who is it who calls to Moses, and if it is presumably God, why not open with the familiar formulation of "God spoke to Moses, saying"? While the traditional commentators have much to say about the "calling," Ḥizkuni offers the simplest, most rational explanation. While Leviticus is clearly a new book, it is a direct continuation of the end of Exodus. In the closing passage of Exodus we read that Moses was unable to enter the Tent of Meeting[1] because the cloud (of God) covered it. God now calls Moses into that tent. Moses's exclusion from the Tent of Meeting was temporary, in effect only for the inaugural moment, after which Moses is invited back for follow-up instruction by God.

1. Prior to the Golden Calf, the *Mishkan* and the Tent of Meeting are interchangeable. Afterward, Exodus 33 clearly identifies the Tent of Meeting as being distinct from the *Mishkan*; the former is far outside the camp and is a place of private meeting between Moses and God while the latter is designed to be inside the camp. Outside of Exodus it is difficult to know if these remain two distinct places or if they get merged. Exodus 40 mentions them repeatedly as a single place, but the closing of that chapter suggests that they are two distinct places.

While the opening of Leviticus is thus clearly a continuation of the end of Exodus, the content of the follow-up instruction is what distinguishes Leviticus from the book which precedes it. The content of God's instruction focuses on the details of the sacrificial order. It opens with private offerings, especially those which can be brought voluntarily – the *ola* (burnt offering), *minḥa* (grain offering), and *shelamim* (peace offering) – and moves on to offerings which are mandatory, such as the *ḥatat* (purification or sin offering) and the *asham* (guilt offering). This guide for individual offerings (Lev. 1–5) is followed by manuals for the *kohanim* who are to process them, which are presented in a different order, which focuses on the relative sanctity of each (Lev. 6–7).

The presentation of these instructions here raises a fundamental question. Was this array of offerings part of God's initial plan or does it represent a new twist on the relationship between God and Israel? To be sure, for mystics like Nahmanides who understand the sacrificial order as linked to the functioning of the universe, it must have been part of an initial plan, and its delay until this point was due to the circumstances on the ground. Rabbi Aharon Lichtenstein offers a variation on this, suggesting that while Exodus is focused on building a "house" for God, Leviticus concentrates on the invitation to serve the Creator.[2]

It is possible, however, that the omission of personal sacrifices – in fact, the omission of *any* sacrifices except for two daily *tamid* offerings – is not the result of circumstances but by design. The description of the *Mishkan* as presented in Exodus is quite unlike what many would imagine. It is a quiet place, God's place. The only people who enter are Moses, to receive further instruction from God, and the *kohanim* who perform a single sacrificial service in the morning and a second one in the afternoon. It functions primarily as God's residence: "They shall make for Me a Sanctuary and I will dwell among them." There are no individual sacrifices, no communal sacrifices, no holiday sacrifices (save for a purification rite once a year on the inner altar). It is a sacred place, off-limits to all except those identified to serve in it.[3]

2. Aharon Lichtenstein, *Shiurei Zevaḥim* (Yeshivat Har Etzion, 2002), 10–12.
3. Yonatan Grossman suggests that the second list of sacrifices in Leviticus (Lev. 6–7)

Experientially, simply knowing that God's presence was in the camp should have been sufficient. In fact, once the Israelites settled into their land, that was effectively their experience as well. The average person had no regular contact with the *Mishkan* or later the Temple. Their religious experience was primarily a vicarious one in knowing that the daily sacrifices were being brought. In Second Temple times there was a practice instituted to enhance people's awareness of the Temple in their lives, whereby there was a rotation among different cities which each took one week a year to demonstrate their identification with what was happening in the Temple. The Mishna describes the development of the practice. Discussing the daily *tamid* offering, an offering of the public, the Mishna states:

> How is it possible that a person's sacrifice is offered and he is not standing over it? The early prophets established twenty-four shifts. For each shift there was a representation in Jerusalem of *kohanim*, of Levites, and of regular Israelites. When the time came for the shift to go up, the *kohanim* and Levites went up to Jerusalem while the Israelites in that shift gathered in their cities and read the Creation. (Taanit 4:2)

It was clear that there was a need to create a personal bond between individuals and the service in Jerusalem, which was far from the daily consciousness of the average person. These shifts brought that awareness to the people throughout the land.

What I am suggesting is that that reality may have been part of God's initial plan. There would be the daily *tamid* offerings and no more. While the people were in the wilderness, they would be aware of those offerings as they camped surrounding the *Mishkan*, and that awareness was enough to let the people know that God was in their presence. Perhaps for this reason the Sages understood that any disruption to

---

predates the first list and was taught to Moses at some earlier stage. See his *Torat HaKorbanot*, 69–79.

the *tamid* was devastating,[4] as it signaled the departure of the Divine Presence.

While the pristine *Mishkan* may have been God's plan, the Golden Calf disrupted that. The covenant with the people as an aggregate could not be sustained without the support of the masses of individual people. Lacking a direct link with God, which is what God had intended at Sinai but was rejected by the people (20:15–18), a significant enough group sought an alternative path. God understood that there needed to be a change; there needed to be an opportunity for individuals – all individuals – to build their personal bonds with Him.

It is for that reason that Exodus closes with ambiguity about the restoration of the covenant. Going through Moses could be a short-term approach but was untenable for establishing and maintaining a long-term relationship. For that to happen, the *Mishkan* needed to be repurposed. Instead of functioning exclusively as God's abode and the locus of communication between God and Moses, the *Mishkan* needed to become accessible to all, albeit with guidance and limitations, but nonetheless a place in which every individual could build a personal bond with God. The covenant with the people would be built on the commitments of a multitude of individual people. Exodus did not provide the medium for that; Leviticus, with its array of individual sacrifices, was God's new vehicle for accomplishing that.

BLESSINGS AND CURSES

The end of Leviticus introduces an entirely new element into the covenant – reward for adherence to it and punishment for violating its terms. This element is markedly absent in Exodus, where Israel's entry into the covenant is entirely voluntary and the reward is the covenant itself, the partnership with God. The Golden Calf introduces God to the possibility of Israel's failure to live up to the terms of the relationship, something which had not been considered earlier.

It is significant that the rewards and punishments, or blessings and curses, are not on the personal level but on the national one. God's

4. Mishna Taanit 4:6 identifies the disruption of the *tamid* as one of the tragedies which occurred on the Seventeenth of Tamuz.

covenant is not with individuals but is based on His relationship with those individuals. How one does the calculus of whether the collective is fulfilling the terms of the covenant or violating them is unknown to humanity; that is God's domain exclusively. How many individuals need to be in breach of the covenant before God can say that the collective has violated its terms? How many people need to be in the process of repairing their relationship before God can say that the corporate entity of Israel is considered as returning to its terms? These are questions to which we will never have answers. What is important, however, is to understand that God's relationship with Israel is built on His relationships with countless individuals. They each bear responsibility for the whole.

Indeed, it seems like God has recommitted to His covenant with Israel, and not just through Moses, but there are changes. It has become necessary for individuals to establish their relationships with God and be provided with tools for repairing breaches in that relationship. Those tools usually come in the form of three types of offerings, offered in proper sequence. The *ḥatat* is first, as it purifies the sinner and hence atones for the sin, repairing the breach. The second is the *ola*, completely burnt on the altar, which represents the individual's acceptance of their status as totally committed to God, like the totally burnt offering. That is capped by the *shelamim*, the offering of partnership, of the restoration of the bilateral relationship with God now that the hierarchy within that relationship has been firmly established. That system for the renewed covenant is established in the opening of Leviticus and puts the onus of maintaining the relationship on the people. The close of Leviticus sets up mechanisms for God to act to reinforce and remind Israel of its commitments to God. That close is introduced as happening at Mount Sinai (25:1), not the Tent of Meeting which marked the opening of the book, indicating that at the end of the book, the covenant of Mount Sinai between God and Israel has been fully restored, albeit altered. It turns out that the framing of Leviticus demonstrates the mutual responsibilities of God and Israel in maintaining the relationship between them.

Perhaps nothing more dramatically highlights the restoration of the covenant than the close of the passage of the curses.

> And yes, even then, when they are in the land of their enemies, I will not have been repelled by them nor disgusted by them to the extent of finishing them off, to abrogate My covenant with them. Rather, I will remember for them the covenant of the first-ones whom I brought out of the land of Egypt, before the eyes of the nations, to be for them a God – I am A-donai! (Lev. 26:44–45)

The covenant of "the first-ones" does not refer to the patriarchs, but to the generation which stood at Mount Sinai, whom God brought out of Egypt. It is extraordinary that these are none other than the people to whom Moses is speaking – they are the "first-ones" in whose merit God provides His solemn reassurance that He will not spurn their descendants. It is the same generation which committed the breach of the Golden Calf and with whom God reestablished His covenant. There can be no greater vote of confidence in that restored covenant than God's reassurance that it is that very reestablished covenant that God assures the people will never be abrogated.

INAUGURATION OF THE *KOHANIM*

Aside from its impact on the covenant between God and Israel, the Golden Calf challenges the status of Aaron and his sons. We've already noted that God identified Aaron as His chief functionary in the *Mishkan* and shared that with Moses. We've also seen that Moses's perception of Aaron may have been damaged when he saw the results of Aaron's leadership failure – even before he realized just how active a role Aaron played. How would Moses take to Aaron's position as chief *kohen* after this event?

When we broaden our view to include the Israelites, they have no idea that God had already identified Aaron as chief *kohen*. What they do know is that he was integrally involved in making the Golden Calf. In that light, it is easy to imagine considerable surprise and skepticism on their part to discover that the man responsible for making the Golden Calf is now the most significant figure in the functioning of the *Mishkan*.

Which brings us to the inauguration of the *kohanim*. This was designed by God and shared with Moses while Moses was still on the mountain. When it came time to assemble the *Mishkan*, God tells Moses:

> You should bring Aaron and his sons close to the entrance of the Tent of Meeting and wash them in water. You shall dress Aaron in the sacred garments; you shall anoint him and set him aside – he will serve Me. (40:12–13)

While the text continues to say that Moses did everything that God had commanded him (40:15), we are surprised in Leviticus to discover that the induction of Aaron and his sons into service has not as yet taken place.

> Take Aaron and his sons with him, and the garments and the anointing oil, and the bull for the *ḥatat* and the two rams and the basket of matzot. Gather together the entire community, to the opening of the Tent of Meeting. (Lev. 8:2–3)

Whatever Moses did earlier, it was not the induction into service described in the chapter which follows. Did Moses hold back on inducting Aaron, concerned that he was no longer fit for this role? Did God command this *miluim* ritual to be performed publicly, in front of the entire community, to quell any qualms about the choice of Aaron for this position?

One thing is for sure. This induction ceremony is inherently linked to the closing chapters of Exodus with all of the uncertainty about whether the *Mishkan* will actually serve as God's dwelling place. As before, Moses follows God's instructions exactly, again fearful of mishap. Seven times in the chapter describing the seven days of *miluim* we hear the refrain "as God commanded Moses," paralleling its frequent use at the end of Exodus. The anxiety about whether God will restore His relationship with Israel is echoed by the anxiety about Aaron and his position.

That anxiety is not only justified but borne out in the continuation of the events. The seven days of *miluim* are completed, but God's presence is still not apparent. On the eighth day, Moses calls Aaron, his sons, and the elders of Israel. He presents them with a new ritual, one which was never heard of before (the only offering featuring a calf!), which is never repeated, and which focuses only on Aaron, not his sons.[5] And even though

5. Although they are not instructed to do so, Aaron's sons do assist him. See Lev. 9:9, 9:12, and 9:18.

Moses claims that God had taught him this ceremony, it is quite telling that there is no mention of it. In fact, the refrain of "as God commanded Moses" is now replaced by a new one, "as Moses commanded."[6] Perhaps even more important, however, is Moses's explanation for this new, one-of-a-kind ritual: "For today God will appear to you" (Lev. 9:4). Aaron had been inducted, but the *Mishkan* seems to not be working. God's presence is still absent.[7] Moses feels the necessity to do something, lest the people suspect that God is not returning to them.

This ceremony, however, still fails to bring the appearance of God's presence. Could it be that after instructing Moses to induct him, God has rejected Aaron? That is highly unlikely, and yet from Aaron's perspective it is easy to see how he would feel responsible for the failure of the *Mishkan* project. Even more, it is easy to see how the people would lay the blame for that failure on Moses's choice of his brother, the one responsible for the mess in the first place. Just before stepping back from his work, Aaron raises his hands and blesses the people. The content of that blessing is left unspecified,[8] but we can only imagine what is happening in Aaron's mind that prompts him to bless them.

That blessing, however, also does not work. The seven days of *miluim* passed, and no Divine Presence. A special eighth day is added, whether by Moses's design or God's, and still no Divine Presence. Aaron blesses the people, and still no Divine Presence. Could it be that this is all retribution for the Golden Calf? In a final, perhaps

6. Twice Moses attributes the commands to God (Lev. 9:6 and 9:7). One action described in this passage is ascribed by the narrator as God's command (Lev. 9:10). Twice the commands are ascribed to Moses himself (Lev. 9:5 and 9:21).
7. It is not clear how this fits with the description at the end of Exodus, in which God's glory filled the *Mishkan*. According to a rabbinic tradition (*Seder Olam Rabba* 7), the seven days of *miluim* described here precede the end of Exodus, so that the appearance of God's glory mentioned in Exodus is the same event described at the end of this scene.
8. Commentators debate this. Rashi and many others assume that it is the priestly blessing mentioned in Numbers (6:22–27). Nahmanides maintains the ambiguity, suggesting that perhaps it is similar to the blessing that Solomon issued to the people upon the inauguration of the Temple (I Kings 8:55–61), in which he prays that the Temple be a place for people to find God.

desperate act, Moses and Aaron go into the Tent of Meeting. Listen to the following midrash:

> When Aaron saw that all the offerings were brought and all the things which had to be done were done and the divine *Shekhina* had still not descended for Israel he stood and was pained. He said, "I know that God is angry with me and because of me the *Shekhina* did not descend for Israel. Look at what my brother, Moses, did to me! I entered and was disgraced and the *Shekhina* did not descend for Israel!" Immediately, Moses went in with him and they begged for mercy. Then the *Shekhina* descended for Israel. That's what it means when it states that "Moses and Aaron entered the Tent of Meeting." (*Mekhilta DeMiluim* 19)

A fire comes from before God and consumes Aaron's offerings; the people explode in joy and fall on their faces in appreciation. The drama which began many months earlier, the tension of whether God will enter the *Mishkan*, is finally and gloriously resolved.

The joy, however, is short-lived. The Divine Presence has arrived, but Aaron's two elder sons are dead. They, too, were apparently concerned about God's non-appearance and decide to try their hand at helping. The number of explanations for their death is astounding; let us stick to what the Torah describes.

> Nadav and Avihu, Aaron's two sons, each took his pan. They placed in them fire and put the incense on top. They brought a strange fire, which they were not commanded. (Lev. 10:1)

Whatever they do, it is unauthorized and involves a fire that they bring. Well-intentioned as they may have been, they are in the wrong place at the wrong time. Perhaps even more, their innocent use of the fire for their incense offering threatens to blunt the impact and meaning of the divine fire, the sign that God is bringing His presence among the people. God's fire consumes them just as it consumes Aaron's offering, in an incontrovertible sign of His return to Israel. Look at the two verses which describe God's fire:

Aaron's offering (Lev. 9:24)	Nadav and Avihu (Lev. 10:2)
A fire came out from before God and consumed on the altar, the *ola* and the fats.	A fire came out from before God and consumed them.

The expression "before God," describing the source of the fire, is often used to describe the place right in front of the Ark, either inside the *Kodesh HaKodashim* or on the other side of the *Parokhet*. When we draw this, we get a visual understanding to supplement the conceptual one.

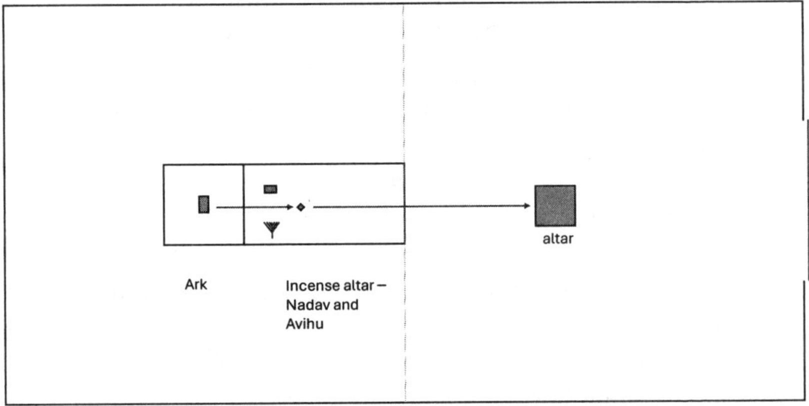

The arrows represent the fire which comes from "before God" and is on its way to the external altar to consume Aaron's offerings. Nadav and Avihu are offering incense, presumably at the incense altar, when God's fire emerges from before the Ark on its way to the external altar. In the process, Nadav and Avihu are consumed by the very fire which is coming to defend their father's dignity and restore hope to Israel.

The Golden Calf clouded the many months prior to the inauguration of the *Mishkan*, and just as the people and Aaron are pulling out from that dark cloud, the cloud of the Golden Calf returns to haunt them all.

The covenant is restored, but it has morphed. The communal bond with God is now predicated on the bonds established with God by masses of individuals. Israel is given tools through which they, as individuals and as a collective, can restore their relationship with God – without Moses the middleman – and God brings reward and punishment as His tools for ensuring that Israel remains faithful to the covenant. But that renewed, reaffirmed, morphed covenant will always carry with it the shadow of the Golden Calf.

MOSES AND THE *KOHANIM*

With all the challenges presented by Aaron and his sons, God not only confirms their role but expands it beyond operating the *Mishkan*. Immediately after the deaths of Nadav and Avihu, the roles of the *kohanim* are defined to include "separating between the holy and the mundane, between the impure and the pure, and to instruct the Israelites" (Lev. 9:10–11). The expansion continues with the extended discussion of *tzaraat* in its various forms, including the diagnostic process and its treatment, in which the *kohanim* play the central role and Moses plays none.

It seems that the *kohanim* play a significant role complementing Moses. Early on, even in Egypt, it was apparent that Aaron had some stature among the people. He was one of them, yet a respected one. He was Moses's mouthpiece to speak to the people, while Moses was the outsider to the people who was in dialogue with God. Aaron's failure at Sinai was precisely because he was attuned to the people and their needs, and it is that same quality which makes him, rather than Moses, fit to be the *kohen*. It is a quality which is simultaneously his weakness and his strength; it makes him vulnerable but it is that very vulnerability which qualifies him for his position.

Moses is the intermediary between the corporate entity of Israel and God. He negotiates with God on their behalf, debates with God about their fate and destiny, and defends them before God when necessary. That being said, he does not do well with individual people. He wears a mask on his face and is unapproachable. He is "other." By contrast, Aaron is of the people. He, and his sons the *kohanim*, are not only functionaries in the *Mishkan* but facilitators of the encounters of individual members of the people with God and the world of sanctity.

Even more, if Israel is to be a nation of *kohanim* serving to bridge between God's word and the rest of humanity, then Aaron and sons are the *kohanim* to the nation of *kohanim*, serving that same function. Just as Leviticus 18–20 details restrictions on Israel as a nation of *kohanim*, Leviticus 21 explicates the laws regulating the behavior of Aaron and sons, the *kohanim* to the nation of *kohanim*.

THE HOLINESS CODE

Those chapters, 1–20 of Leviticus, are often identified as the core of Leviticus and are also known as "The Holiness Code." They contain a range of laws, many of which focus on sexual ethics, and have been compared to the list of laws following the Decalogue. In fact, a midrash compares them to the Decalogue, in that "the main body of the Torah is in it."[9] Here, in the book dedicated to the *kohanim*, we find the code for the people who accepted God's offer to be a kingdom of *kohanim*. This is where the cycle is completed, as we return to the introduction to the covenant in Exodus. God's instructions in the Leviticus holiness code complete the renewal of the covenant.

This is highlighted by the opening of Leviticus 25 – "God spoke to Moses at Mount Sinai."[10] With the reworked covenant, Israel's ability to restore its relationship with God in the sacrificial system, and the installation of the class of *kohanim* and the nation of *kohanim*, we return to Mount Sinai, having learned and grown from the Golden Calf and to build on the strengths and weaknesses of the nation's individuals to build a people which is greater than the sum of its parts – a people which can be in covenant with God.

It is not surprising that the Mount Sinai section, including the curses and blessings, closes with God's reassuring words.

---

9. *Sifra* 1:1.
10. The identification of this passage being said at Mount Sinai caught the attention of many commentators. It contrasts with the opening of Leviticus, which identifies the communication of most of Leviticus as happening in the Tent of Meeting. Ibn Ezra suggests that this final passage is chronologically out of order, and identifies it as thematically linked to Exodus 23.

> And even with all this, as they are in the lands of the enemies, I have neither rejected them nor despised them to bring about their end in cancellation of My covenant with them, for I am A-donai their God. (Lev. 26:44)

God's covenant with Israel is eternal. It was not and never will be canceled.

Epilogue 2

Numbers

From a narrative perspective, Numbers is the continuation of the story begun in the beginning of Exodus. The people recently freed from slavery face a series of challenges as they begin their trek through the wilderness. Sparse natural sources of food and water plague them almost immediately and continue to plague them, especially when they complain about what God is providing. That first tumultuous year in the wilderness, which was itself part of the delay generated by the Golden Calf, climaxes with an extreme display of lack of confidence – in both themselves and in God – and an open rebellion against Israel's leadership.[11] After a hiatus of thirty-eight years of which we know nothing at all,[12] the journey continues as Israel has learned from its mistakes and a new generation prepares to face its own challenges.

---

11. Number 11–17 presents a series of events, beginning with unspecified grumblings and climaxing with the open rebellion against both Moses and Aaron.
12. Those years are when the old generation, which lacks confidence in itself and in God to conquer the Promised Land, dies out and is replaced by a new one. In all likelihood, that transition is marked by Numbers 19, which details the process of purification from contact with death – a most befitting topic relating to what most occupies Israel during that period.

One snapshot stands as an example. Both Exodus and Numbers feature an attack upon Israel. In Exodus it is Amalek. While we hear about Joshua's heroic battling and Moses's efforts on the mountain, there is barely a mention of Israel's response, and it is God who vows to take up the battle against Amalek (17:8–16). In Numbers, some forty years later, Israel is attacked by the Canaanites from Arad, who actually take some Israelites captive. Rather than wait for divine intervention or Moses's magic, the Israelites themselves vow revenge and ask for divine assistance. They lead the charge and trounce their enemy (Num. 21:1–3).

As for Moses, his leadership evolves as well. When the story closed at the end of Exodus, he was essentially inaccessible – he was a half-man/half-god who could survive extended stretches with no food or drink and whose face radiated to the extent that he wore a mask at most times – hardly a formula for effective, communicative leadership. The continuation of the saga in Numbers picks up with that theme, as Moses faces a series of challenges which are fueled by his distance from the people.[1] Over the course of time the barriers between himself and the people begin to fall as he learns more about them and understands his role as one who needs to be sympathetic even as he sticks to his core values. His own path climaxes in two incidents. One is a mostly private matter, in which he demonstrates extraordinary sensitivity to the plight of five sisters seeking to preserve their father's legacy in the Promised Land (Num. 27:1–11). The second is a very public affair, in which he negotiates with two renegade tribes and prevents their secession from the nation (Num. 32).[2] For Moses, however, despite his growth as a leader, his change was too slow. The new generation needs a new leadership, and he is destined to be buried with the people he led through the wilderness.

Beyond the narrative arc, however, there are broader themes introduced in Exodus, including God's reentry into human affairs, the election-selection of Israel as God's covenantal partner, the *Mishkan*, and the challenges presented by the Golden Calf. These, too, are developed further in Numbers.

---

1. For a fuller explication of this, see Grumet, *Moses and the Path to Leadership*, 65–98.
2. For more on this, see Grumet, *Moses and the Path to Leadership*, 145–74.

MISHKAN

Leviticus opens with God calling to Moses from the Tent of Meeting and speaking with him. Numbers also begins with a communication from God from the Tent of Meeting.[3] While Leviticus provides closure for the saga of the covenant, especially from God's perspective, Numbers functions largely as a sequel to Exodus from the people's perspective. What is Israel's relationship with God? What role does the *Mishkan* play in their lives? What lasting impact does the incident of the Golden Calf have on the Israelite collective?

Numbers opens with what appears to be a thoroughly uninteresting topic, a census of Israel.

> God spoke to Moses in the Wilderness of Sinai in the Tent of Meeting on the first of the second month in the second year after leaving the land of Egypt, saying: Take up the head count of the entire community of Israelites, by their clans, the households, by the number of names, every male per capita, from the age of twenty years and upward. (Num. 1:2–3)

As the text unfolds it seems like this is preparation for the battle to conquer the Promised Land. They are to count "everyone going out to the armed forces" and they are to be counted "according to their forces." Moses and Aaron, who are to lead the census, will be assisted by the princes of each of the tribes, twelve in all. The counting takes place in a number of phases. In the first phase, they are listed by tribe and the number of members in each; in the second the order is changed and the tribes – along with their tribal leaders – are grouped into four camps of three tribes each,[4] each camp taking up a different flank around the *Mishkan* as follows:

---

3. As I noted in the previous chapter, it is unclear if the Tent of Meeting refers to the private tent set up by Moses outside the camp in Exodus 23 or if it refers to the *Mishkan*. The incident in Numbers 12 (especially v. 4) clearly demonstrates that there is still a Tent of Meeting, distinct from the *Mishkan*, outside the camp.
4. The four camps are apparently based mostly on the birth mothers of Jacob's children, with some modification. Judah, who was given leadership by Jacob, takes up the lead role and is accompanied by a pair of his maternal siblings (see Deut. 33:18).

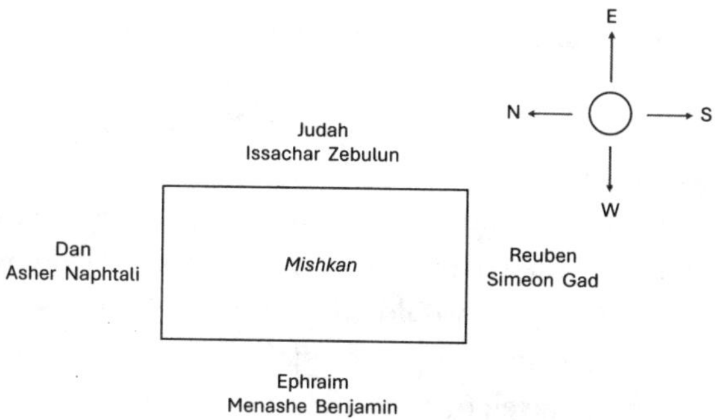

Immediately clear is that the *Mishkan* is taking on an entirely new dimension as the center of the Israelite camp. Everyone in the camp is effectively equidistant from the *Mishkan* as it takes on a defining role for the camp of Israel – Israel is the nation marked by the *Mishkan* at its core. This is true both as the camp rests and as it travels – the eastern and southern flanks travel first, followed by the *Mishkan* in the center, with the western and northern flanks taking up the rear. This identification of the camp is especially significant as Israel prepares their march toward their promised destination – they are conquering that land not as a liberated people seeking refuge but as God's partners fulfilling their destiny.

The role of the *Mishkan* as the center of the camp is best demonstrated in a passage we earlier saw briefly as it related to the closing two lines of Exodus. The extended presentation in Numbers is quite telling as it describes the dependency of the Israelite camp and its travels on the *Mishkan*:

> On the day the *Mishkan* was put up the cloud covered the *Mishkan* (Dwelling) of the Tent of Testimony; in the evening it was over the *Mishkan* with an appearance of fire until morning. That's the way it was perpetually; the cloud would cover it and at night with the appearance of fire. As the cloud lifted from above the

Ephraim, Menashe, and Benjamin are all Rachel's descendants. Reuben and Simeon, two disgraced sons of Leah (Gen. 49:3–7), are joined by the eldest son of Leah's maidservant. Finally, Dan, Asher, and Naphtali are the remaining children of the maidservants. See Ibn Ezra on Num. 1:5–14.

> tent, afterward the Israelites would travel; and where the cloud settled, that's where the Israelites would camp; all the days that the cloud dwelled over the *Mishkan* they would camp. If the cloud lingered for a lengthy time over the *Mishkan*, the Israelites would keep watch for God and not travel. Sometimes the cloud would remain for a few days; based on God Israel would travel and based on God they would camp. Sometimes the cloud would be from evening until morning and would rise in the morning, then they would travel; or a day and a night and the cloud would rise, then they would travel. Or two days, or a month, or a year – the length of time the cloud lingered over the *Mishkan* determined the length of time the Israelites camped and did not travel; only when it rose did they travel. Based on God Israel would travel and based on God they would camp; they would keep watch for God based on what God had told Moses. (Num. 9:15–23)

The lengthy description, with its multitude of details and examples, powerfully displays the level of dependence the Israelites felt regarding the *Mishkan*. God does not need to instruct them to wait for His cloud to move; they choose to make sure that they are never distanced from God. They keep watch, perhaps even having a rotation of people who are tasked with watching the cloud, and are prepared to move at a moment's notice.

Aside from its spiritual and symbolic functions, the *Mishkan* served an important social component as well. We've already seen that it sits at the center of the camp, providing a center of gravity for the camp so that everyone is in its orbit. Later (Num. 5:1–10) the Torah briefly mentions those who may not be in the proximity of the *Mishkan* and are thus excluded from the camp. The status of the stranger (*ger*), outsiders who joined the Israelite people, is especially sensitive, as they do not fit into the schematic of the camp. They become a particular focus in Numbers, as God wants to ensure that their lack of place in any of the flanks does not translate into discriminatory practice or exclusion from religious practice. Thus, the Torah explicitly includes the *ger* in the *pesaḥ* (Num. 9:14), libations for sacrifices (Num. 15:14–16 – five times!), public atonement offerings (15:26–29 – twice), red heifer purification (Num.

19:10), and refuge for unintentional killing (Num. 35:15), and Moses's endeavors to ensure that his wife's relative, Ḥovav, feels welcome in the camp (Num. 10:29–32).[5]

Finally, just as there are accounts of the dedication of the *Mishkan* in Exodus (40:34–35) and Leviticus (8:1–10:20), there is an account of that event in Numbers as well – and each has its own focus.[6] The description in Exodus focuses on the appearance of the Divine Presence in the *Mishkan*, the one in Leviticus focuses on the roles of Aaron and his sons in that dedication, while the account in Numbers (ch. 7) – unsurprisingly – focuses on the role of the tribes and especially their leaders. On each of twelve successive days the tribal princes bring their tributes to the *Mishkan*, each described in detail, and all are identical. The exaggerated repetition, which has drawn the attention of commentators throughout the ages, seems to be highlighting the lack of competition between the tribes. Without instruction, each brings a tribute identical to those which preceded them. Even more, there seems to be an organic consensus about the order in which those tributes are offered. No order was prescribed, yet there is no record of any discussion, debate, or tension about who gets precedence.[7]

It seems that while Exodus highlights the *Mishkan*'s role in God's relationship with Israel, Numbers sees the *Mishkan* as addressing Israel's relationship with God, and with itself. The *Mishkan* defines their camp,

---

5. For more on the status of the *ger* in the camp, and especially Ḥovav, see my article "Within and Without Our Encampment in the Desert: The Ambivalent Acceptance of a Biblical Convert" in *Tradition* 28: 370–78. I thank Chaim Frazer for pointing out that in Ezekiel's prophecy (Ezek. 47:21–23), the *ger* will ultimately be granted a portion in the land like native-born Israelites.
6. The timing of these three accounts is a source of considerable debate. Rashi understands that the eight days of the *miluim* for Aaron and his sons culminated on the first day of the first month, with the appearance of the Divine Presence and the deaths of Nadav and Avihu. That was followed by the tributes of the princes, which began on that same day and continued for twelve days afterward. Ibn Ezra disagrees, arguing that all three accounts began on the first day of the first month, so that the eight days of *miluim* of Aaron and his sons overlap the first eight days of tributes brought by the tribal leaders. For a full discussion of the issue, including other alternatives, see Rabbi Samet, *Iyunim BeFarashat HaShavua,* Series 3, Volume 2, 27–45.
7. The order is identical to the one describing their encampment in Numbers 2.

defines their experience in the wilderness, defines Israel's understanding of how they will conduct the battle for their promised land, is a force for contending with antisocial behavior, and serves as a catalyst for fostering pro-social attitudes and national cohesion.

THE TRIBE OF LEVI

The census in the beginning of Numbers raises a serious question for the readers, one which likely bothered Moses as well. God tells Moses to count "the entire community of Israelites" (Num. 1:2) and assign twelve princes – one for each tribe – to assist in the census. When those tribes and their leaders are enumerated, however, it turns out that Joseph's tribe has been split into two – Menashe and Ephraim – while the tribe of Levi is missing. Those who have been following the Torah text carefully will have noted that up until this point the tribe of Levi has not been identified as special in any way – not in Genesis, not in Exodus, and surprisingly (even ironically), not even in Leviticus. Leviticus addresses Aaron and his sons, the *kohanim*, at great length, but with the exception of a single reference to Levite cities at the very end, the book makes no mention of any special role or status for the Levite tribe.[8] Neither the reader nor Moses himself has any reason to believe that Levi should be treated differently from any other tribe, and their omission from the census is jarring.

The omission takes on an entirely different dimension in light of how the text describes the census after it is complete. "The total accounting of the Israelites from the age of twenty and upward, all those going out to war in Israel, the total accounting was 603,550" (Num. 1:46). How can an accounting be total if an entire tribe is left out?

There is acute awareness of this problem in the text. In what sounds like an afterthought, it adds: "However the Levites, by the tribe of their fathers, were not counted among them" (Num. 1:47). In other words, when we take a census of Israel, *all* of Israel, Levi is not included.

8. This upends the classical notion that Israel is chosen from among the nations, Levi is chosen from among Israel, and the *kohanim* are chosen from Levi. When the *kohanim* are selected, Levi has no status. In fact, as we will soon see, the status of Levi is derived from their relationship to the *kohanim* and not the other way around.

In fact, if we missed the point, once the entire counting is completed God adds an addendum: "However, you shall not take account of the tribe of Levi nor take up a head count of them among the Israelites" (Num. 1:48). They will ultimately be counted, but not among Israel. It is almost as if they are a separate nation. Read the following carefully:

> The Israelites shall camp, each according to his camp and each according to his flag, by their battalions. But the Levites will camp surrounding the Dwelling of Testimony so that there will not be fury at the Israelites. (Num. 1:52–53)

There are Israelites and there are Levites. Not only are the Levites not counted numerically as part of Israel; they do not count as part of Israel. They are a separate entity. This idea is later reinforced multiple times in the opening of Numbers, both explicitly and implicitly. Consider that when Israel are counted they are subdivided into tribes, each with its own leader; when the Levites are counted they are subdivided into clans, each with its own leader (Num. 3:14–39).

Much of the first ten chapters of Numbers deals with the Levites and their special status. They are counted separately (Num. 3:14–39, 26:57–62) and are tasked with both assisting the *kohanim* (3:9, 8:19–22) and ensuring that the Israelites are protected from God's wrath, which will be incurred if they violate the space of the *Mishkan* (Num. 1:53, 3:7–8, 18:2–6). They are charged to disassemble the *Mishkan*, transport it, and reassemble it when Israel camps (Num. 1:50–51, 4:1–49, 7:5–9). Part of their election includes their sanctified status as a replacement for the firstborns, and they serve as a redemption for the firstborns (3:11–13, 40–51).[9] Like the *kohanim*, they go through a process of purification and sanctification (8:5–22). They are to benefit from tithes brought by the people (18:21–24) but are not accorded land in the Promised Land together with the rest of the people (26:62). More than any other book

9. The issue with the firstborns is complex. There was an initial redemption, as the Levites en masse redeemed the firstborns who came from Egypt (Num. 3:11–13, 40–51), but there are additional redemptions of firstborns involving only the *kohanim* (18:16).

in the Bible, the name Leviticus would have been appropriate for the one known as Numbers.

All this begs the question of what sparked this. Why is it now, after Exodus and the extensive focus on *kohanim* in the third book of the Torah, that the tribe of Levi is singled out for exceptional treatment?

There is only one prior incident which can provide background – the story of the Golden Calf.[10] Moses descends the mountain to find the people dancing around Aaron's handiwork, claiming it to be their God. After destroying both the tablets and the calf he calls out, "Whoever is for God – to me!" and it is the Levites who answer his call and do his bidding, killing three thousand worshippers of the abomination.

This one group distinguishes itself in its devotion to God, which makes it a likely candidate for an elevated position as assisting the *kohanim* and protecting the divine space.[11] At the same time, from a different perspective, the Levite action may have precipitated a significant social rift. How would the masses relate to a group which ran through the camp slaughtering violators?[12] Would the Levites be seen as murderers, true to their distant past as partners in the massacre of Shechem? Which tribe would want Levi as a neighbor, whether in the wilderness or in the Promised Land? Would people be afraid or unwilling to have social interactions with Levites?

The double-edged sword of their loyalty to God brings potential for elevation in God's eyes but ostracism in the eyes of the people. As Numbers is a sequel to Exodus, it needs to deal with this new reality. Indeed, Levi is promoted to a special position protecting God; its devotion to God is rewarded by legislated opportunities to demonstrate that devotion. The price, however, is that it cannot be counted as part of Israel. It is separate, perhaps a nation within a nation or even a separate nation bound to and parallel to Israel. It is not another tribe; it does not

10. Some might point to the massacre of Shechem in Genesis 34, but there Simeon was Levi's partner and receives no similar affirmation. In fact, Jacob's blessing to both at the end of his life (Gen. 49:5–7) sounds more like a condemnation than a blessing.
11. See Exodus Rabba 31:8.
12. Ironically, their role in the story of the Golden Calf may have protected Israel from God's wrath, which is precisely their function in camping around the *Mishkan*.

live together with other tribes in the wilderness; it has its own encampment – surrounding the *Mishkan*; it is not granted land.

In an unusual twist, there are two types of people who stand out in Numbers – the *ger* and the Levite. Neither lives within the camp of Israel – the *ger* is outside of it while the Levite lives in an inner circle in the camp. Deuteronomy is acutely aware of the special status of these two people and repeatedly includes them both in the list of the unfortunates who need to be cared for by society, along with the widow and the orphan.[13]

The story of the *Mishkan* completes one part of Exodus. The story of the Levites tells an untold story spun off the Golden Calf.

GOD'S PRESENCE

There is no sustained narrative in the Bible in which God's presence is as overt as in Exodus. God speaks with Moses regularly and performs a series of wonders designed to publicly demonstrate His dominion over all. From the plagues through the Splitting of the Sea, God sought to teach the Egyptians that he was Master of all, and from the water and the manna and the Revelation at Sinai through His appearance in the final verses of the book He presented Himself to Israel as their God who is desirous of establishing a covenant with them. In fact, after the Golden Calf, Moses insists that He show Israel explicit signs that He is sticking with His choice of them as His people.

In Numbers we begin to see a shift. True, His presence is experienced by Israel on a daily basis – the manna continues to fall and the cloud hovers over the *Mishkan*. But as we know from our own experience, daily miracles are no longer perceived as miraculous; they become part of what we expect as natural. We've all experienced the wonder of nature in some extraordinary view, but when we have that view daily it no longer moves us. Familiarity and regularity breed normalization of the unusual and special. The special appearances, however, are reserved for special occasions – mostly in response to the Israelites' rebellions against Him or Moses. And as much as we think that their complaining is endless, it is actually limited to a few special occasions – food (Num.

13. Deut. 14:29, 16:11, 16:14, and 26:11–13.

11), fear of war (Num. 13–14), rejection of Moses and Aaron (Num. 16), water (Num. 20:1–12), travel (Num. 21:4–9). Considering that these five events are spread out over a thirty-nine-year span, their behavior does not seem excessive for a young nation just finding its way.

Where we see the greatest change, however, is when it comes to God demonstrating His presence to non-Israelites. In contrast to Exodus, where that motif dominates the opening fifteen chapters, in Numbers it is completely absent. This is most apparent in the unusual story of Balak, the Moabite king, who hires Balaam the sorcerer to curse Israel. God intervenes multiple times – He tells Balaam not to go, places obstacles in his way, and eventually makes sure that Balaam pronounces blessings rather than curses – but Balaam is the only one aware of these events. Not even his sponsor, Balak, understands that God is involved.

Numbers marks the beginning of a new phase in God's revelation to humanity. His revelation to Israel is mostly quiet, hidden in its regularity. His revelation to the rest of the world is hidden in what appears to be normal human events. This is a process which will continue throughout the rest of the Bible, and the rest of human history. God's involvement in human affairs will gradually become less apparent; the responsibility to reveal God's involvement in human affairs will slowly shift from God to people. If God is to have a relationship with people, and if that relationship is going to be a meaningful one, it must be because people seek it out, not a result of God imposing Himself on humanity.

HOLIDAYS

With the exception of Genesis, there is a discussion of the holidays in every book of the Torah. In Exodus they are introduced, not only to populate the calendar of the emerging nation with commemorations of its unique history and the origins of its relationship with God, but as an integral component of the covenant between Israel and God. Transforming the holidays from pagan agricultural celebrations into historical events credited to God is a declaration of covenantal commitment. In Leviticus, with its focus on cultivating Israel as a sanctified nation, the holidays take on a new dimension as sanctified time with requirements, mitzvot, and prohibitions (Lev. 23). Deuteronomy adds specifically how the holidays are to be celebrated in the Promised Land – with emphasis especially on their agricultural aspects and the pilgrimage to the "place which God will choose" to have His name dwell. Numbers adds a twist to the holidays that is surprising because it appears in Numbers rather than in Leviticus – sacrificial offerings.

In a passage spanning two chapters (Num. 28:1–31:1), the Torah articulates a complex system of special holiday offerings.[14] Parallel to the daily *tamid* offerings, these (each called a *musaf*, or additional offering) are communal offerings brought exclusively on the holidays. In fact, the link between these holiday offerings and the *tamid* is explicit, as the Torah introduces the holiday offering with a description of the *tamid* (Num. 28:1–8) which is nearly identical to the *tamid* passage in Exodus (29:38–41).

We've learned that, in Exodus, God builds a covenant with Israel, which is soon afterward threatened by the Golden Calf. God hesitated to commit to having His presence in the camp because He decided that the covenant with the corporate entity of Israel must be built on a mass of commitments by individuals to being in a relationship with Him. The sacrificial system established in Leviticus focuses primarily on creating the vehicles for every Israelite to manage and repair his or her own relationship with God. It is those individual relationships which are the core of Leviticus.

Numbers brings us back to the group identity of Israel. Every individual is counted, but as part of a family, a tribe, a cluster of three tribes, and the national entity. Numbers completes the cycle in which the corporate identity of Israel and its relationship with God are built on the multitude of individuals.[15] The complaint that their impurity prevents them from bringing the *pesaḥ* (Num. 9:1–14) emanates from the fear of being excluded from membership in the communal identity – which is precisely the consequence for neglecting to bring the *pesaḥ*.[16] Similarly, the plea by the five sisters emerges from their fear that their family's

14. For a partial discussion of the system, see Yoel Bin-Nun, *Zakhor VeShamor* (Tevunot, 1984), 155–71.
15. This may also help explain why Leviticus must precede Numbers.
16. Num. 9:13 explicates that the punishment for neglecting to bring the *pesaḥ* is to be cut off from the people.

name will not be associated with and grounded in the Promised Land.[17] The *musaf* offerings, which are fixed offerings brought by the community (like the *tamid*) on the holidays, are the final affirmation that God is prepared to fully reengage covenantally with Israel as a corporate entity.

The tension of the end of Exodus finally finds its resolution. After forty years of relationship building, Israel is prepared to accept God's offer more authentically than they were at Sinai, and God is finally prepared to fully engage with His people, His nation of *kohanim.* All that is left is to prepare for the entry into the land so that they can begin to engage with the world as God's ambassadors.

17. In fact, the stories are linked linguistically. The impure men complain *lama nigara* ("Why should we be excluded?") and the five daughters of Zelophehad cry *lama yigara* ("Why should our father's name be excluded?").

Afterword

This book traces the emergence of God's people from a family to a nation and from a nation to a nation set apart – a sanctified people. It explores cultivating national identity and sacred identity, the relationship between individuals and the nation, and the emergence of leadership. It examines how law and narrative build on each other to tell a story and how acts and objects become symbols embodying that story. It probes how a God who cares about all humanity can, and must, choose a particular people and build a relationship with it.

Much of Exodus focuses on God's interactions with people, as does the entire Torah. After all, without people the Torah is irrelevant. But precisely because people are so central to the very premise of the Torah, and because people are imperfect, the story will get messy. Very little will go as God planned. People need to learn, and that learning process is both slow and non-linear. Two steps forward and one step back, and there are always new mistakes to be made, both by the masses and by their leadership.

God, who contracted Himself and self-limited His knowledge to enable the existence of people, also learns. Pharaoh will never really come around, and He needs to adjust for that. Israel will waver between believing and not trusting His promises, between faith and fear, between hope and despair – and He learns tolerance for that too. Just as the creation of man caused God pain and frustration (Gen. 6:6), so does the forging of the Israelite people – His chosen people – bring frustration. But that frustration is just a springboard for God to adjust, to learn about His people. God sets Himself up as the ultimate model of the lifelong learner, which is fairly impressive for the Omniscient One.

Genesis ends with resolution of the family crisis but the beginning of an extended period of uncertainty, as the covenantal family settles into a foreign, uncovenantal land. Exodus brings God's chosen people into a new covenant, but that relationship is shaky and may be completely dependent on the effort of a single man. It, too, closes with a note of false climax. Truthfully, the five books of Torah end with uncertainty, as Israel is still not in its promised land and the Abrahamic covenant is as yet to be fulfilled. In fact, the entire biblical narrative ends with an unfinished project – Israel is exiled, begins to return, but hesitatingly, while the masses of the people remain in their lands of exile. I suspect that none of this is accidental.

The second paragraph of the *Aleinu* prayer lays out a grand vision:

> When the world will be perfected under the sovereignty of the Almighty, when all of humanity will call on Your name, to turn all the earth's wicked toward You.... They will accept the yoke of Your kingdom and You will reign over them soon and forever.

This utopian vision drives the essence of creation and of the story told in the Bible. It is a story with a beginning, with many twists and turns on the tortured path toward helping to bring that vision to fruition, a path laid out in sometimes painful detail throughout the entire Bible, a story which continues until today. It is my hope and dream that learning about this vision will help move it one step closer to fulfillment.

Other books in the Maggid Studies in Tanakh series:

Genesis: From Creation to Covenant
Zvi Grumet

Exodus: The Genesis of God's People
Zvi Grumet

Joshua: The Challenge of the Promised Land
Michael Hattin

Judges: The Perils of Possession
Michael Hattin

I Samuel: A King in Israel
Amnon Bazak

II Samuel (forthcoming)
Amnon Bazak

I Kings: Torn in Two
Alex Israel

II Kings: In a Whirlwind
Alex Israel

Isaiah: Prophet of Righteousness and Justice
Yoel Bin-Nun and Binyamin Lau

Jeremiah: The Fate of a Prophet
Binyamin Lau

Ezekiel: From Destruction to Restoration
Tova Ganzel

Joel, Obadiah, and Micah: Facing the Storm
Yaakov Beasley

Amos: The Genius of Prophetic Rhetoric
Yitzchak Etshalom

Jonah: The Reluctant Prophet
Erica Brown

Nahum, Habakkuk, and Zephaniah: Lights in the Valley
Yaakov Beasley

Haggai, Zechariah, and Malachi: Prophecy in an Age of Uncertainty
Hayyim Angel

Ruth: From Alienation to Monarchy
Yael Ziegler

Lamentations: Faith in a Turbulent World
Yael Ziegler

Ecclesiastes and the Search for Meaning
Erica Brown

Esther: Power, Fate, and Fragility in Exile
Erica Brown

Nehemiah: Statesman and Sage
Dov S. Zakheim

Ezra-Nehemiah: Retrograde Revolution
Yael Leibowitz

Maggid Books
The best of contemporary Jewish thought from
Koren Publishers Jerusalem Ltd.